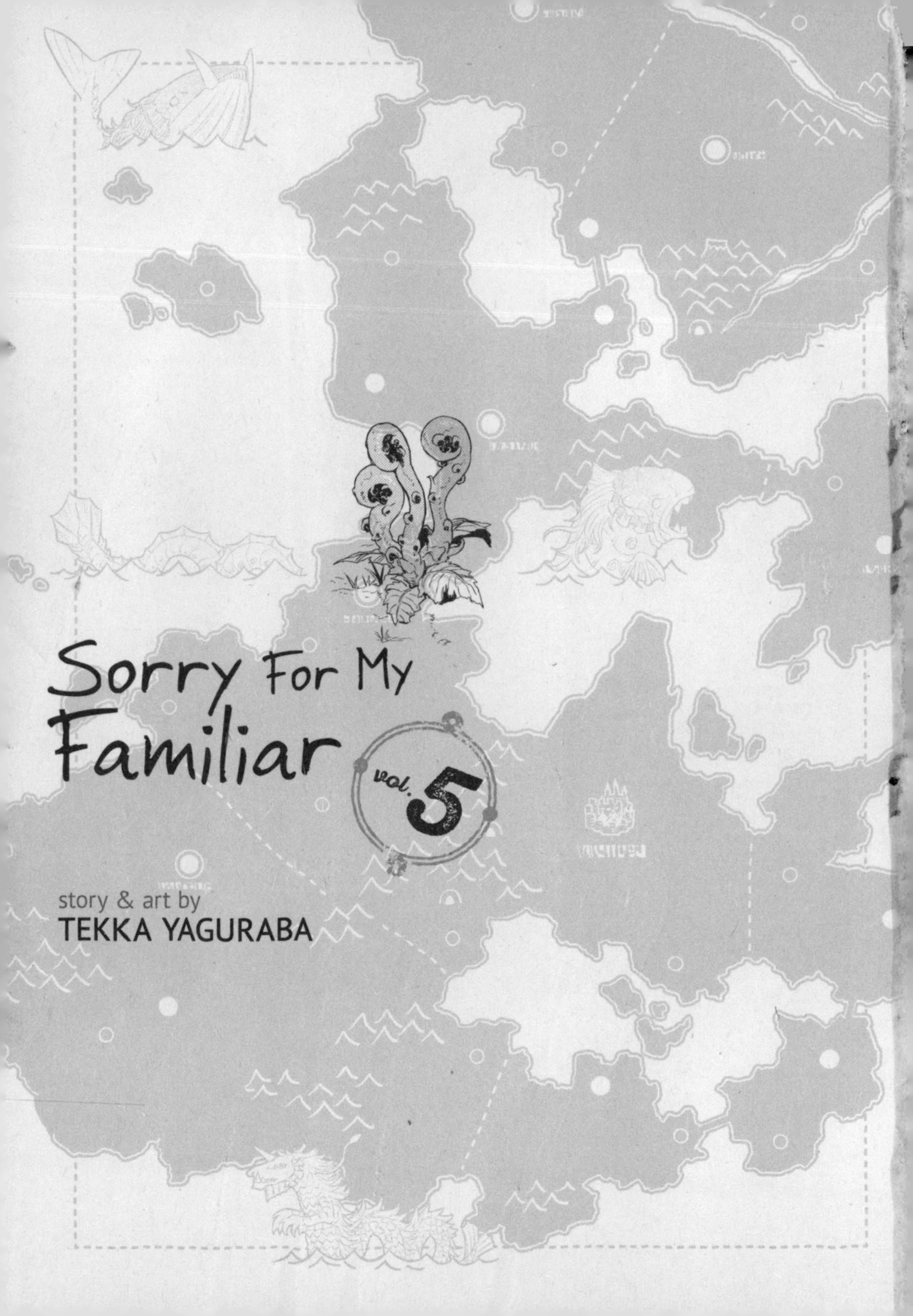

Sorry For My Familiar

vol. 5

story & art by
TEKKA YAGURABA

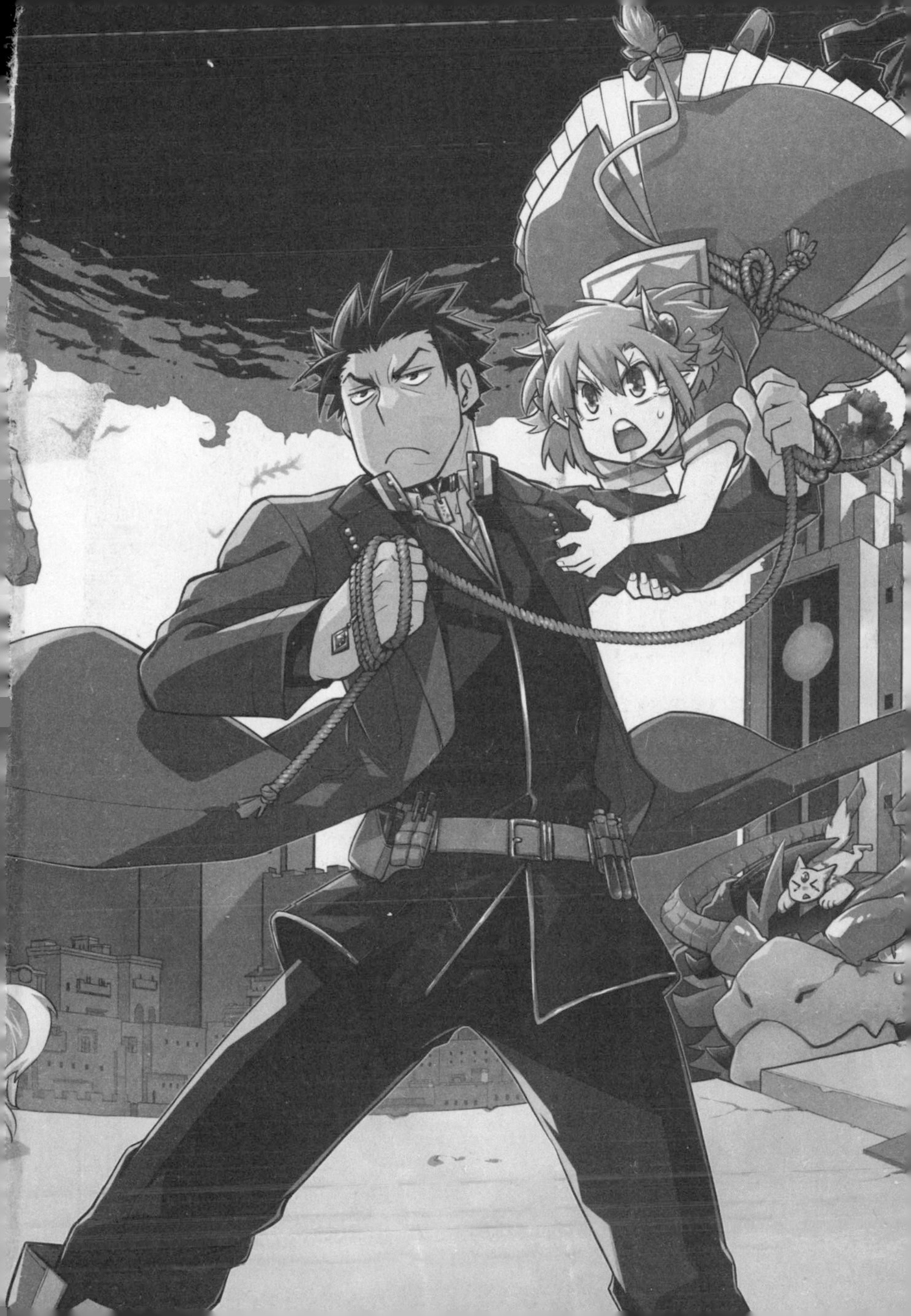

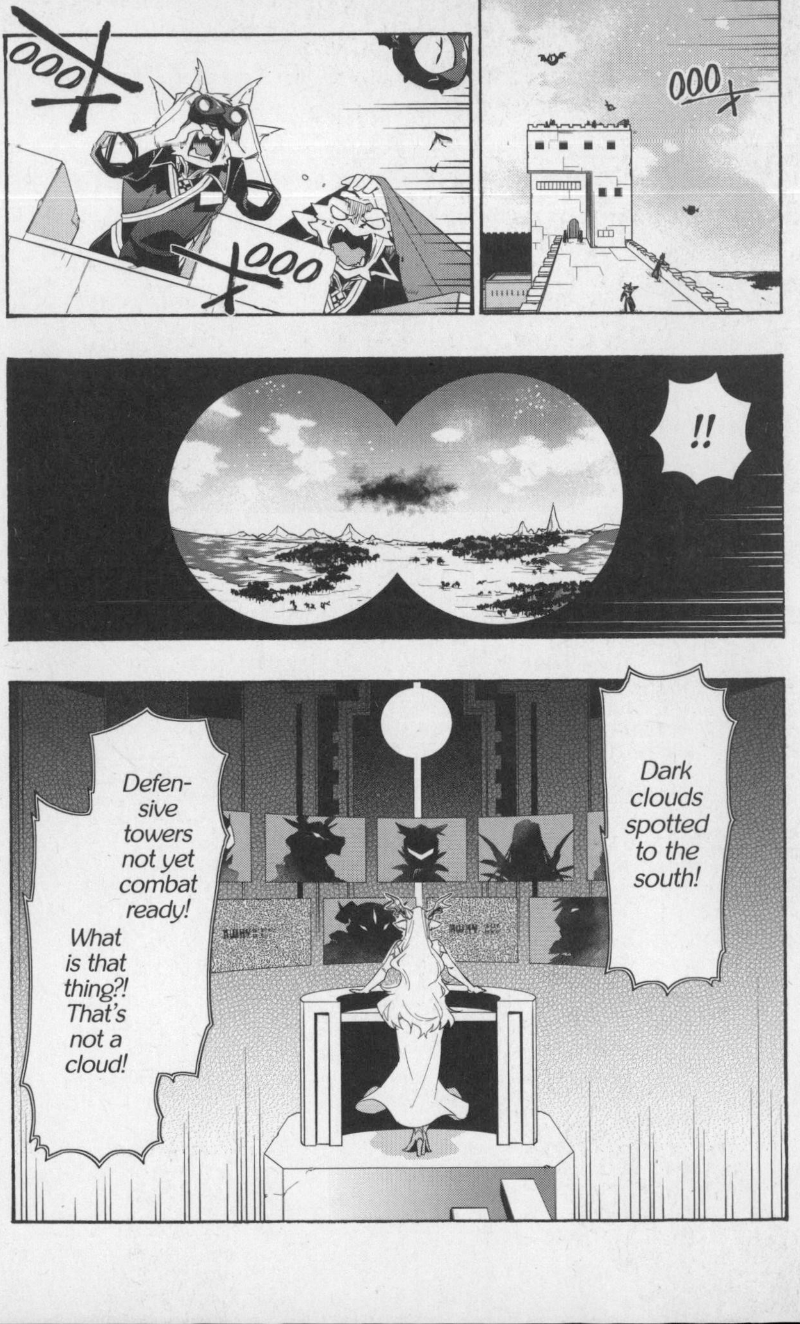
OOO
OOO
OOO
!!
Dark clouds spotted to the south!
Defensive towers not yet combat ready!
What is that thing?! That's not a cloud!

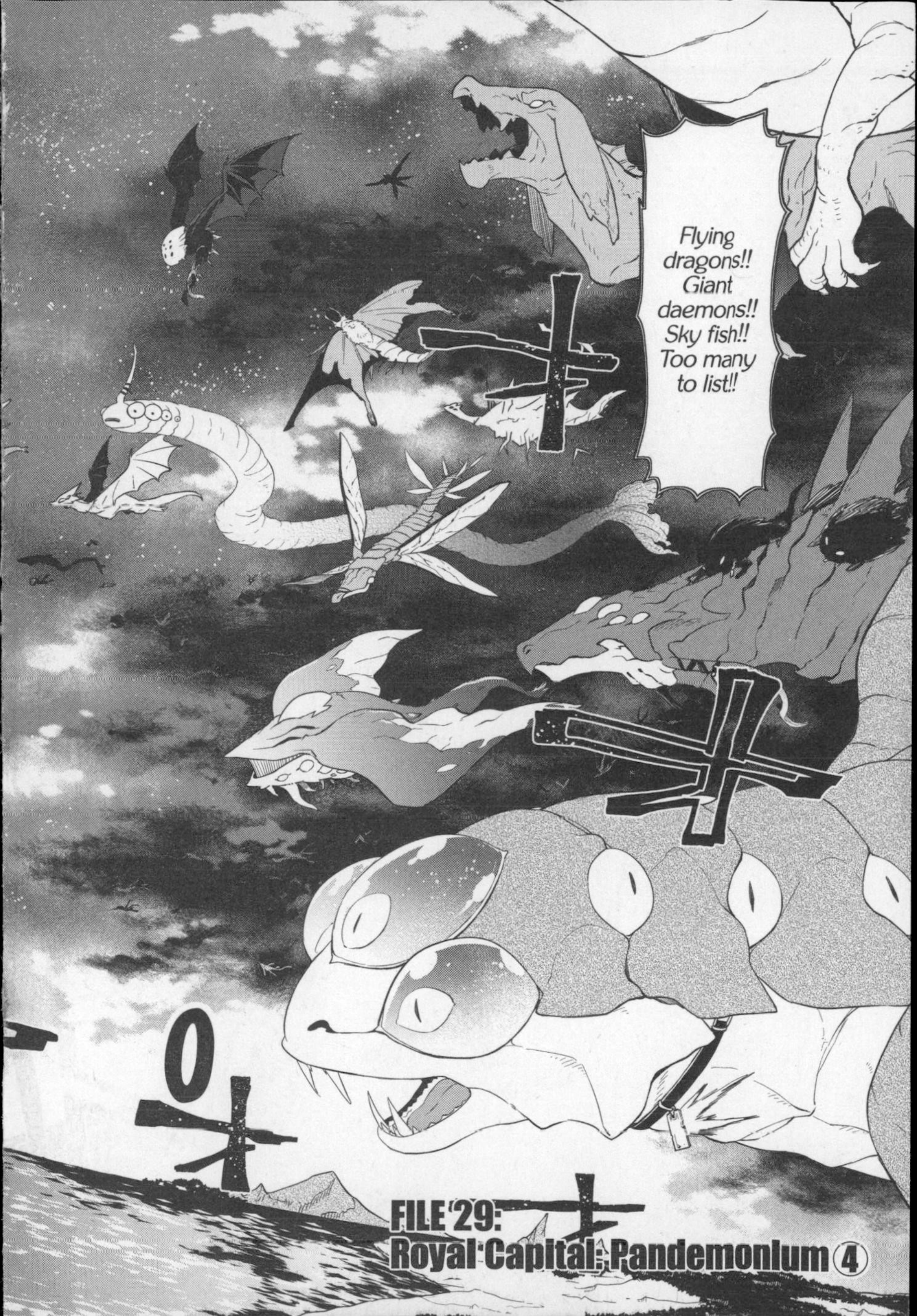
Flying dragons!! Giant daemons!! Sky fish!! Too many to list!!
FILE 29:
Royal Capital: Pandemonium ④

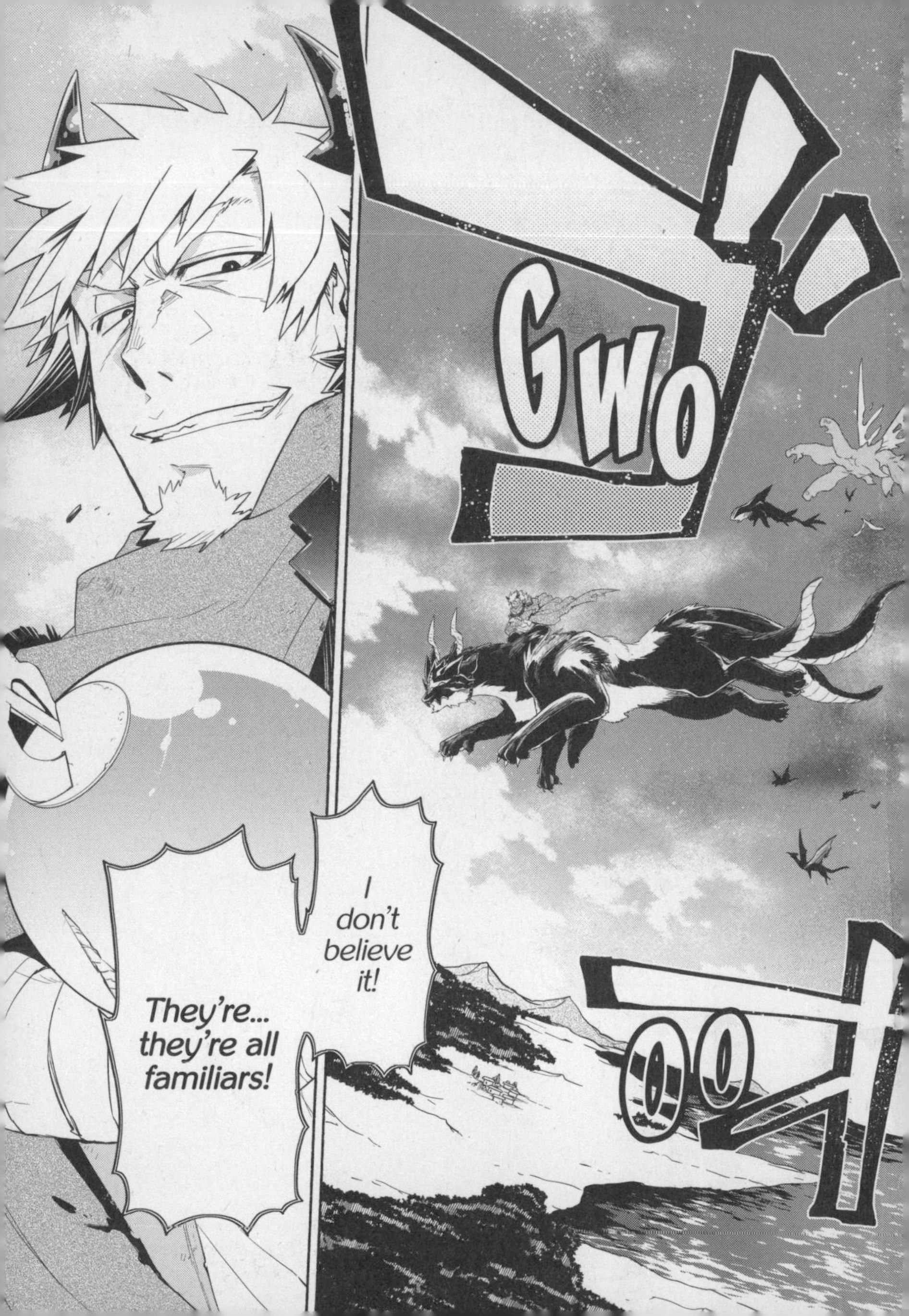
GWO
OO
I don't believe it!
They're... they're all familiars!

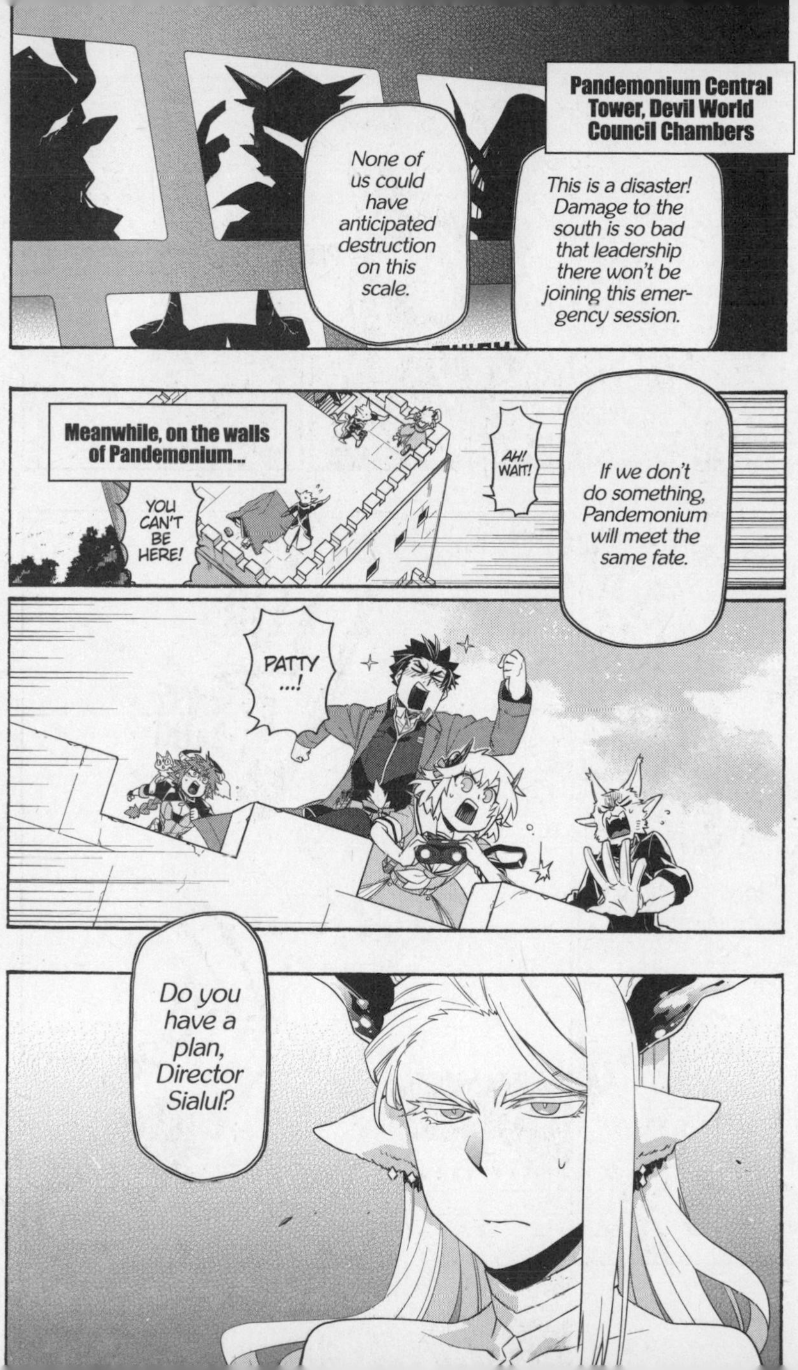
Pandemonium Central Tower, Devil World Council Chambers
This is a disaster! Damage to the south is so bad that leadership there won't be joining this emergency session.
None of us could have anticipated destruction on this scale.
If we don't do something, Pandemonium will meet the same fate.
AH! WAIT!
Meanwhile, on the walls of Pandemonium...
YOU CAN'T BE HERE!
PATTY ...!
Do you have a plan, Director Sialul?

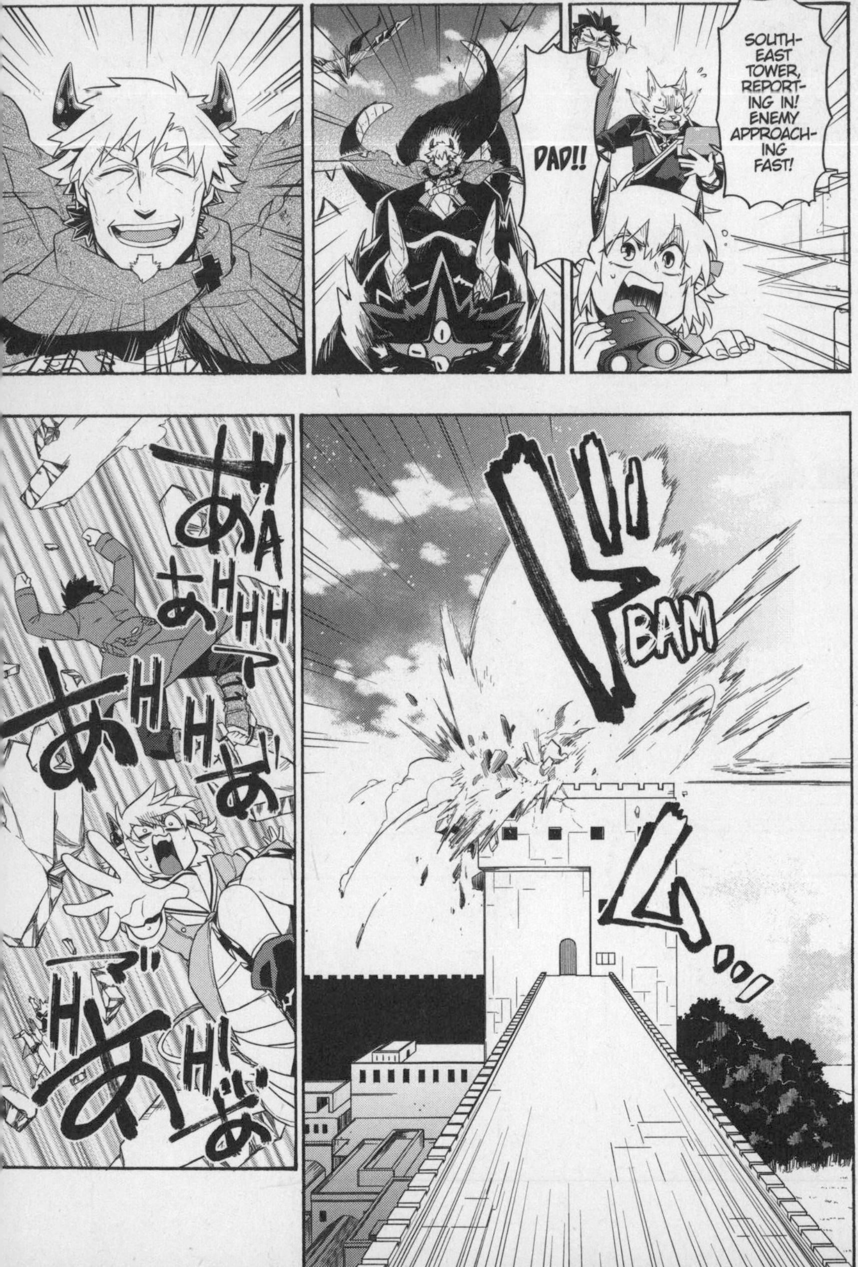
SOUTH-EAST TOWER, REPORTING IN! ENEMY APPROACHING FAST!
DAD!!
BAM

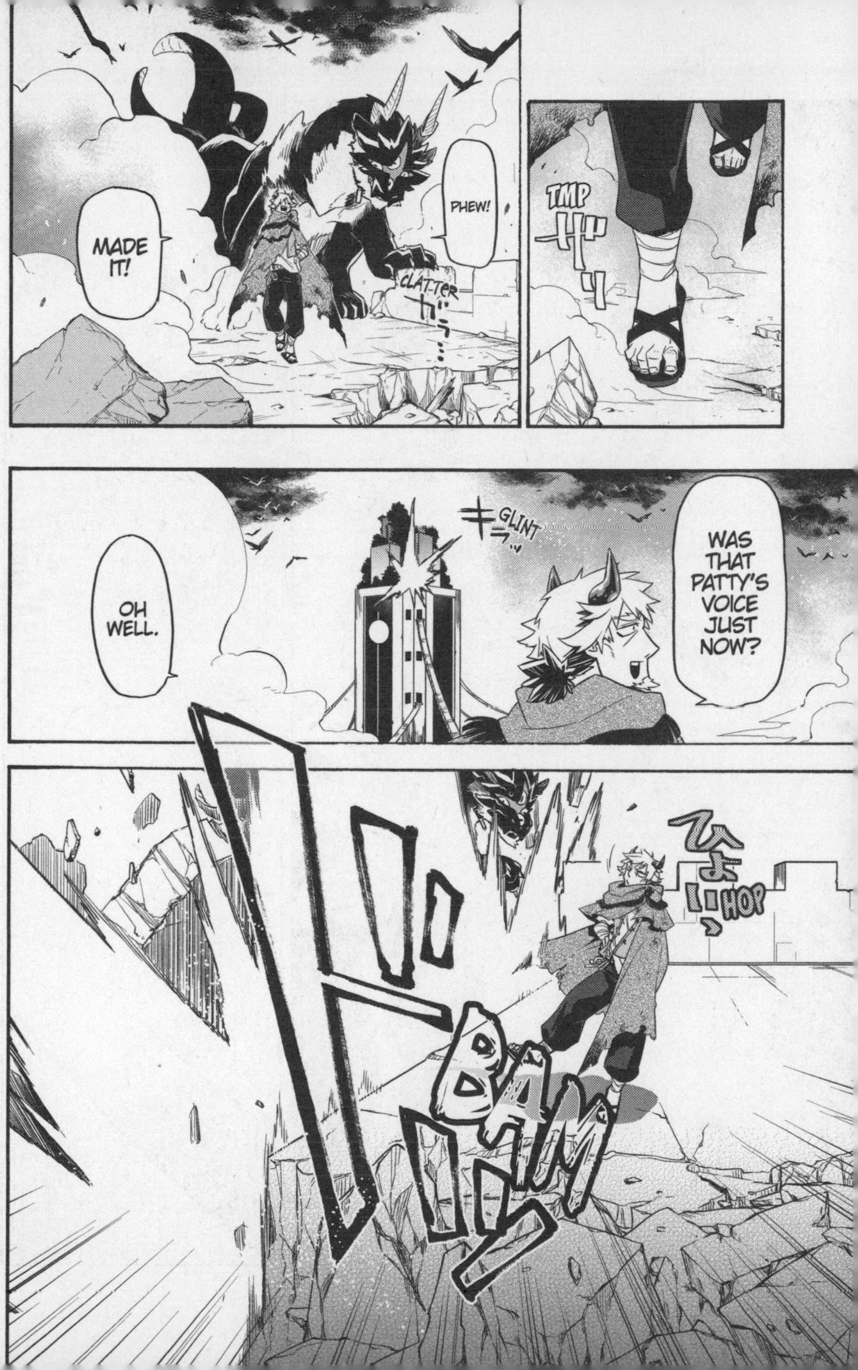
TMP
PHEW!
MADE IT!
CLATTER
WAS THAT PATTY'S VOICE JUST NOW?
GLINT
OH WELL.
ひょい
HOP
BAM

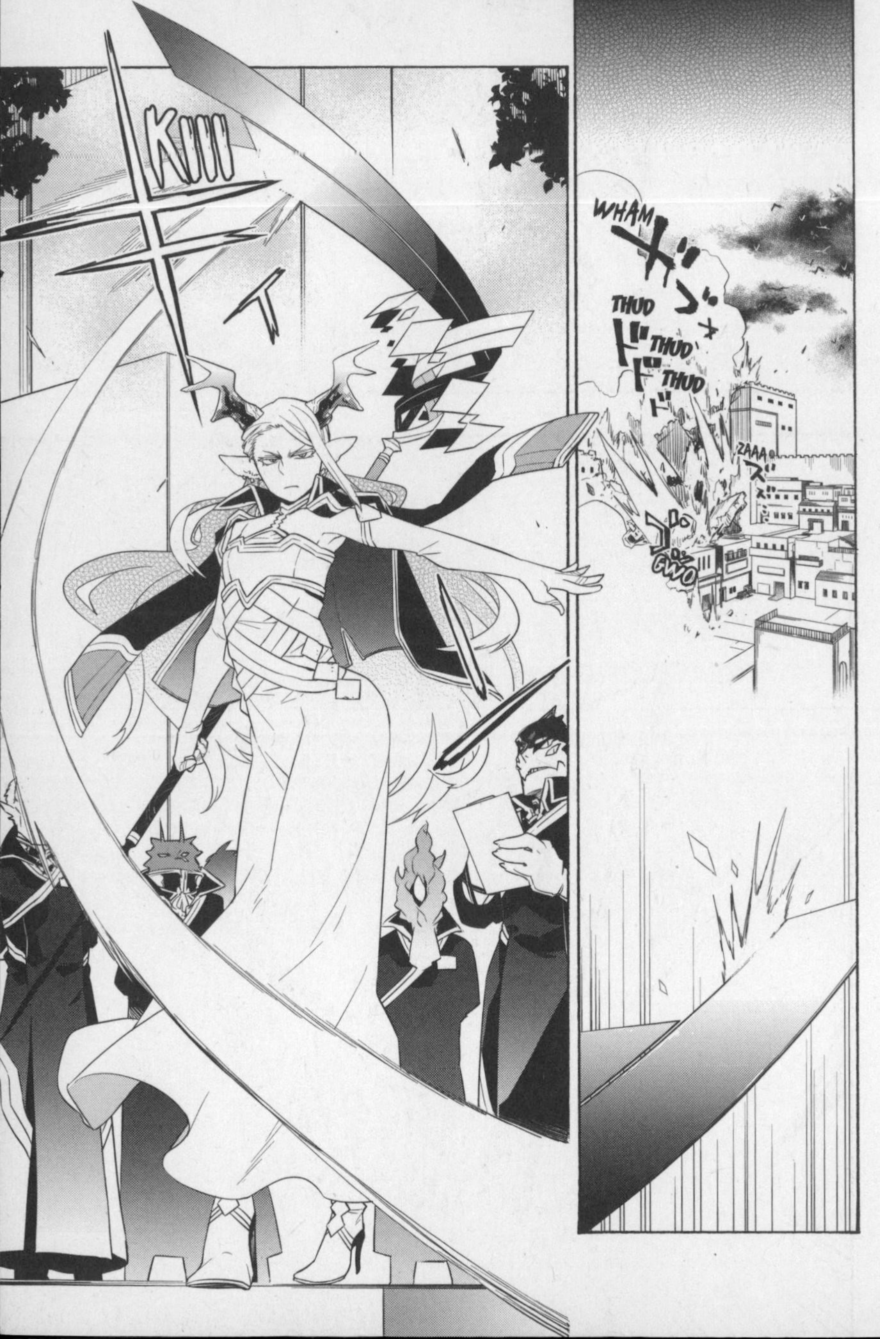
WHAM
THUD
THUD
THUD
ZAAA
GWO
KIIII

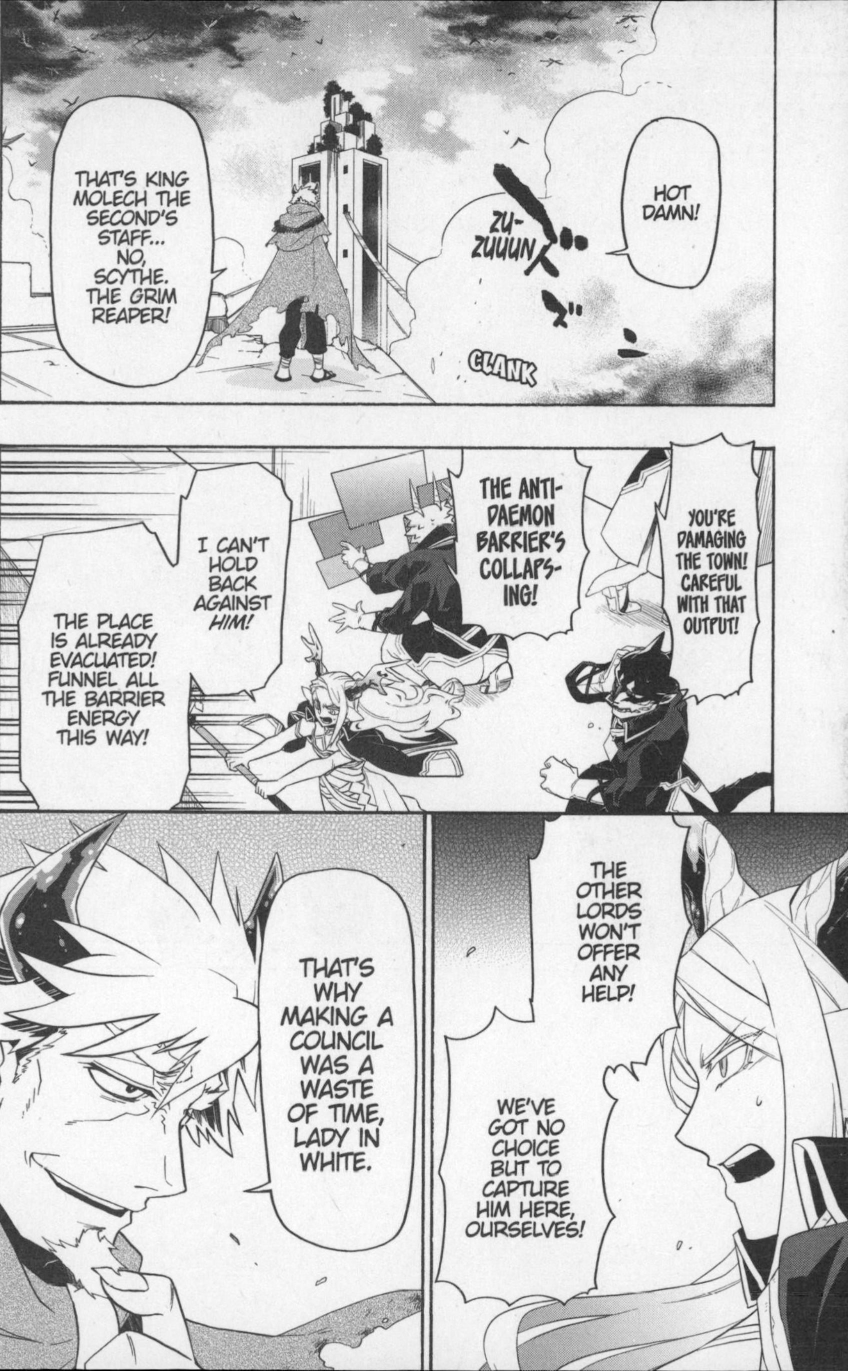
HOT DAMN!
ZU-ZUUUN
CLANK
THAT'S KING MOLECH THE SECOND'S STAFF... NO, SCYTHE. THE GRIM REAPER!
YOU'RE DAMAGING THE TOWN! CAREFUL WITH THAT OUTPUT!
THE ANTI-DAEMON BARRIER'S COLLAPS-ING!
I CAN'T HOLD BACK AGAINST *HIM!*
THE PLACE IS ALREADY EVACUATED! FUNNEL ALL THE BARRIER ENERGY THIS WAY!
THE OTHER LORDS WON'T OFFER ANY HELP!
WE'VE GOT NO CHOICE BUT TO CAPTURE HIM HERE, OURSELVES!
THAT'S WHY MAKING A COUNCIL WAS A WASTE OF TIME, LADY IN WHITE.

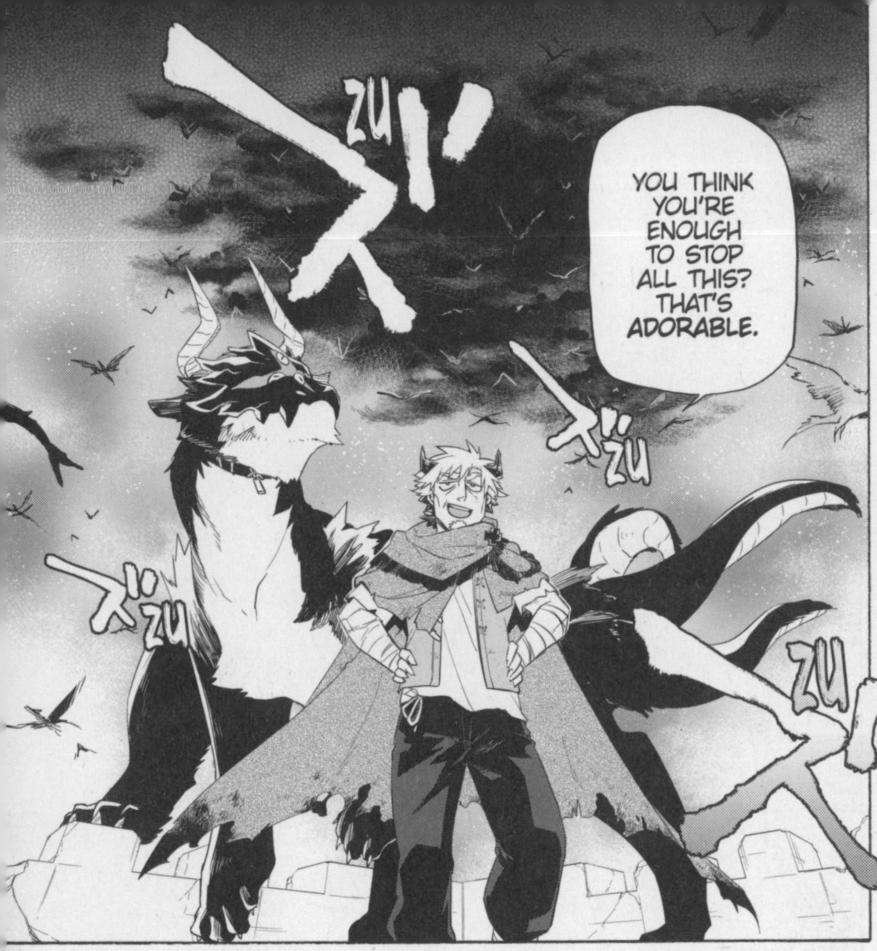
ZU
YOU THINK YOU'RE ENOUGH TO STOP ALL THIS? THAT'S ADORABLE.
ZU
ZU
ZU
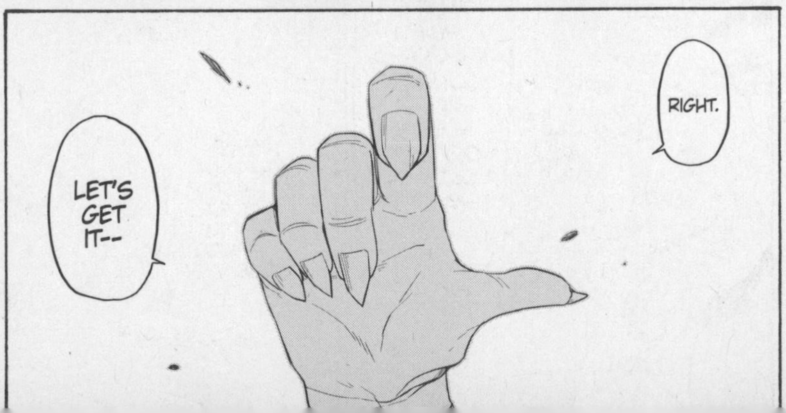
RIGHT.
LET'S GET IT--

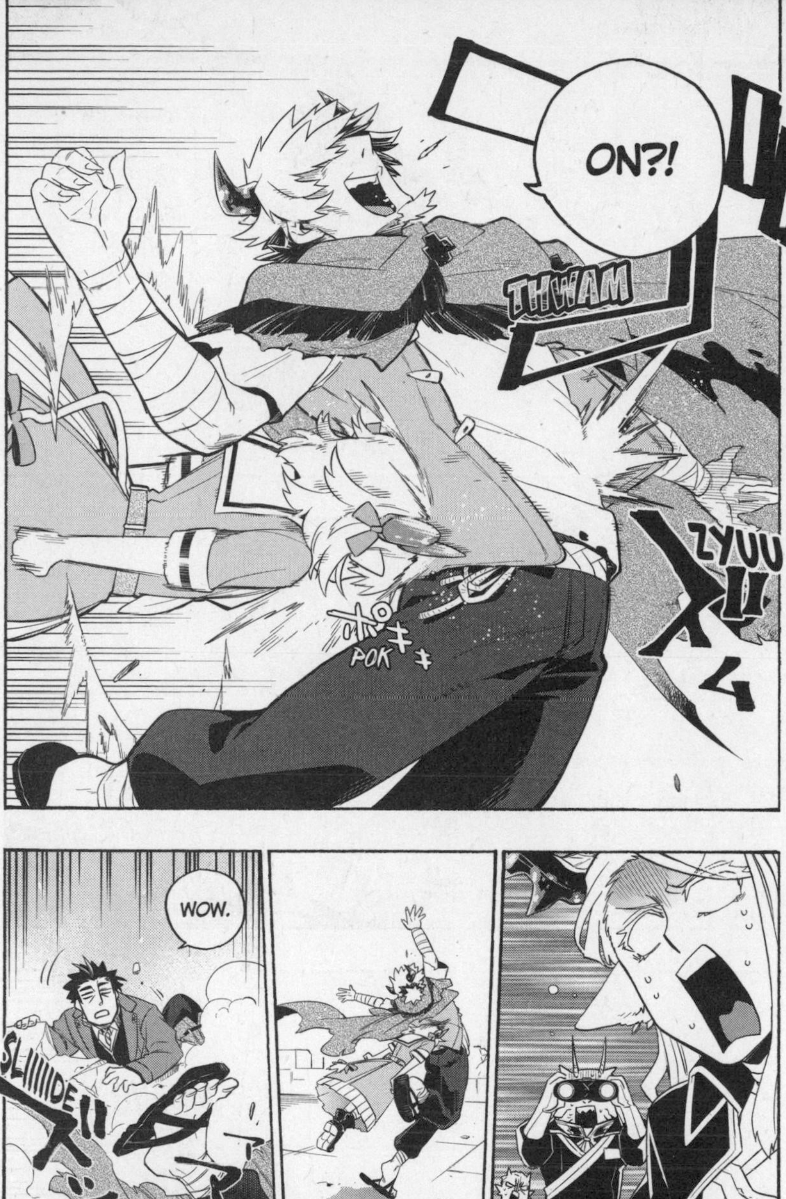
ON?!
THWAM
ZYUU
POK
WOW.
SLIIIIIDE!!

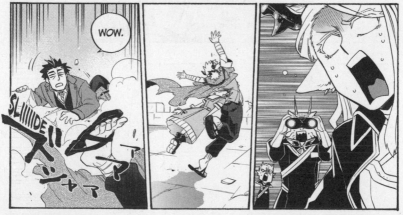

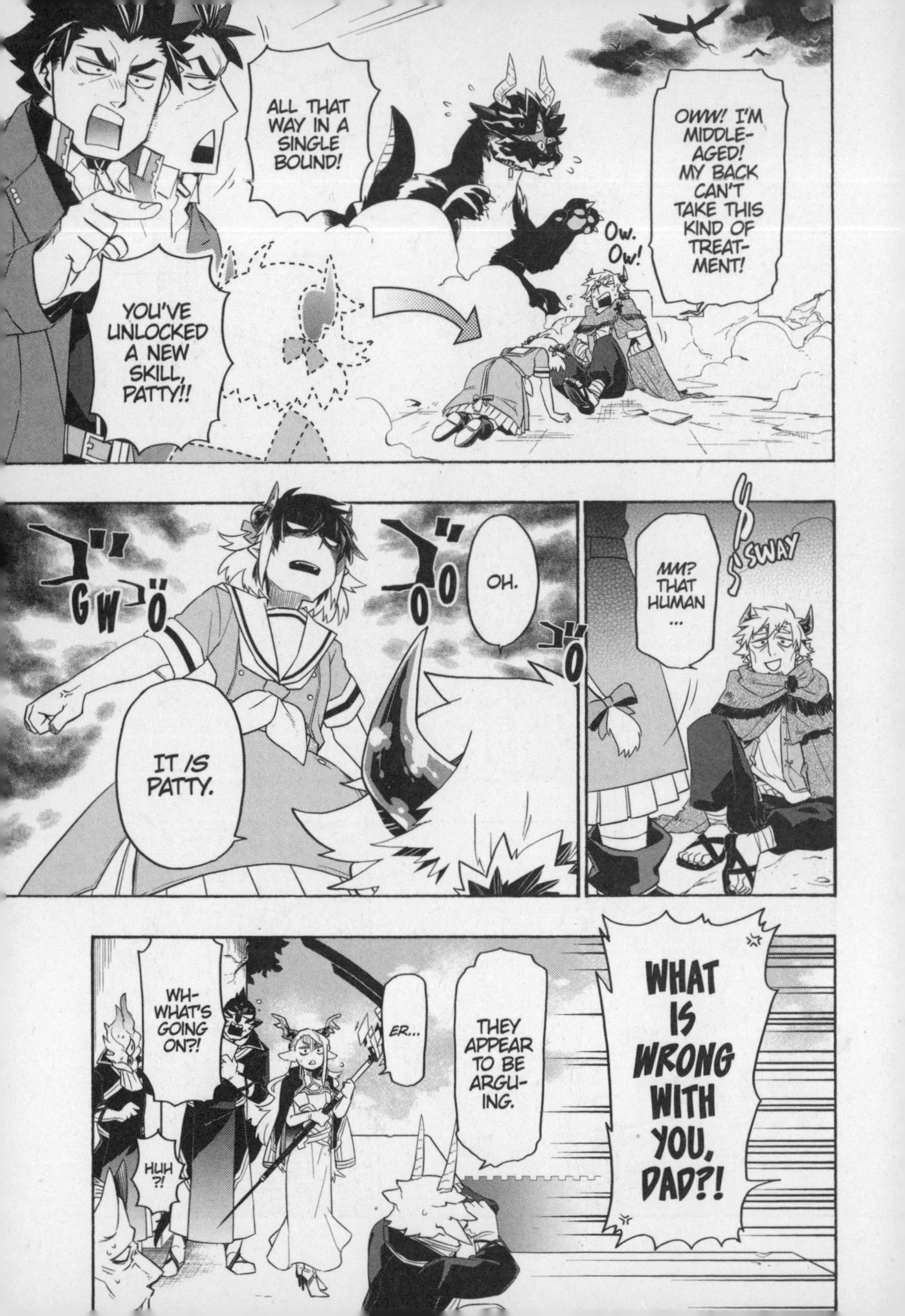
OWW! I'M MIDDLE-AGED! MY BACK CAN'T TAKE THIS KIND OF TREATMENT!
OW. OW!
ALL THAT WAY IN A SINGLE BOUND!
YOU'VE UNLOCKED A NEW SKILL, PATTY!!
SWAY
MM? THAT HUMAN ...
OH.
GWÖ
IT IS PATTY.
WHAT IS WRONG WITH YOU, DAD?!
THEY APPEAR TO BE ARGUING.
ER...
WH-WHAT'S GOING ON?!
HUH?!

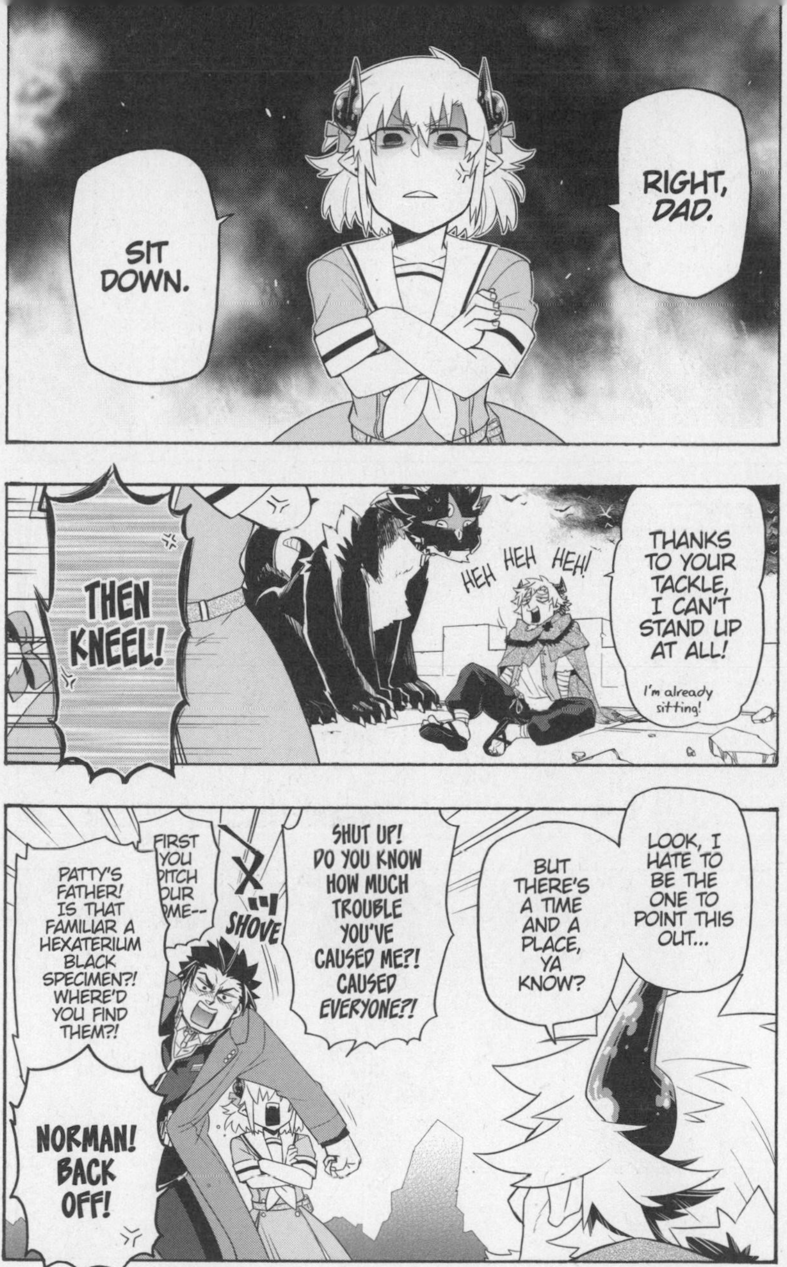
RIGHT, DAD.
SIT DOWN.
THANKS TO YOUR TACKLE, I CAN'T STAND UP AT ALL!
I'm already sitting!
HEH HEH HEH!
THEN KNEEL!
LOOK, I HATE TO BE THE ONE TO POINT THIS OUT...
BUT THERE'S A TIME AND A PLACE, YA KNOW?
SHUT UP! DO YOU KNOW HOW MUCH TROUBLE YOU'VE CAUSED ME?! CAUSED EVERYONE?!
SHOVE
FIRST YOU
PATTY'S FATHER! IS THAT FAMILIAR A HEXATERIUM BLACK SPECIMEN?! WHERE'D YOU FIND THEM?!
NORMAN! BACK OFF!

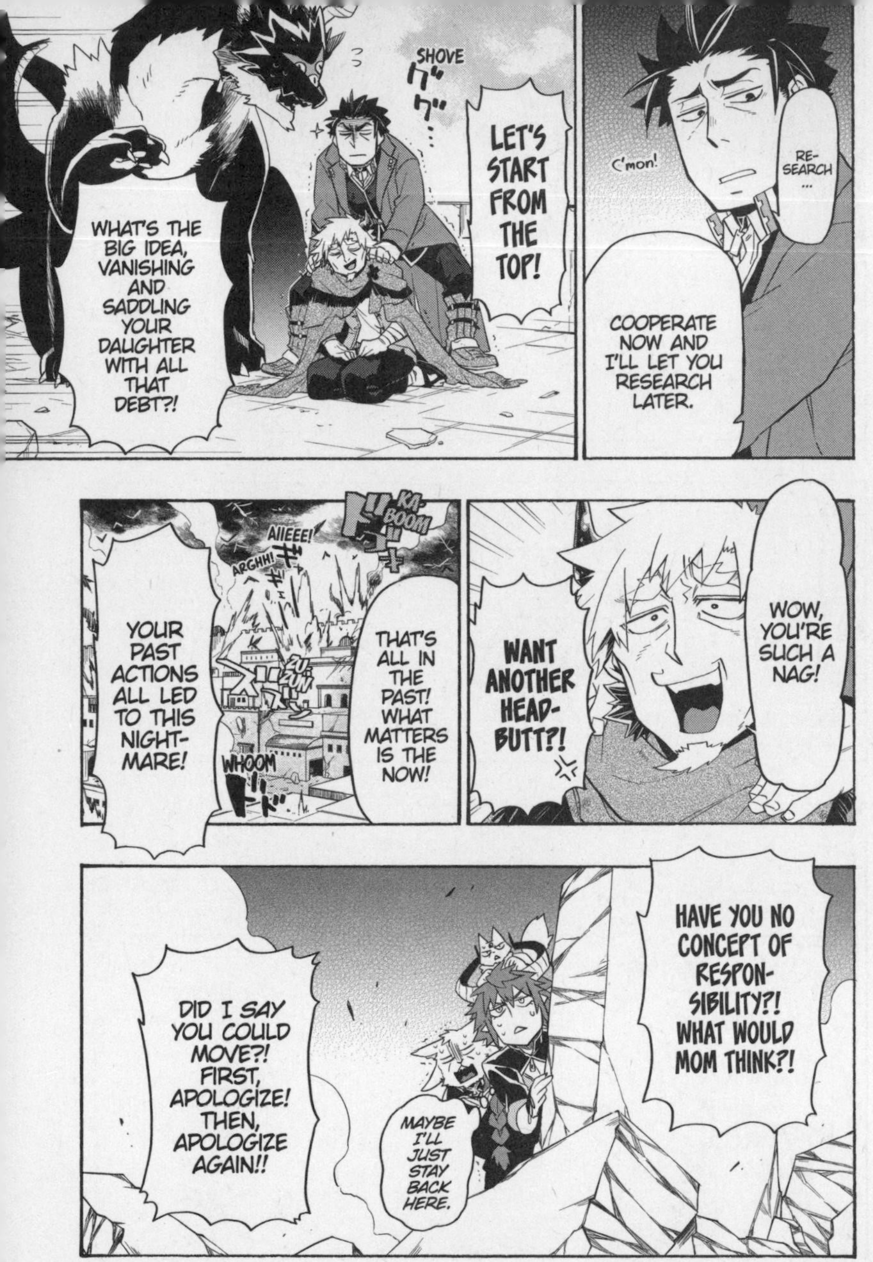
RE-SEARCH ...
C'mon!
COOPERATE NOW AND I'LL LET YOU RESEARCH LATER.
SHOVE
LET'S START FROM THE TOP!
WHAT'S THE BIG IDEA, VANISHING AND SADDLING YOUR DAUGHTER WITH ALL THAT DEBT?!
WOW, YOU'RE SUCH A NAG!
WANT ANOTHER HEAD-BUTT?!
KA-BOOM
AIIEEE!
ARGHH!
THAT'S ALL IN THE PAST! WHAT MATTERS IS THE NOW!
ZUZUN
WHOOM
YOUR PAST ACTIONS ALL LED TO THIS NIGHT-MARE!
HAVE YOU NO CONCEPT OF RESPON-SIBILITY?! WHAT WOULD MOM THINK?!
MAYBE I'LL JUST STAY BACK HERE.
DID I SAY YOU COULD MOVE?! FIRST, APOLOGIZE! THEN, APOLOGIZE AGAIN!!

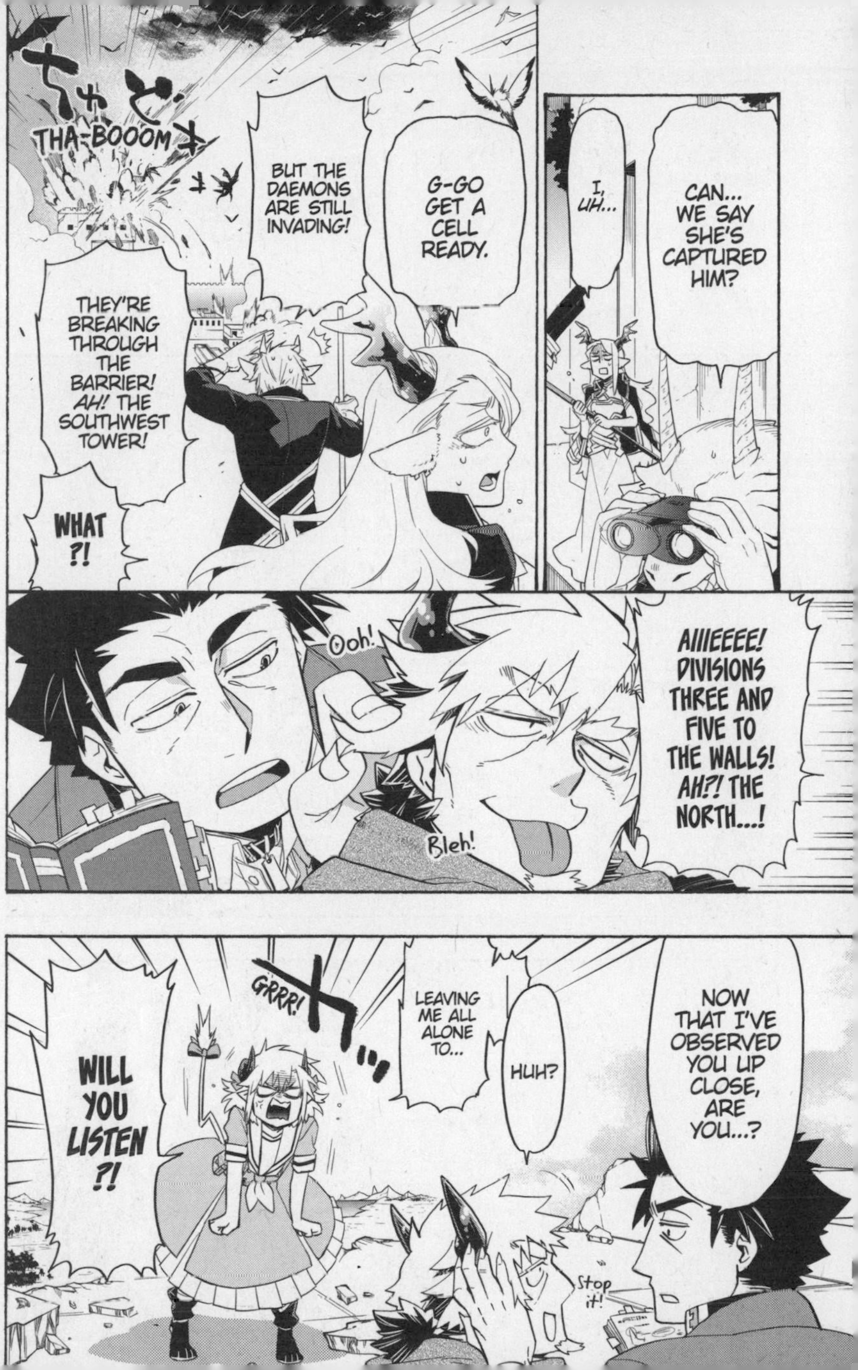
CAN... WE SAY SHE'S CAPTURED HIM?
I, UH...
THA-BOOOM
G-GO GET A CELL READY.
BUT THE DAEMONS ARE STILL INVADING!
THEY'RE BREAKING THROUGH THE BARRIER! AH! THE SOUTHWEST TOWER!
WHAT?!
AIIIEEEE! DIVISIONS THREE AND FIVE TO THE WALLS! AH?! THE NORTH...!
Ooh!
Bleh!
NOW THAT I'VE OBSERVED YOU UP CLOSE, ARE YOU...?
HUH?
LEAVING ME ALL ALONE TO...
GRRR!
WILL YOU LISTEN?!
Stop it!

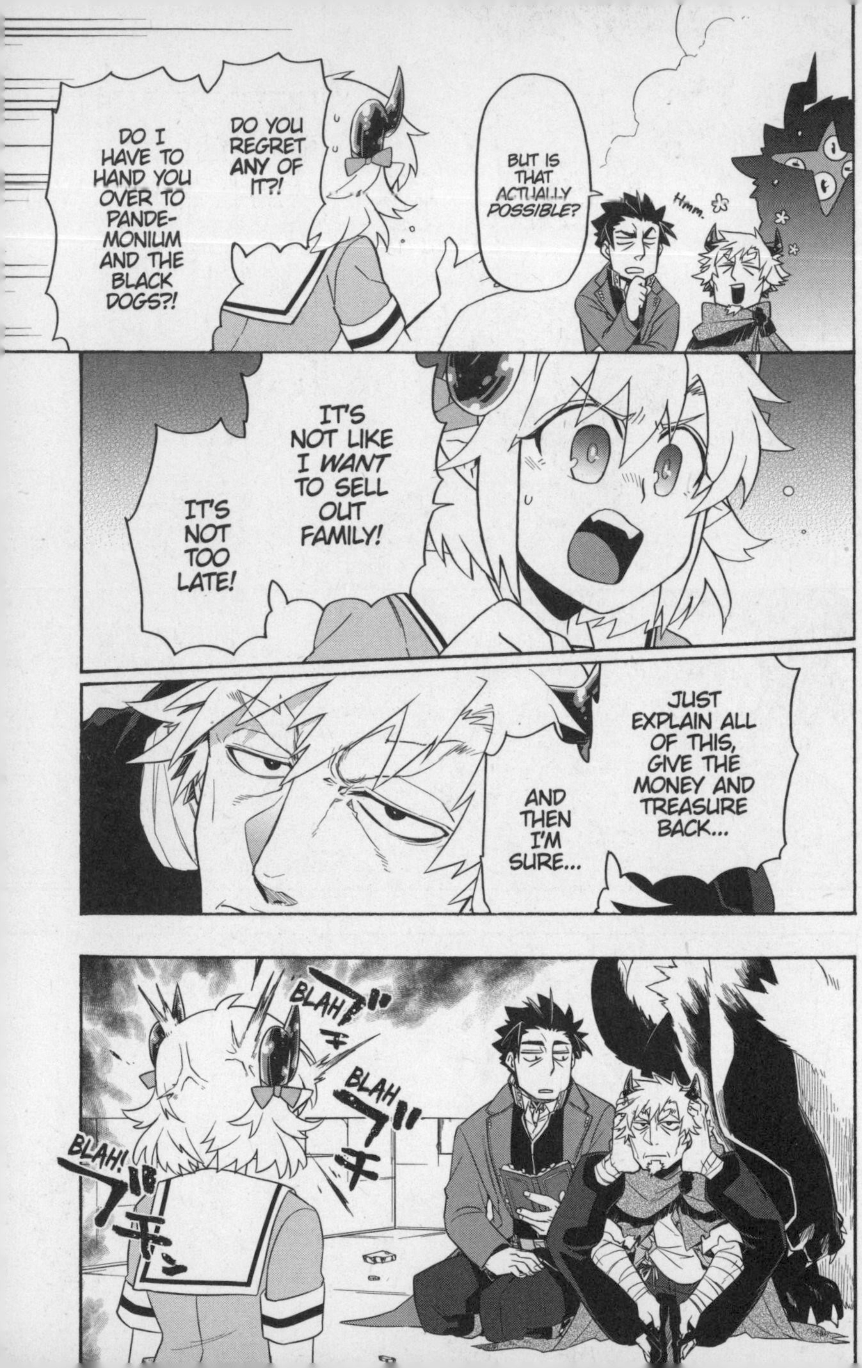
Hmm.
BUT IS THAT ACTUALLY *POSSIBLE?*
DO YOU REGRET ANY OF IT?!
DO I HAVE TO HAND YOU OVER TO PANDEMONIUM AND THE BLACK DOGS?!
IT'S NOT LIKE I *WANT* TO SELL OUT FAMILY!
IT'S NOT TOO LATE!
JUST EXPLAIN ALL OF THIS, GIVE THE MONEY AND TREASURE BACK...
AND THEN I'M SURE...
BLAH
BLAH
BLAH!

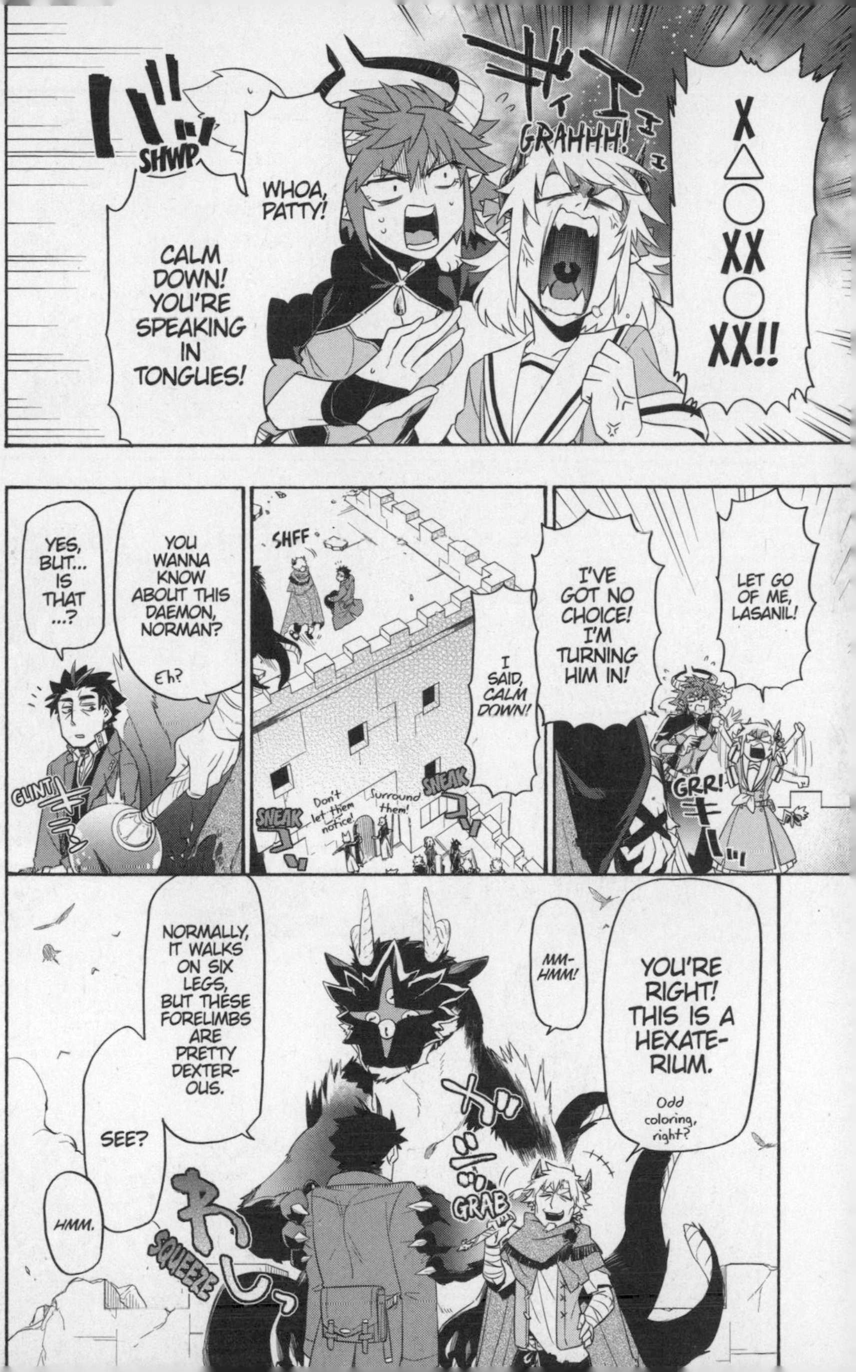
X△○XX○XX!!
GRAHHH!
WHOA, PATTY!
CALM DOWN! YOU'RE SPEAKING IN TONGUES!
SHWP
LET GO OF ME, LASANIL!
I'VE GOT NO CHOICE! I'M TURNING HIM IN!
GRR!
I SAID, CALM DOWN!
SHFF
SNEAK
Surround them!
Don't let them notice!
SNEAK
YOU WANNA KNOW ABOUT THIS DAEMON, NORMAN?
YES, BUT... IS THAT ...?
Eh?
GLINT
YOU'RE RIGHT! THIS IS A HEXATE-RIUM.
Odd coloring, right?
MM-HMM!
NORMALLY, IT WALKS ON SIX LEGS, BUT THESE FORELIMBS ARE PRETTY DEXTER-OUS.
GRAB
SEE?
HMM.
SQUEEZE

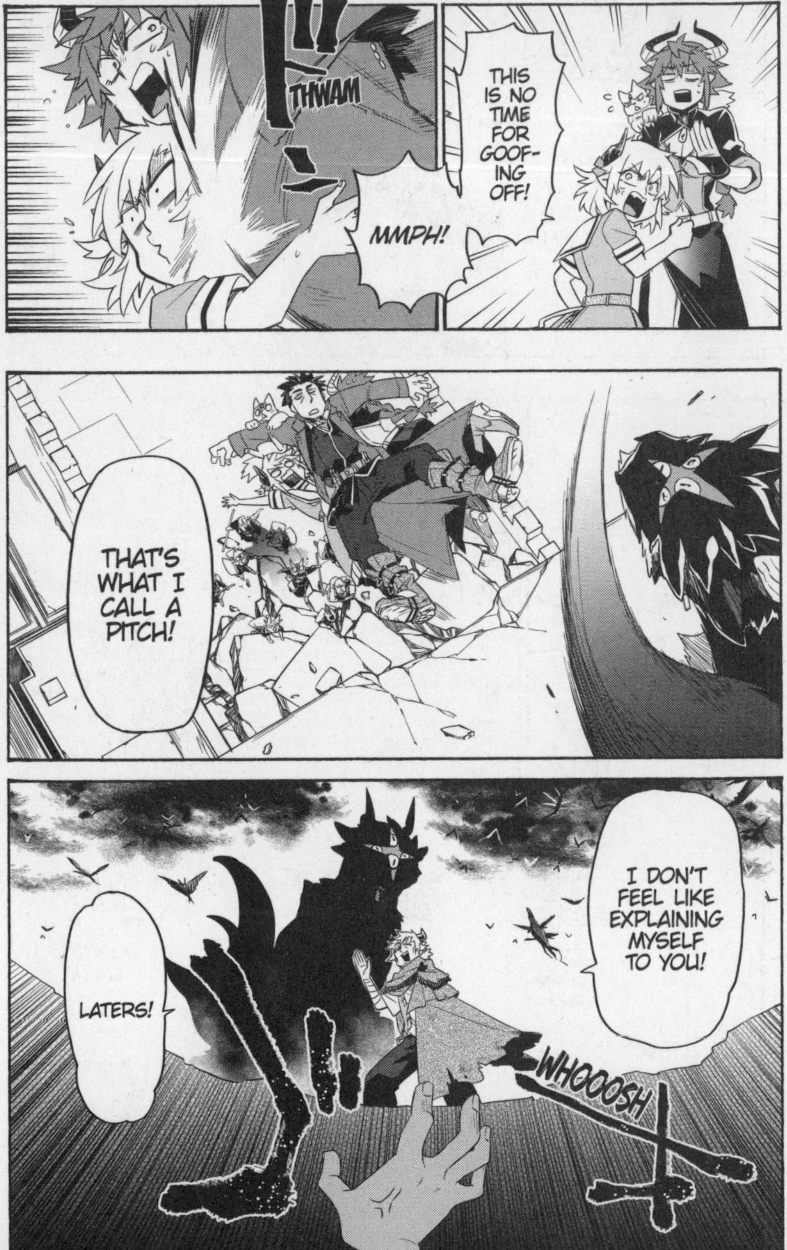
THIS IS NO TIME FOR GOOF-ING OFF!
THWAM
MMPH!
THAT'S WHAT I CALL A PITCH!
I DON'T FEEL LIKE EXPLAINING MYSELF TO YOU!
WHOOOOSH
LATERS!

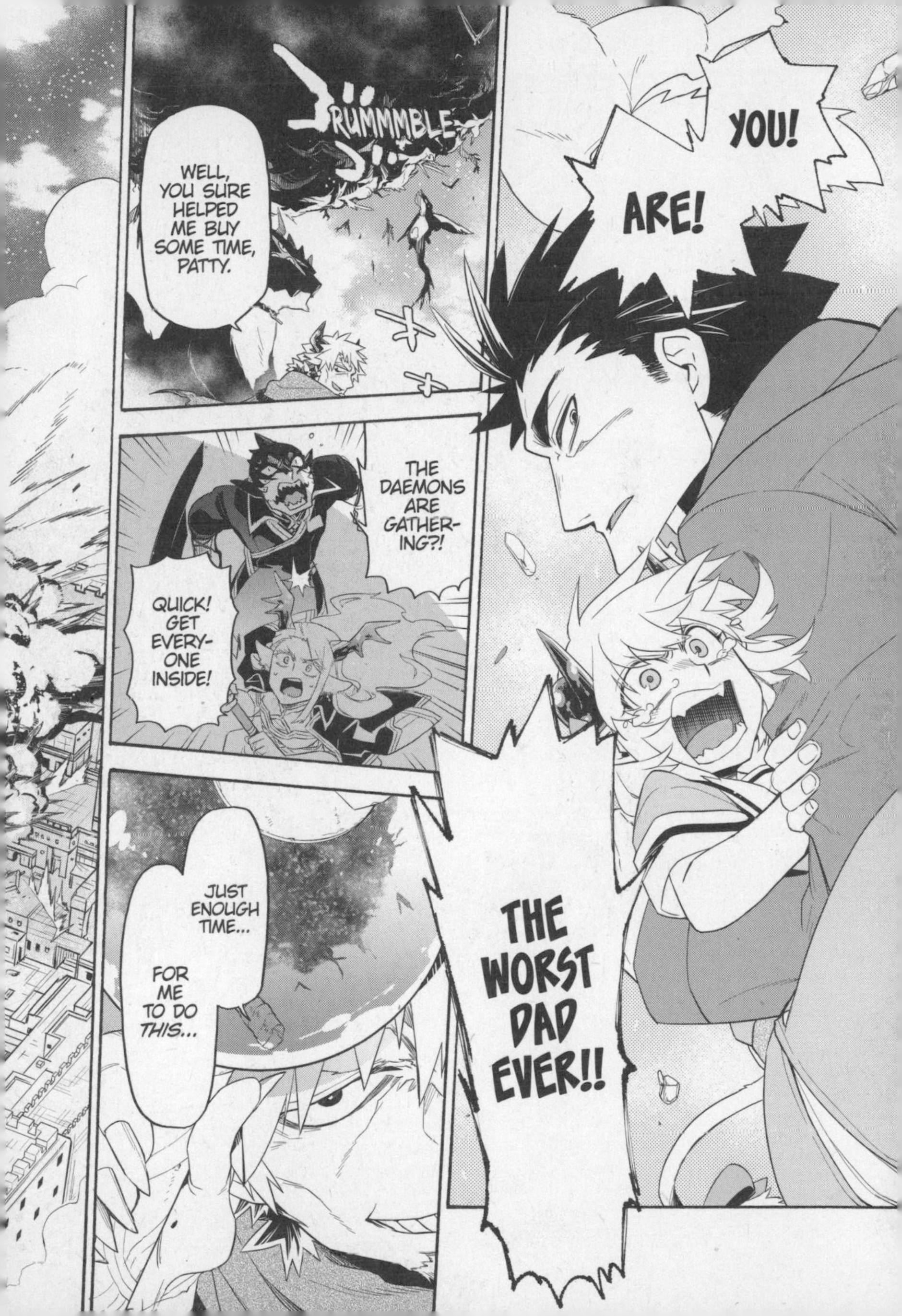
YOU!
ARE!
THE WORST DAD EVER!!
RUMMMBLE
WELL, YOU SURE HELPED ME BUY SOME TIME, PATTY.
THE DAEMONS ARE GATHERING?!
QUICK! GET EVERY-ONE INSIDE!
JUST ENOUGH TIME...
FOR ME TO DO THIS...

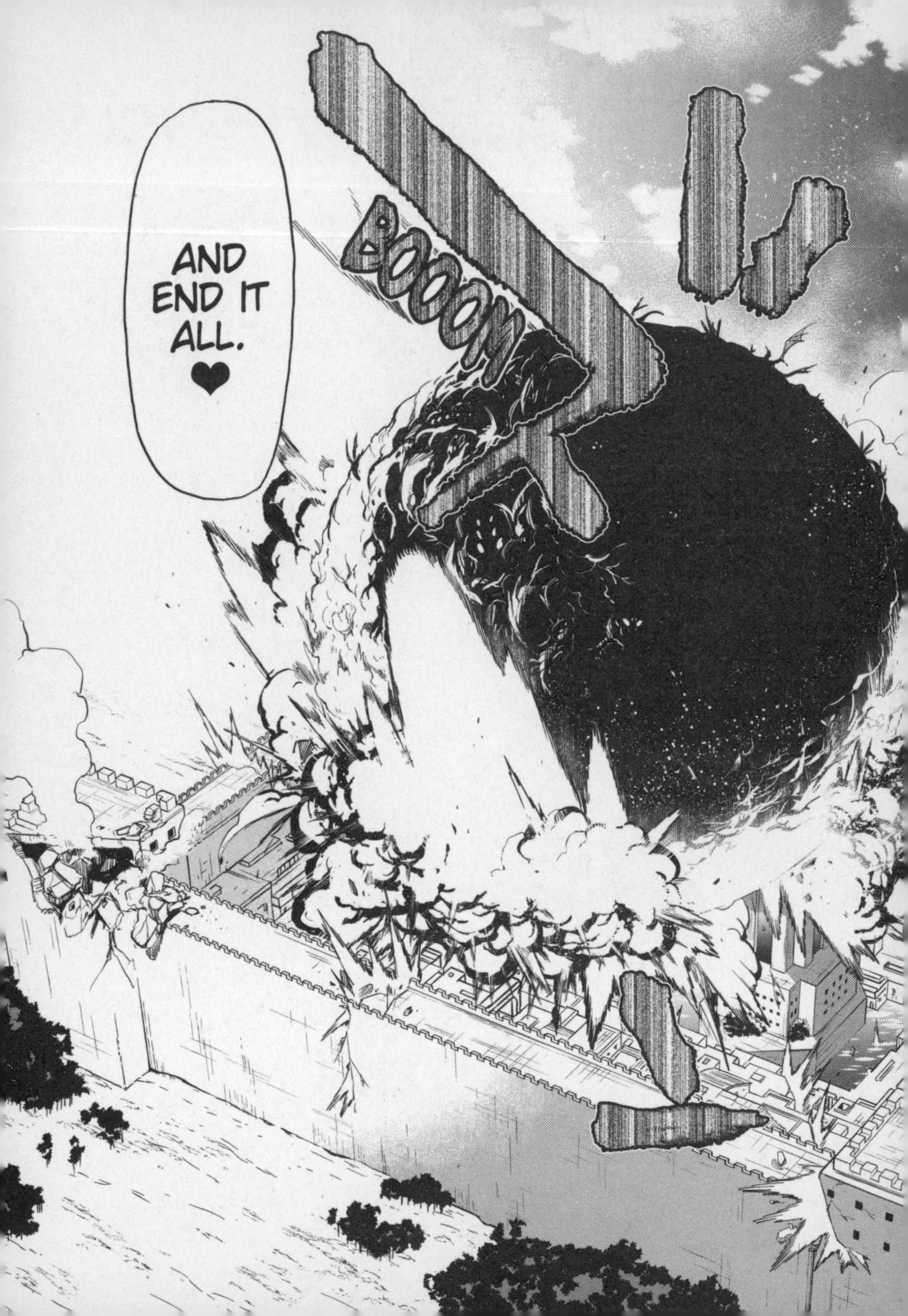
AND END IT ALL. ❤
BOOOOM

Sorry For My Familiar

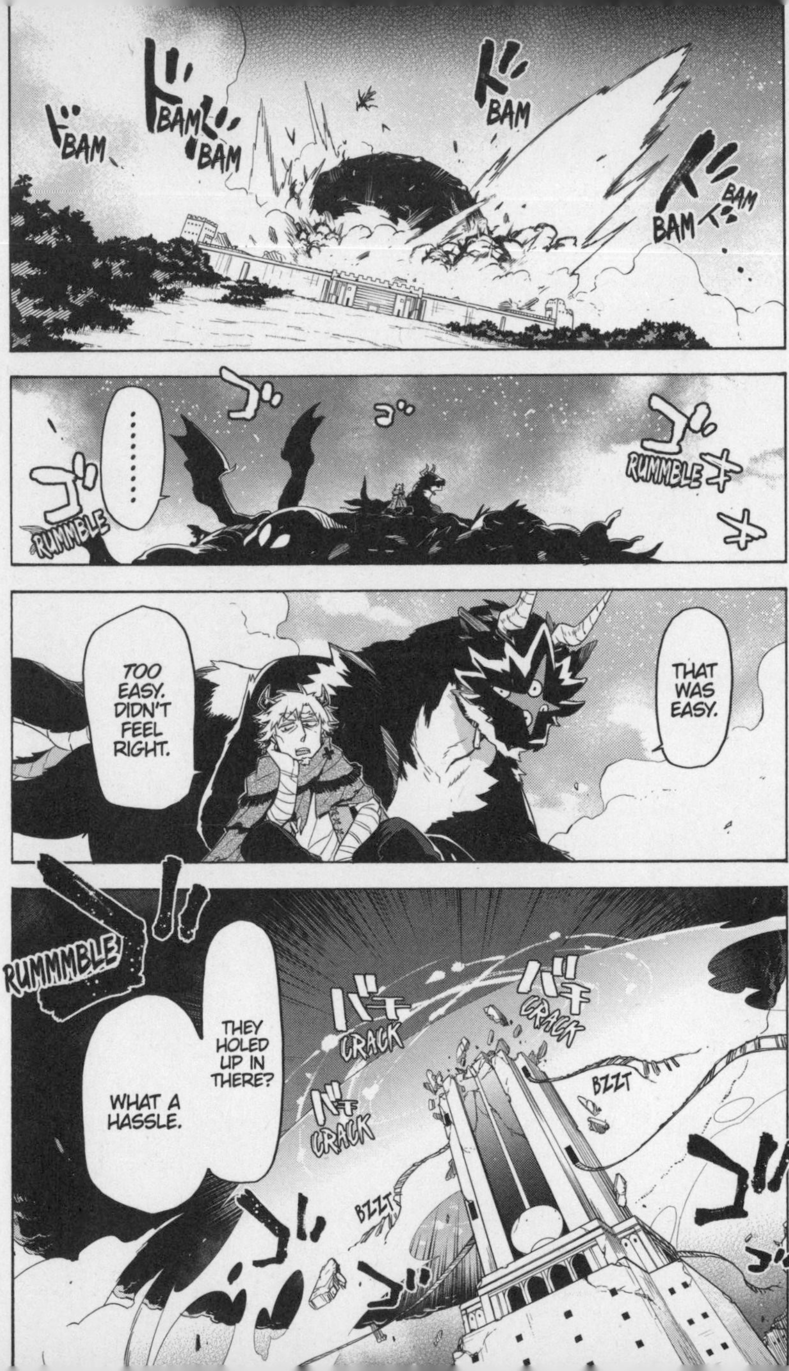
BAM
BAM
BAM
BAM
BAM
BAM
RUMMBLE
......
RUMMBLE
THAT WAS EASY.
TOO EASY. DIDN'T FEEL RIGHT.
CRACK
BZZT
CRACK
THEY HOLED UP IN THERE?
WHAT A HASSLE.
CRACK
BZZT
RUMMMBLE

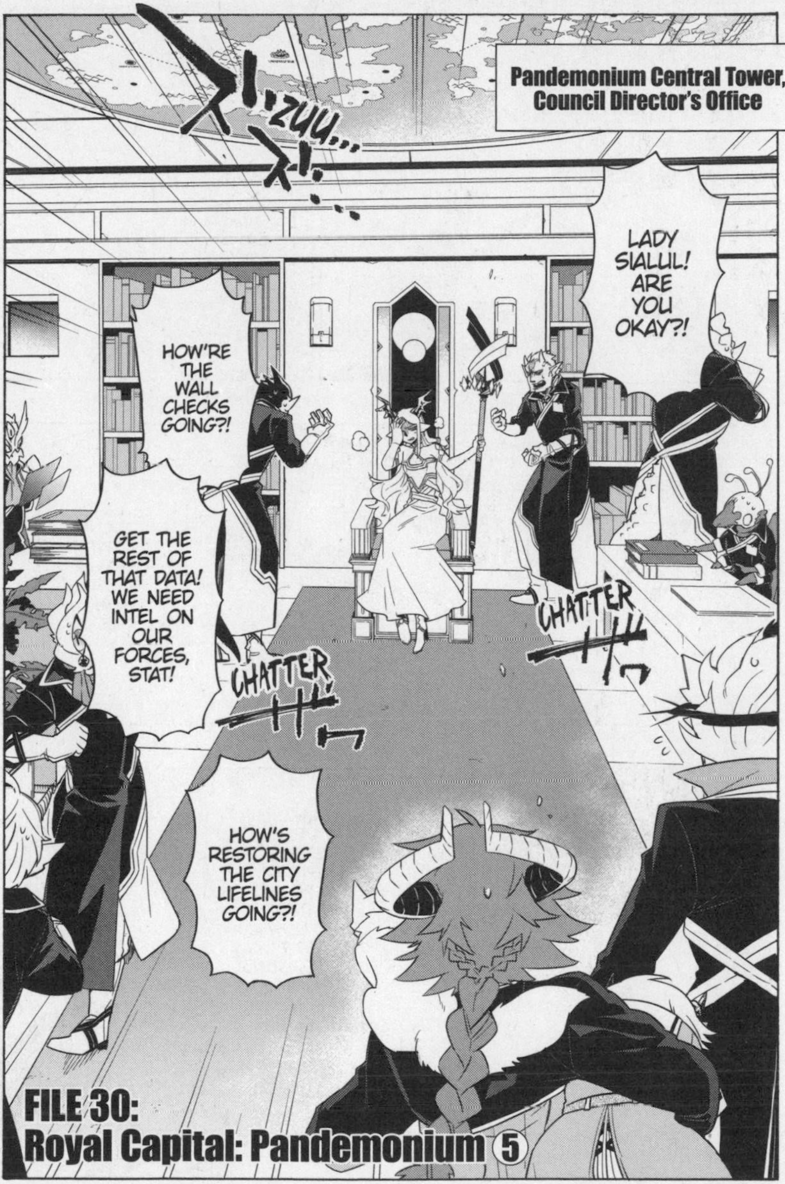
Pandemonium Central Tower, Council Director's Office
ZUU...
ZUU...
LADY SIALUL! ARE YOU OKAY?!
HOW'RE THE WALL CHECKS GOING?!
GET THE REST OF THAT DATA! WE NEED INTEL ON OUR FORCES, STAT!
CHATTER
CHATTER
HOW'S RESTORING THE CITY LIFELINES GOING?!
FILE 30:
Royal Capital: Pandemonium 5

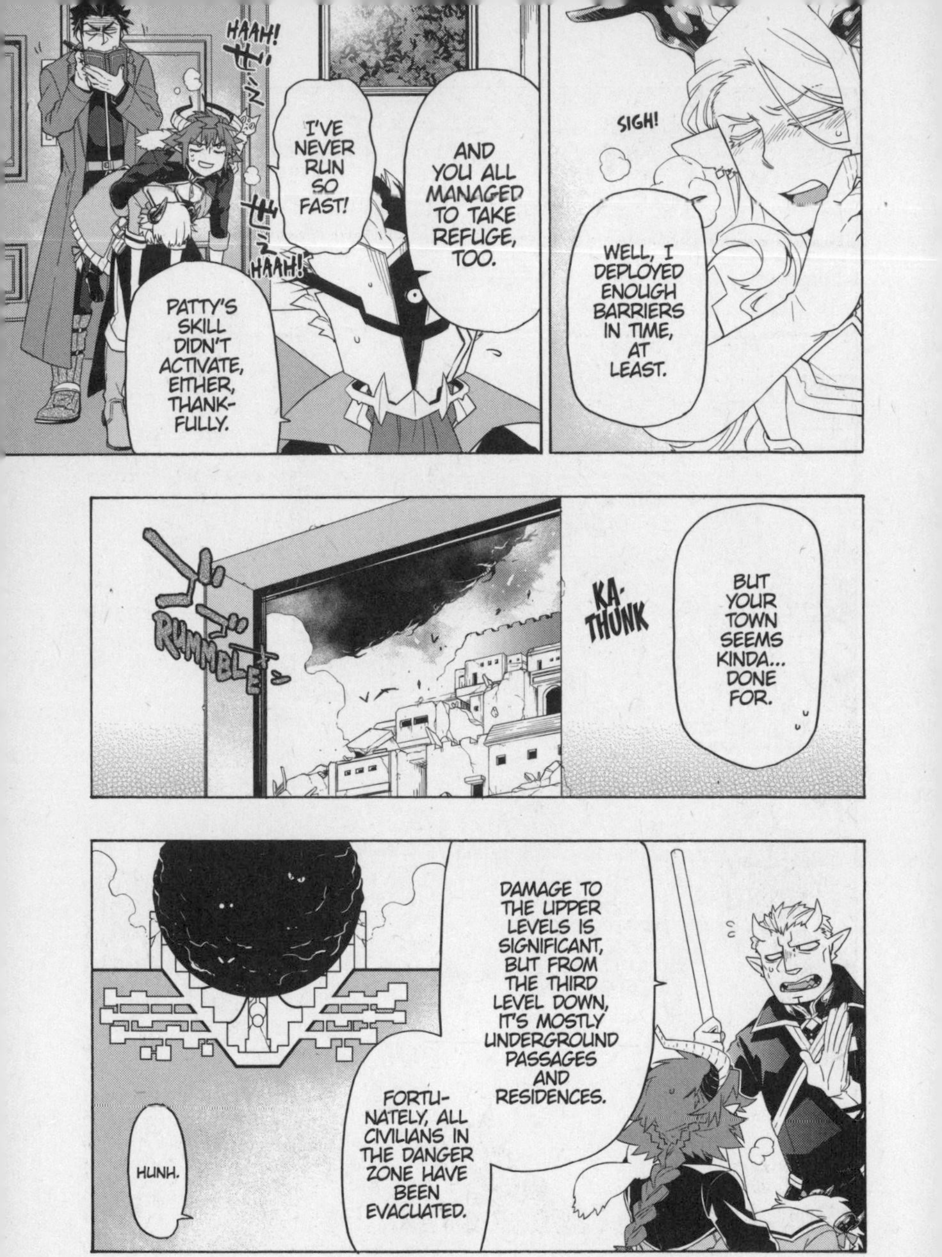
SIGH!
WELL, I DEPLOYED ENOUGH BARRIERS IN TIME, AT LEAST.
AND YOU ALL MANAGED TO TAKE REFUGE, TOO.
I'VE NEVER RUN SO FAST!
HAAH!
HAAH!
PATTY'S SKILL DIDN'T ACTIVATE, EITHER, THANKFULLY.
KA-THUNK
BUT YOUR TOWN SEEMS KINDA... DONE FOR.
RUMMBLE
DAMAGE TO THE UPPER LEVELS IS SIGNIFICANT, BUT FROM THE THIRD LEVEL DOWN, IT'S MOSTLY UNDERGROUND PASSAGES AND RESIDENCES.
FORTUNATELY, ALL CIVILIANS IN THE DANGER ZONE HAVE BEEN EVACUATED.
HUNH.

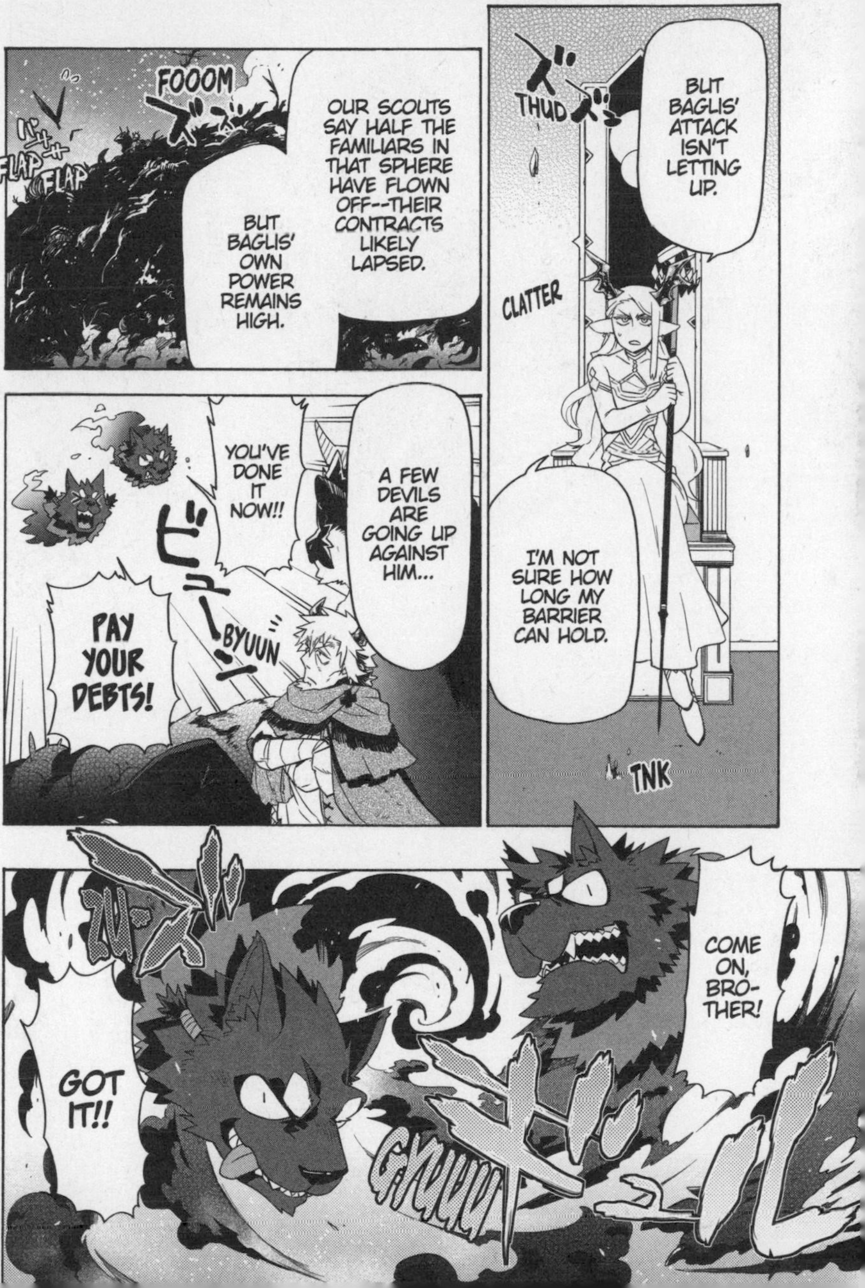
THUD
BUT BAGLIS' ATTACK ISN'T LETTING UP.
CLATTER
I'M NOT SURE HOW LONG MY BARRIER CAN HOLD.
TNK
FOOOM
OUR SCOUTS SAY HALF THE FAMILIARS IN THAT SPHERE HAVE FLOWN OFF--THEIR CONTRACTS LIKELY LAPSED.
BUT BAGLIS' OWN POWER REMAINS HIGH.
FLAP FLAP
A FEW DEVILS ARE GOING UP AGAINST HIM...
YOU'VE DONE IT NOW!!
BYUUN
PAY YOUR DEBTS!
COME ON, BRO-THER!
GYUUUN
GOT IT!!

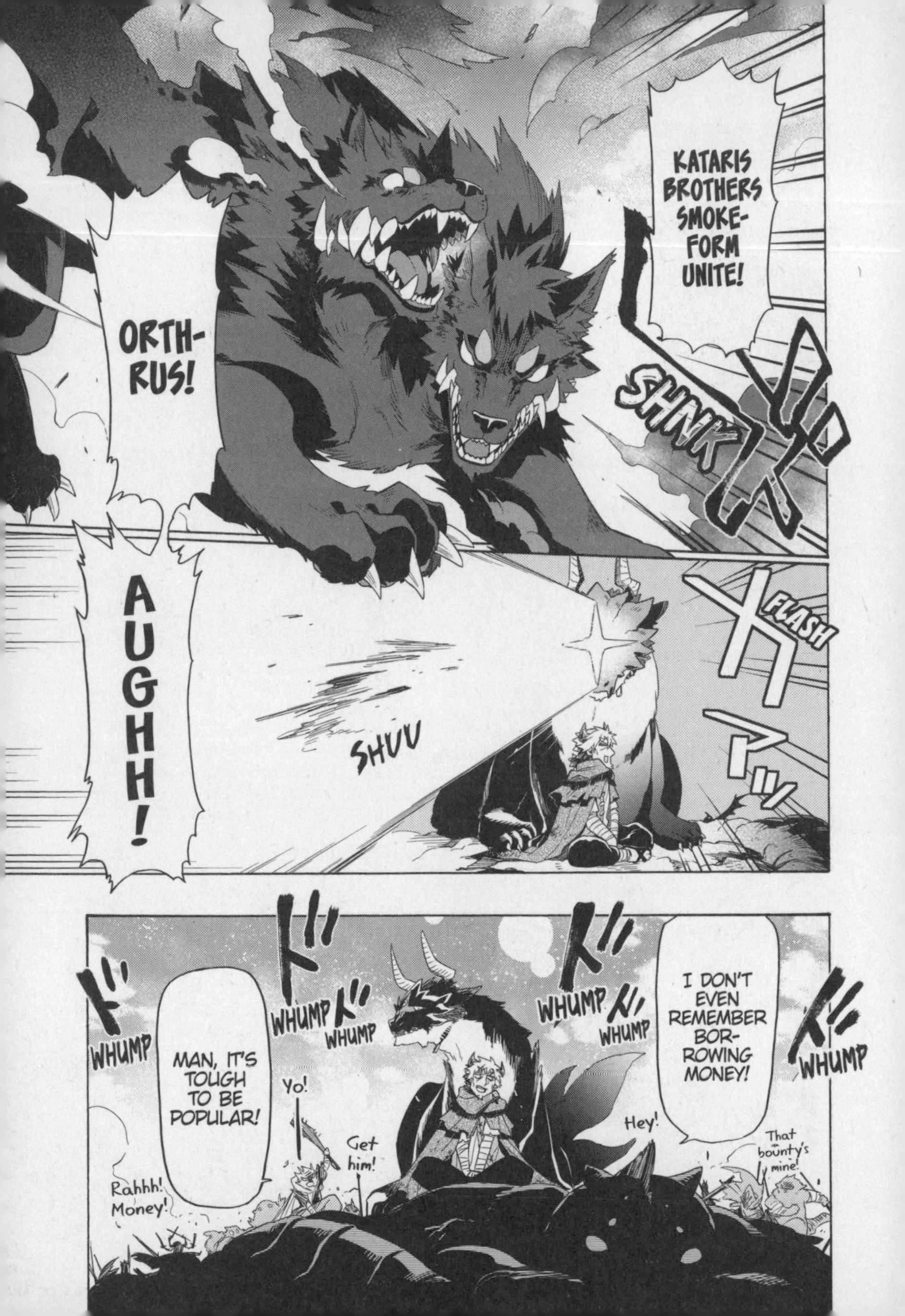
KATARIS BROTHERS SMOKE-FORM UNITE!
SHNK
ORTH-RUS!
FLASH
SHUU
AUGHH!
WHUMP
I DON'T EVEN REMEMBER BOR-ROWING MONEY!
That bounty's mine!
Hey!
WHUMP
WHUMP
Get him!
Yo!
MAN, IT'S TOUGH TO BE POPULAR!
WHUMP
WHUMP
WHUMP
Rahhh! Money!

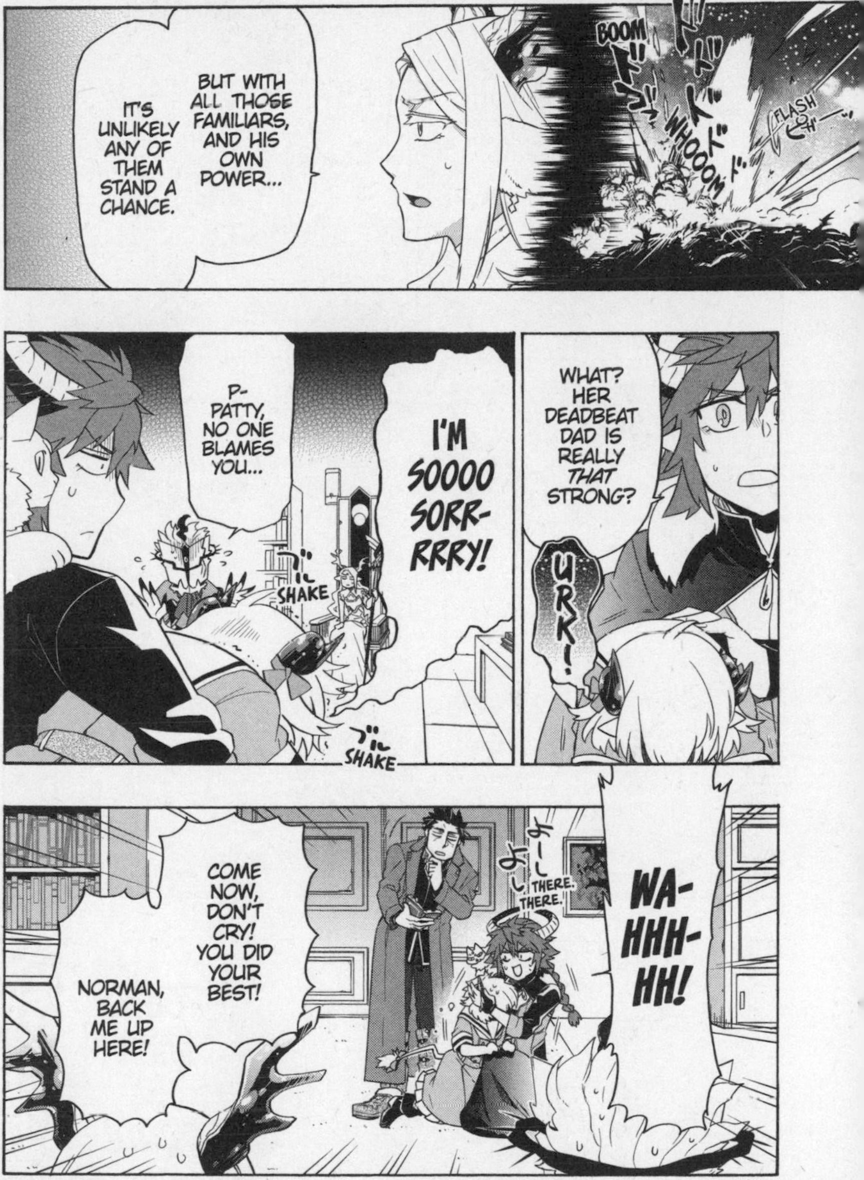
BOOM
WHOOOM
FLASH
BUT WITH ALL THOSE FAMILIARS, AND HIS OWN POWER...
IT'S UNLIKELY ANY OF THEM STAND A CHANCE.
WHAT? HER DEADBEAT DAD IS REALLY *THAT* STRONG?
URK!
I'M SOOOO SORR-RRRY!
P-PATTY, NO ONE BLAMES YOU...
SHAKE
SHAKE
WA-HHH-HH!
THERE. THERE.
COME NOW, DON'T CRY! YOU DID YOUR BEST!
NORMAN, BACK ME UP HERE!

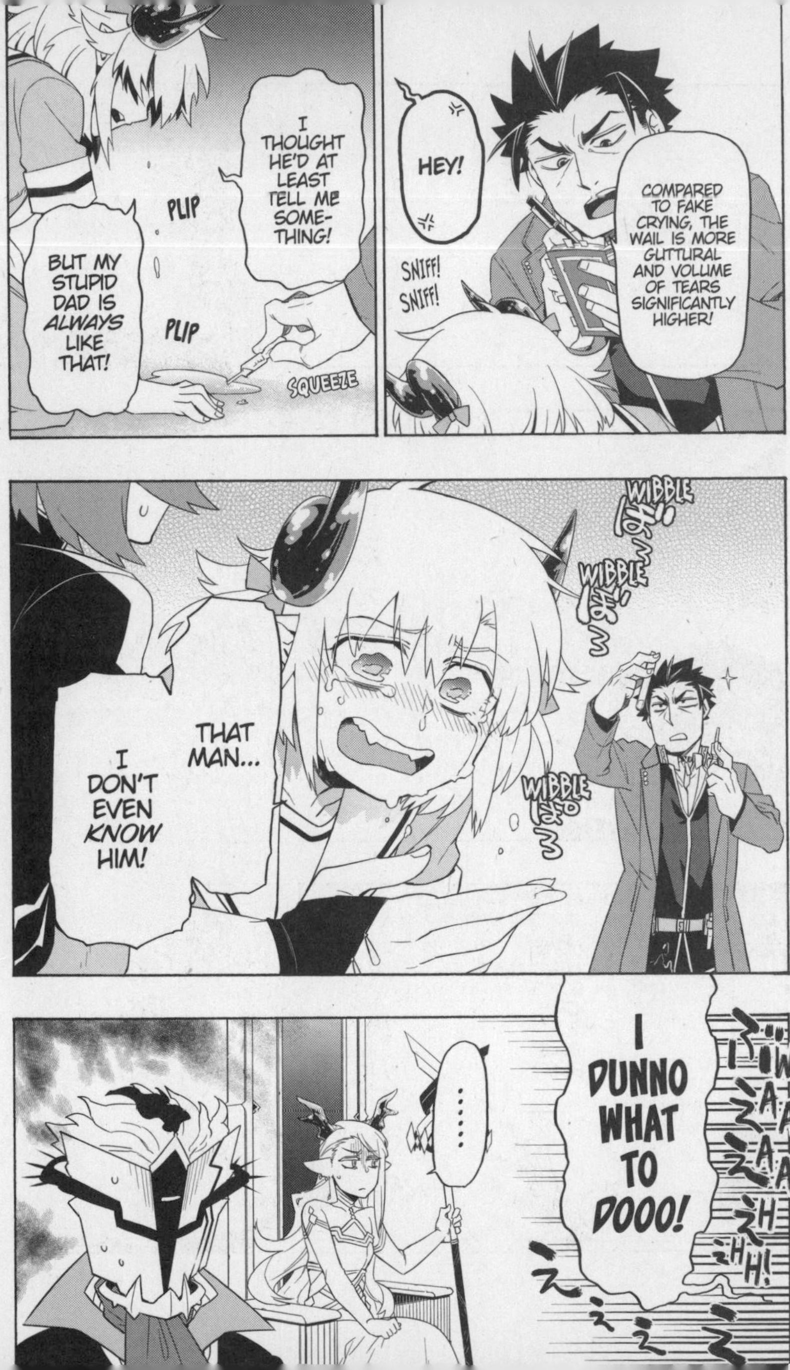
COMPARED TO FAKE CRYING, THE WAIL IS MORE GUTTURAL AND VOLUME OF TEARS SIGNIFICANTLY HIGHER!
HEY!
SNIFF! SNIFF!
I THOUGHT HE'D AT LEAST TELL ME SOME-THING!
PLIP
PLIP
BUT MY STUPID DAD IS ALWAYS LIKE THAT!
SQUEEZE
WIBBLE
WIBBLE
THAT MAN...
I DON'T EVEN KNOW HIM!
WIBBLE
I DUNNO WHAT TO DOOO!
WAAAAAHHH!
......

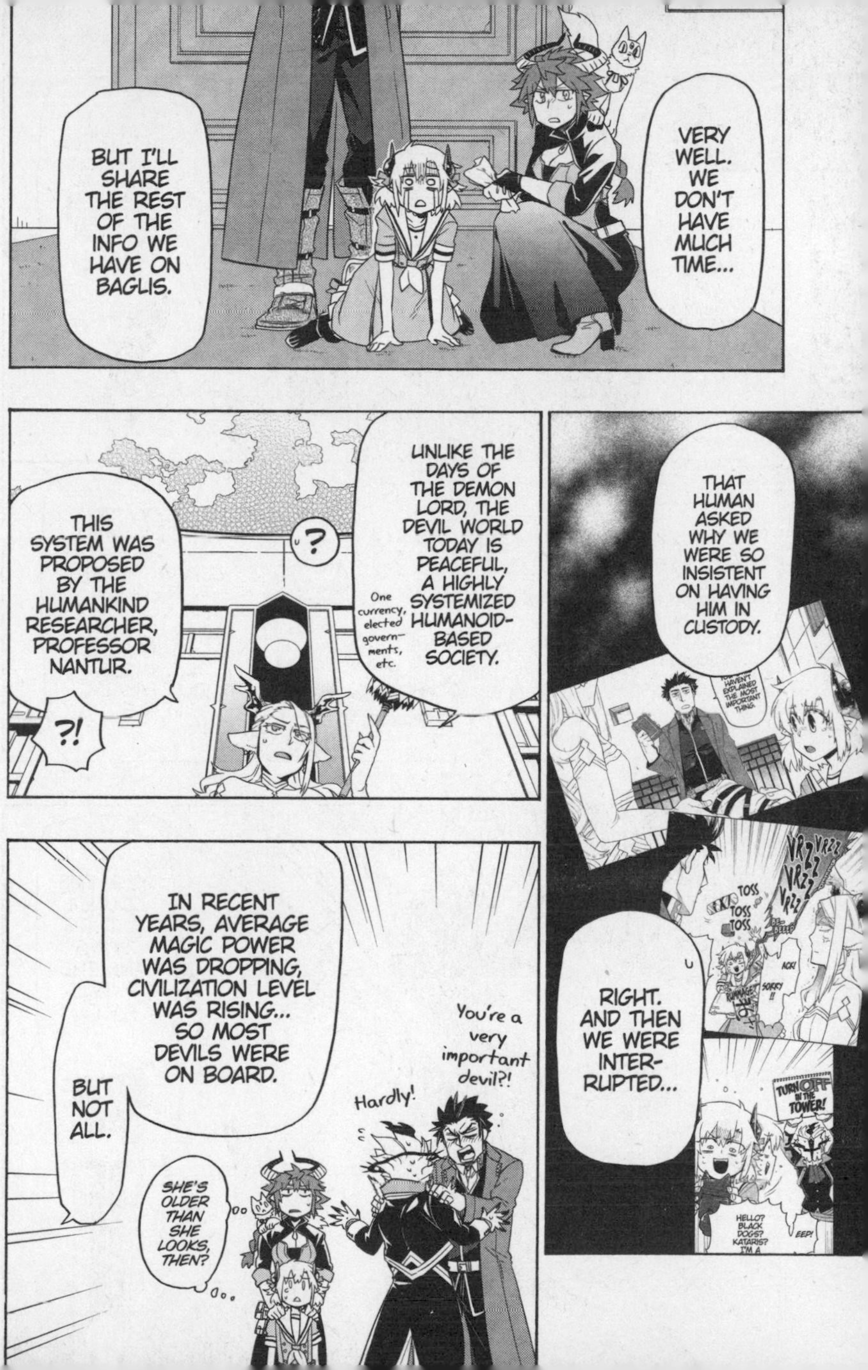
VERY WELL. WE DON'T HAVE MUCH TIME...
BUT I'LL SHARE THE REST OF THE INFO WE HAVE ON BAGLIS.
THAT HUMAN ASKED WHY WE WERE SO INSISTENT ON HAVING HIM IN CUSTODY.
YOU HAVEN'T EXPLAINED THE MOST IMPORTANT THING.
VRZZ VRZZ VRZZ
TOSS TOSS TOSS
BE-EEEP
ACK!
SORRY!!
RUMMAGE
RIGHT. AND THEN WE WERE INTER-RUPTED...
TURN OFF IN THE TOWER!
HELLO? BLACK DOGS? KATARIS? I'M A
EEP!
UNLIKE THE DAYS OF THE DEMON LORD, THE DEVIL WORLD TODAY IS PEACEFUL, A HIGHLY SYSTEMIZED HUMANOID-BASED SOCIETY.
One currency, elected govern-ments, etc.
?
THIS SYSTEM WAS PROPOSED BY THE HUMANKIND RESEARCHER, PROFESSOR NANTUR.
?!
IN RECENT YEARS, AVERAGE MAGIC POWER WAS DROPPING, CIVILIZATION LEVEL WAS RISING... SO MOST DEVILS WERE ON BOARD.
BUT NOT ALL.
You're a very important devil?!
Hardly!
SHE'S OLDER THAN SHE LOOKS, THEN?

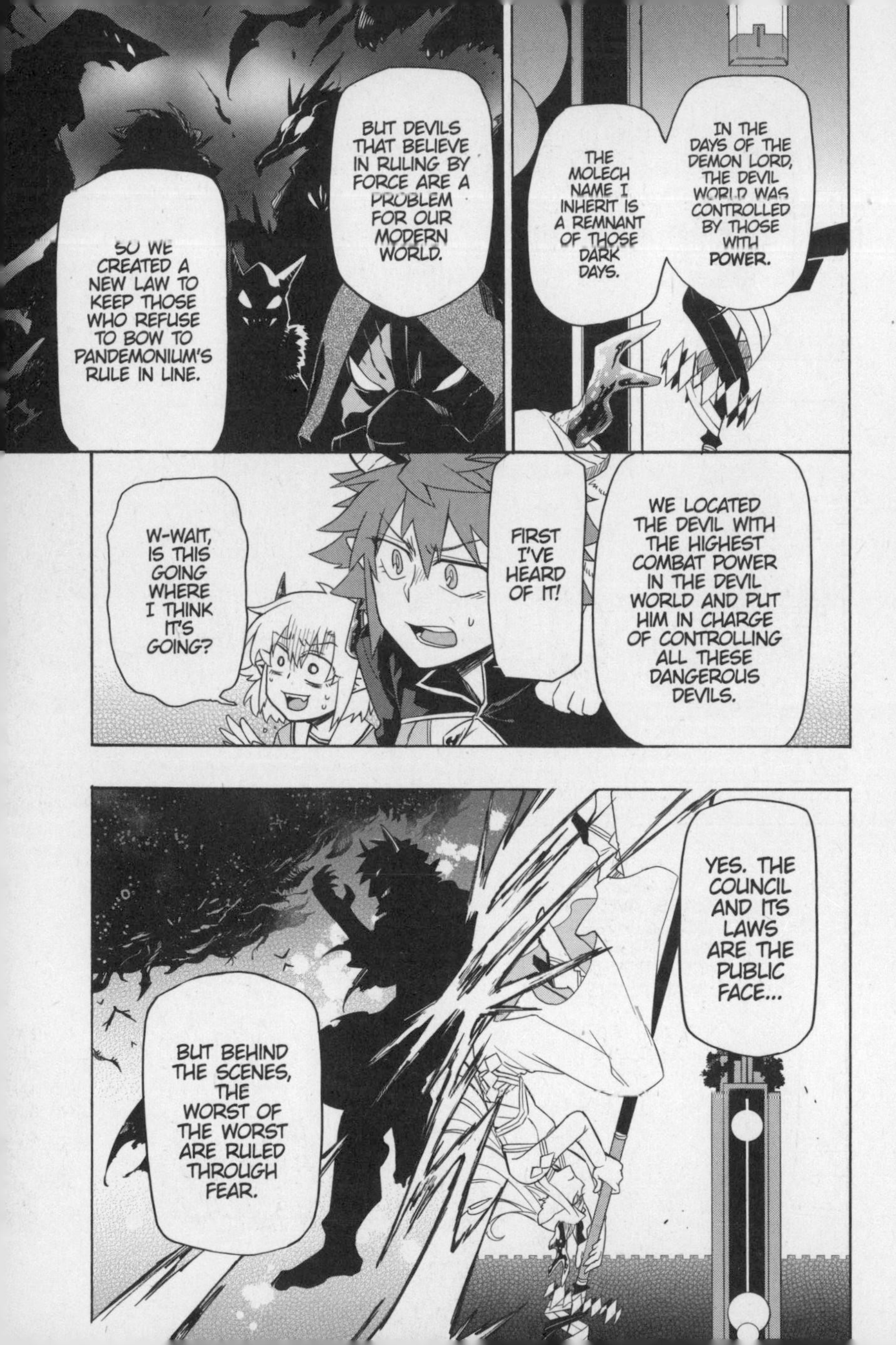
IN THE DAYS OF THE DEMON LORD, THE DEVIL WORLD WAS CONTROLLED BY THOSE WITH POWER.
THE MOLECH NAME I INHERIT IS A REMNANT OF THOSE DARK DAYS.
BUT DEVILS THAT BELIEVE IN RULING BY FORCE ARE A PROBLEM FOR OUR MODERN WORLD.
SO WE CREATED A NEW LAW TO KEEP THOSE WHO REFUSE TO BOW TO PANDEMONIUM'S RULE IN LINE.
WE LOCATED THE DEVIL WITH THE HIGHEST COMBAT POWER IN THE DEVIL WORLD AND PUT HIM IN CHARGE OF CONTROLLING ALL THESE DANGEROUS DEVILS.
FIRST I'VE HEARD OF IT!
W-WAIT, IS THIS GOING WHERE I THINK IT'S GOING?
YES. THE COUNCIL AND ITS LAWS ARE THE PUBLIC FACE...
BUT BEHIND THE SCENES, THE WORST OF THE WORST ARE RULED THROUGH FEAR.

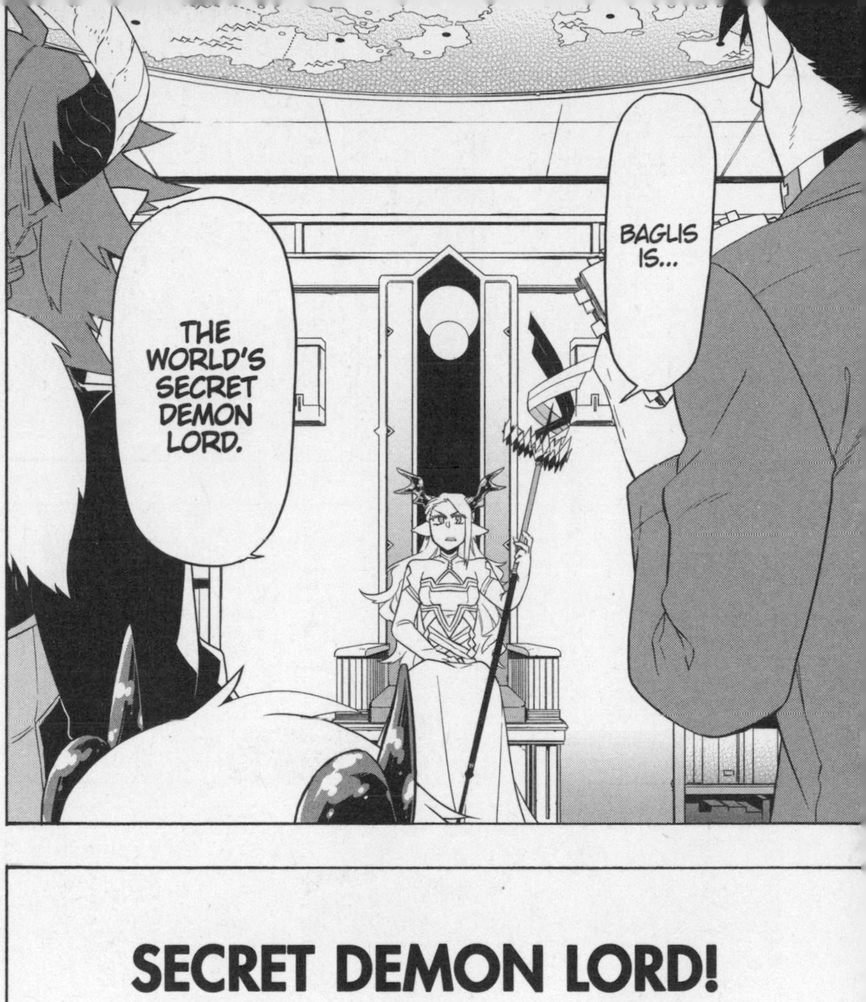
BAGLIS IS...
THE WORLD'S SECRET DEMON LORD.

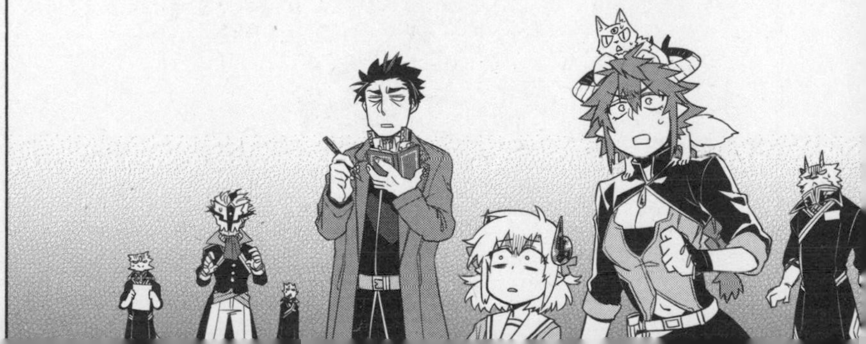
SECRET DEMON LORD!

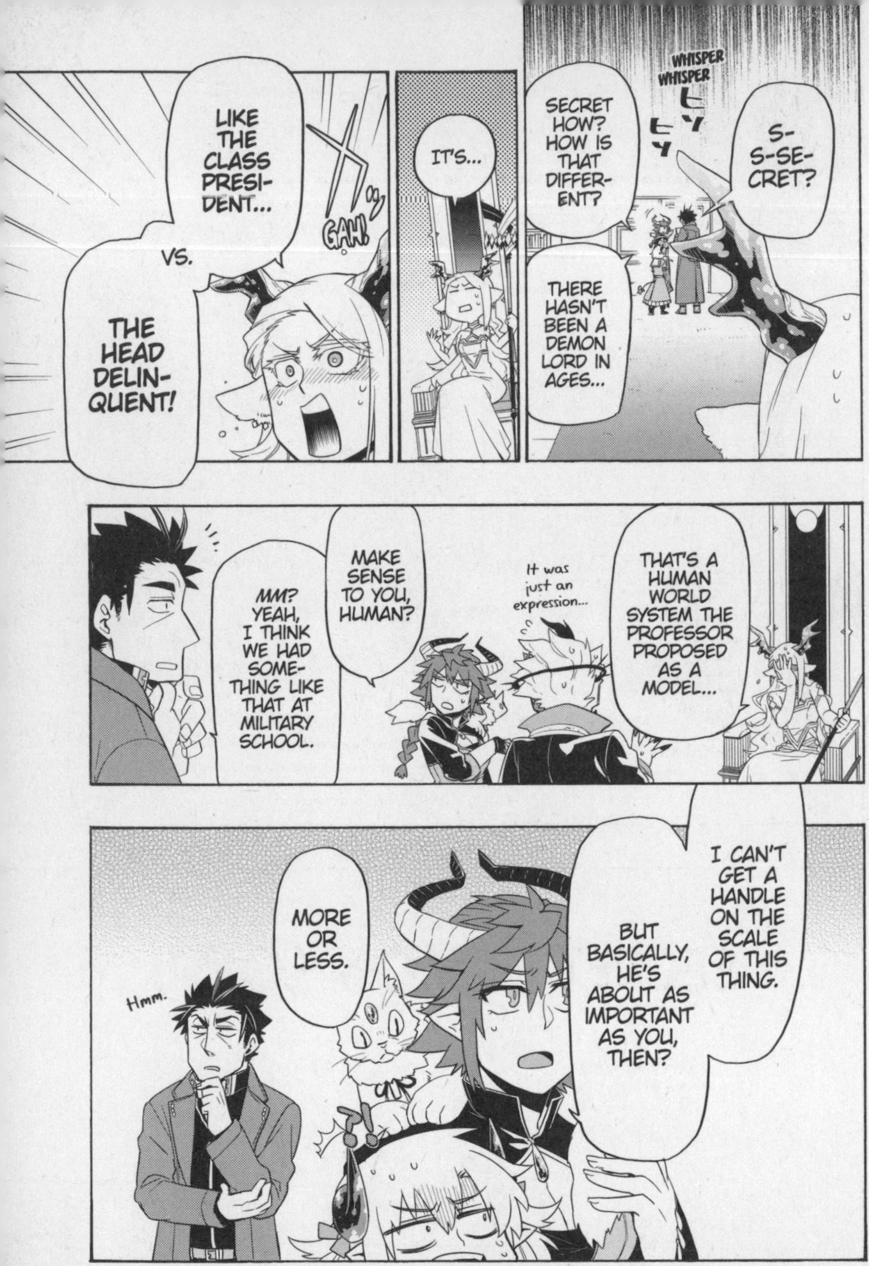
WHISPER WHISPER
ヒソヒソ
S-S-SE-CRET?
SECRET HOW? HOW IS THAT DIFFER-ENT?
THERE HASN'T BEEN A DEMON LORD IN AGES...
IT'S...
GAH!
LIKE THE CLASS PRESI-DENT...
VS.
THE HEAD DELIN-QUENT!
THAT'S A HUMAN WORLD SYSTEM THE PROFESSOR PROPOSED AS A MODEL...
It was just an expression...
MAKE SENSE TO YOU, HUMAN?
MM? YEAH, I THINK WE HAD SOME-THING LIKE THAT AT MILITARY SCHOOL.
I CAN'T GET A HANDLE ON THE SCALE OF THIS THING.
BUT BASICALLY, HE'S ABOUT AS IMPORTANT AS YOU, THEN?
MORE OR LESS.
Hmm.

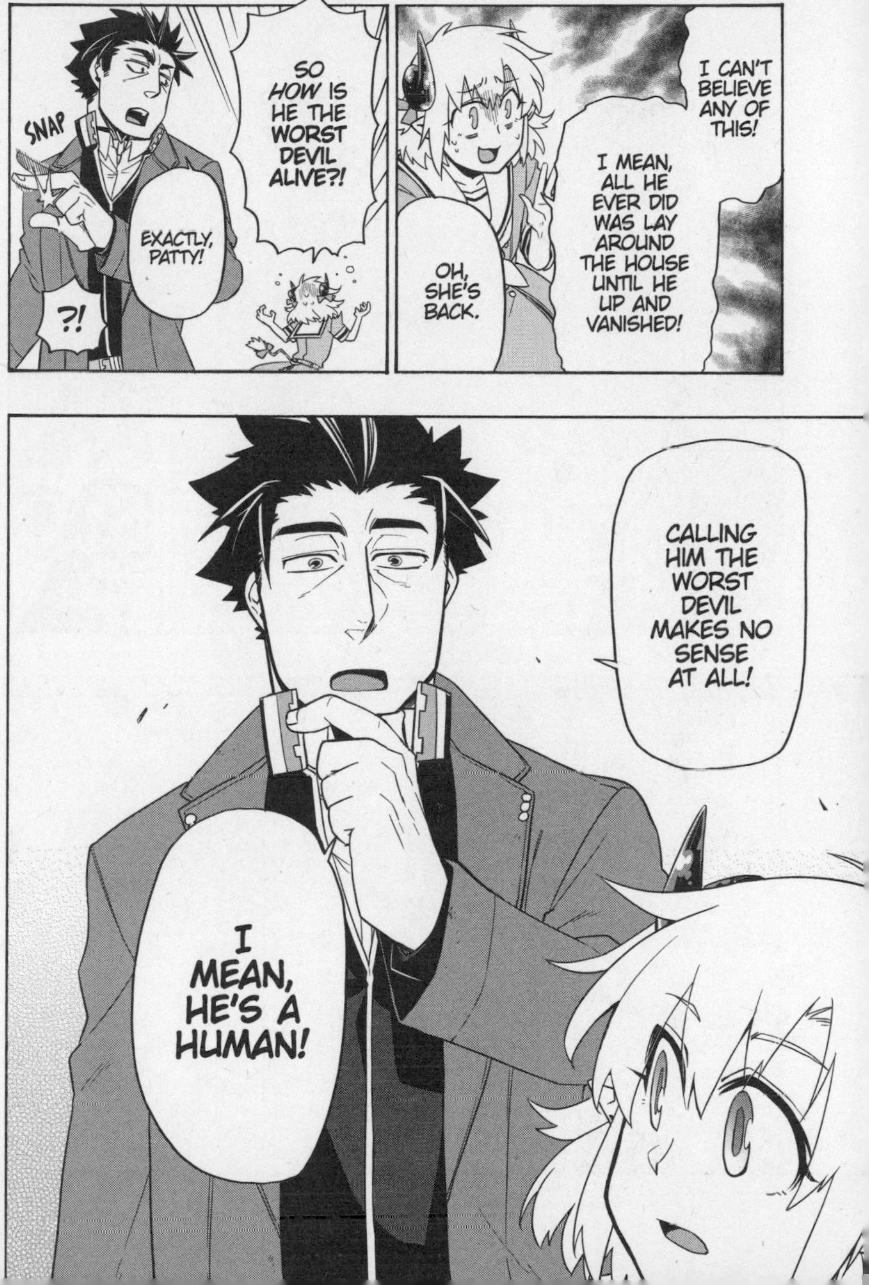
I CAN'T BELIEVE ANY OF THIS!
I MEAN, ALL HE EVER DID WAS LAY AROUND THE HOUSE UNTIL HE UP AND VANISHED!
OH, SHE'S BACK.
SO *HOW* IS HE THE WORST DEVIL ALIVE?!
SNAP
EXACTLY, PATTY!
?!
CALLING HIM THE WORST DEVIL MAKES NO SENSE AT ALL!
I MEAN, HE'S A HUMAN!

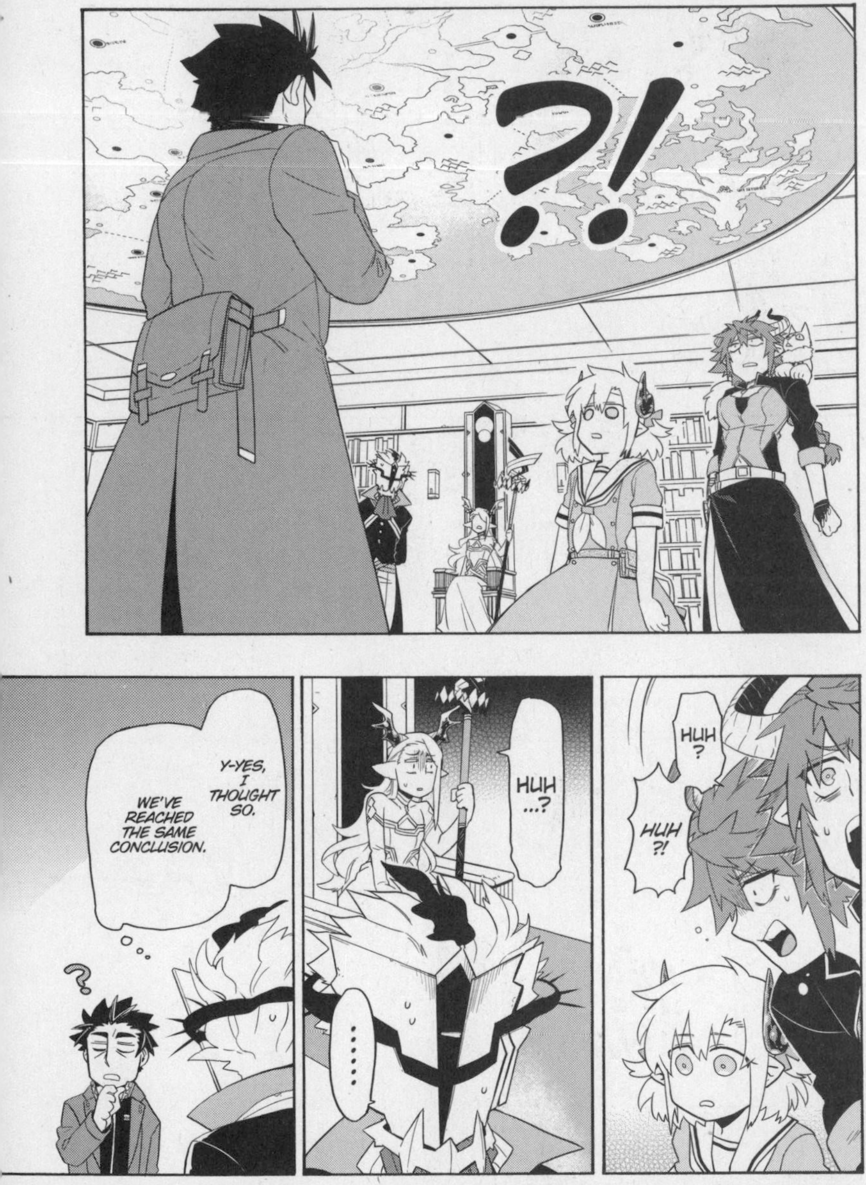
?!
HUH?
HUH?!
HUH...?
......
Y-YES, I THOUGHT SO.
WE'VE REACHED THE SAME CONCLUSION.
?

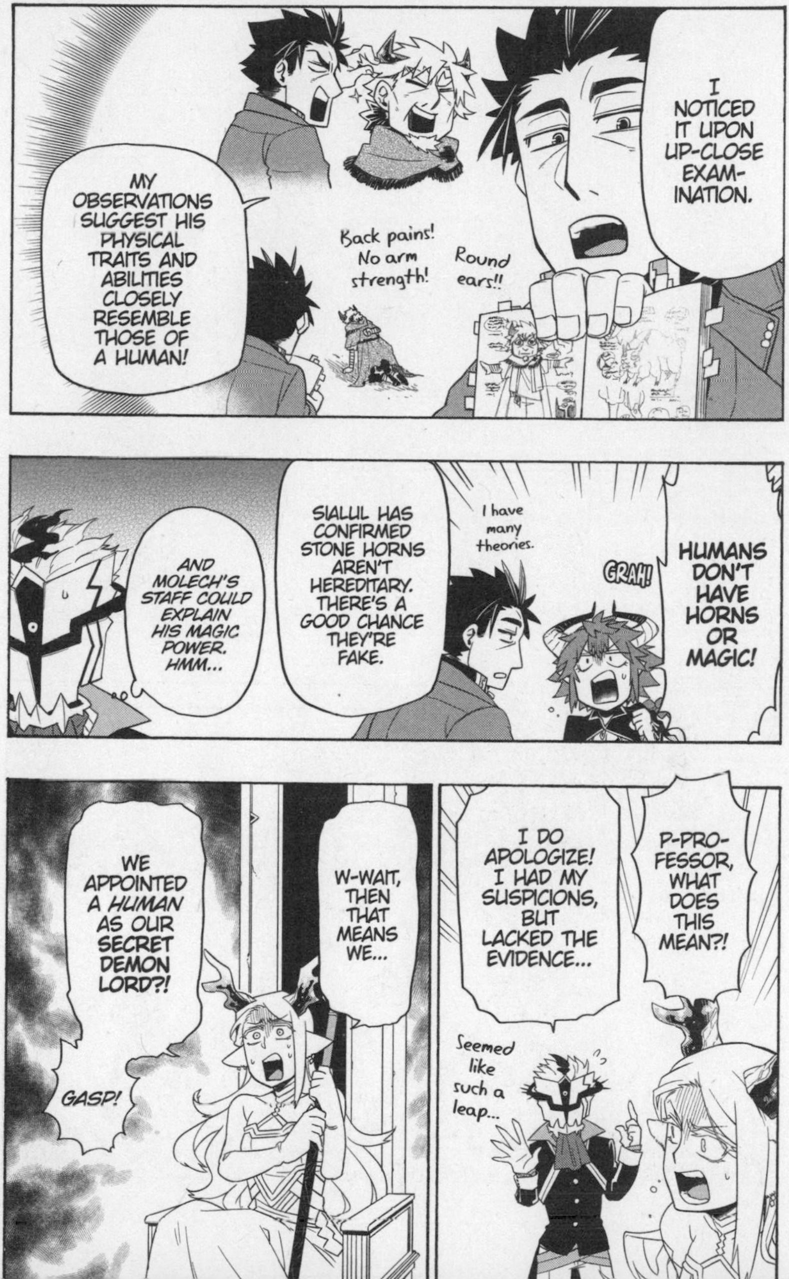
I NOTICED IT UPON UP-CLOSE EXAMINATION.
Round ears!!
Back pains! No arm strength!
MY OBSERVATIONS SUGGEST HIS PHYSICAL TRAITS AND ABILITIES CLOSELY RESEMBLE THOSE OF A HUMAN!
HUMANS DON'T HAVE HORNS OR MAGIC!
GRAH!
I have many theories.
SIALUL HAS CONFIRMED STONE HORNS AREN'T HEREDITARY. THERE'S A GOOD CHANCE THEY'RE FAKE.
AND MOLECH'S STAFF COULD EXPLAIN HIS MAGIC POWER. HMM...
P-PROFESSOR, WHAT DOES THIS MEAN?!
I DO APOLOGIZE! I HAD MY SUSPICIONS, BUT LACKED THE EVIDENCE...
Seemed like such a leap...
W-WAIT, THEN THAT MEANS WE...
WE APPOINTED A *HUMAN* AS OUR SECRET DEMON LORD?!
GASP!

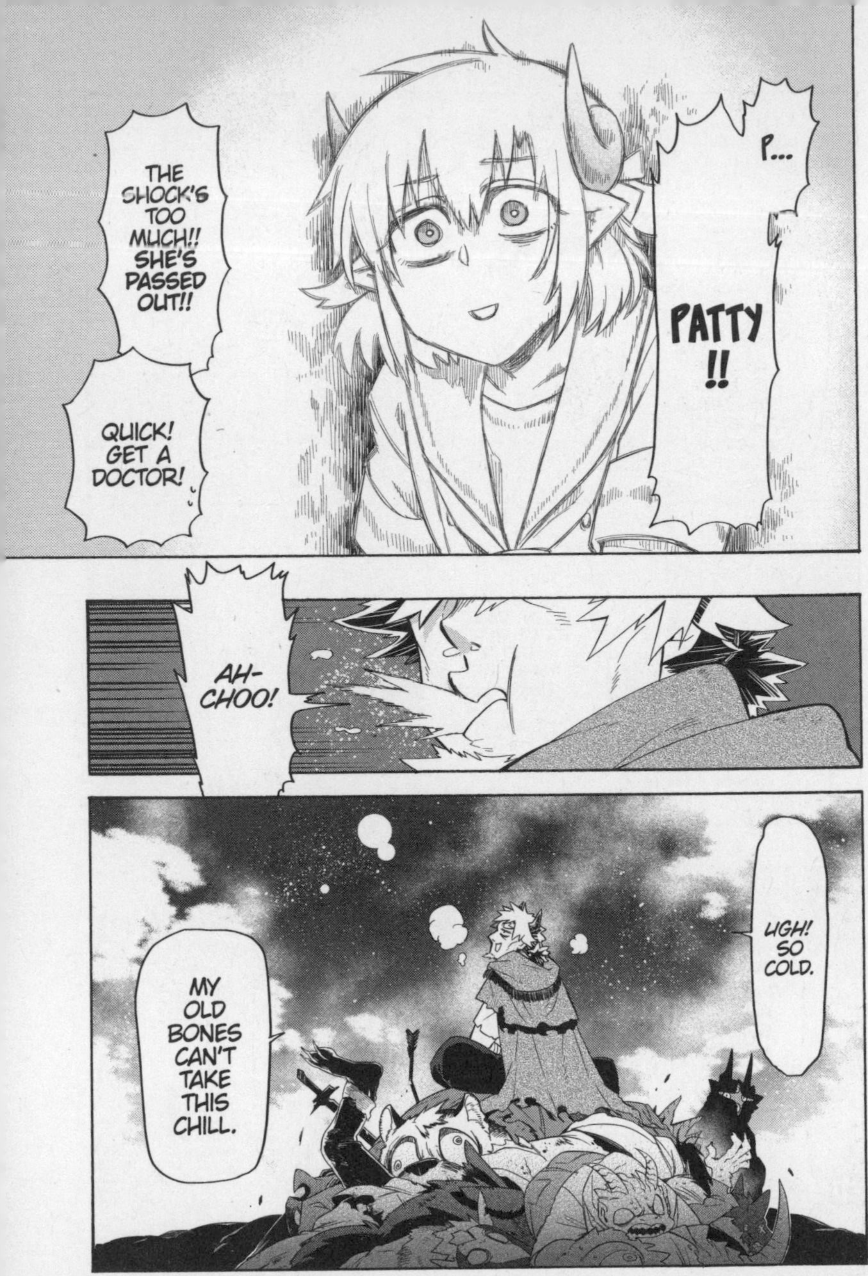
P...
PATTY!!
THE SHOCK'S TOO MUCH!! SHE'S PASSED OUT!!
QUICK! GET A DOCTOR!
AH-CHOO!
UGH! SO COLD.
MY OLD BONES CAN'T TAKE THIS CHILL.

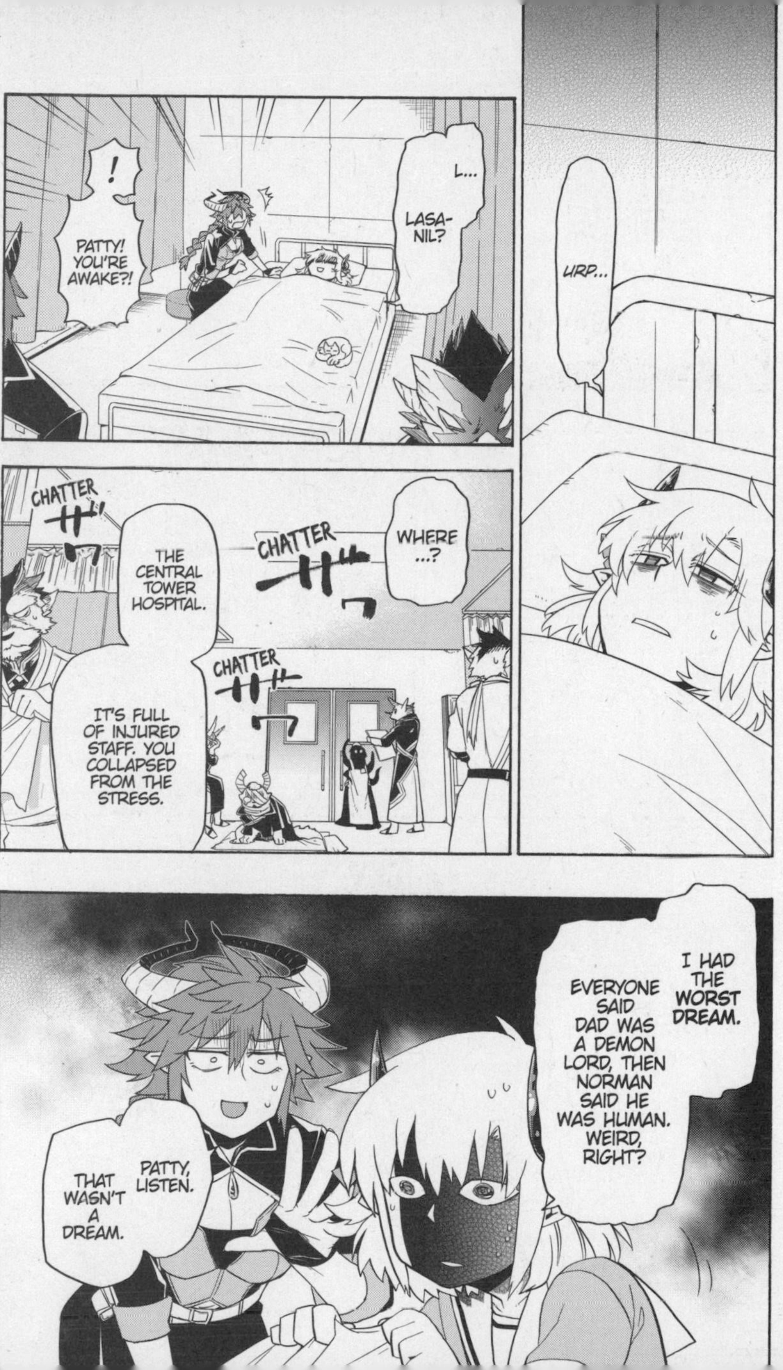
URP...
...
L...
LASA-NIL?
!
PATTY! YOU'RE AWAKE?!
WHERE ...?
CHATTER
THE CENTRAL TOWER HOSPITAL.
CHATTER
CHATTER
IT'S FULL OF INJURED STAFF. YOU COLLAPSED FROM THE STRESS.
I HAD THE WORST DREAM.
EVERYONE SAID DAD WAS A DEMON LORD, THEN NORMAN SAID HE WAS HUMAN. WEIRD, RIGHT?
PATTY, LISTEN.
THAT WASN'T A DREAM.

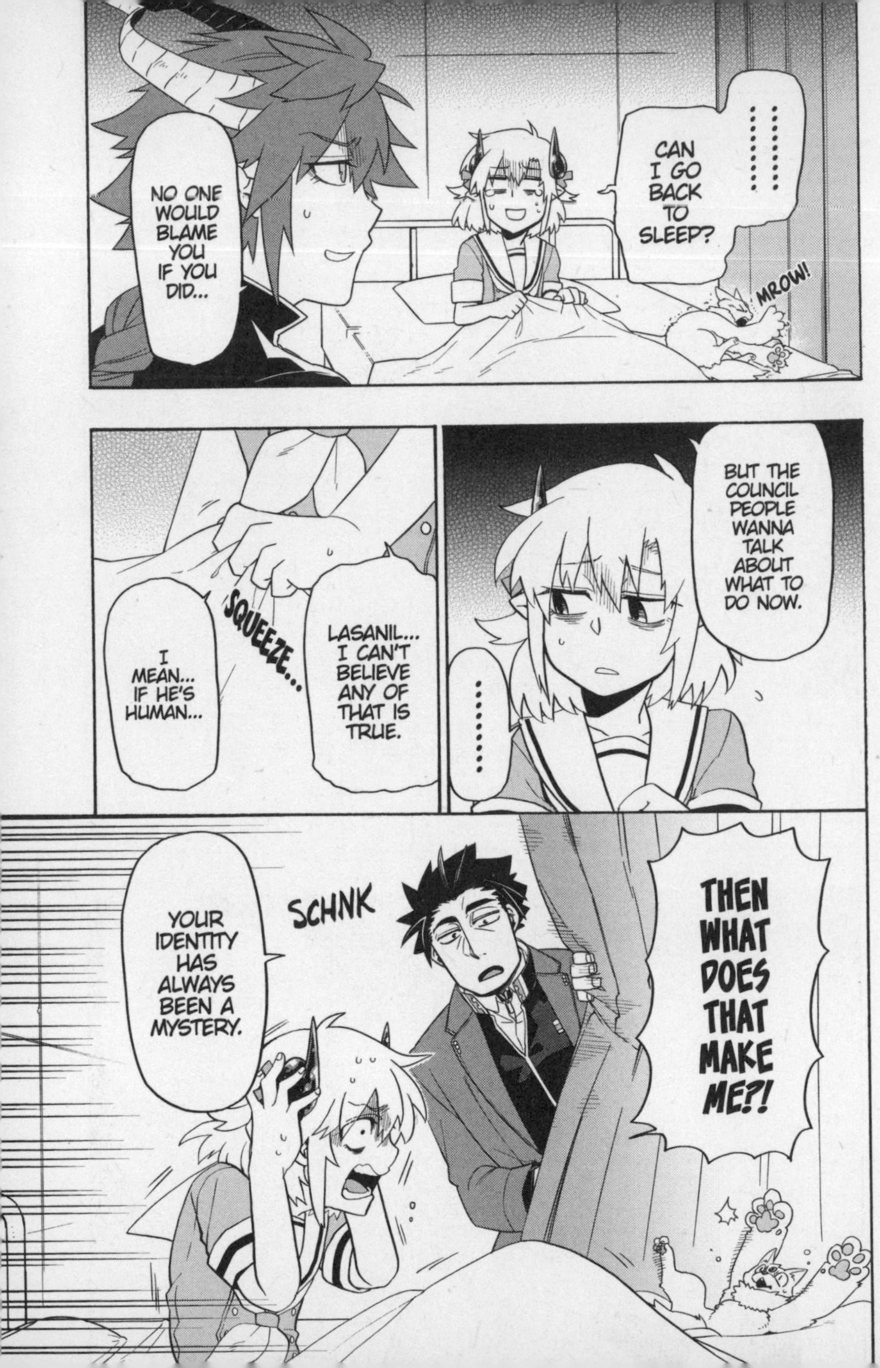
......
CAN I GO BACK TO SLEEP?
MROW!
NO ONE WOULD BLAME YOU IF YOU DID...
BUT THE COUNCIL PEOPLE WANNA TALK ABOUT WHAT TO DO NOW.
......
LASANIL... I CAN'T BELIEVE ANY OF THAT IS TRUE.
SQUEEZE...
I MEAN... IF HE'S HUMAN...
THEN WHAT DOES THAT MAKE ME?!
SCHNK
YOUR IDENTITY HAS ALWAYS BEEN A MYSTERY.

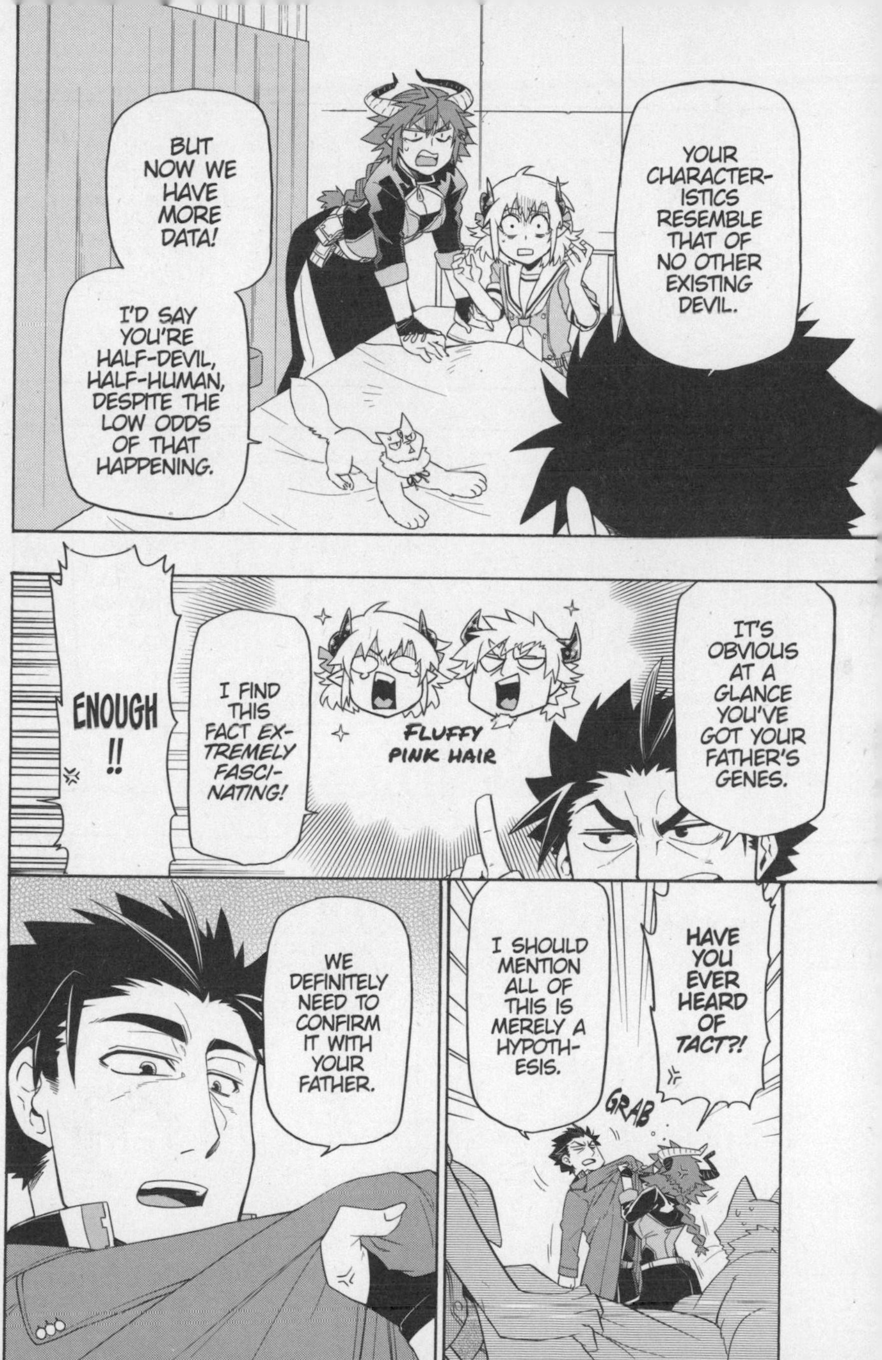
YOUR CHARACTER-ISTICS RESEMBLE THAT OF NO OTHER EXISTING DEVIL.
BUT NOW WE HAVE MORE DATA!
I'D SAY YOU'RE HALF-DEVIL, HALF-HUMAN, DESPITE THE LOW ODDS OF THAT HAPPENING.
IT'S OBVIOUS AT A GLANCE YOU'VE GOT YOUR FATHER'S GENES.
FLUFFY PINK HAIR
I FIND THIS FACT EXTREMELY FASCINATING!
ENOUGH!!
HAVE YOU EVER HEARD OF TACT?!
I SHOULD MENTION ALL OF THIS IS MERELY A HYPOTHESIS.
GRAB
WE DEFINITELY NEED TO CONFIRM IT WITH YOUR FATHER.

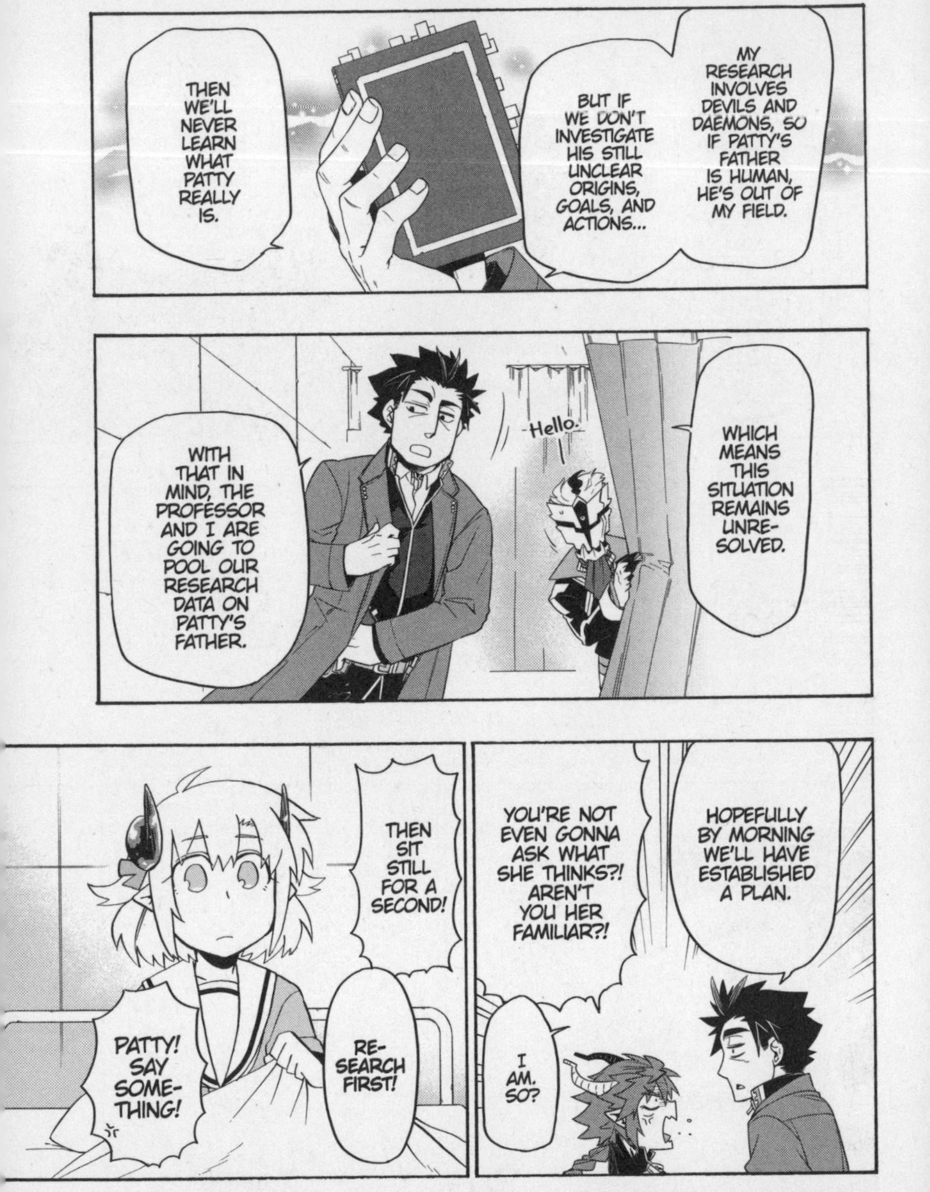
MY RESEARCH INVOLVES DEVILS AND DAEMONS, SO IF PATTY'S FATHER IS HUMAN, HE'S OUT OF MY FIELD.
BUT IF WE DON'T INVESTIGATE HIS STILL UNCLEAR ORIGINS, GOALS, AND ACTIONS...
THEN WE'LL NEVER LEARN WHAT PATTY REALLY IS.
WHICH MEANS THIS SITUATION REMAINS UNRE-SOLVED.
Hello.
WITH THAT IN MIND, THE PROFESSOR AND I ARE GOING TO POOL OUR RESEARCH DATA ON PATTY'S FATHER.
HOPEFULLY BY MORNING WE'LL HAVE ESTABLISHED A PLAN.
YOU'RE NOT EVEN GONNA ASK WHAT SHE THINKS?! AREN'T YOU HER FAMILIAR?!
I AM. SO?
THEN SIT STILL FOR A SECOND!
RE-SEARCH FIRST!
PATTY! SAY SOME-THING!

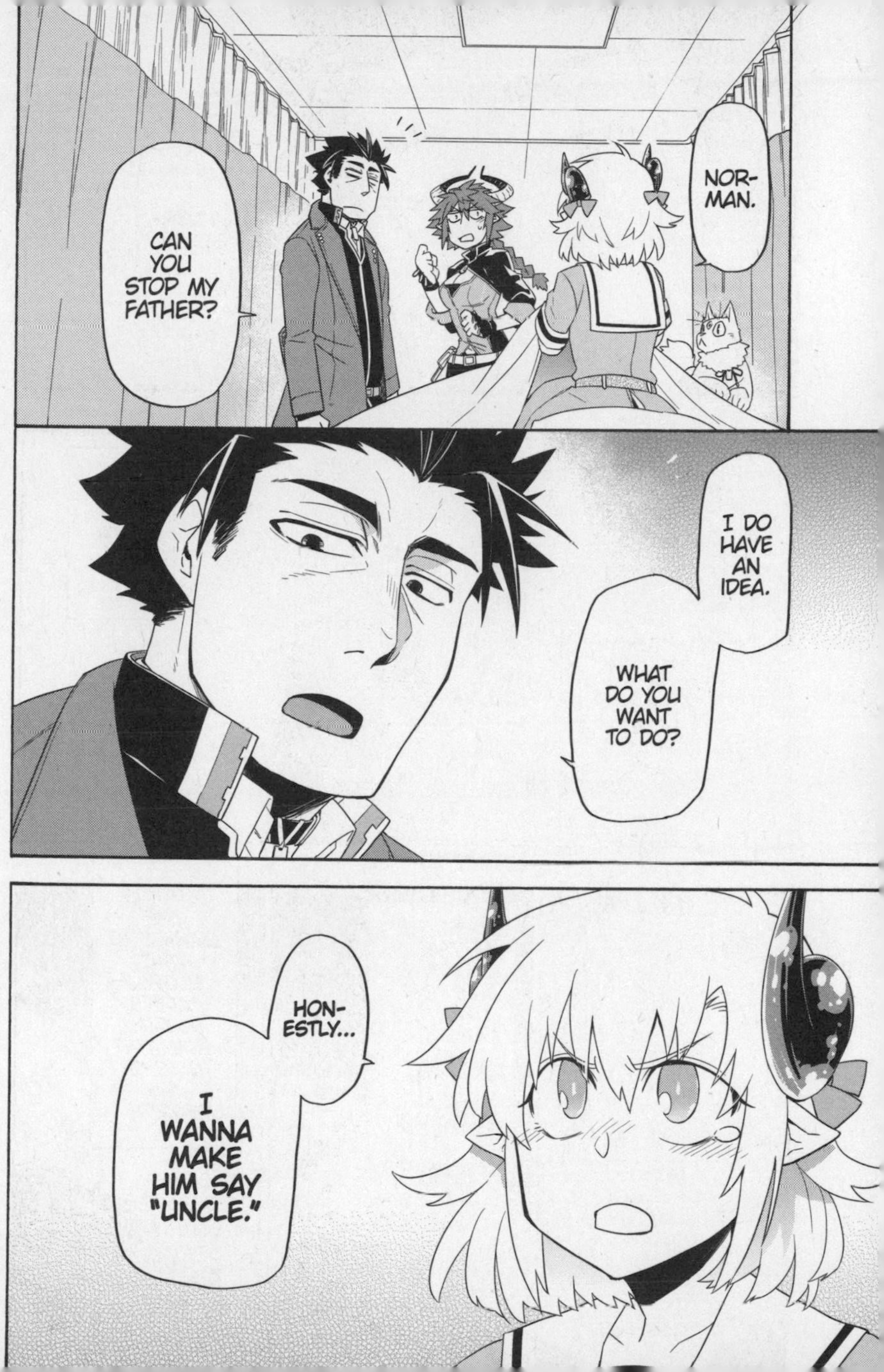
NOR-MAN.
CAN YOU STOP MY FATHER?
I DO HAVE AN IDEA.
WHAT DO YOU WANT TO DO?
HON-ESTLY...
I WANNA MAKE HIM SAY "UNCLE."

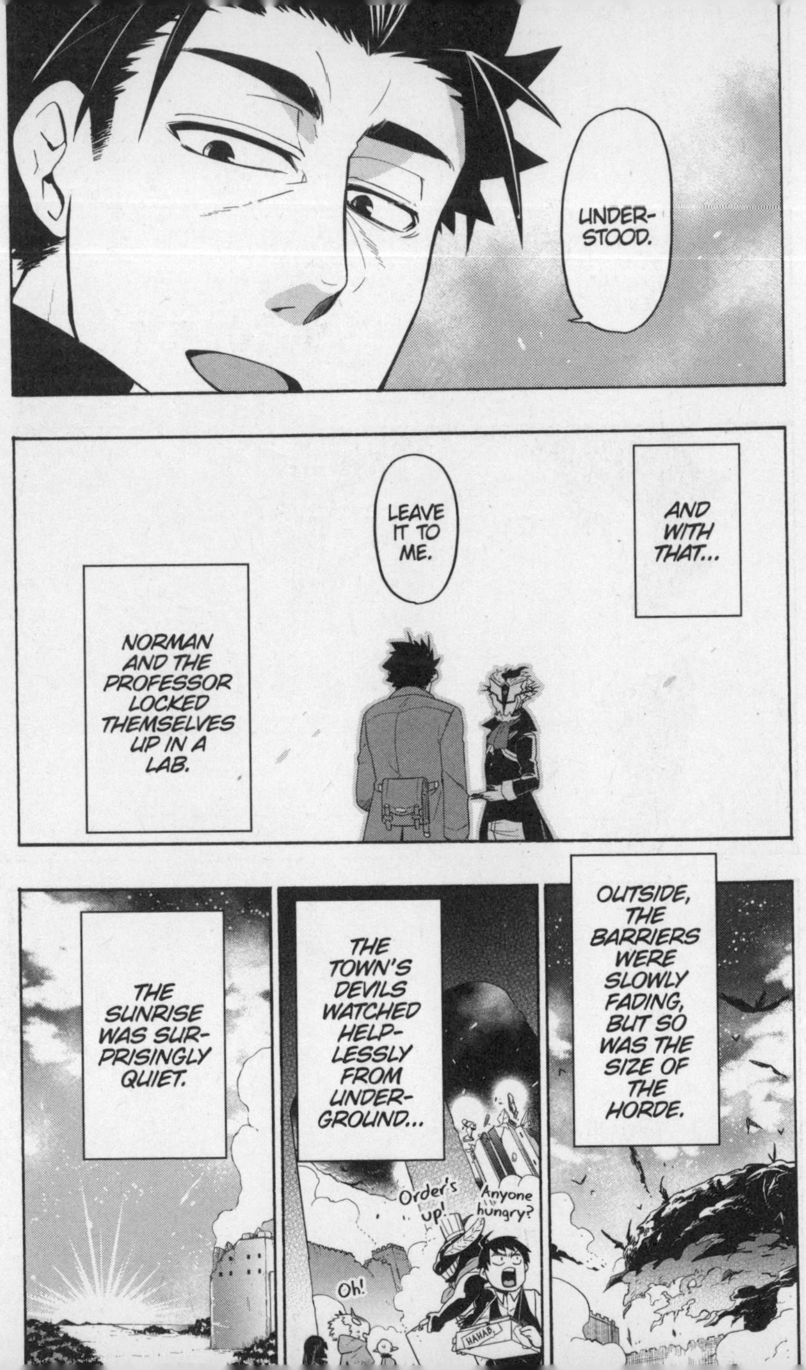
UNDER-STOOD.
AND WITH THAT...
LEAVE IT TO ME.
NORMAN AND THE PROFESSOR LOCKED THEMSELVES UP IN A LAB.
OUTSIDE, THE BARRIERS WERE SLOWLY FADING, BUT SO WAS THE SIZE OF THE HORDE.
THE TOWN'S DEVILS WATCHED HELP-LESSLY FROM UNDER-GROUND...
Anyone hungry?
Order's up!
Oh!
THE SUNRISE WAS SUR-PRISINGLY QUIET.

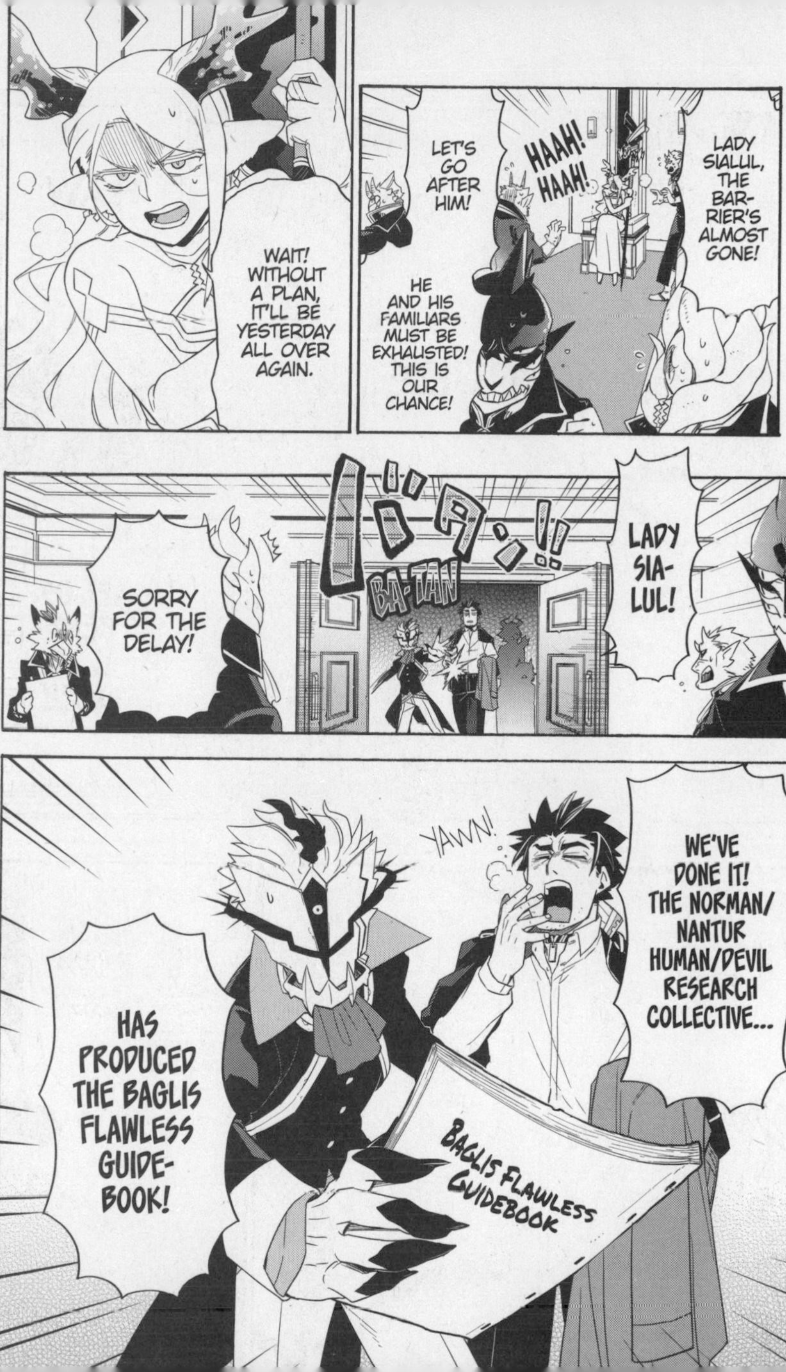
LADY SIALUL, THE BARRIER'S ALMOST GONE!
HAAH! HAAH!
LET'S GO AFTER HIM!
HE AND HIS FAMILIARS MUST BE EXHAUSTED! THIS IS OUR CHANCE!
WAIT! WITHOUT A PLAN, IT'LL BE YESTERDAY ALL OVER AGAIN.
LADY SIALUL!
バタン!!
BA-TAN
SORRY FOR THE DELAY!
WE'VE DONE IT! THE NORMAN/NANTUR HUMAN/DEVIL RESEARCH COLLECTIVE...
YAWN!
HAS PRODUCED THE BAGLIS FLAWLESS GUIDEBOOK!
BAGLIS FLAWLESS GUIDEBOOK

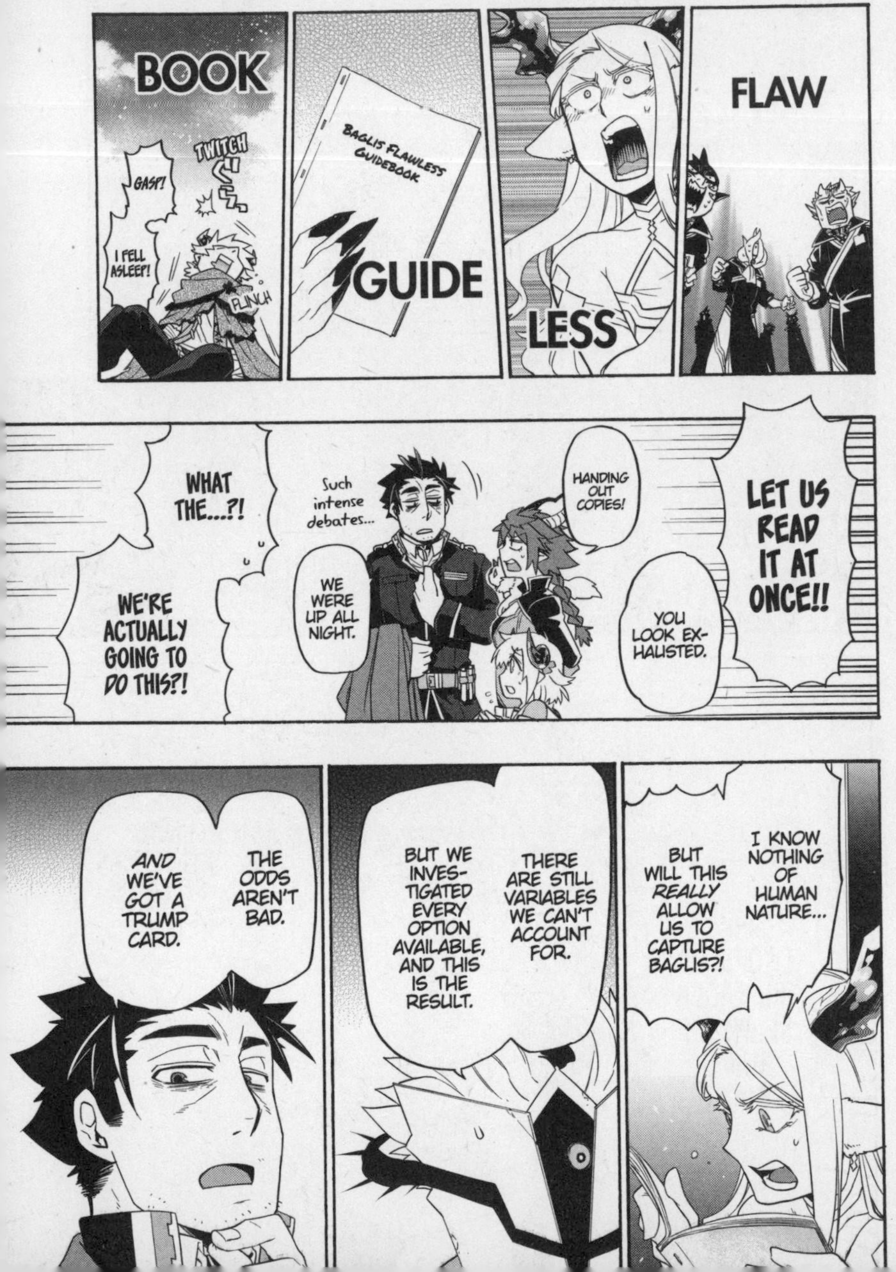
FLAW
LESS
BAGLIS FLAWLESS GUIDEBOOK
GUIDE
BOOK
TWITCH
GASP!
I FELL ASLEEP!
FLINCH
LET US READ IT AT ONCE!!
HANDING OUT COPIES!
YOU LOOK EX-HAUSTED.
Such intense debates...
WE WERE UP ALL NIGHT.
WHAT THE...?!
WE'RE ACTUALLY GOING TO DO THIS?!
I KNOW NOTHING OF HUMAN NATURE...
BUT WILL THIS *REALLY* ALLOW US TO CAPTURE BAGLIS?!
THERE ARE STILL VARIABLES WE CAN'T ACCOUNT FOR.
BUT WE INVES-TIGATED EVERY OPTION AVAILABLE, AND THIS IS THE RESULT.
THE ODDS AREN'T BAD.
AND WE'VE GOT A TRUMP CARD.

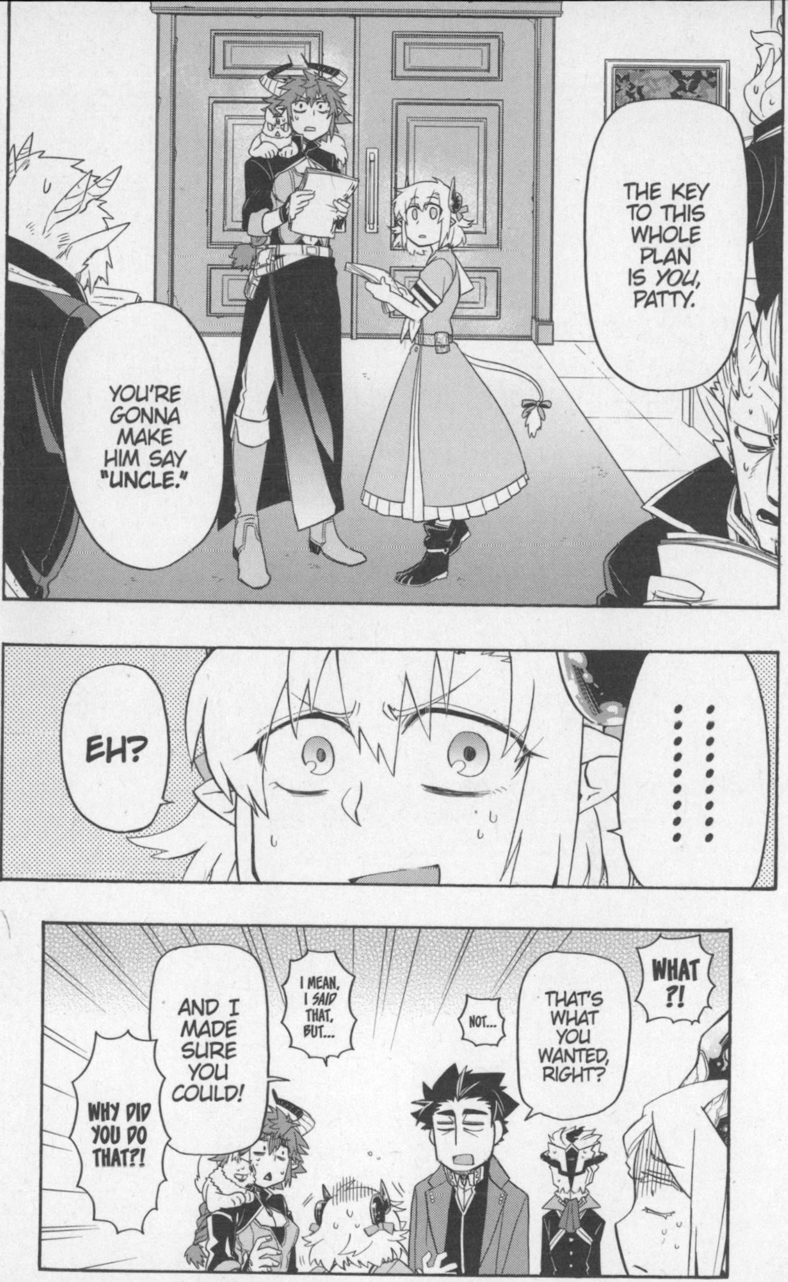
THE KEY TO THIS WHOLE PLAN IS YOU, PATTY.
YOU'RE GONNA MAKE HIM SAY "UNCLE."
......
EH?
WHAT ?!
THAT'S WHAT YOU WANTED, RIGHT?
NOT...
I MEAN, I SAID THAT, BUT...
AND I MADE SURE YOU COULD!
WHY DID YOU DO THAT?!

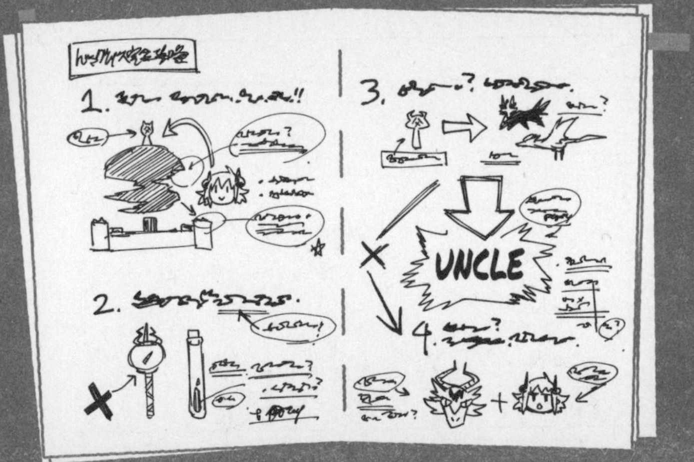
UNCLE

Sorry For My Familiar

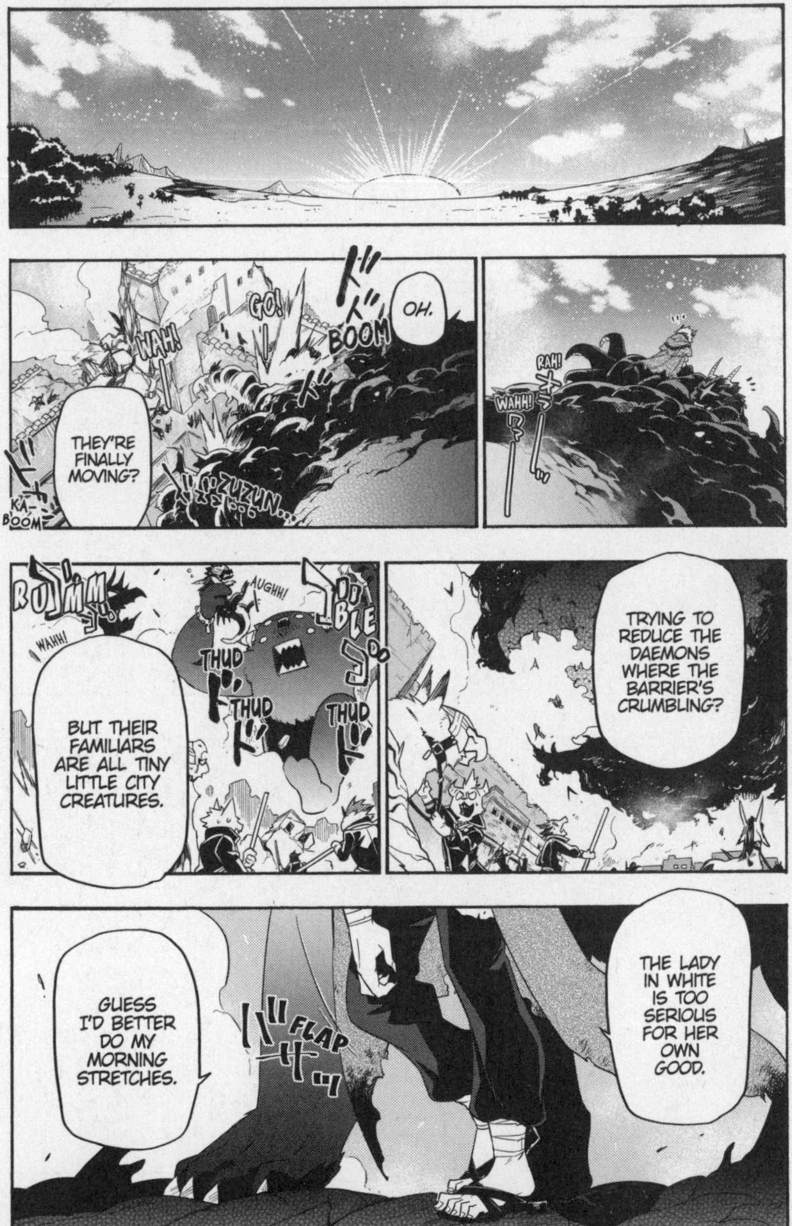
RAH!
WAHH!
OH.
BOOM
GO!
WAHH!
THEY'RE FINALLY MOVING?
ZUZUN...
KA-BOOM
TRYING TO REDUCE THE DAEMONS WHERE THE BARRIER'S CRUMBLING?
BLE
AUGHH!
THUD
THUD
THUD
RUMM
WAHH!
BUT THEIR FAMILIARS ARE ALL TINY LITTLE CITY CREATURES.
THE LADY IN WHITE IS TOO SERIOUS FOR HER OWN GOOD.
FLAP
GUESS I'D BETTER DO MY MORNING STRETCHES.

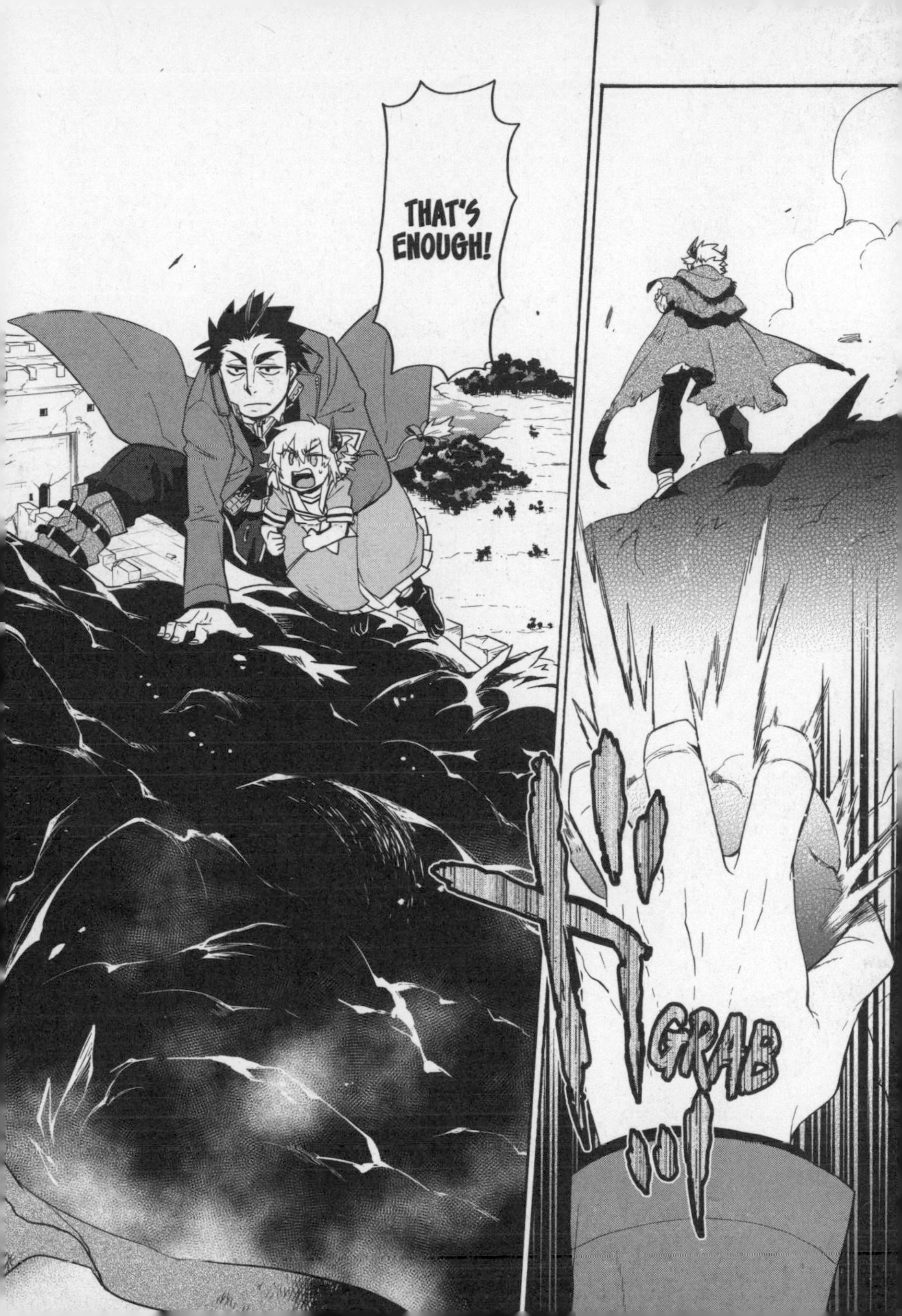
GRAB
THAT'S ENOUGH!

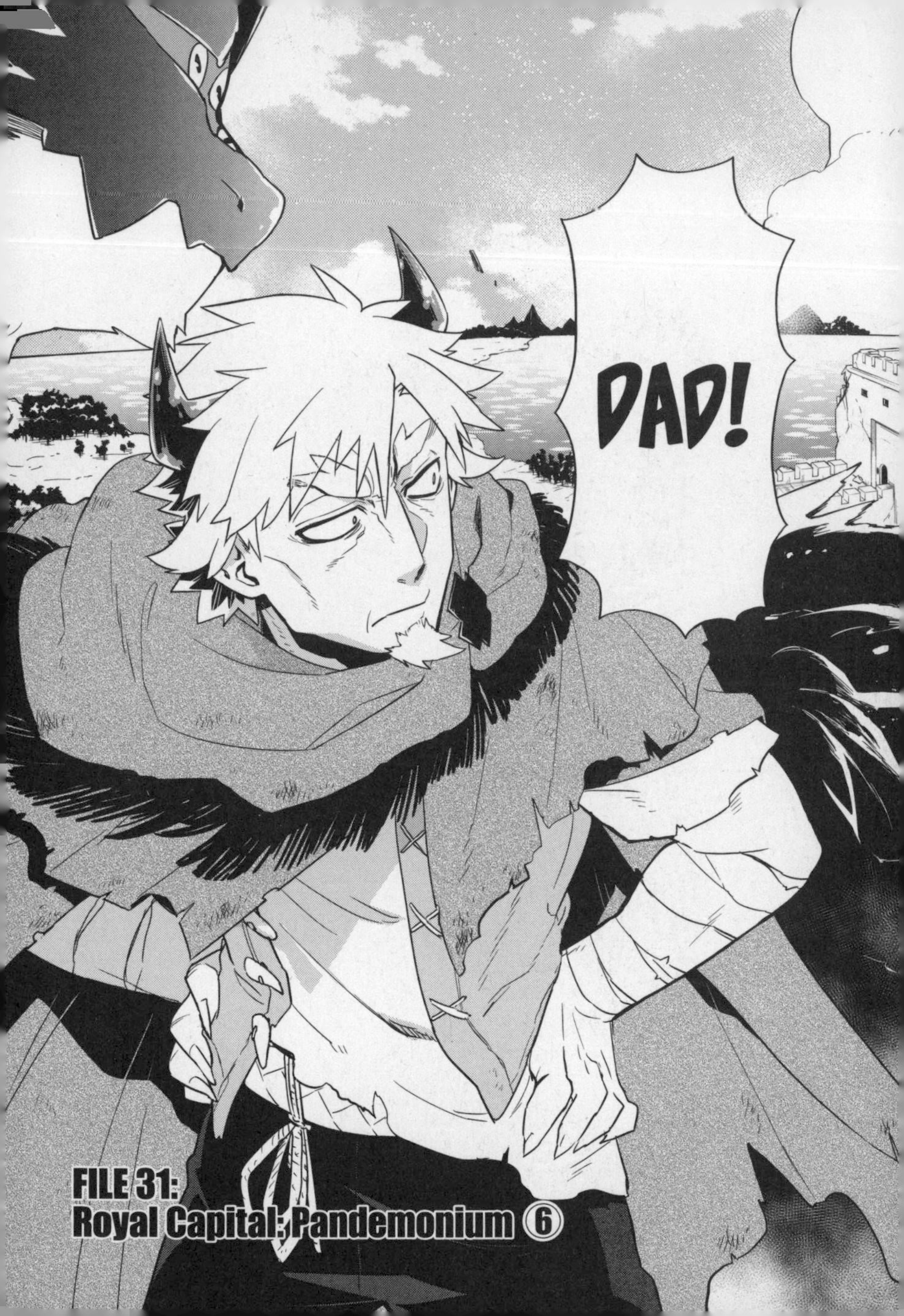
DAD!
FILE 31:
Royal Capital: Pandemonium ⑥

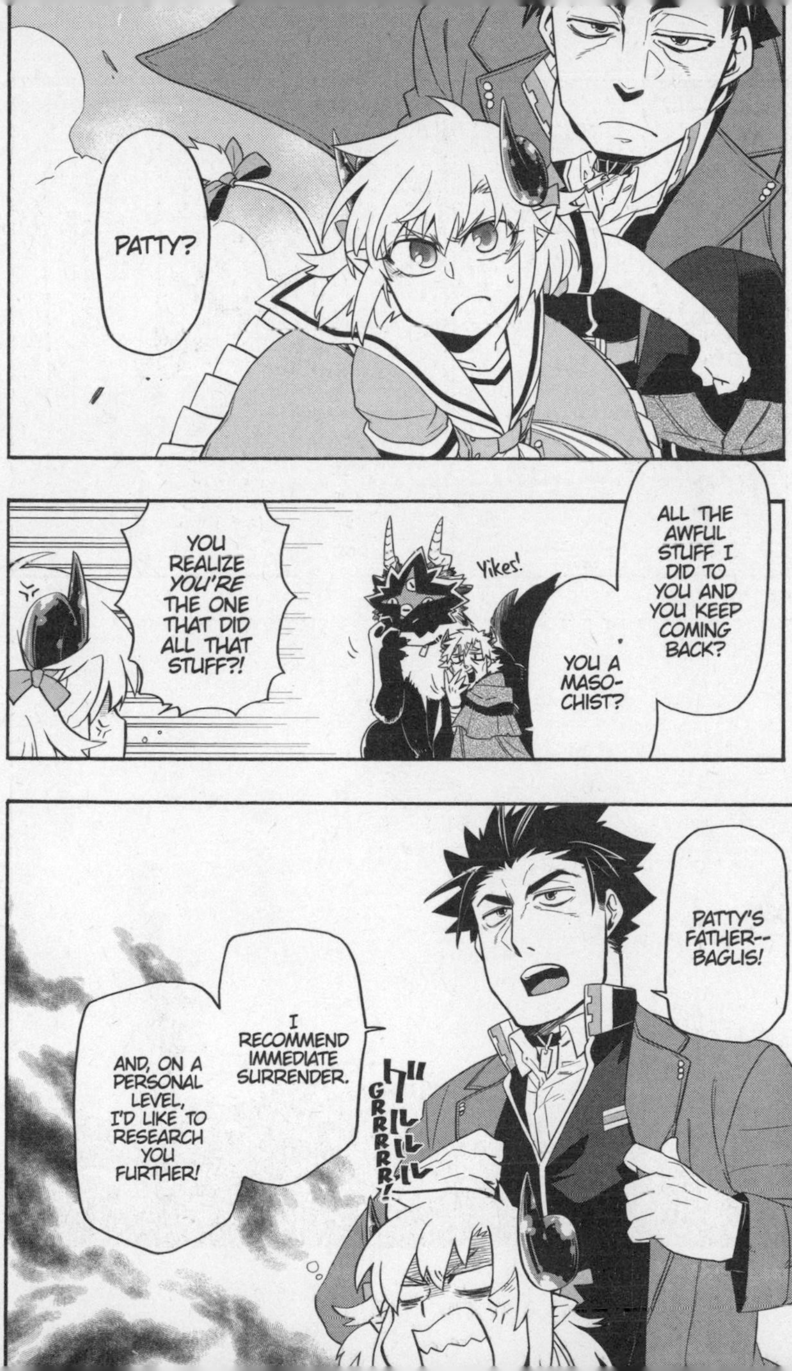
PATTY?
ALL THE AWFUL STUFF I DID TO YOU AND YOU KEEP COMING BACK?
YOU A MASO-CHIST?
Yikes!
YOU REALIZE *YOU'RE* THE ONE THAT DID ALL THAT STUFF?!
PATTY'S FATHER--BAGLIS!
I RECOMMEND IMMEDIATE SURRENDER.
AND, ON A PERSONAL LEVEL, I'D LIKE TO RESEARCH YOU FURTHER!
GRRRRR!

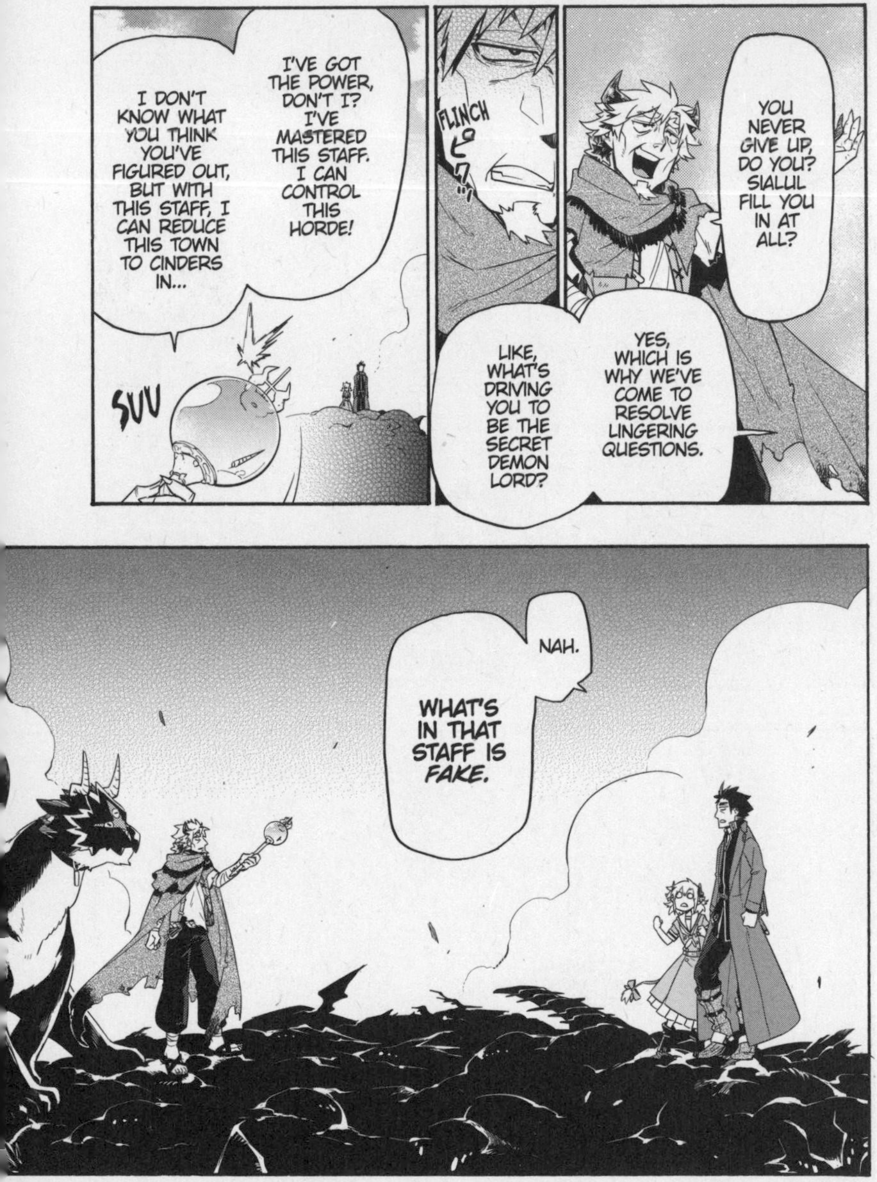
YOU NEVER GIVE UP, DO YOU? SIALUL FILL YOU IN AT ALL?
YES, WHICH IS WHY WE'VE COME TO RESOLVE LINGERING QUESTIONS.
LIKE, WHAT'S DRIVING YOU TO BE THE SECRET DEMON LORD?
FLINCH
I'VE GOT THE POWER, DON'T I? I'VE MASTERED THIS STAFF. I CAN CONTROL THIS HORDE!
I DON'T KNOW WHAT YOU THINK YOU'VE FIGURED OUT, BUT WITH THIS STAFF, I CAN REDUCE THIS TOWN TO CINDERS IN...
SUU
NAH.
WHAT'S IN THAT STAFF IS *FAKE.*

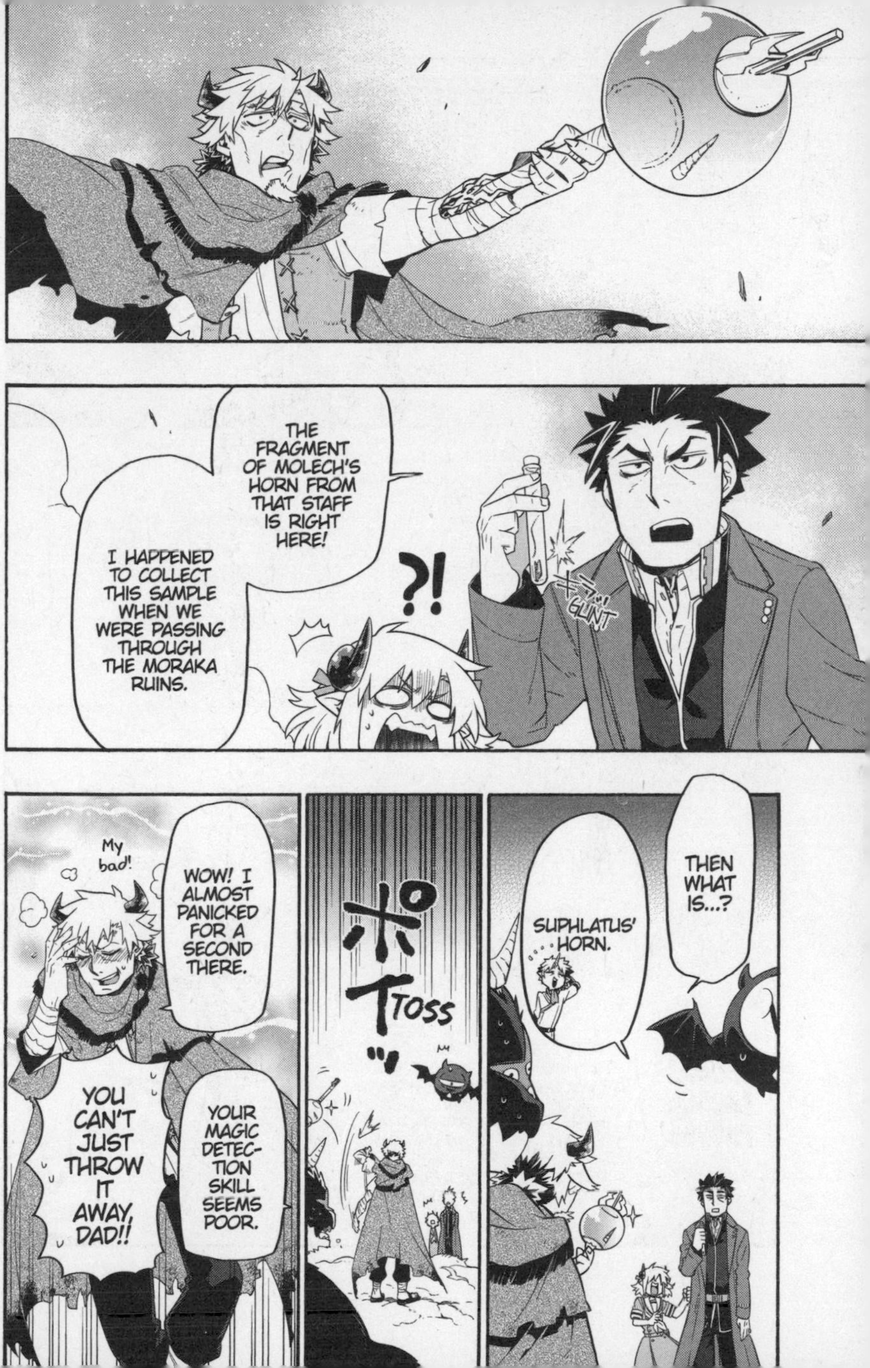
THE FRAGMENT OF MOLECH'S HORN FROM THAT STAFF IS RIGHT HERE!
I HAPPENED TO COLLECT THIS SAMPLE WHEN WE WERE PASSING THROUGH THE MORAKA RUINS.
GLINT
?!
THEN WHAT IS...?
SUPHLATUS' HORN.
TOSS
WOW! I ALMOST PANICKED FOR A SECOND THERE.
My bad!
YOUR MAGIC DETECTION SKILL SEEMS POOR.
YOU CAN'T JUST THROW IT AWAY, DAD!!

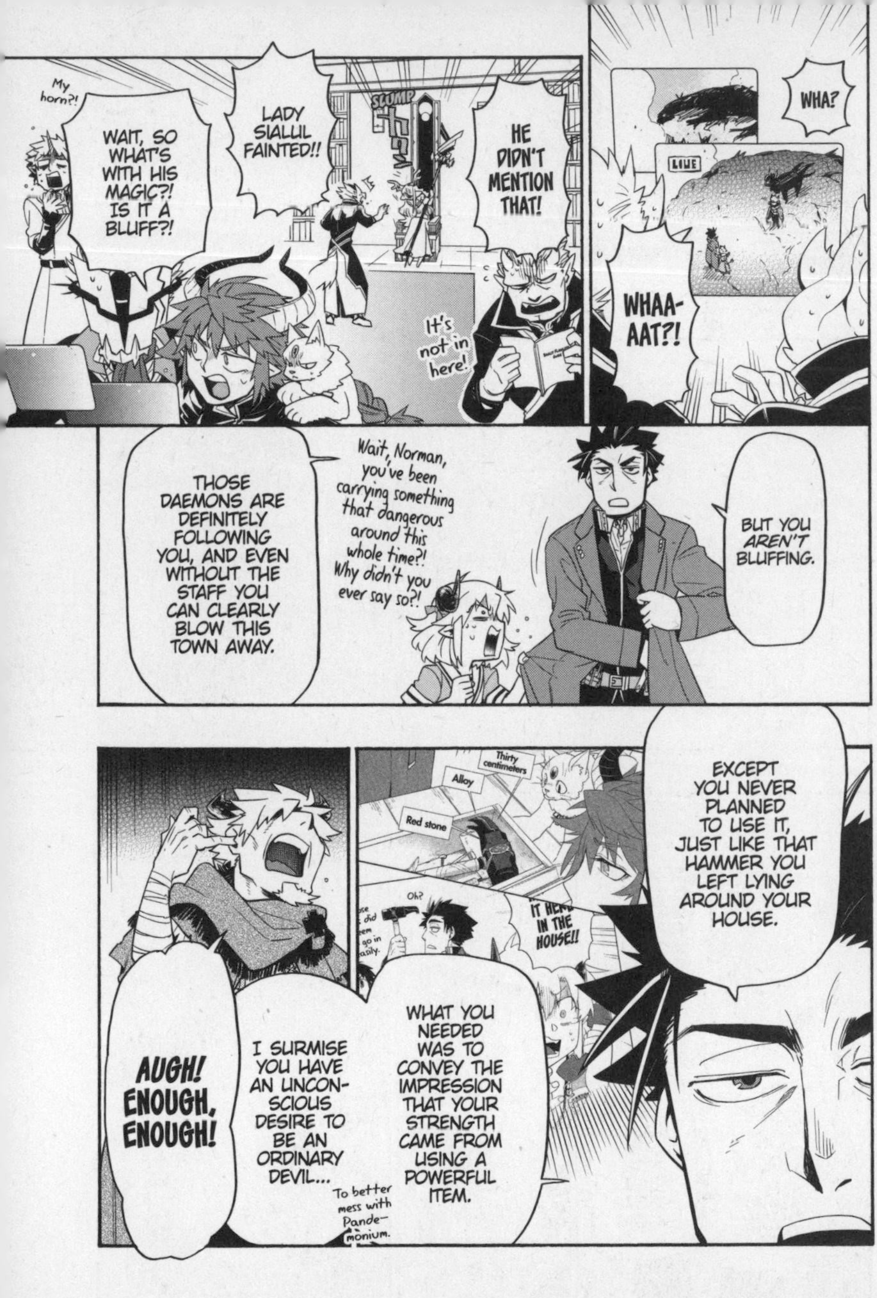
WHA?
LIVE
WHAA-AAT?!
HE DIDN'T MENTION THAT!
It's not in here!
LADY SIALUL FAINTED!!
SLUMP
My horn?!
WAIT, SO WHAT'S WITH HIS MAGIC?! IS IT A BLUFF?!
BUT YOU AREN'T BLUFFING.
Wait, Norman, you've been carrying something that dangerous around this whole time?! Why didn't you ever say so?!
THOSE DAEMONS ARE DEFINITELY FOLLOWING YOU, AND EVEN WITHOUT THE STAFF YOU CAN CLEARLY BLOW THIS TOWN AWAY.
EXCEPT YOU NEVER PLANNED TO USE IT, JUST LIKE THAT HAMMER YOU LEFT LYING AROUND YOUR HOUSE.
Thirty centimeters
Alloy
Red stone
IN THE HOUSE!!
Oh?
WHAT YOU NEEDED WAS TO CONVEY THE IMPRESSION THAT YOUR STRENGTH CAME FROM USING A POWERFUL ITEM.
I SURMISE YOU HAVE AN UNCON-SCIOUS DESIRE TO BE AN ORDINARY DEVIL...
To better mess with Pande-monium.
AUGH! ENOUGH, ENOUGH!

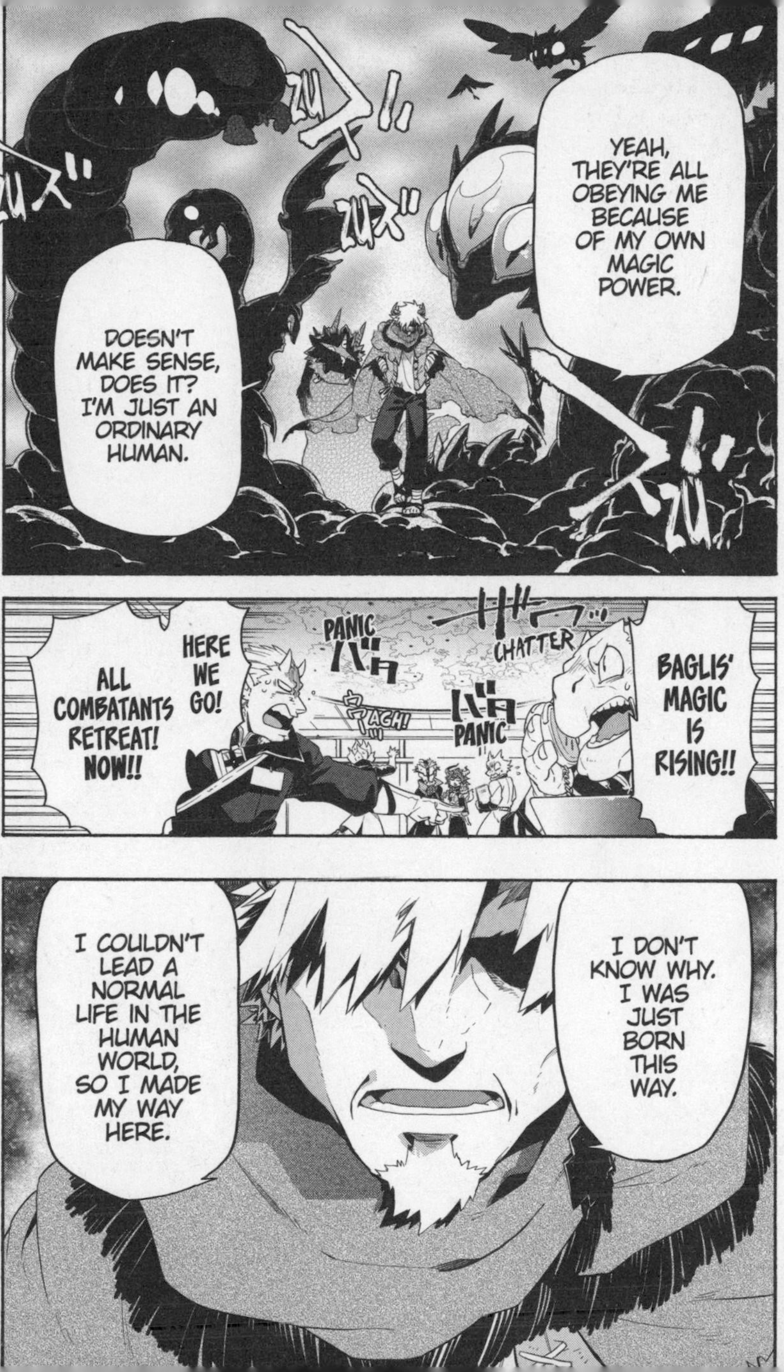
ZU
YEAH, THEY'RE ALL OBEYING ME BECAUSE OF MY OWN MAGIC POWER.
ZU
ZU
ZU
DOESN'T MAKE SENSE, DOES IT? I'M JUST AN ORDINARY HUMAN.
CHATTER
BAGLIS' MAGIC IS RISING!!
PANIC
PANIC
AGH!
HERE WE GO!
ALL COMBATANTS RETREAT! NOW!!
I DON'T KNOW WHY. I WAS JUST BORN THIS WAY.
I COULDN'T LEAD A NORMAL LIFE IN THE HUMAN WORLD, SO I MADE MY WAY HERE.

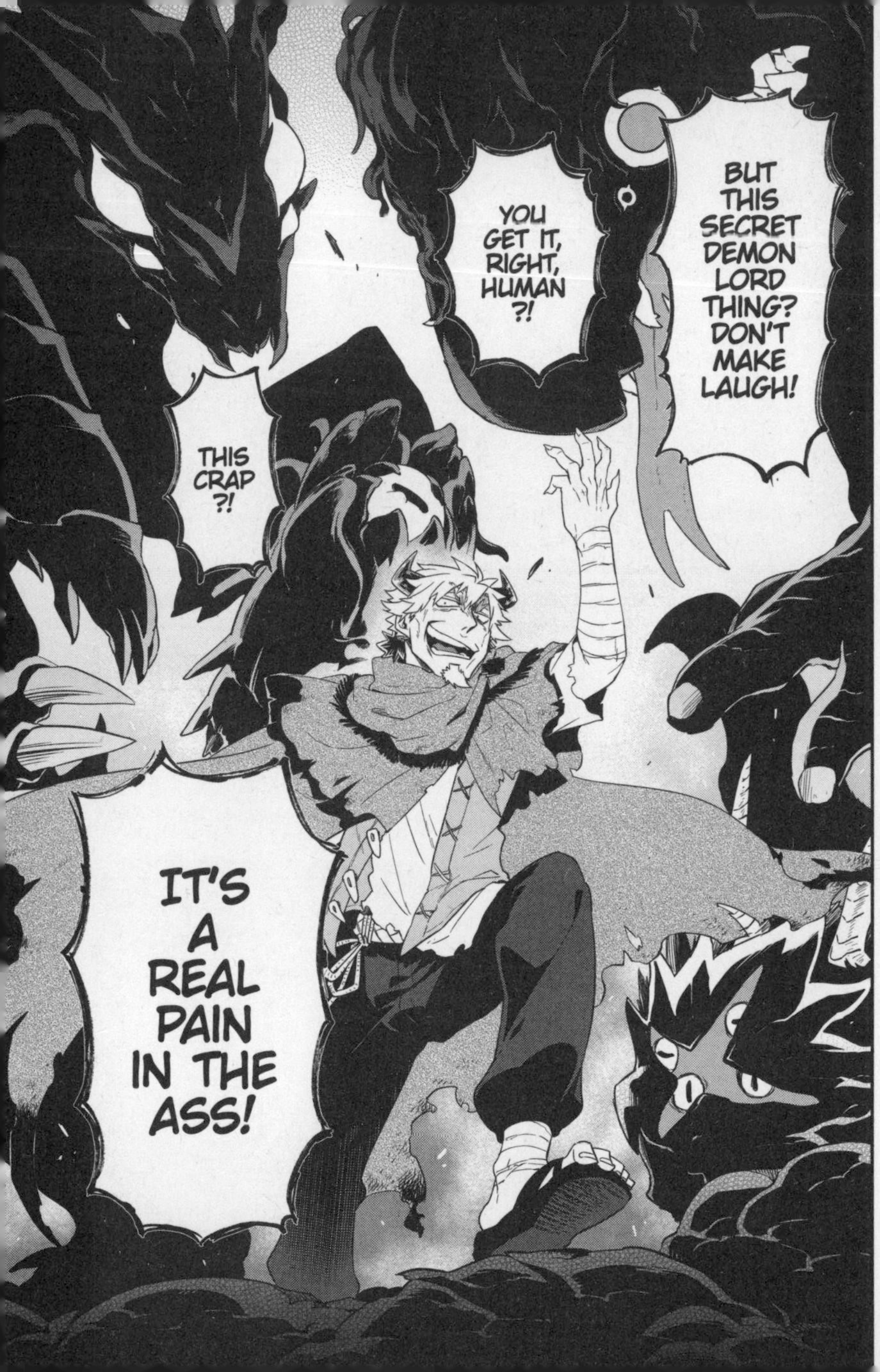
BUT THIS SECRET DEMON LORD THING? DON'T MAKE LAUGH!
YOU GET IT, RIGHT, HUMAN?!
THIS CRAP?!
IT'S A REAL PAIN IN THE ASS!

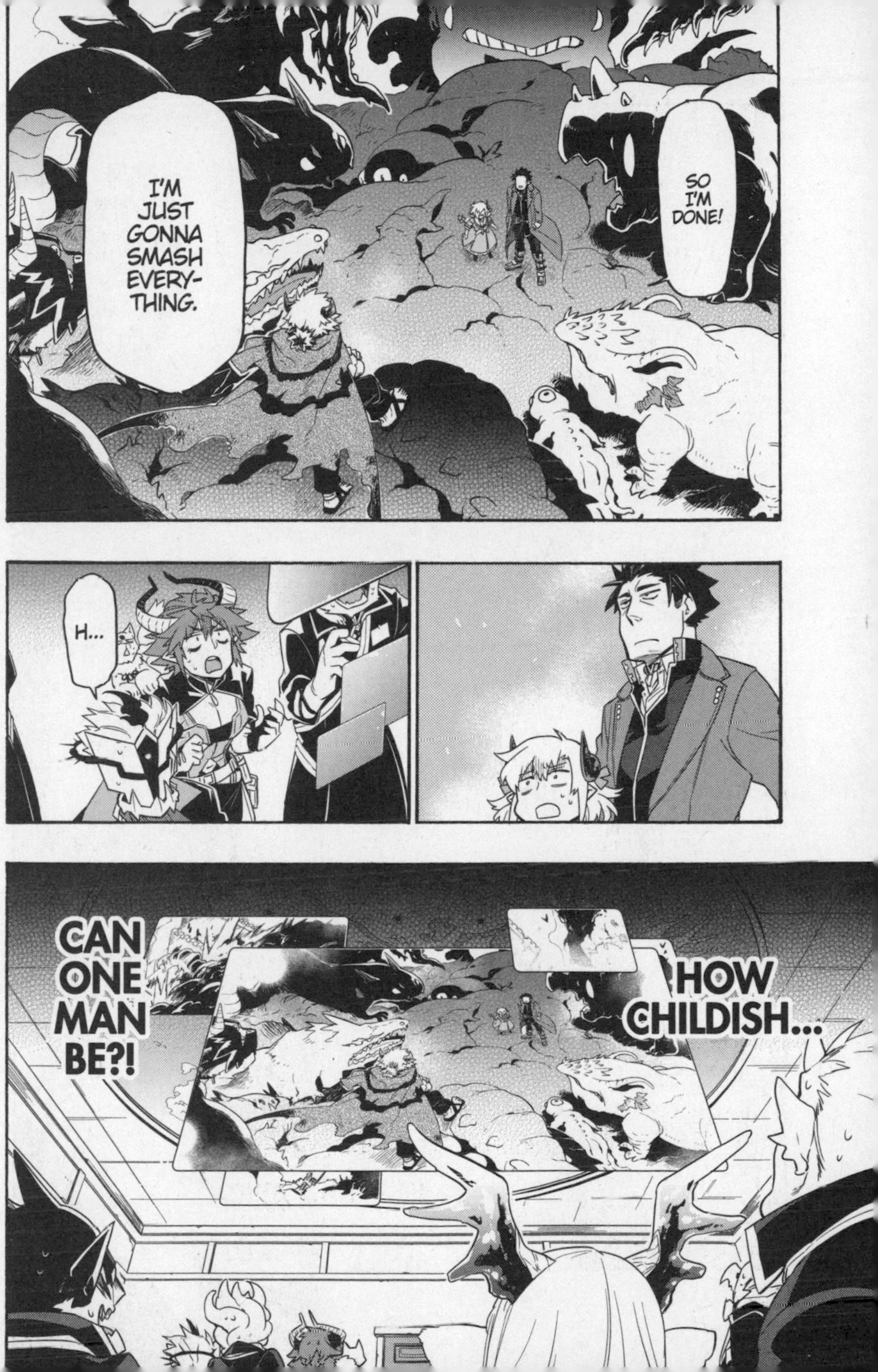
SO I'M DONE!
I'M JUST GONNA SMASH EVERYTHING.
H...
HOW CHILDISH...
CAN ONE MAN BE?!

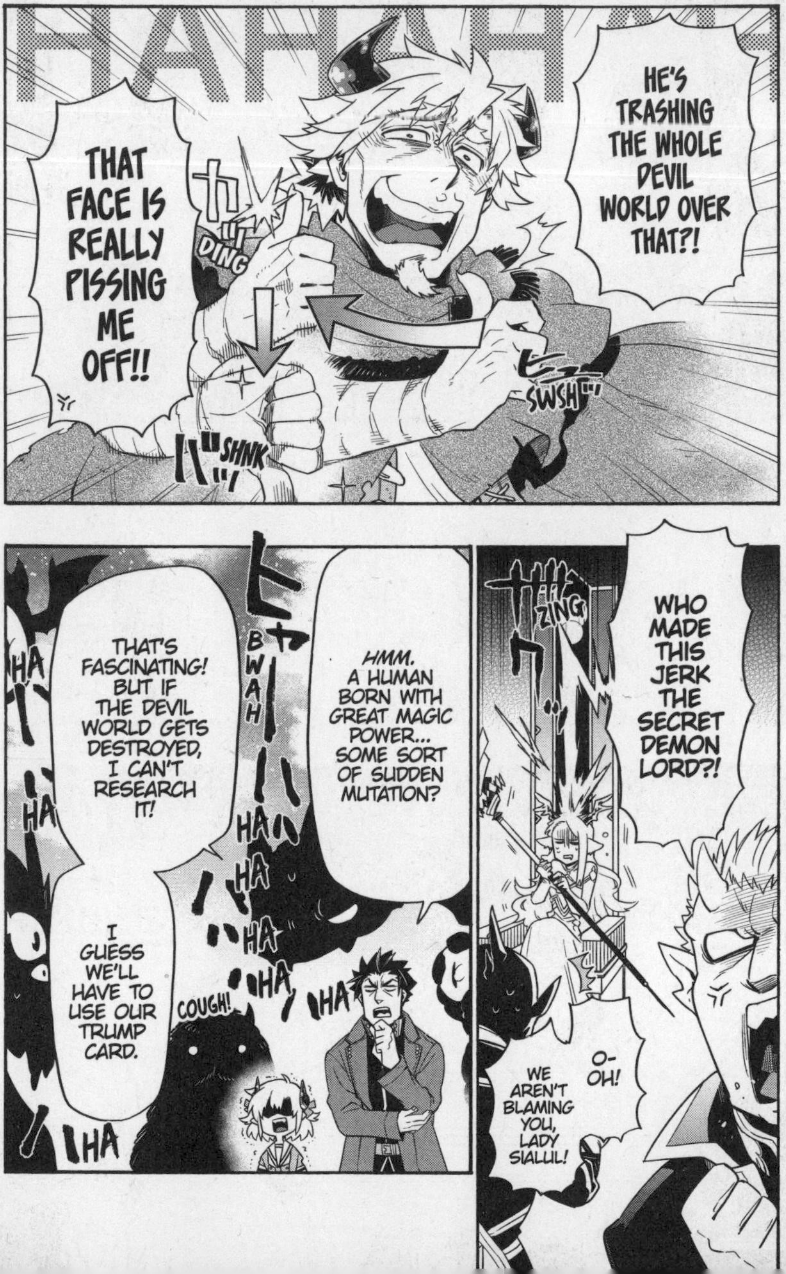
HE'S TRASHING THE WHOLE DEVIL WORLD OVER THAT?!
DING
THAT FACE IS REALLY PISSING ME OFF!!
SWSH
SHNK
WHO MADE THIS JERK THE SECRET DEMON LORD?!
ZING
O-OH!
WE AREN'T BLAMING YOU, LADY SIALUL!
BWAH
HMM. A HUMAN BORN WITH GREAT MAGIC POWER... SOME SORT OF SUDDEN MUTATION?
THAT'S FASCINATING! BUT IF THE DEVIL WORLD GETS DESTROYED, I CAN'T RESEARCH IT!
HA HA HA HA HA HA HA HA
I GUESS WE'LL HAVE TO USE OUR TRUMP CARD.
COUGH!
HA

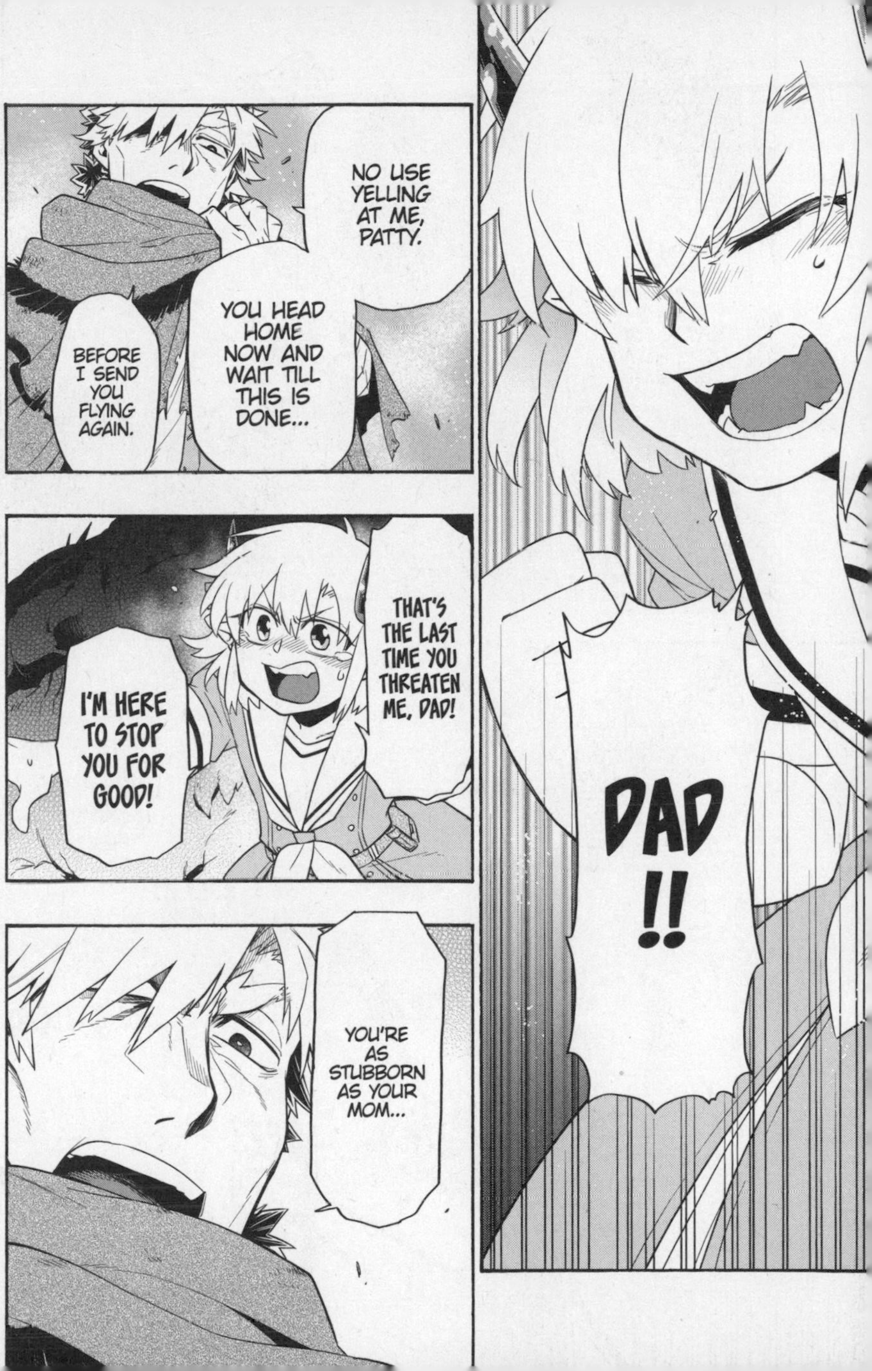
DAD!!
NO USE YELLING AT ME, PATTY.
YOU HEAD HOME NOW AND WAIT TILL THIS IS DONE...
BEFORE I SEND YOU FLYING AGAIN.
THAT'S THE LAST TIME YOU THREATEN ME, DAD!
I'M HERE TO STOP YOU FOR GOOD!
YOU'RE AS STUBBORN AS YOUR MOM...

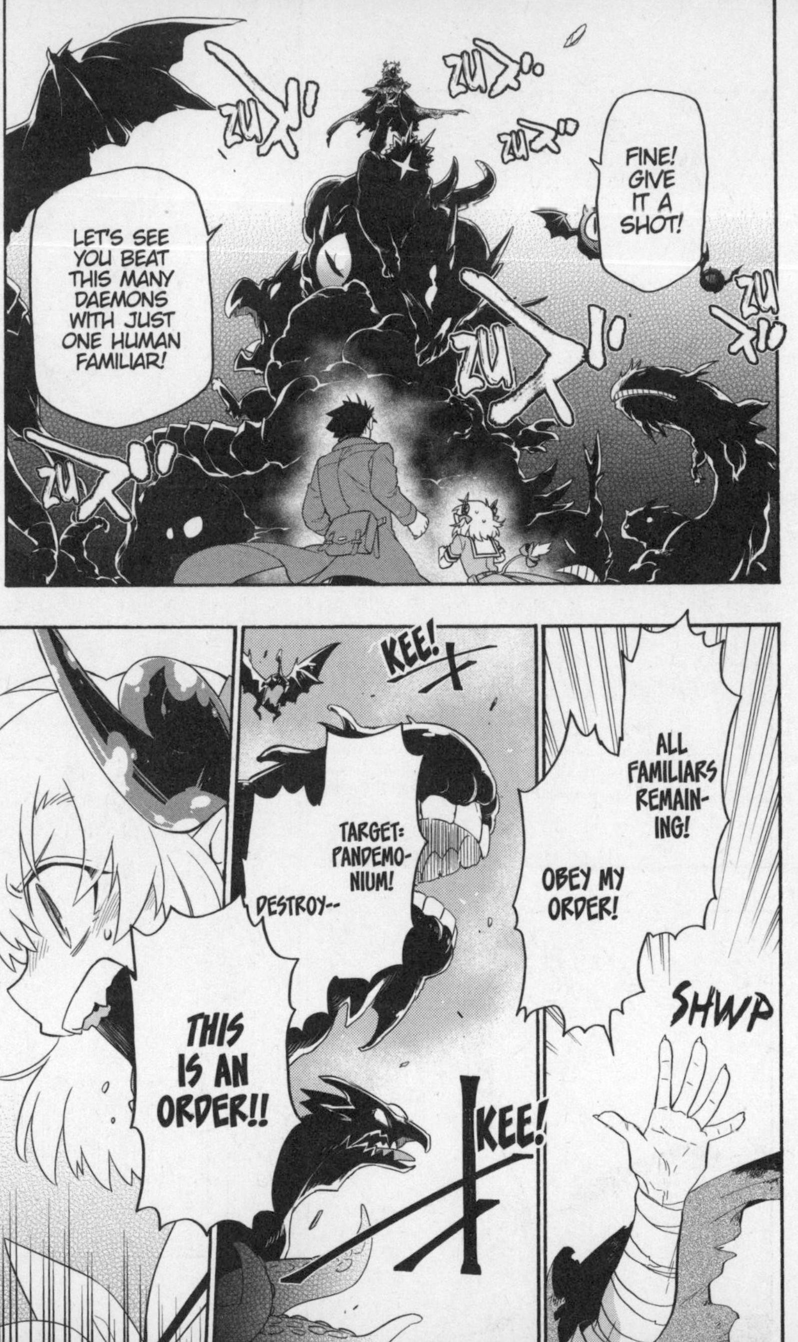
ZUズ
ZUズ
FINE! GIVE IT A SHOT!
ZUズ
ZUズ
LET'S SEE YOU BEAT THIS MANY DAEMONS WITH JUST ONE HUMAN FAMILIAR!
ZUズ
ZUズ
ALL FAMILIARS REMAIN-ING!
OBEY MY ORDER!
SHWP
KEE!
TARGET: PANDEMO-NIUM!
DESTROY--
KEE!
THIS IS AN ORDER!!

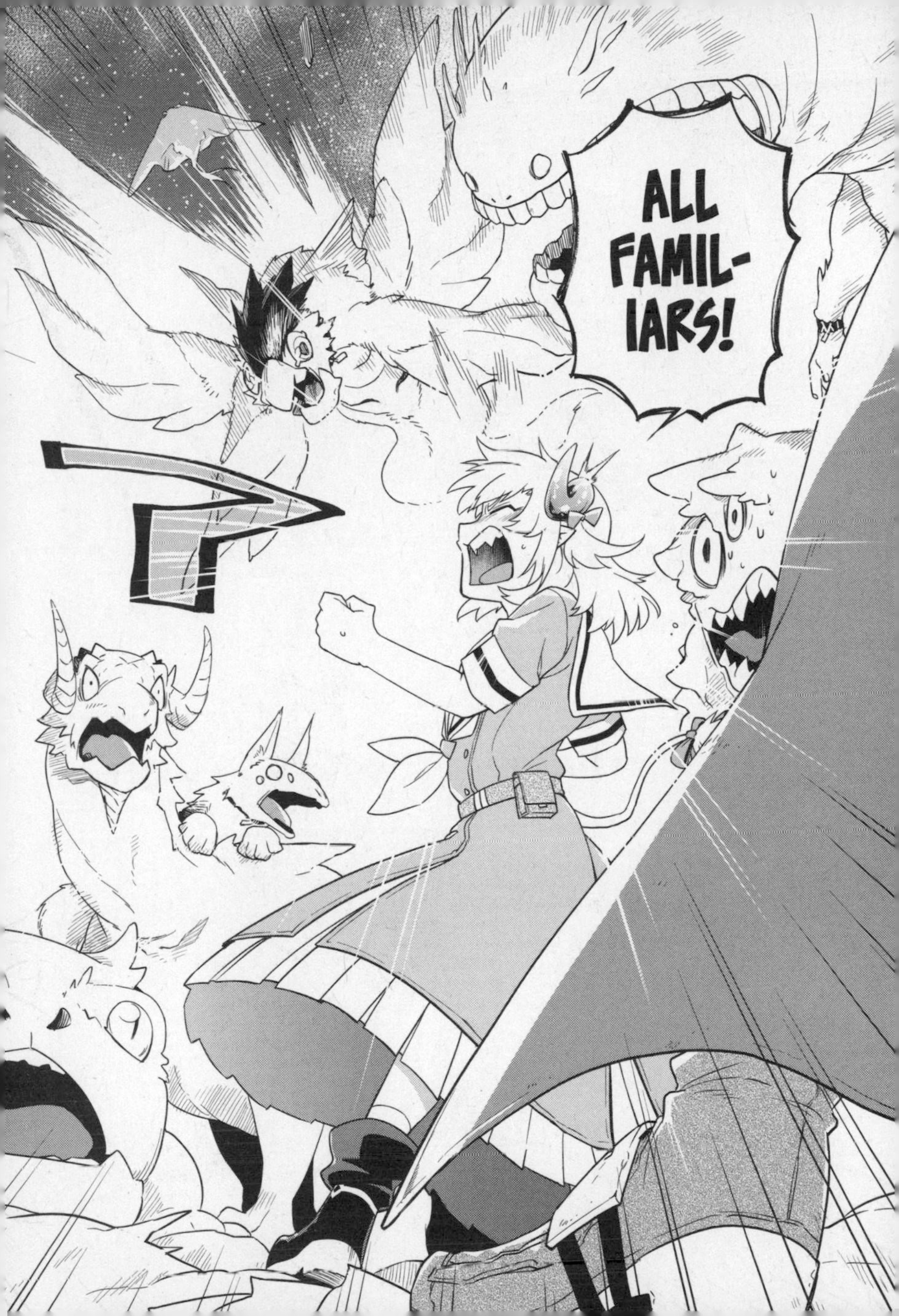
ALL FAMIL-IARS!

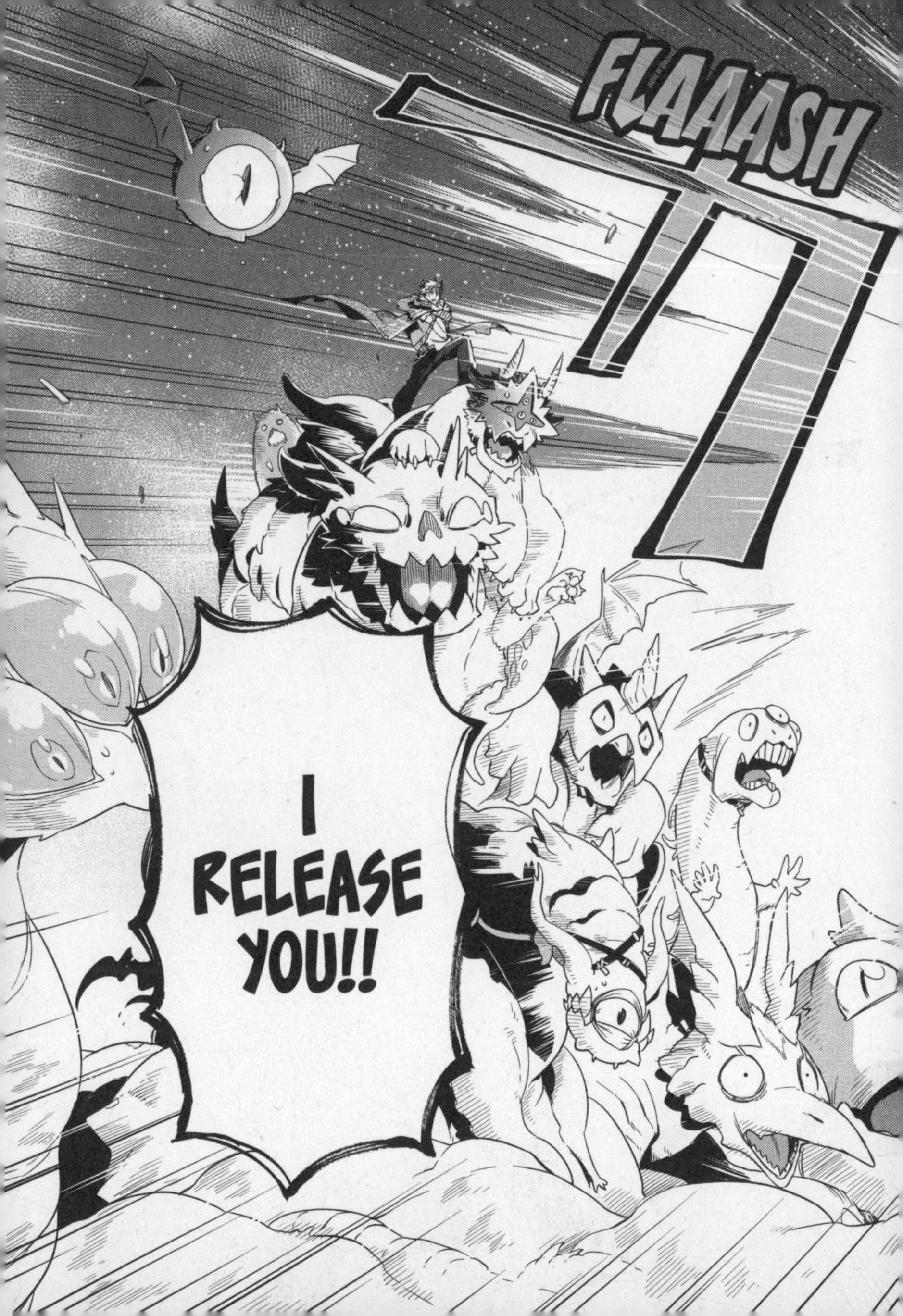
FLAAAASH
I RELEASE YOU!!

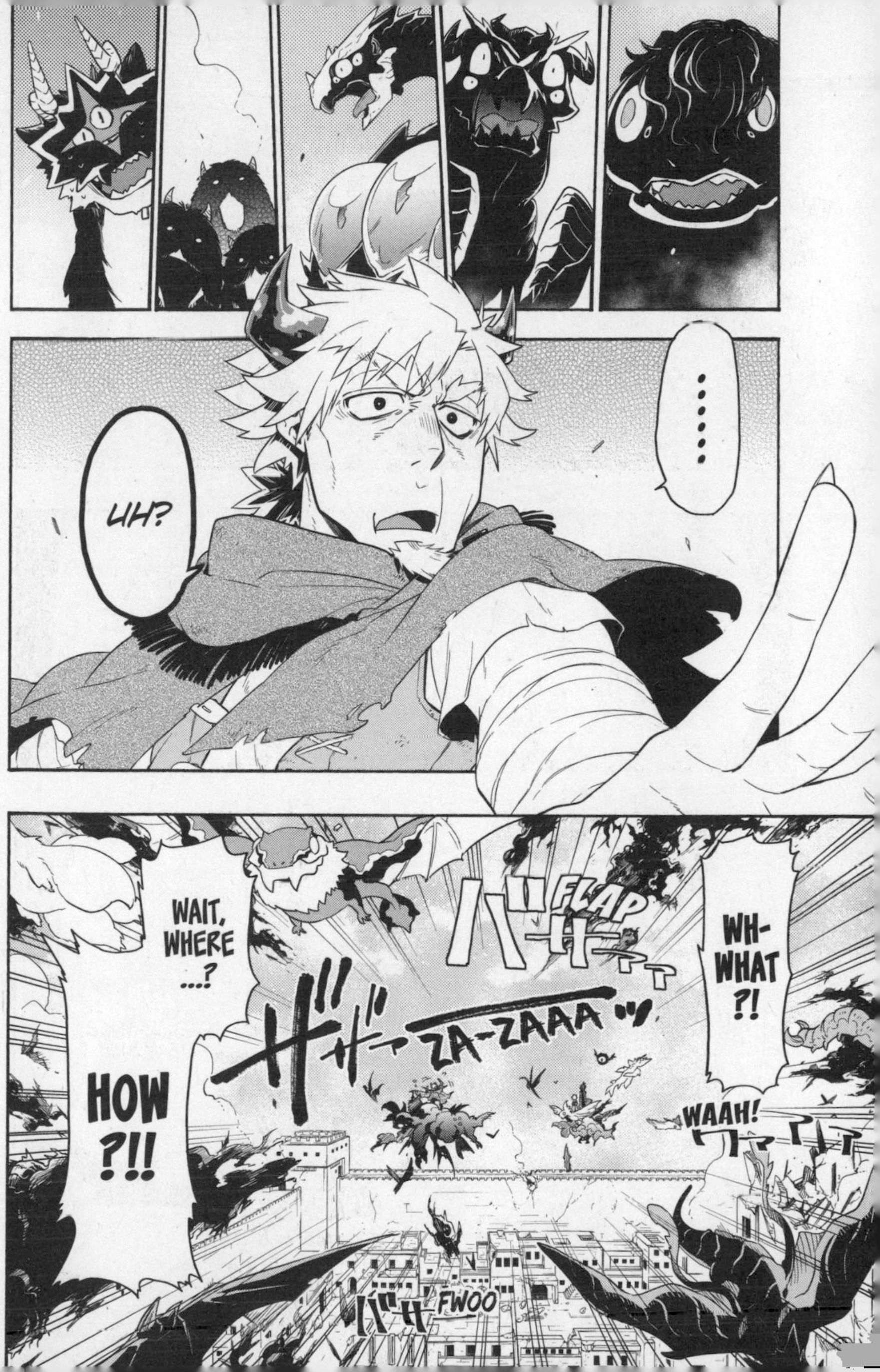
......
UH?
WH-WHAT?!
FLAP
WAIT, WHERE ...?
ZA-ZAAA
WAAH!
HOW?!!
FWOO

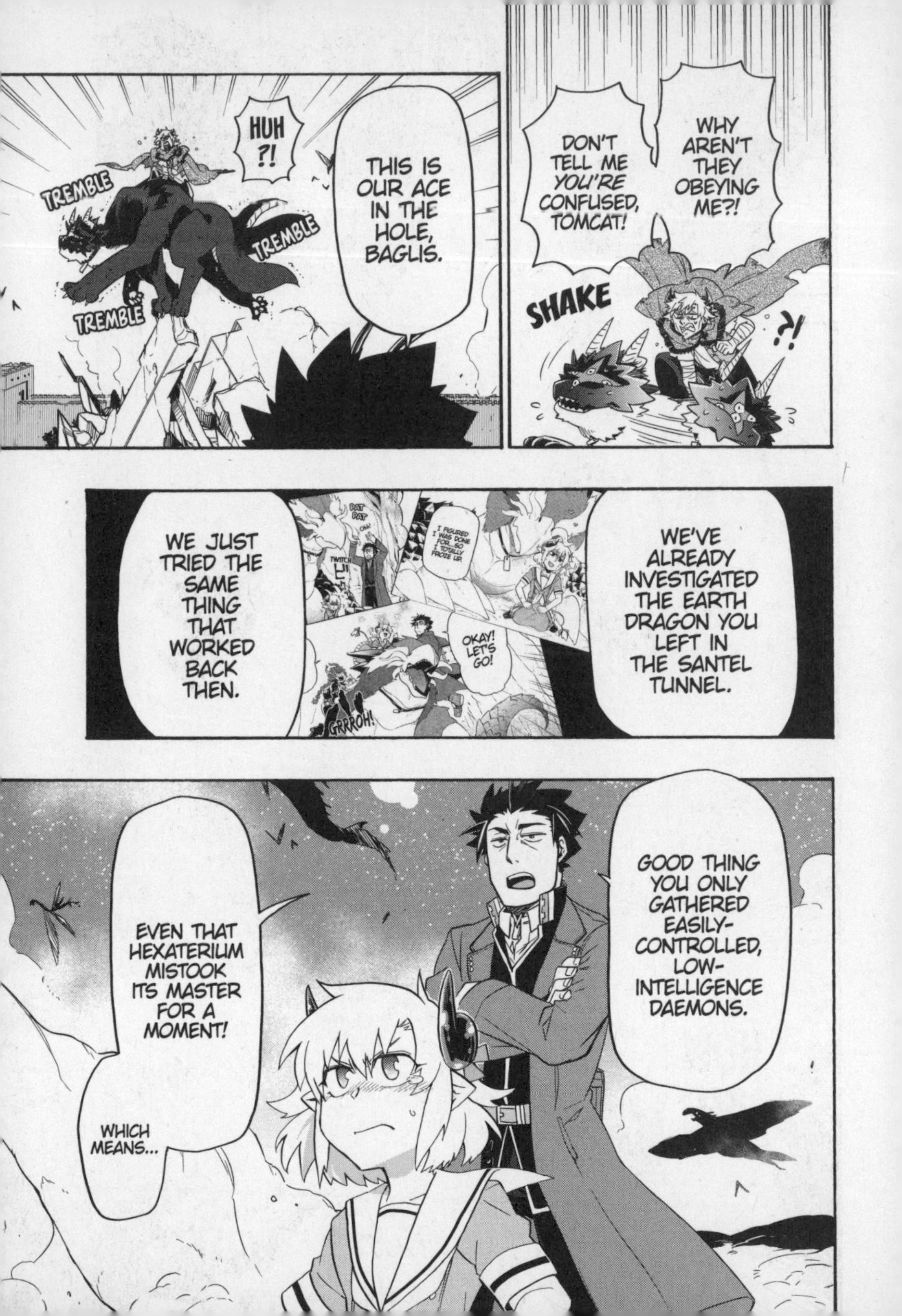
WHY AREN'T THEY OBEYING ME?!
DON'T TELL ME YOU'RE CONFUSED, TOMCAT!
SHAKE
?!
THIS IS OUR ACE IN THE HOLE, BAGLIS.
HUH ?!
TREMBLE
TREMBLE
TREMBLE
WE'VE ALREADY INVESTIGATED THE EARTH DRAGON YOU LEFT IN THE SANTEL TUNNEL.
I FIGURED I WAS DONE FOR... SO I TOTALLY FROZE UP.
PAT PAT
TWITCH
OKAY! LET'S GO!
GRRROH!
WE JUST TRIED THE SAME THING THAT WORKED BACK THEN.
GOOD THING YOU ONLY GATHERED EASILY-CONTROLLED, LOW-INTELLIGENCE DAEMONS.
EVEN THAT HEXATERIUM MISTOOK ITS MASTER FOR A MOMENT!
WHICH MEANS...

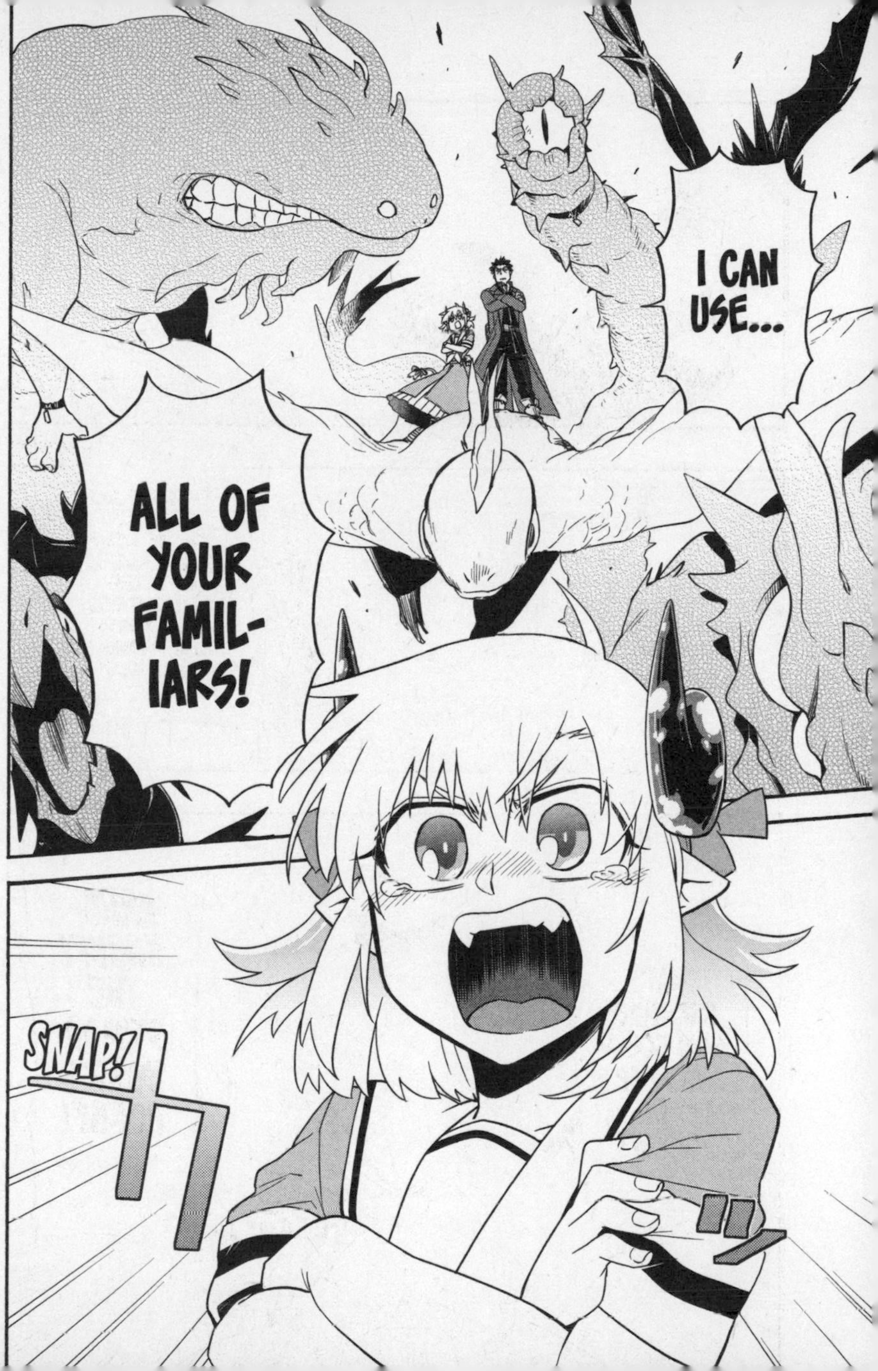
I CAN USE...
ALL OF YOUR FAMIL-IARS!
SNAP!

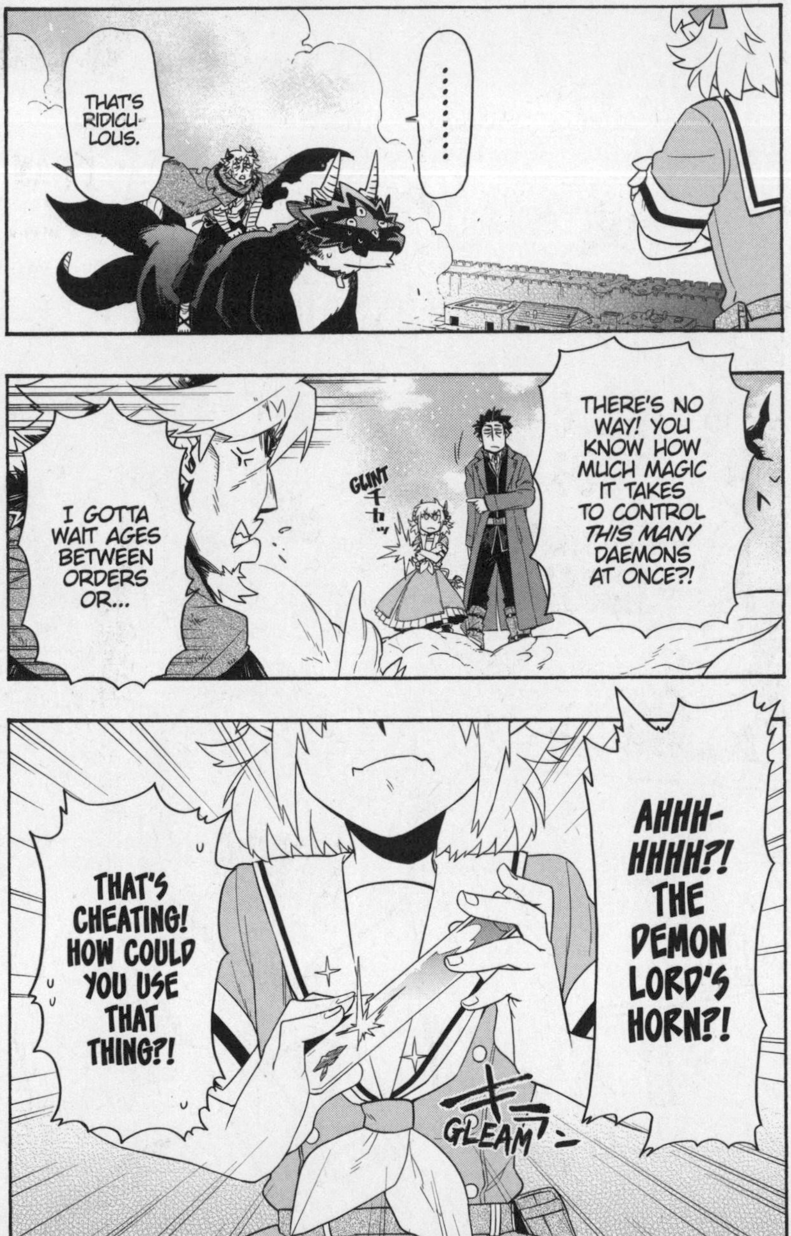
......
THAT'S RIDICULOUS.
THERE'S NO WAY! YOU KNOW HOW MUCH MAGIC IT TAKES TO CONTROL *THIS MANY* DAEMONS AT ONCE?!
GLINT
I GOTTA WAIT AGES BETWEEN ORDERS OR...
AHHHHHHH?! THE DEMON LORD'S HORN?!
THAT'S CHEATING! HOW COULD YOU USE THAT THING?!
GLEAM

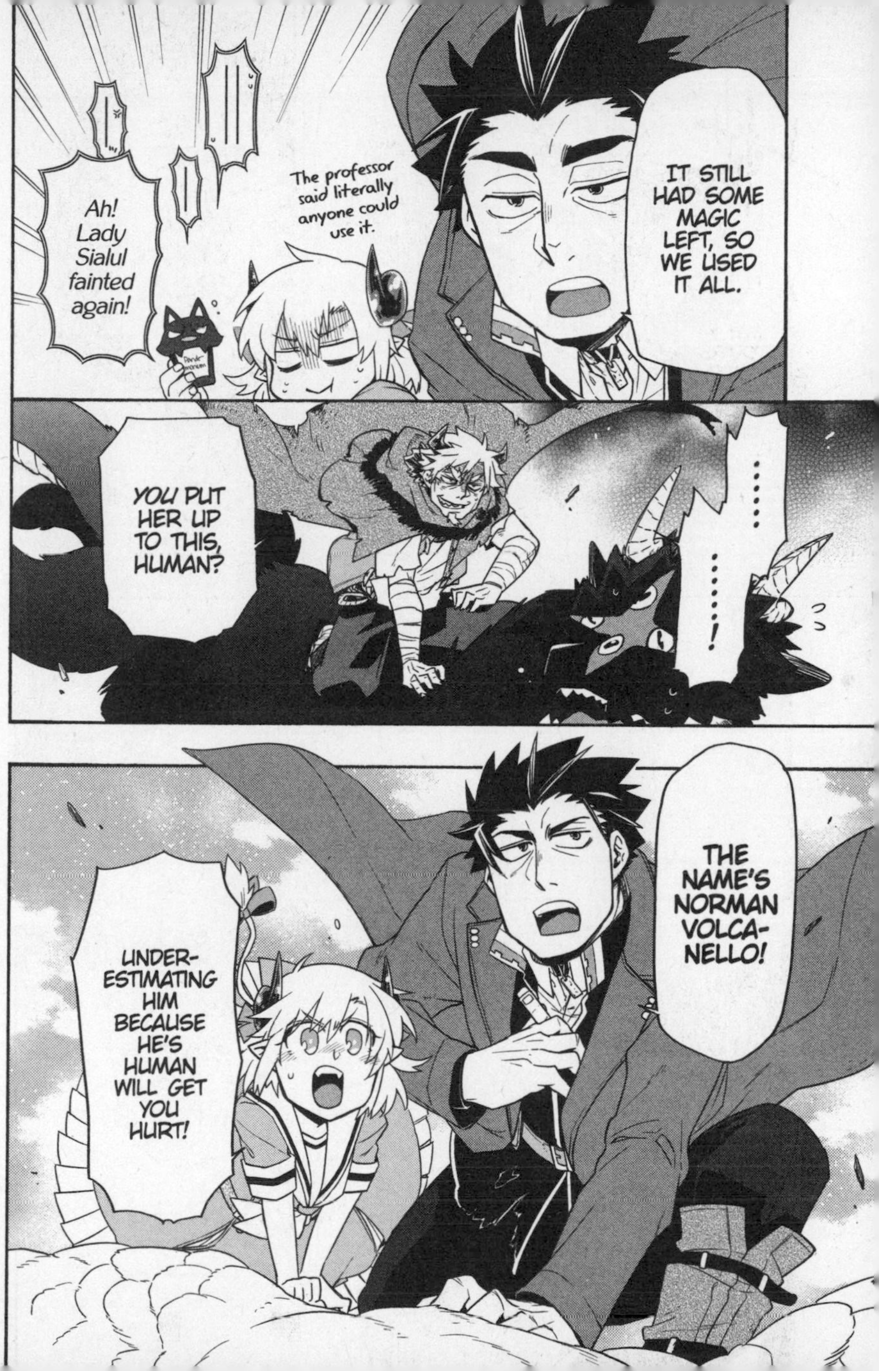
IT STILL HAD SOME MAGIC LEFT, SO WE USED IT ALL.
The professor said literally anyone could use it.
Ah! Lady Sialul fainted again!
......!
YOU PUT HER UP TO THIS, HUMAN?
THE NAME'S NORMAN VOLCA-NELLO!
UNDER-ESTIMATING HIM BECAUSE HE'S HUMAN WILL GET YOU HURT!

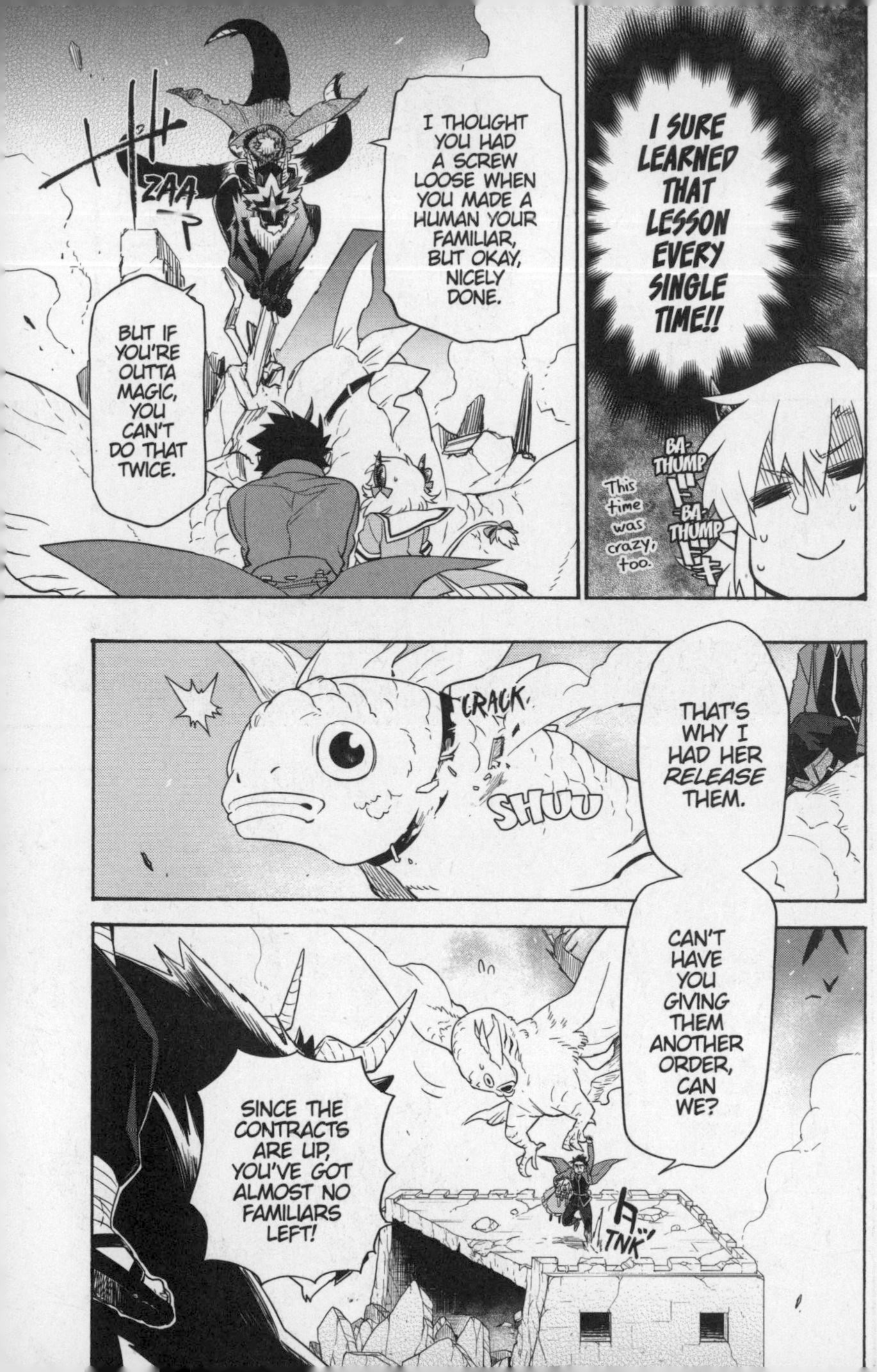
I SURE LEARNED THAT LESSON EVERY SINGLE TIME!!
BA-THUMP
BA-THUMP
This time was crazy, too.
I THOUGHT YOU HAD A SCREW LOOSE WHEN YOU MADE A HUMAN YOUR FAMILIAR, BUT OKAY, NICELY DONE.
ZAAP
BUT IF YOU'RE OUTTA MAGIC, YOU CAN'T DO THAT TWICE.
THAT'S WHY I HAD HER *RELEASE* THEM.
CRACK
SHUU
CAN'T HAVE YOU GIVING THEM ANOTHER ORDER, CAN WE?
TNK
SINCE THE CONTRACTS ARE UP, YOU'VE GOT ALMOST NO FAMILIARS LEFT!

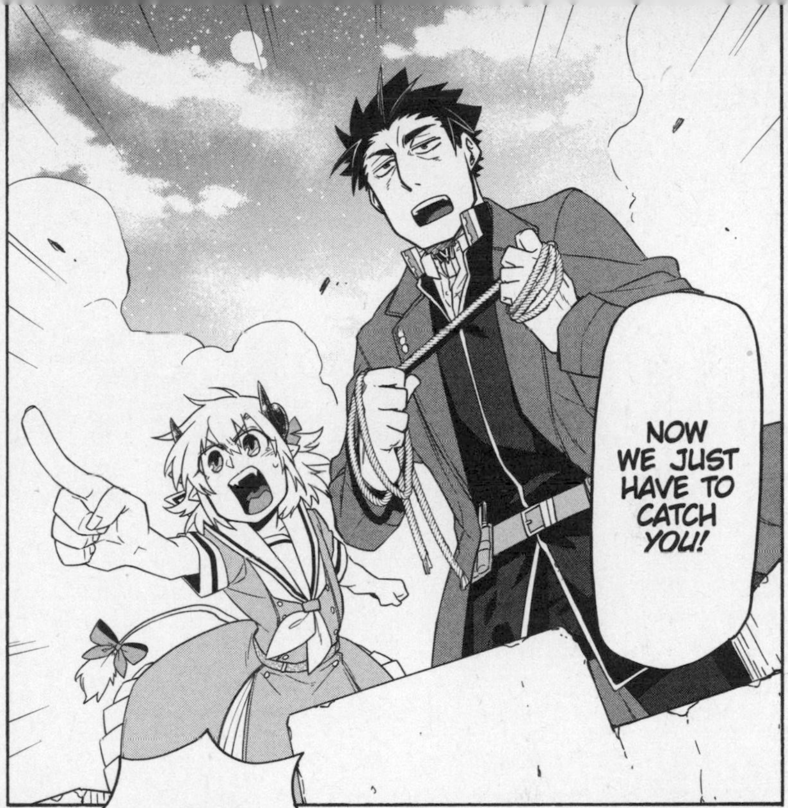
NOW WE JUST HAVE TO CATCH YOU!
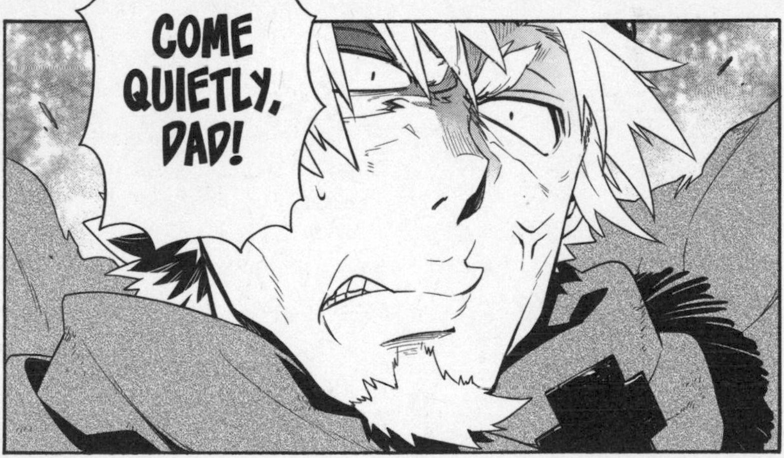
COME QUIETLY, DAD!

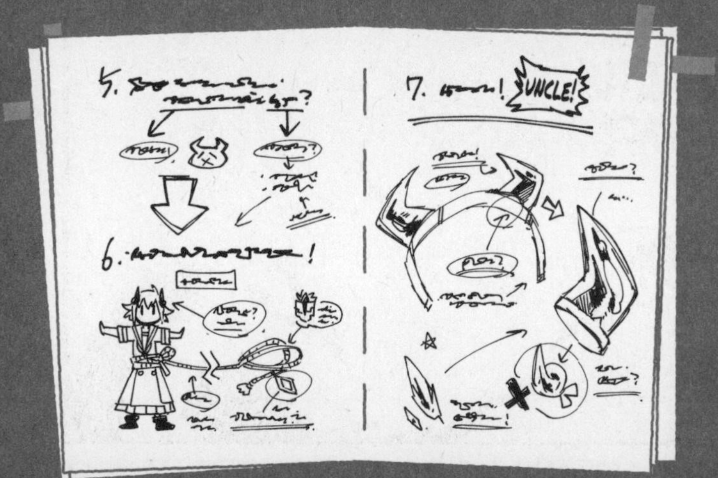
UNCLE!

Sorry For My Familiar

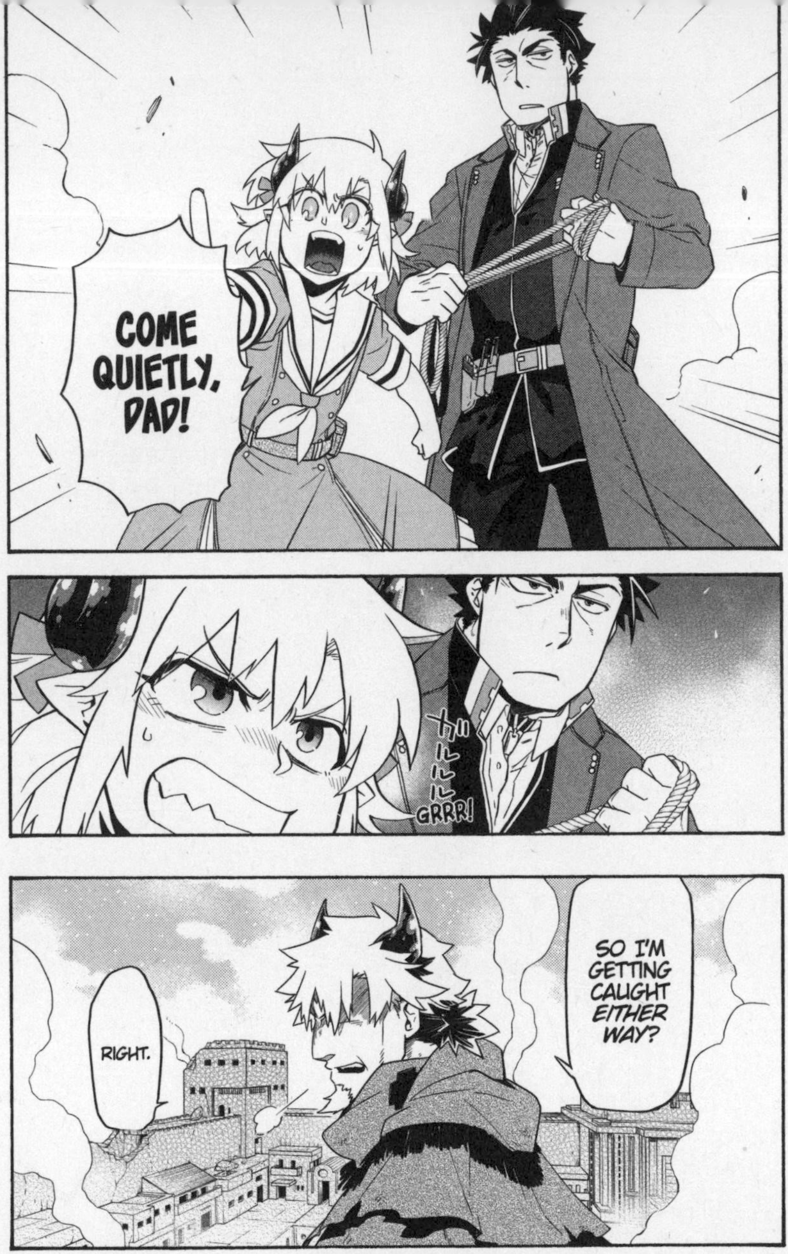
COME QUIETLY, DAD!
ガルルル
GRRR!
SO I'M GETTING CAUGHT EITHER WAY?
RIGHT.

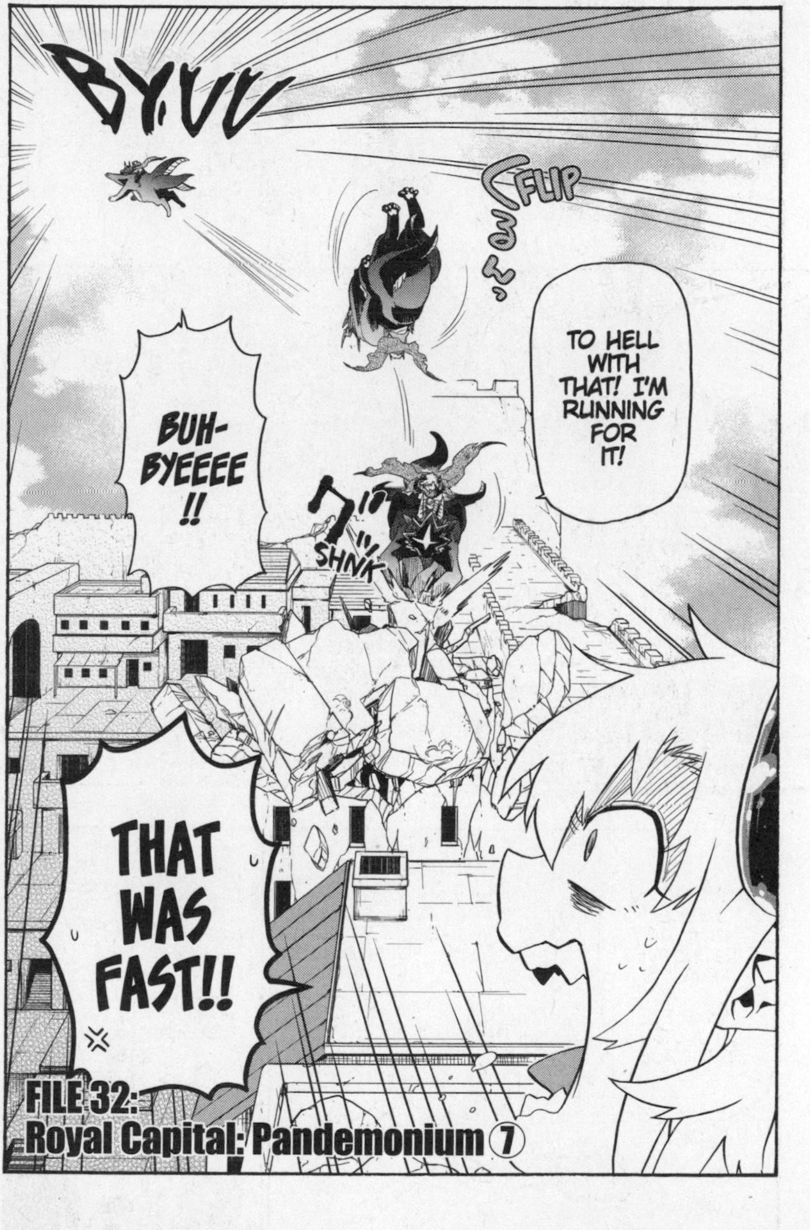
FLIP
TO HELL WITH THAT! I'M RUNNING FOR IT!
BYUU
BUH-BYEEEE!!
SHNK
THAT WAS FAST!!
FILE 32:
Royal Capital: Pandemonium 7

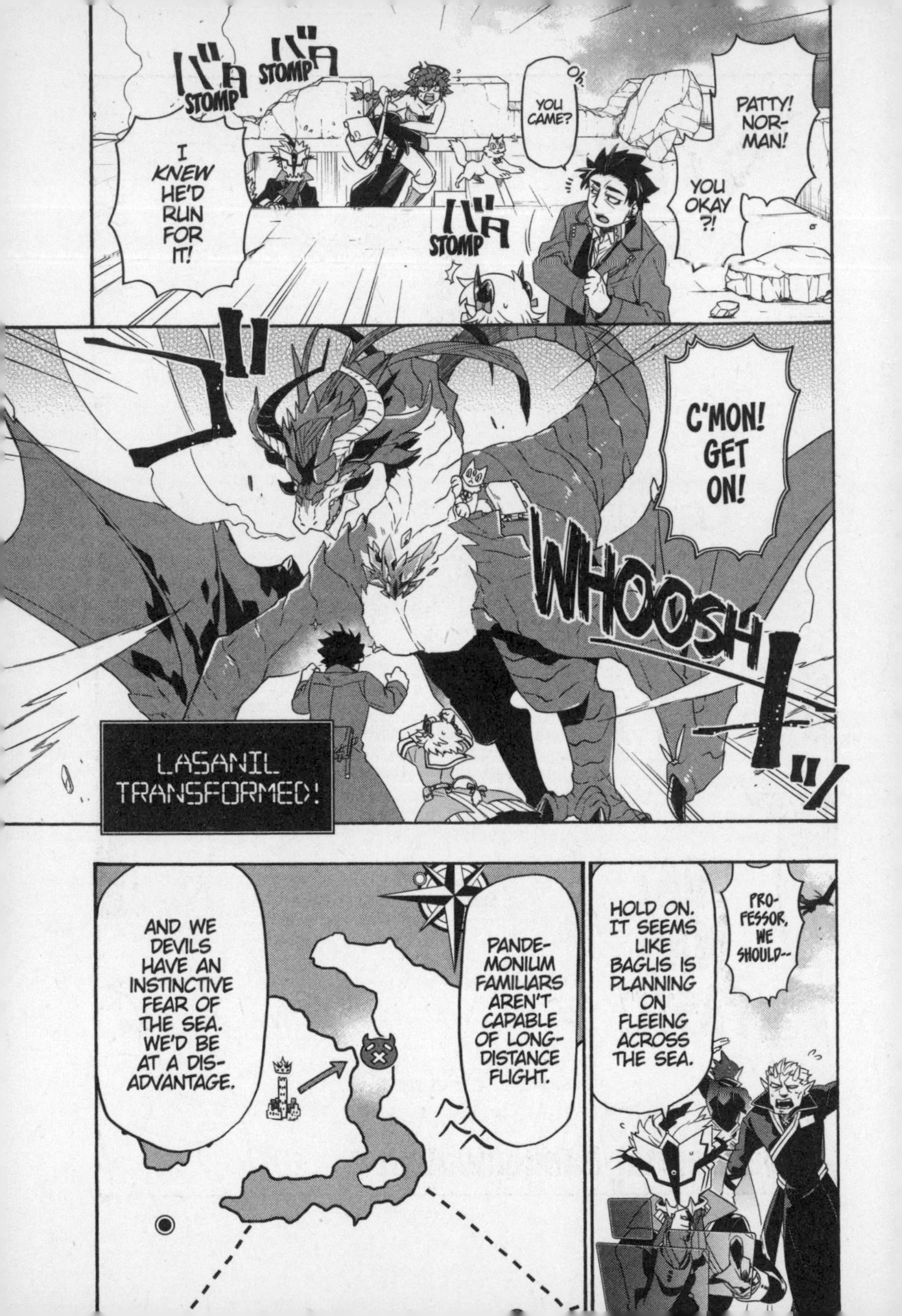
PATTY! NOR-MAN!
YOU OKAY ?!
Oh. YOU CAME?
STOMP
STOMP
STOMP
I KNEW HE'D RUN FOR IT!
C'MON! GET ON!
WHOOSH
LASANIL TRANSFORMED!
PRO-FESSOR, WE SHOULD--
HOLD ON. IT SEEMS LIKE BAGLIS IS PLANNING ON FLEEING ACROSS THE SEA.
PANDE-MONIUM FAMILIARS AREN'T CAPABLE OF LONG-DISTANCE FLIGHT.
AND WE DEVILS HAVE AN INSTINCTIVE FEAR OF THE SEA. WE'D BE AT A DIS-ADVANTAGE.

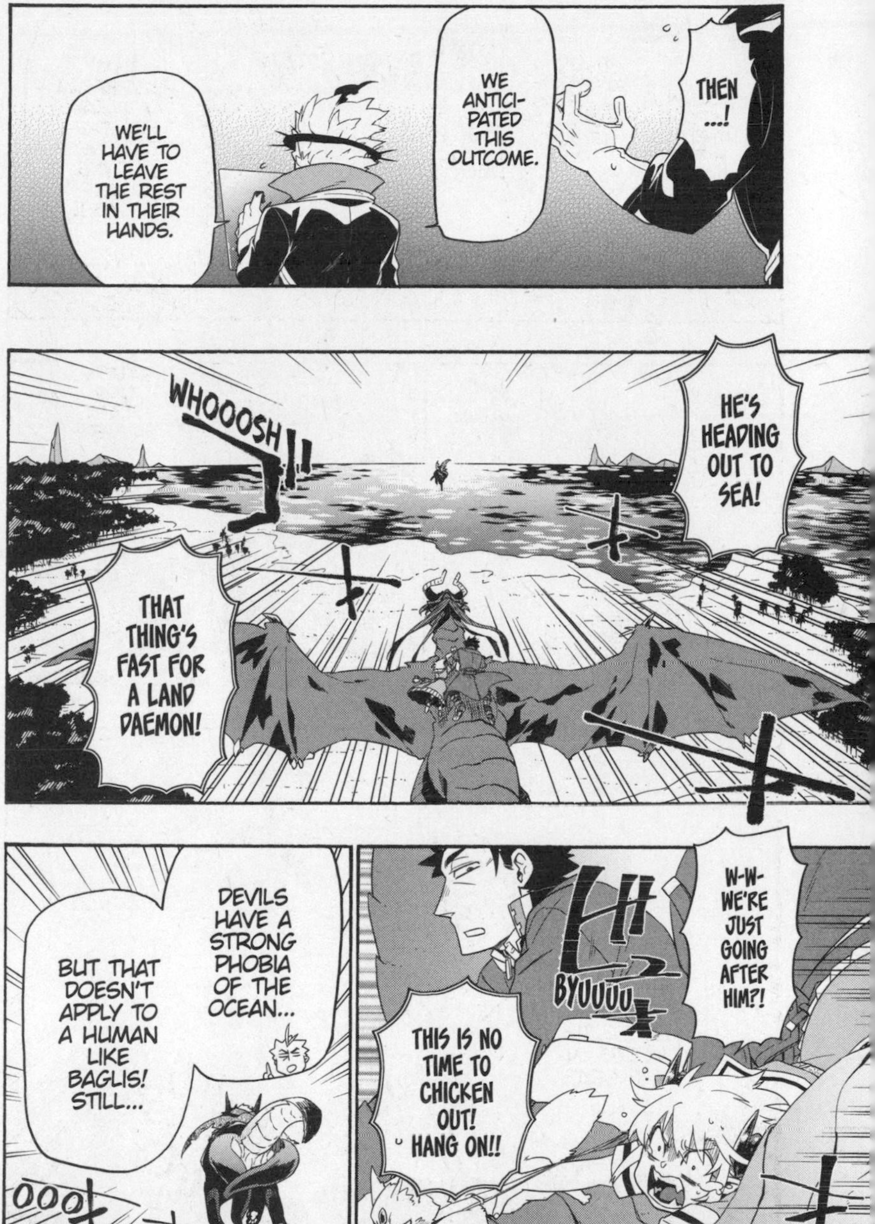
THEN ...!
WE ANTICI-PATED THIS OUTCOME.
WE'LL HAVE TO LEAVE THE REST IN THEIR HANDS.
HE'S HEADING OUT TO SEA!
WHOOOSH!!
THAT THING'S FAST FOR A LAND DAEMON!
W-W-WE'RE JUST GOING AFTER HIM?!
BYUUUU
THIS IS NO TIME TO CHICKEN OUT! HANG ON!!
DEVILS HAVE A STRONG PHOBIA OF THE OCEAN...
BUT THAT DOESN'T APPLY TO A HUMAN LIKE BAGLIS! STILL...
OOO

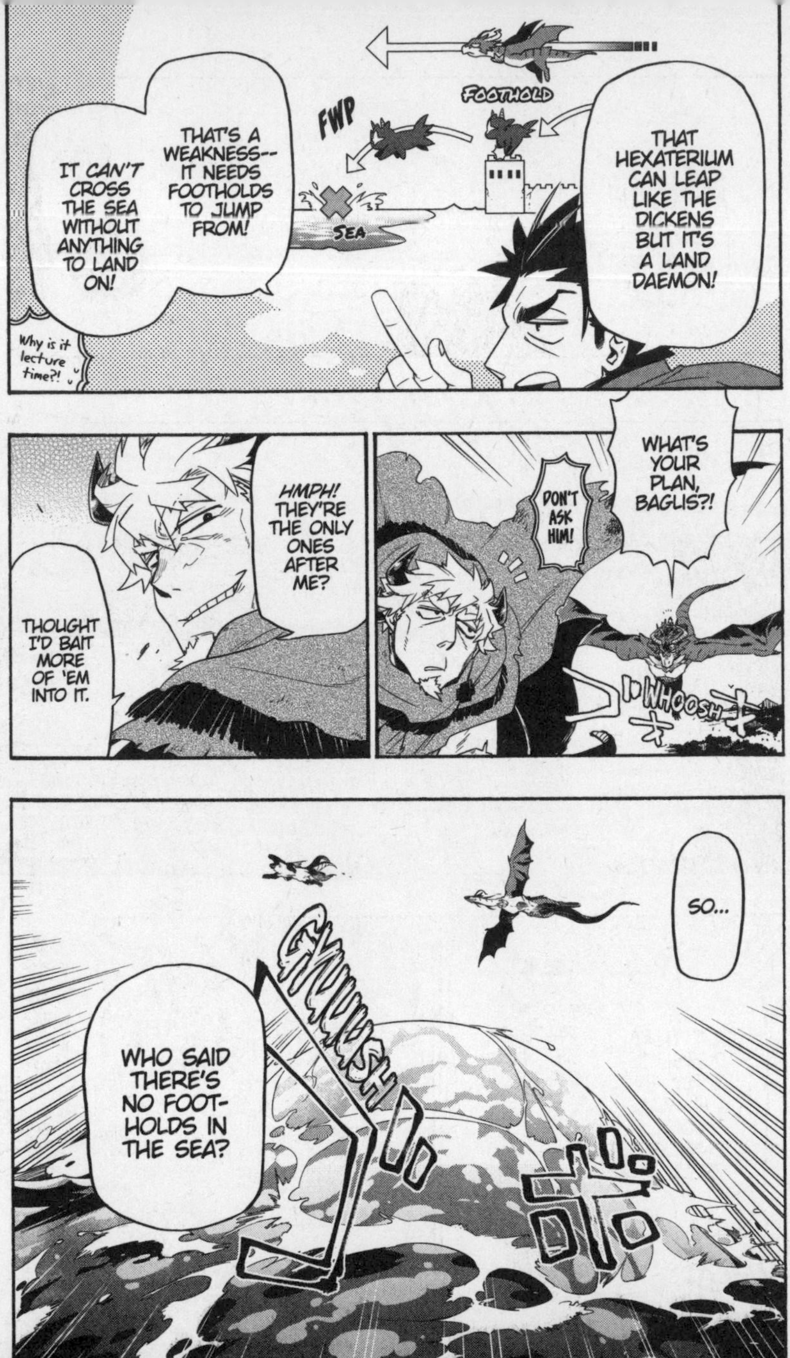
FOOTHOLD
THAT HEXATERIUM CAN LEAP LIKE THE DICKENS BUT IT'S A LAND DAEMON!
FWP
SEA
THAT'S A WEAKNESS-- IT NEEDS FOOTHOLDS TO JUMP FROM!
IT CAN'T CROSS THE SEA WITHOUT ANYTHING TO LAND ON!
Why is it lecture time?!
WHAT'S YOUR PLAN, BAGLIS?!
DON'T ASK HIM!
WHOOSH
HMPH! THEY'RE THE ONLY ONES AFTER ME?
THOUGHT I'D BAIT MORE OF 'EM INTO IT.
SO...
WHO SAID THERE'S NO FOOT-HOLDS IN THE SEA?

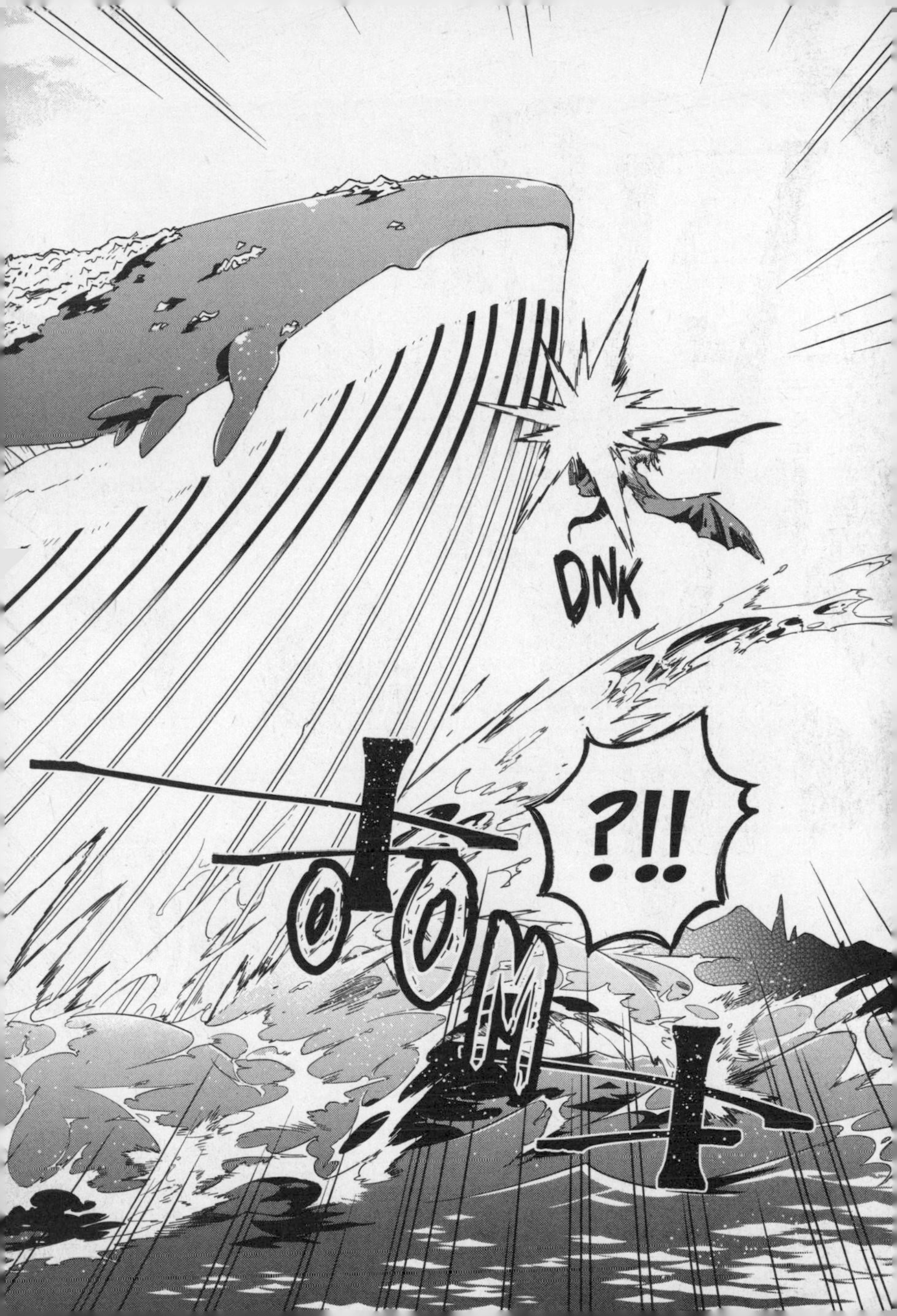
DNK
?!!
DOOM

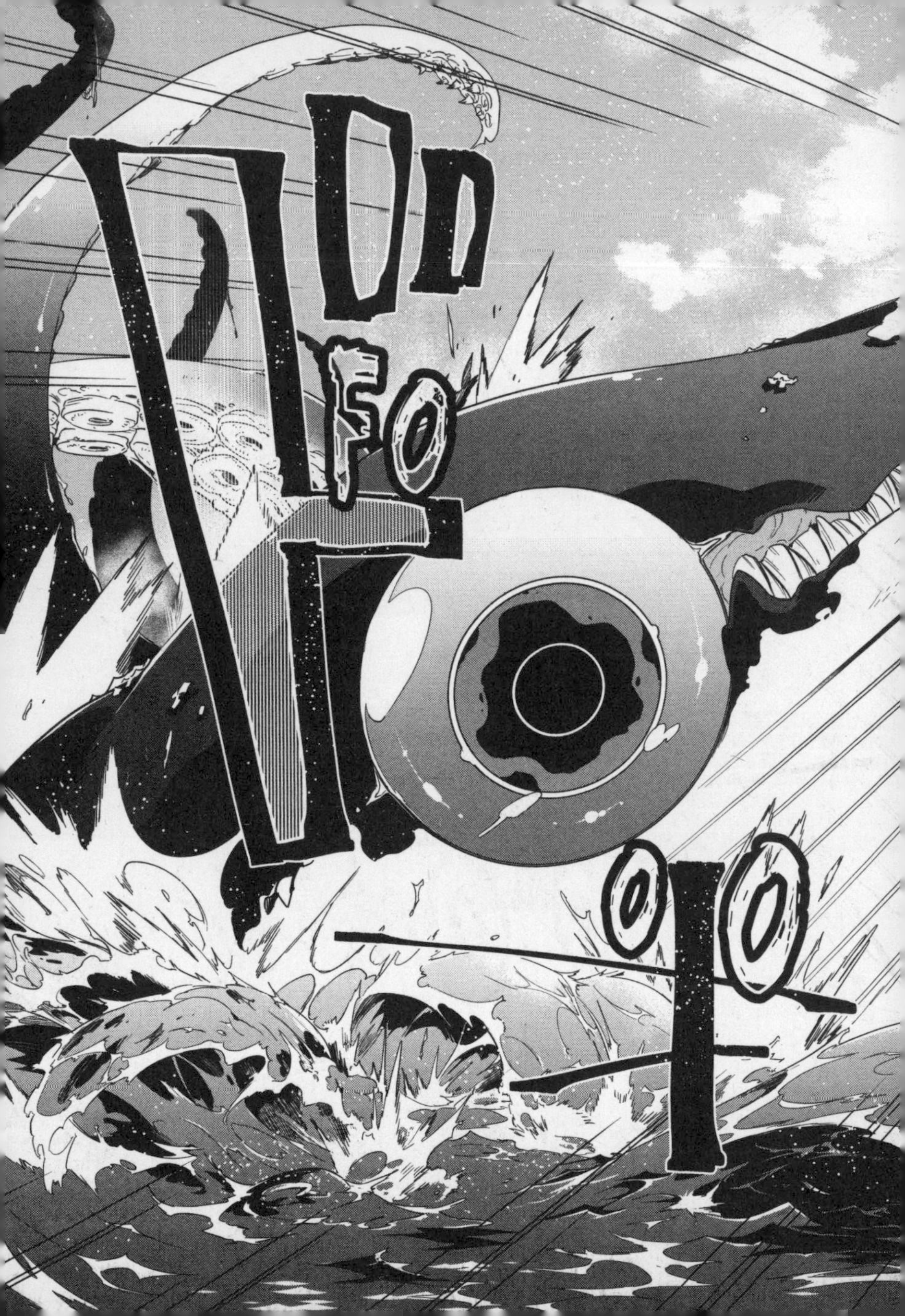

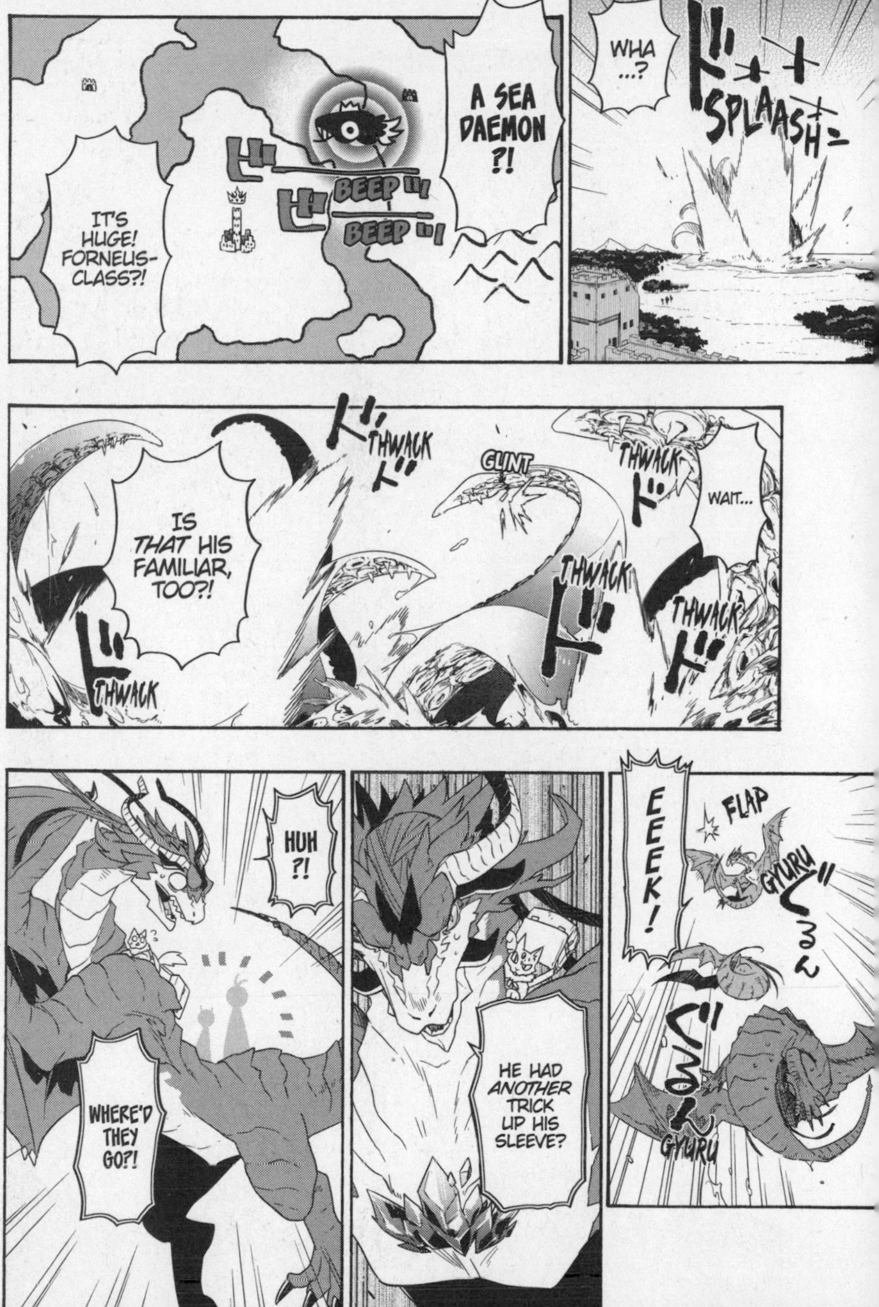
WHA ...?
SPLAASH
A SEA DAEMON ?!
BEEP
BEEP
IT'S HUGE! FORNEUS-CLASS?!
WAIT...
THWACK
THWACK
THWACK
GLINT
THWACK
IS THAT HIS FAMILIAR, TOO?!
THWACK
EEEEK!
FLAP
GYURU
GYURU
HUH ?!
HE HAD ANOTHER TRICK UP HIS SLEEVE?
WHERE'D THEY GO?!

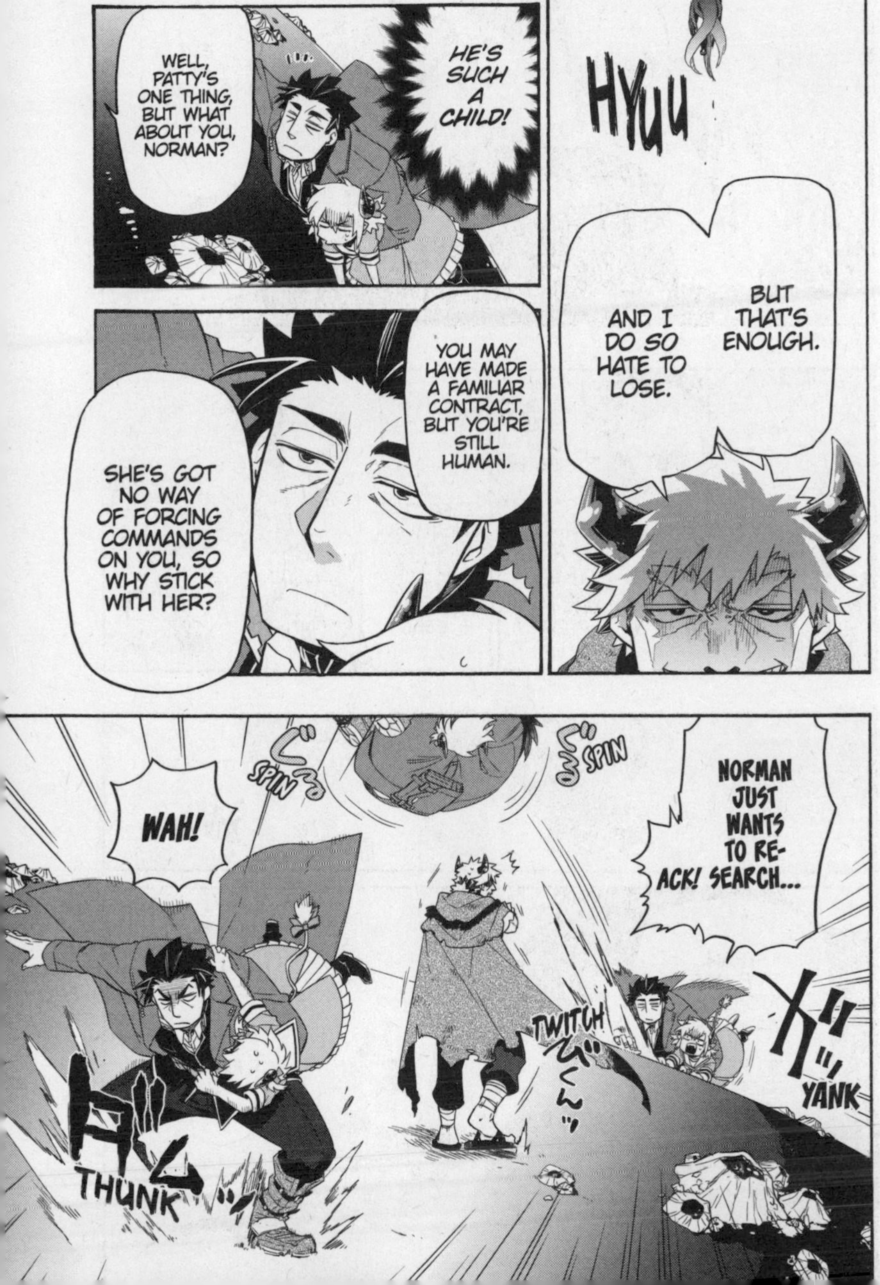
HYUU
BUT THAT'S ENOUGH.
AND I DO SO HATE TO LOSE.
HE'S SUCH A CHILD!
WELL, PATTY'S ONE THING, BUT WHAT ABOUT YOU, NORMAN?
YOU MAY HAVE MADE A FAMILIAR CONTRACT, BUT YOU'RE STILL HUMAN.
SHE'S GOT NO WAY OF FORCING COMMANDS ON YOU, SO WHY STICK WITH HER?
NORMAN JUST WANTS TO RE- ACK! SEARCH...
SPIN
SPIN
WAH!
YANK
TWITCH
THUNK

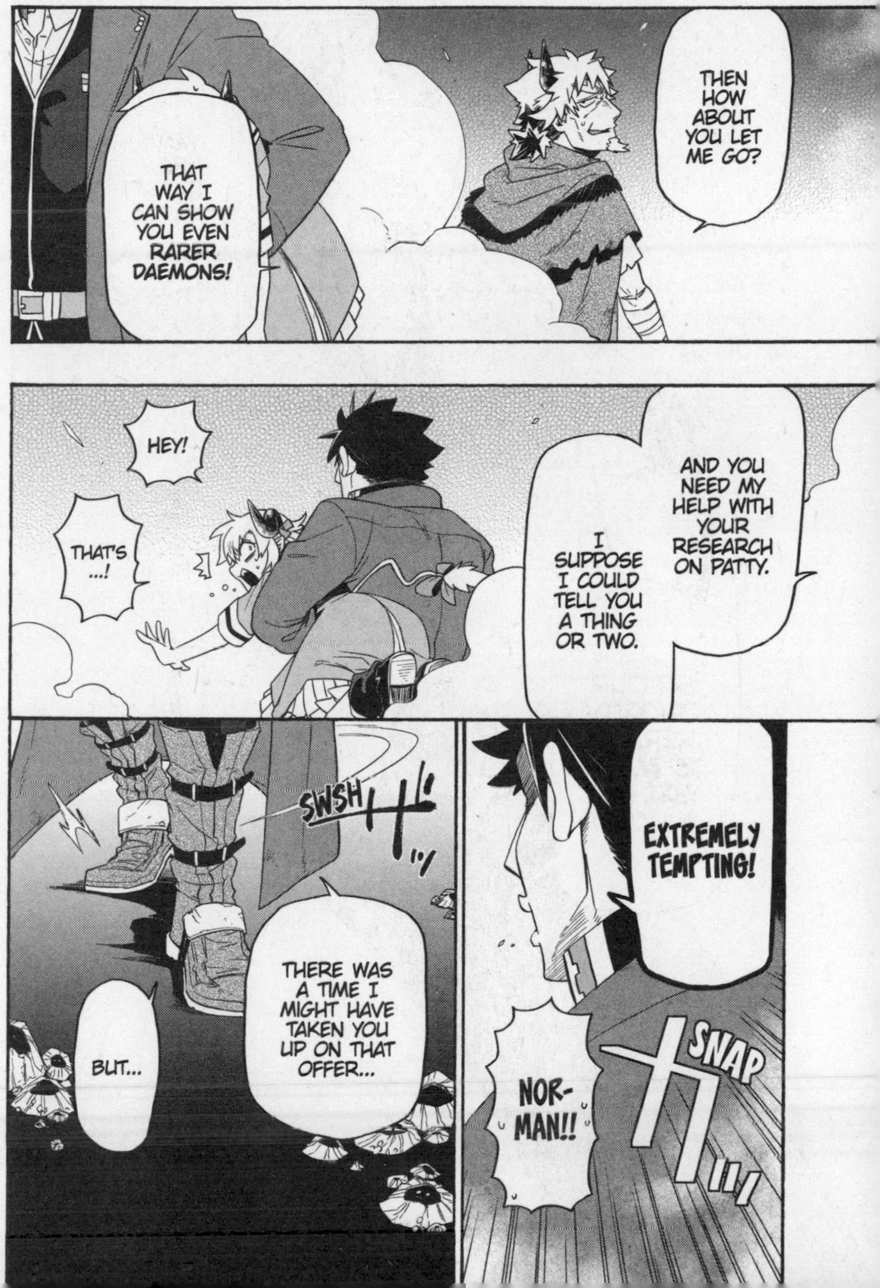
THEN HOW ABOUT YOU LET ME GO?
THAT WAY I CAN SHOW YOU EVEN RARER DAEMONS!
AND YOU NEED MY HELP WITH YOUR RESEARCH ON PATTY.
I SUPPOSE I COULD TELL YOU A THING OR TWO.
HEY!
THAT'S ...!
EXTREMELY TEMPTING!
SNAP
NOR-MAN!!
SWSH
THERE WAS A TIME I MIGHT HAVE TAKEN YOU UP ON THAT OFFER...
BUT...

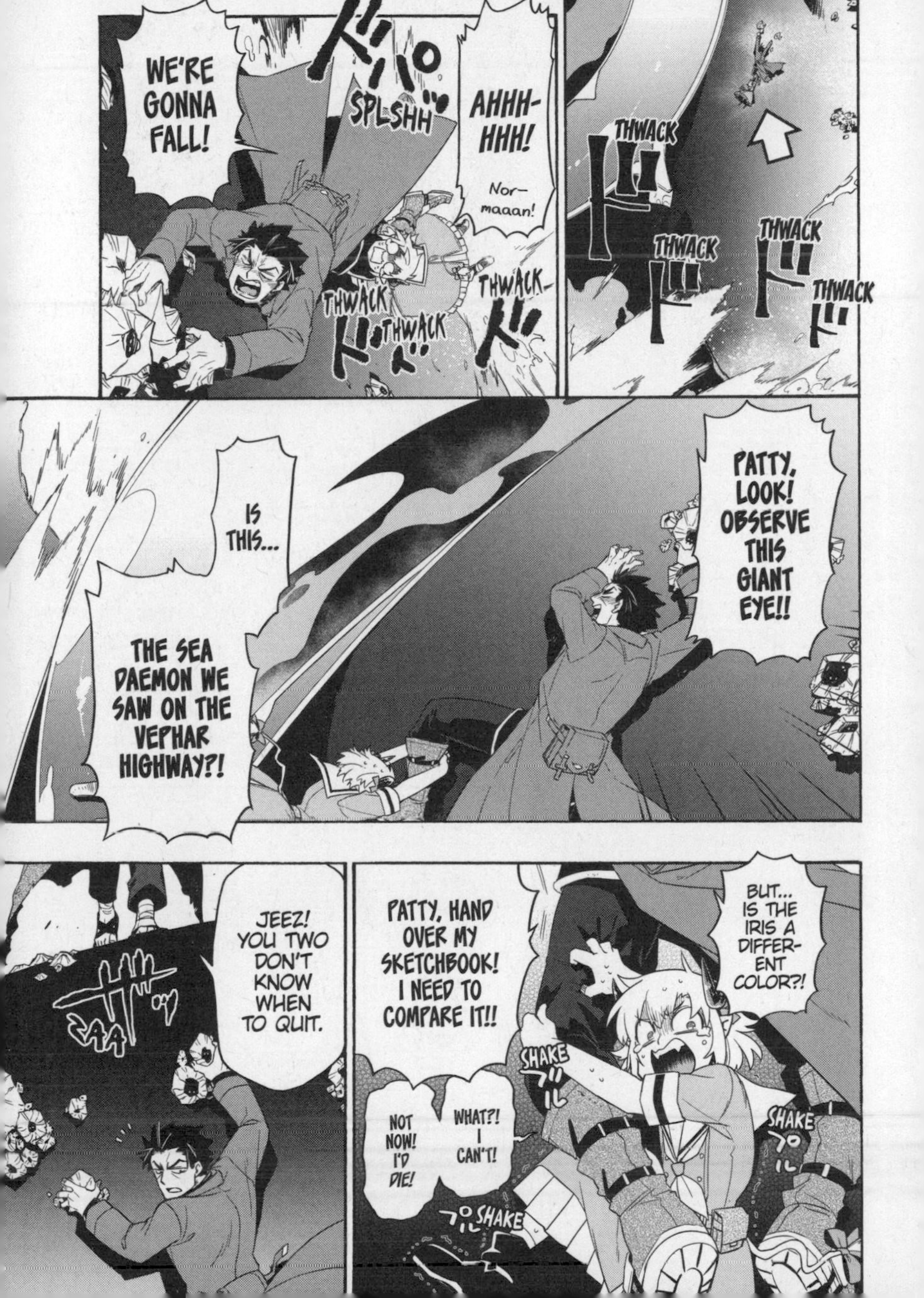
THWACK
THWACK
THWACK
THWACK
AHHH-HHH!
Nor-maaan!
SPLSHH
WE'RE GONNA FALL!
THWACK
THWACK
THWACK
PATTY, LOOK! OBSERVE THIS GIANT EYE!!
IS THIS...
THE SEA DAEMON WE SAW ON THE VEPHAR HIGHWAY?!
BUT... IS THE IRIS A DIFFERENT COLOR?!
PATTY, HAND OVER MY SKETCHBOOK! I NEED TO COMPARE IT!!
SHAKE
SHAKE
WHAT?! I CAN'T!
NOT NOW! I'D DIE!
SHAKE
JEEZ! YOU TWO DON'T KNOW WHEN TO QUIT.

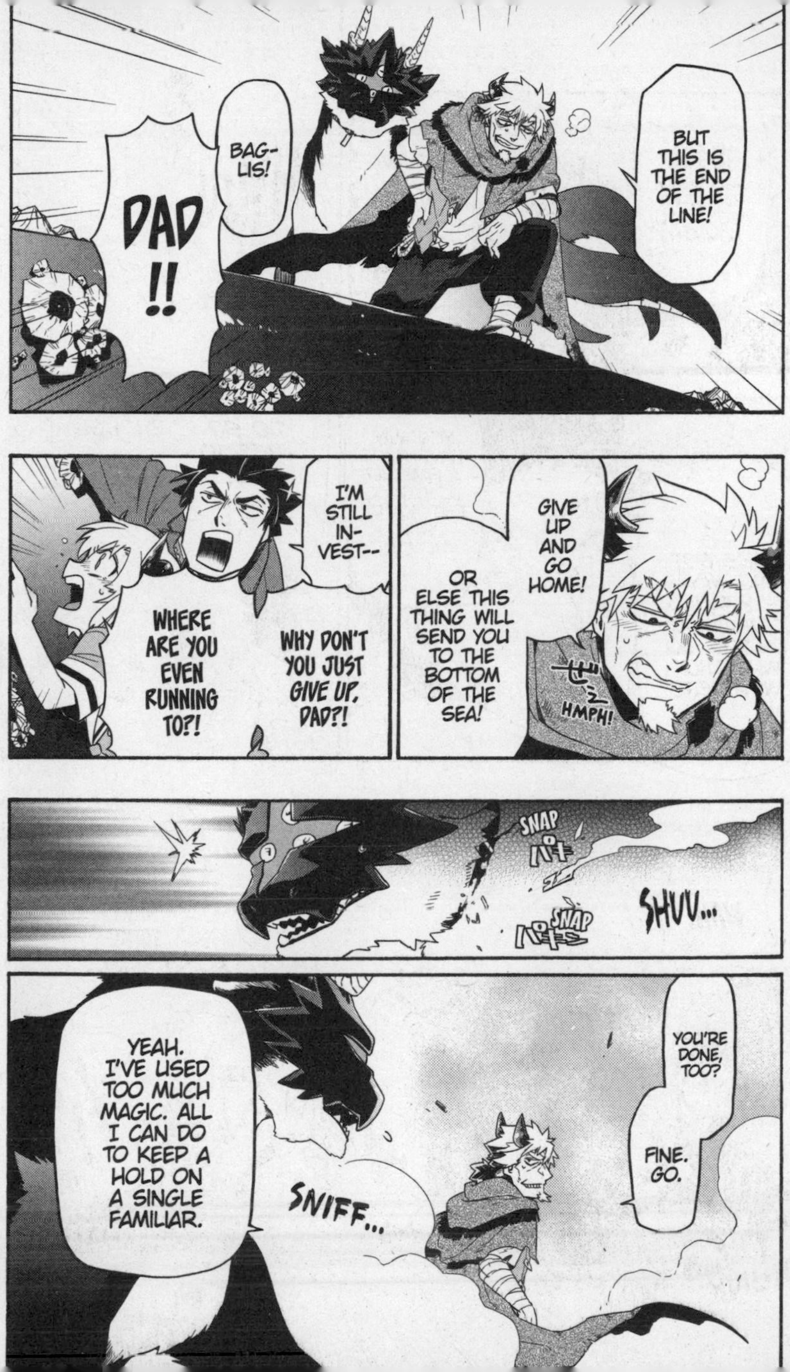
BUT THIS IS THE END OF THE LINE!
BAG-LIS!
DAD!!
GIVE UP AND GO HOME!
OR ELSE THIS THING WILL SEND YOU TO THE BOTTOM OF THE SEA!
HMPH!
I'M STILL IN-VEST--
WHY DON'T YOU JUST GIVE UP, DAD?!
WHERE ARE YOU EVEN RUNNING TO?!
SHUU...
SNAP
SNAP
YOU'RE DONE, TOO?
FINE. GO.
SNIFF...
YEAH. I'VE USED TOO MUCH MAGIC. ALL I CAN DO TO KEEP A HOLD ON A SINGLE FAMILIAR.

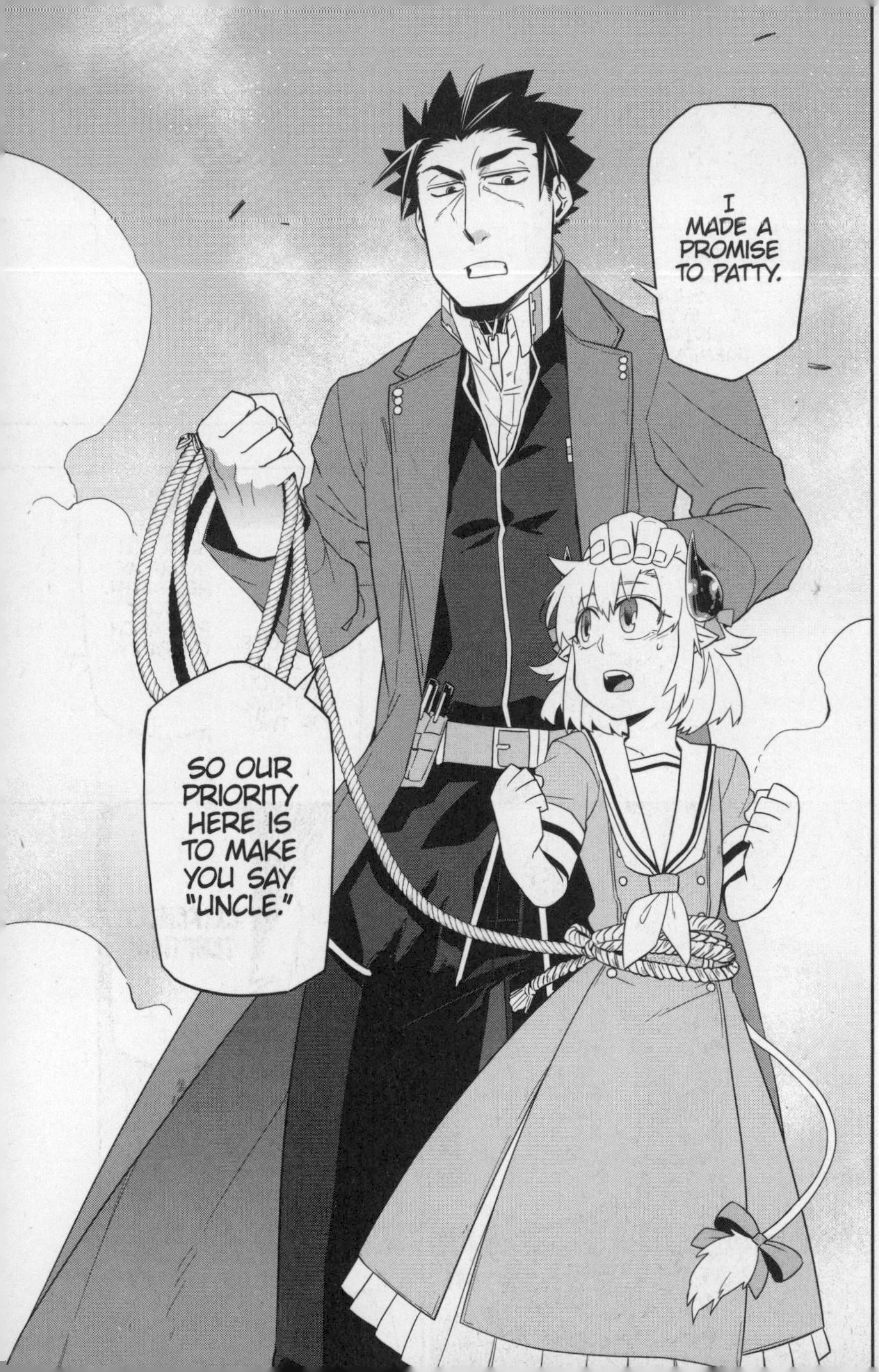
I MADE A PROMISE TO PATTY.
SO OUR PRIORITY HERE IS TO MAKE YOU SAY "UNCLE."

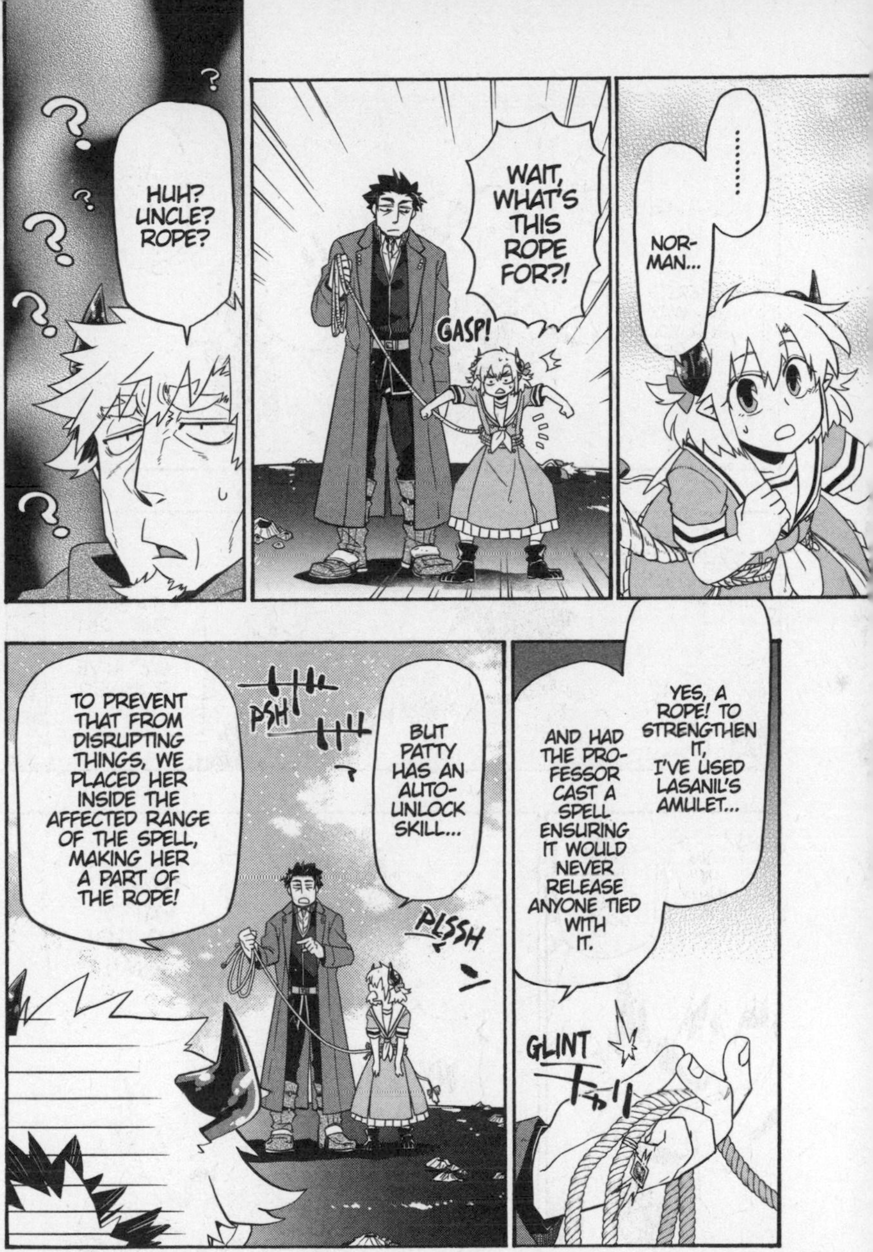
......
NOR-MAN...
WAIT, WHAT'S THIS ROPE FOR?!
GASP!
HUH? UNCLE? ROPE?
YES, A ROPE! TO STRENGTHEN IT, I'VE USED LASANIL'S AMULET...
AND HAD THE PRO-FESSOR CAST A SPELL ENSURING IT WOULD NEVER RELEASE ANYONE TIED WITH IT.
GLINT
BUT PATTY HAS AN AUTO-UNLOCK SKILL...
PLSSH
PSH
TO PREVENT THAT FROM DISRUPTING THINGS, WE PLACED HER INSIDE THE AFFECTED RANGE OF THE SPELL, MAKING HER A PART OF THE ROPE!

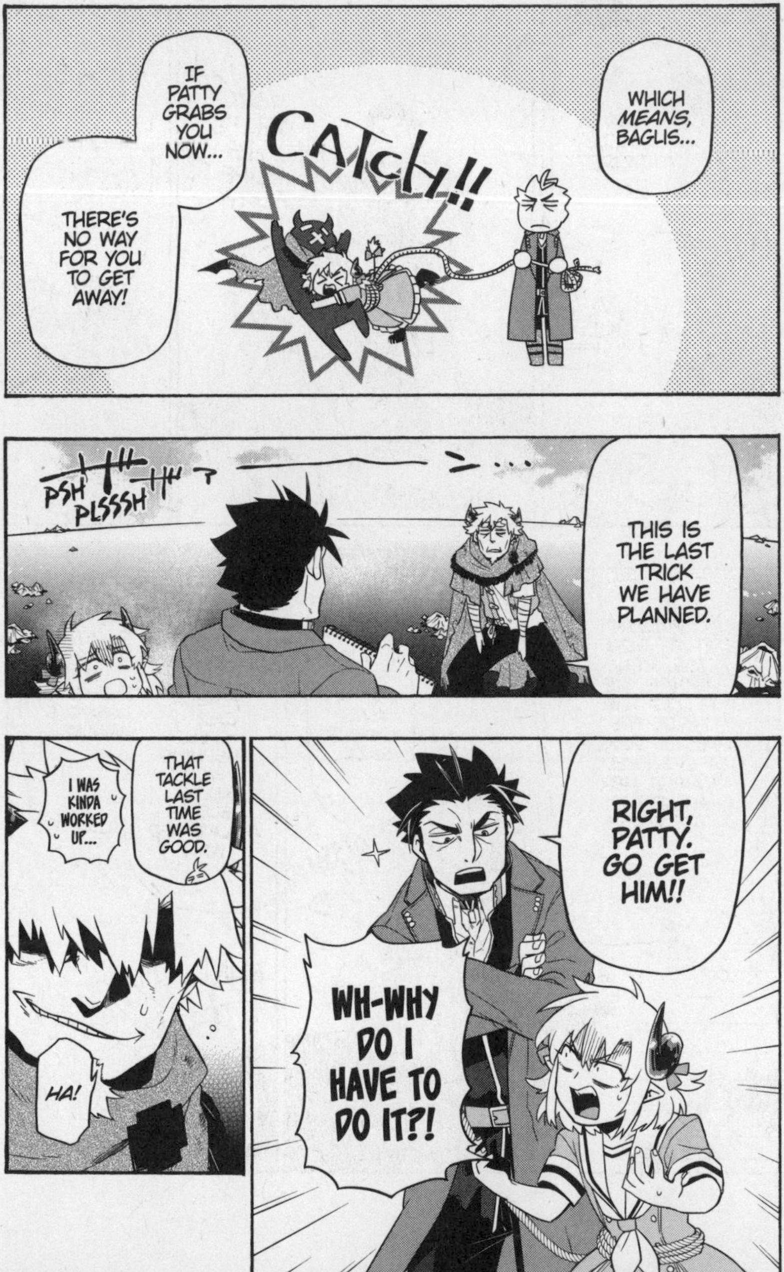
WHICH MEANS, BAGLIS...
CATCH!!
IF PATTY GRABS YOU NOW...
THERE'S NO WAY FOR YOU TO GET AWAY!
THIS IS THE LAST TRICK WE HAVE PLANNED.
PSH PLSSSH
RIGHT, PATTY. GO GET HIM!!
WH-WHY DO I HAVE TO DO IT?!
THAT TACKLE LAST TIME WAS GOOD.
I WAS KINDA WORKED UP...
HA!

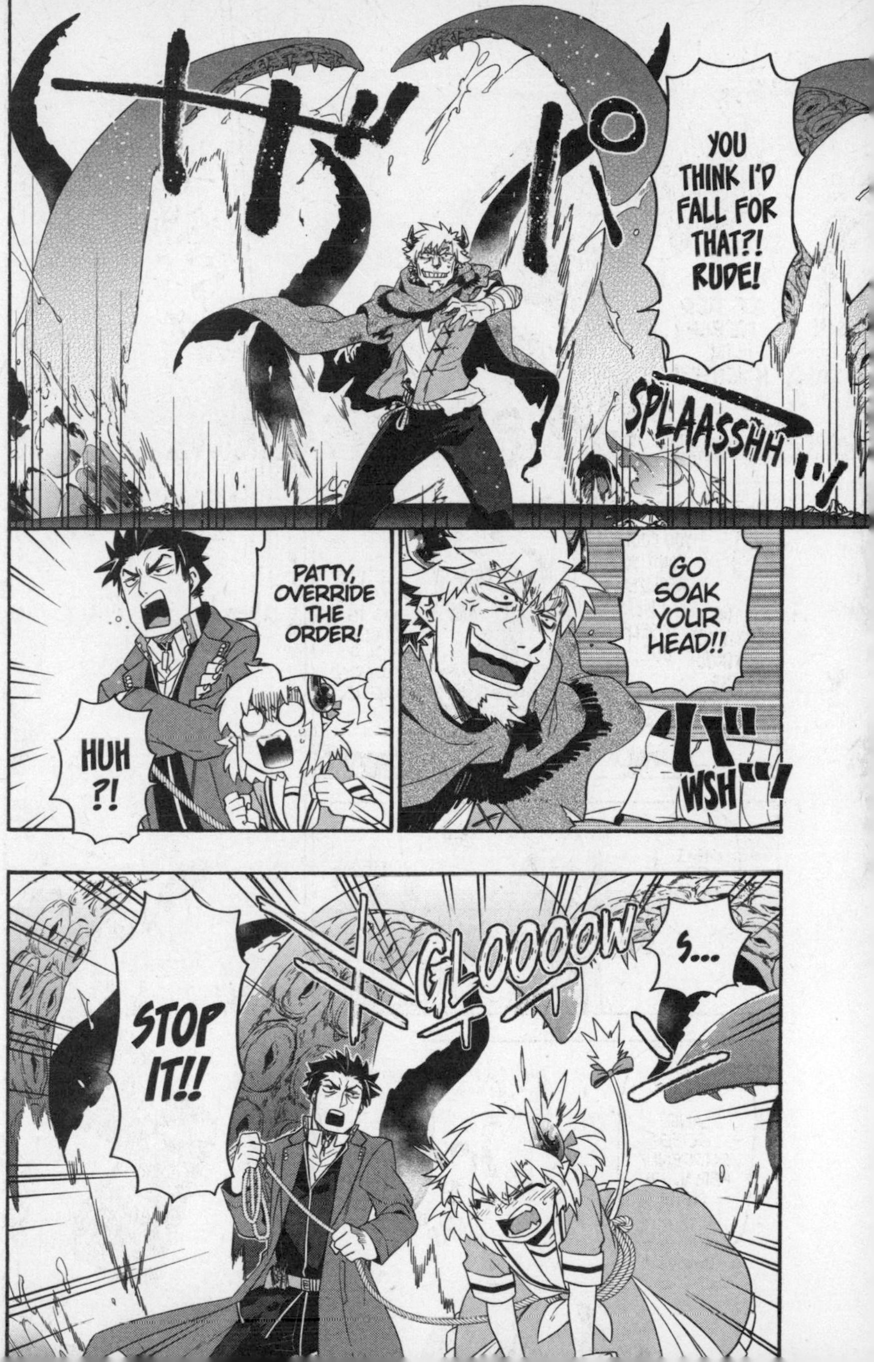
YOU THINK I'D FALL FOR THAT?! RUDE!
SPLAASSHH!
GO SOAK YOUR HEAD!!
WSH!
PATTY, OVERRIDE THE ORDER!
HUH?!
S...
GLOOOOW
STOP IT!!

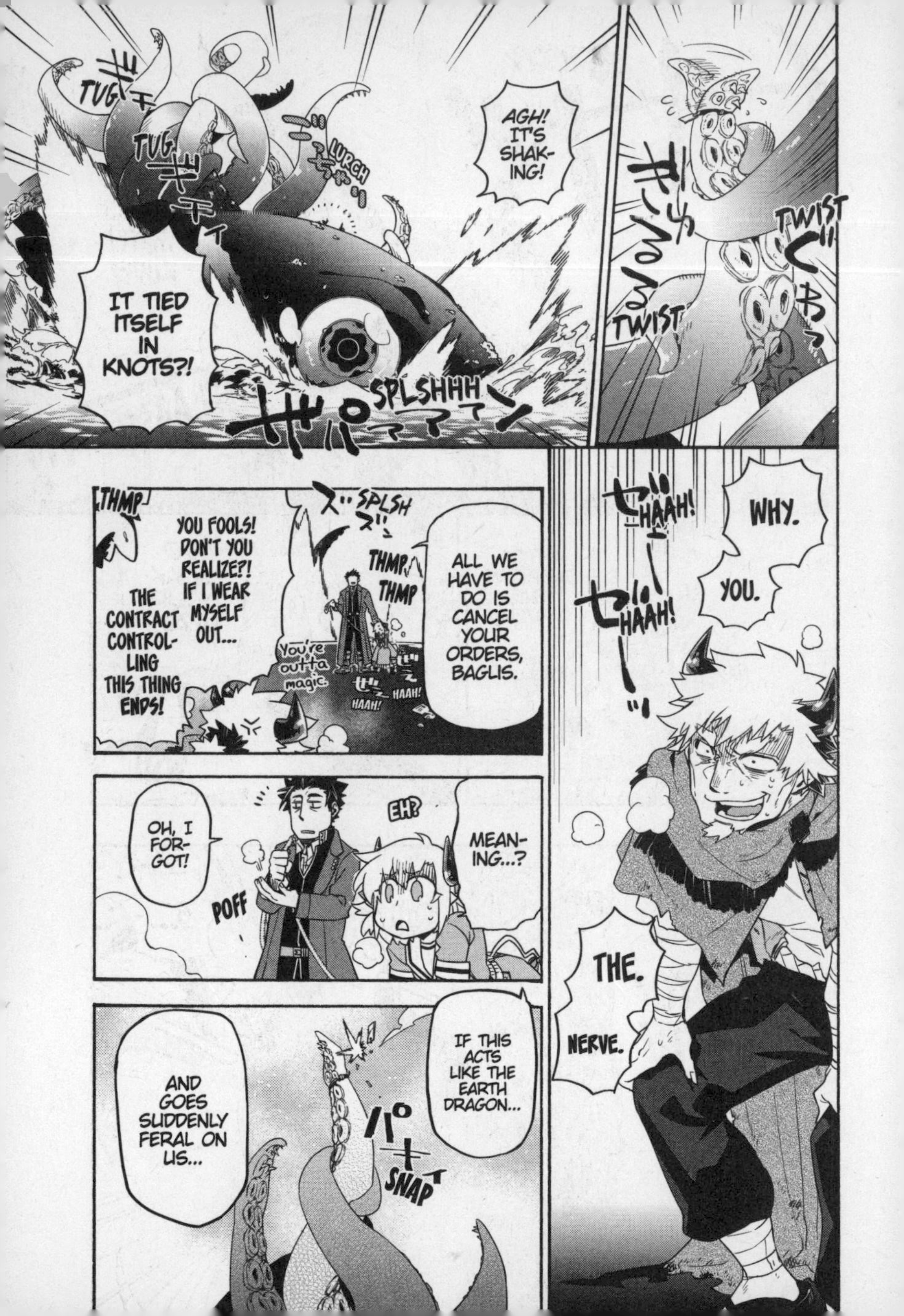
TWIST
TWIST
AGH! IT'S SHAKING!
TUG
TUG
LURCH
IT TIED ITSELF IN KNOTS?!
SPLSHHH
WHY.
YOU.
HAAH!
HAAH!
THE.
NERVE.
ALL WE HAVE TO DO IS CANCEL YOUR ORDERS, BAGLIS.
SPLSH
THMP THMP
You're outta magic.
HAAH!
HAAH!
THMP
YOU FOOLS! DON'T YOU REALIZE?! IF I WEAR MYSELF OUT...
THE CONTRACT CONTROLLING THIS THING ENDS!
MEANING...?
EH?
OH, I FORGOT!
POFF
IF THIS ACTS LIKE THE EARTH DRAGON...
SNAP
AND GOES SUDDENLY FERAL ON US...

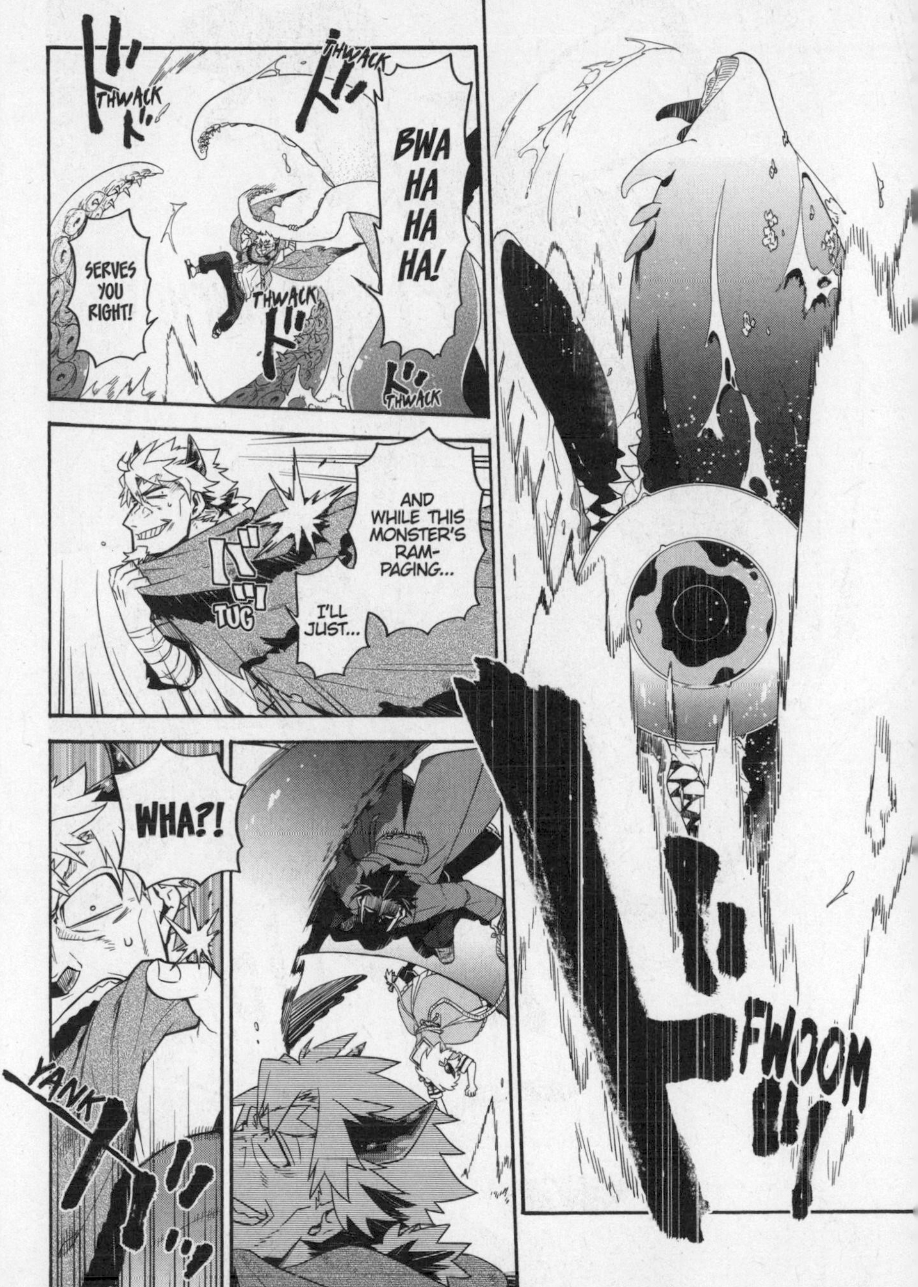

FWOOM
THWACK
BWA HA HA HA!
THWACK
THWACK
SERVES YOU RIGHT!
THWACK
AND WHILE THIS MONSTER'S RAM-PAGING...
I'LL JUST...
TUG
WHA?!
YANK

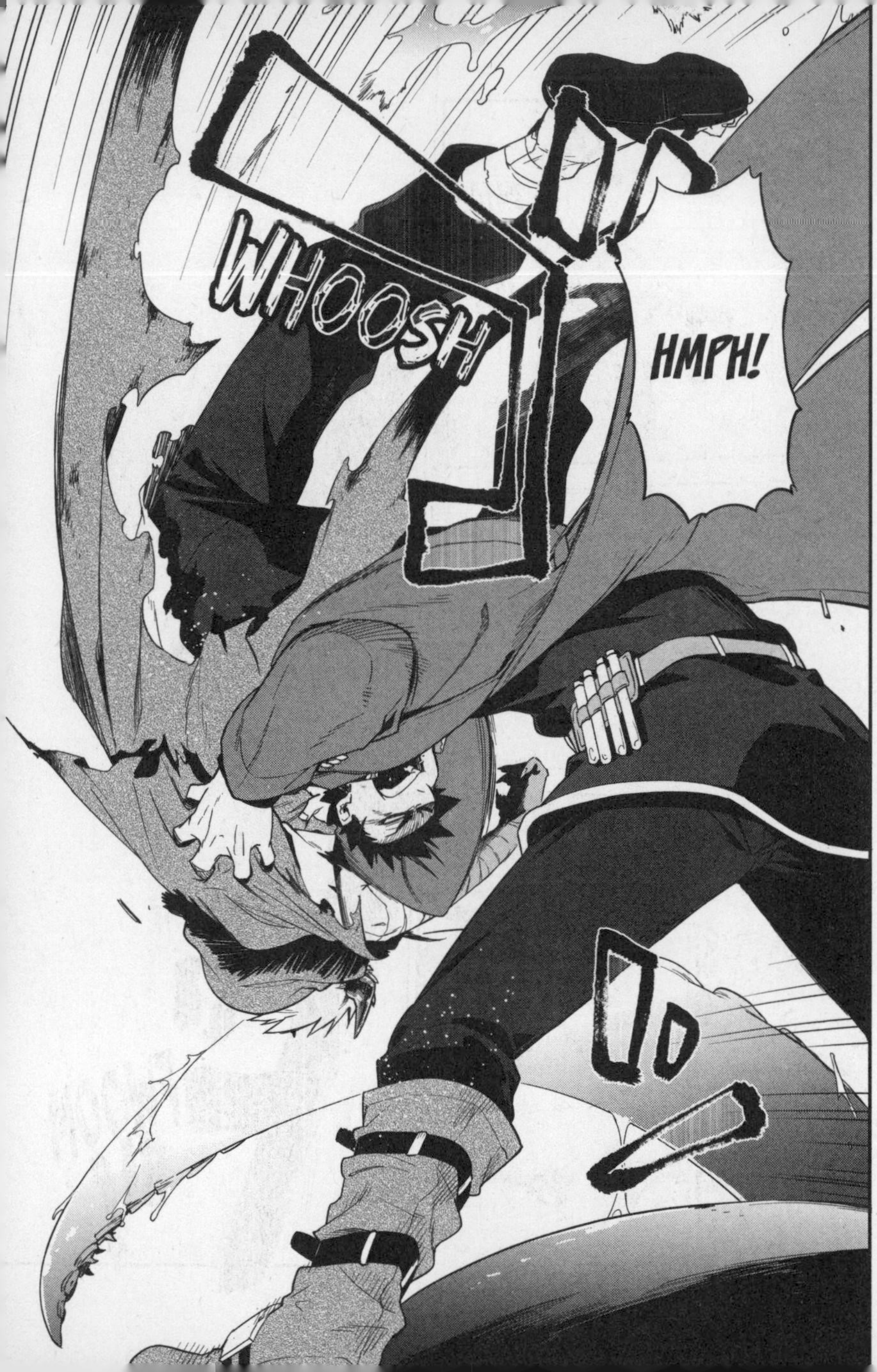
HMPH!
WHOOSH

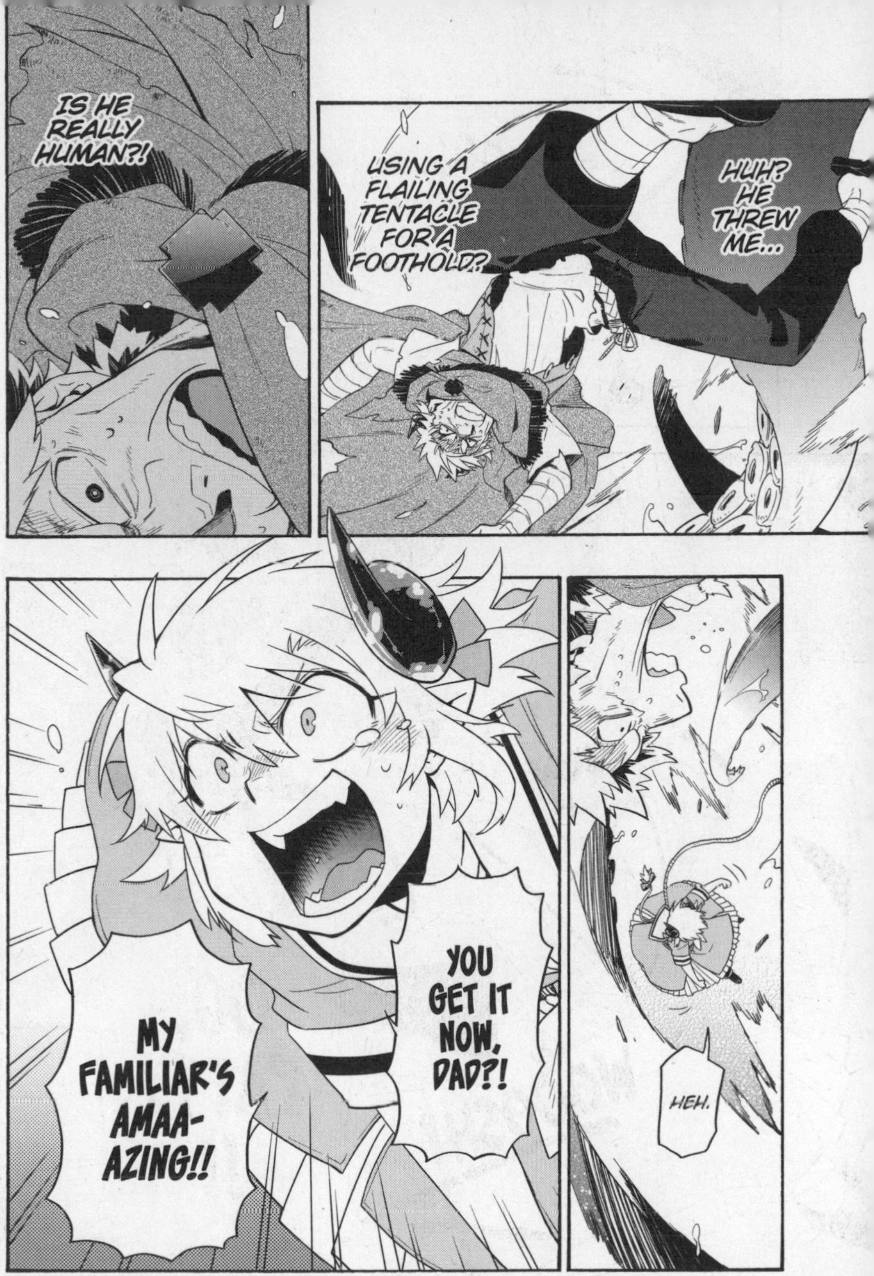
HUH? HE THREW ME...
USING A FLAILING TENTACLE FOR A FOOTHOLD?
IS HE REALLY HUMAN?!
HEH.
YOU GET IT NOW, DAD?!
MY FAMILIAR'S AMAA-AZING!!

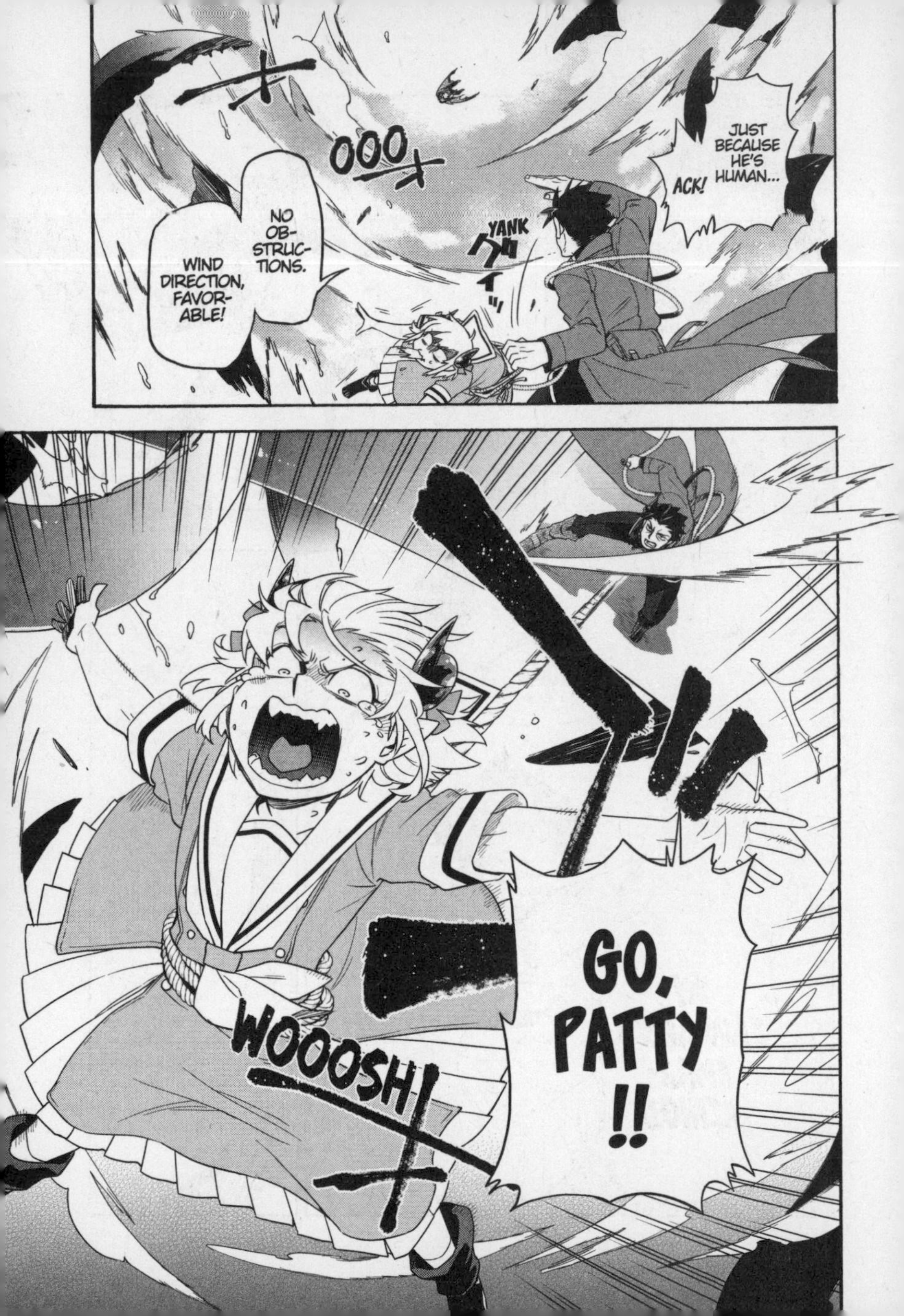
JUST BECAUSE HE'S HUMAN...
ACK!
YANK
OOO
NO OB-STRUC-TIONS.
WIND DIRECTION, FAVOR-ABLE!
GO, PATTY!!
WOOOSH!

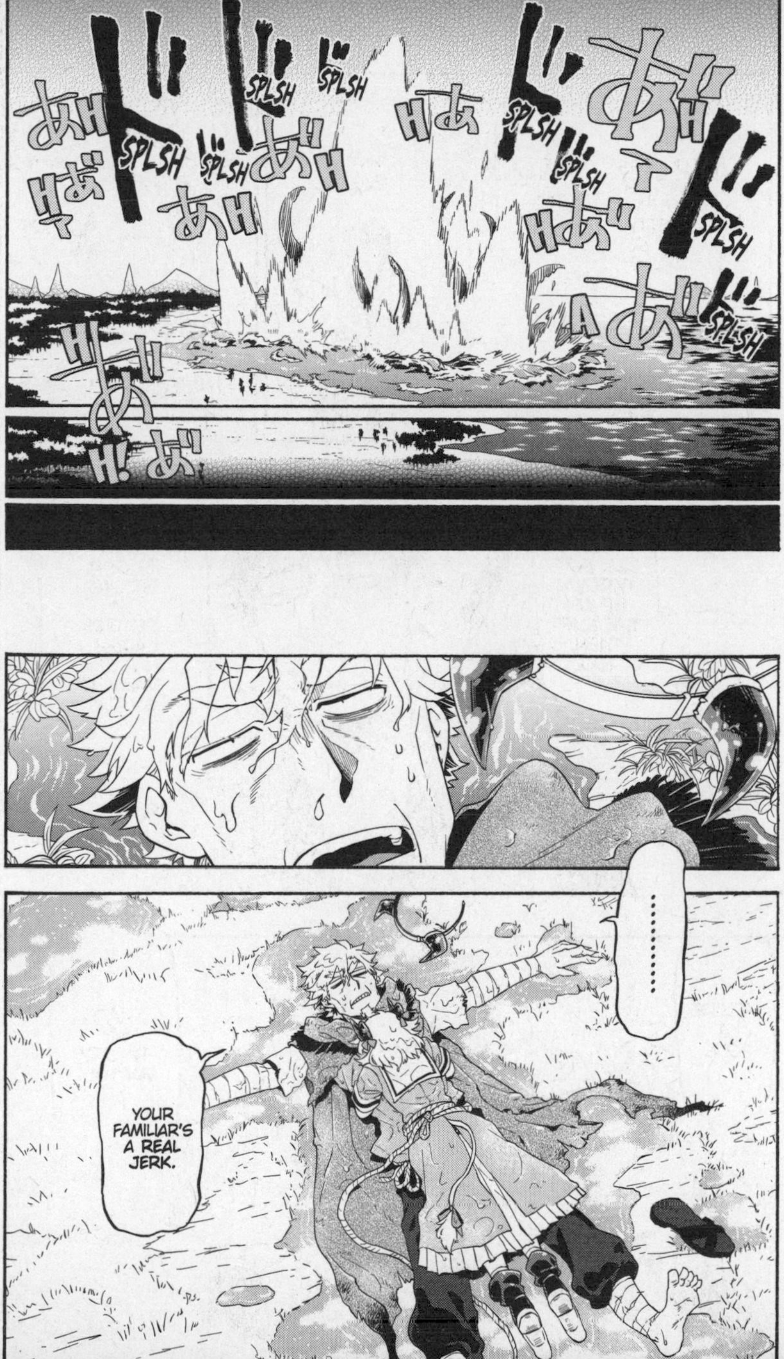

SPLSH
SPLSH
SPLSH
SPLSH
SPLSH
SPLSH
SPLSH
SPLSH
......
YOUR FAMILIAR'S A REAL JERK.

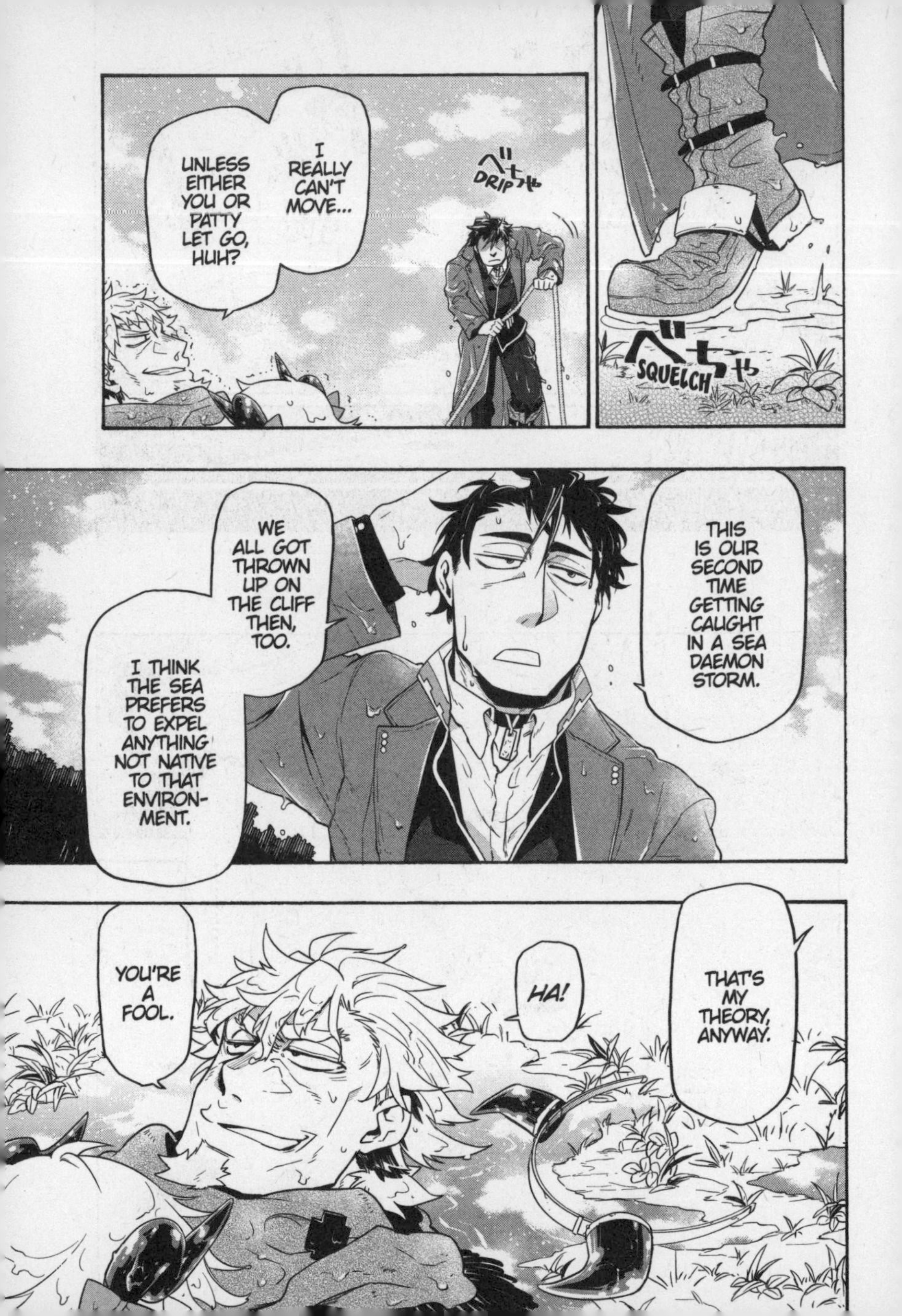
SQUELCH
べちゃ
DRIP
べちゃ
I REALLY CAN'T MOVE...
UNLESS EITHER YOU OR PATTY LET GO, HUH?
THIS IS OUR SECOND TIME GETTING CAUGHT IN A SEA DAEMON STORM.
WE ALL GOT THROWN UP ON THE CLIFF THEN, TOO.
I THINK THE SEA PREFERS TO EXPEL ANYTHING NOT NATIVE TO THAT ENVIRONMENT.
THAT'S MY THEORY, ANYWAY.
HA!
YOU'RE A FOOL.

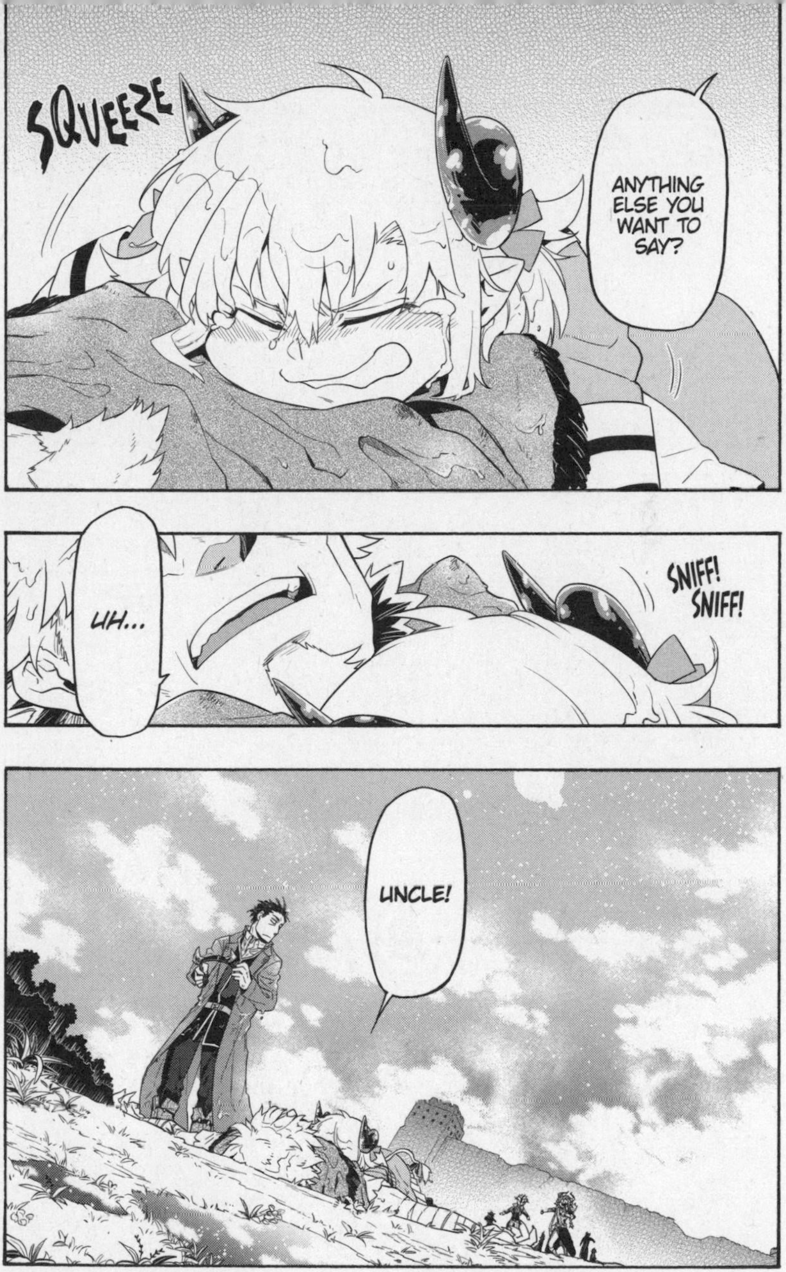
ANYTHING ELSE YOU WANT TO SAY?
SQUEEZE
SNIFF! SNIFF!
UH...
UNCLE!

Sorry For My Familiar

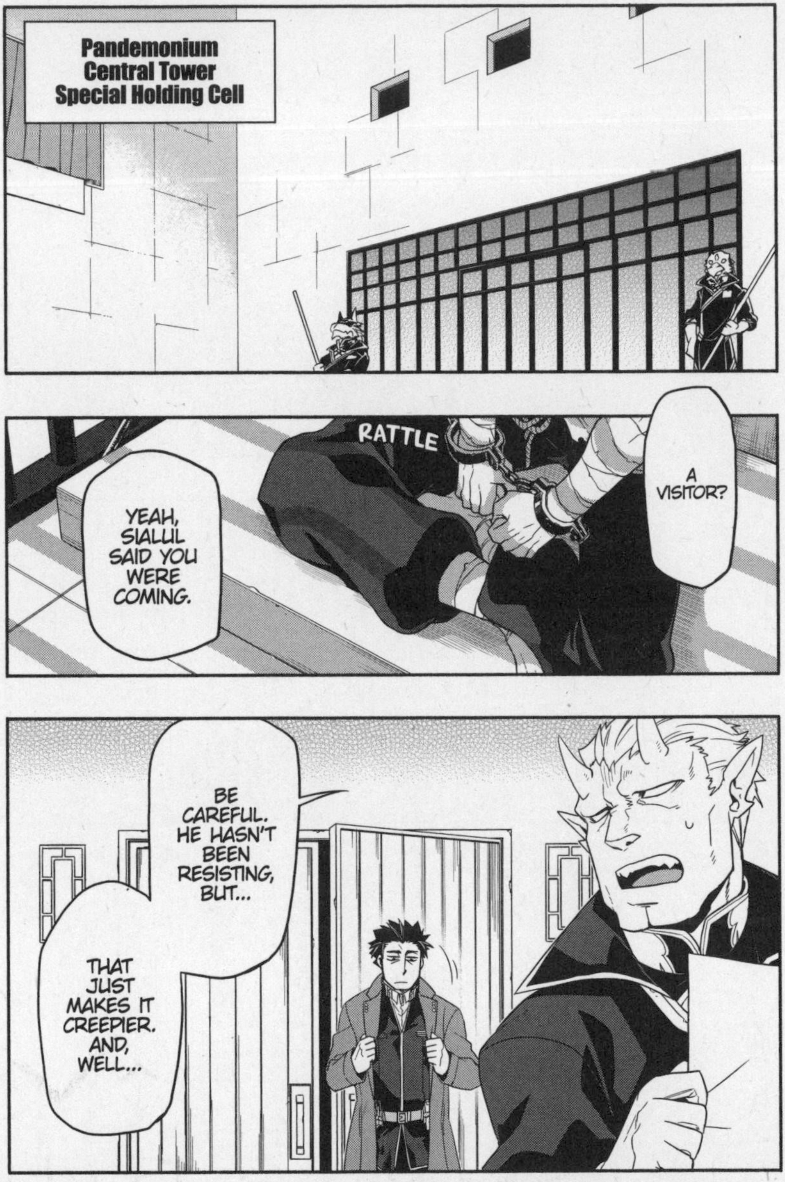
Pandemonium Central Tower Special Holding Cell
A VISITOR?
RATTLE
YEAH, SIALUL SAID YOU WERE COMING.
BE CAREFUL. HE HASN'T BEEN RESISTING, BUT...
THAT JUST MAKES IT CREEPIER. AND, WELL...

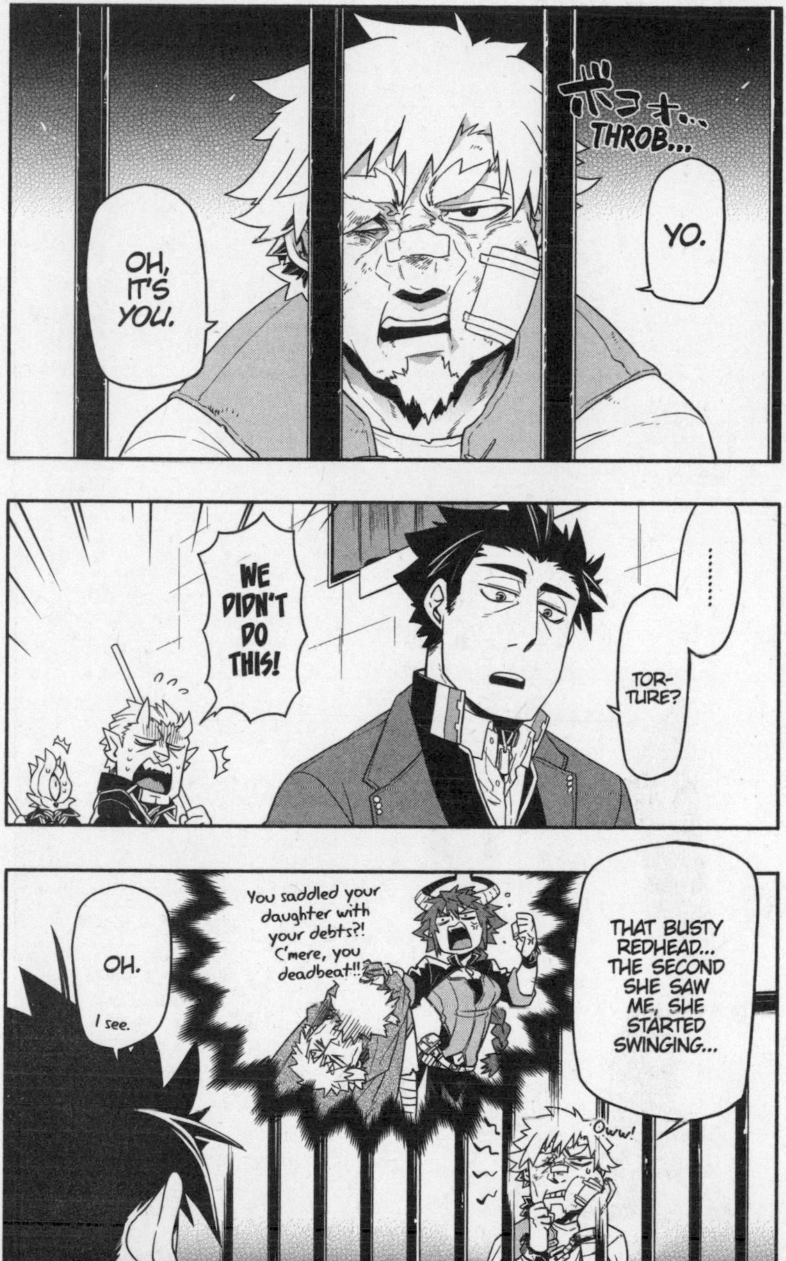
ボコォ…
THROB...
YO.
OH, IT'S YOU.
......
TOR-TURE?
WE DIDN'T DO THIS!
THAT BUSTY REDHEAD... THE SECOND SHE SAW ME, SHE STARTED SWINGING...
You saddled your daughter with your debts?! C'mere, you deadbeat!!
Owww!
OH.
I see.

FILE 33:
Royal Capital: Pandemonium ⑧

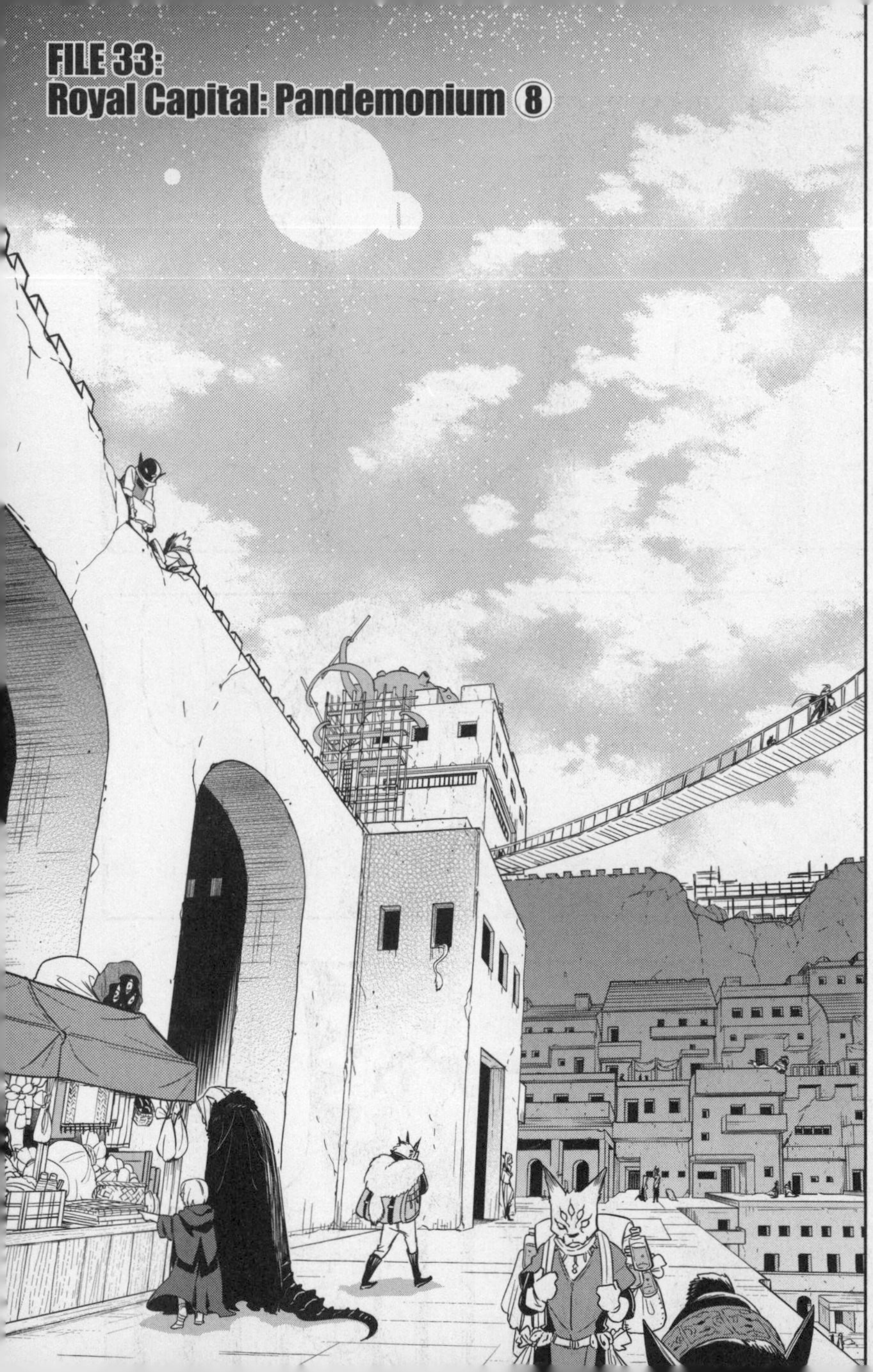

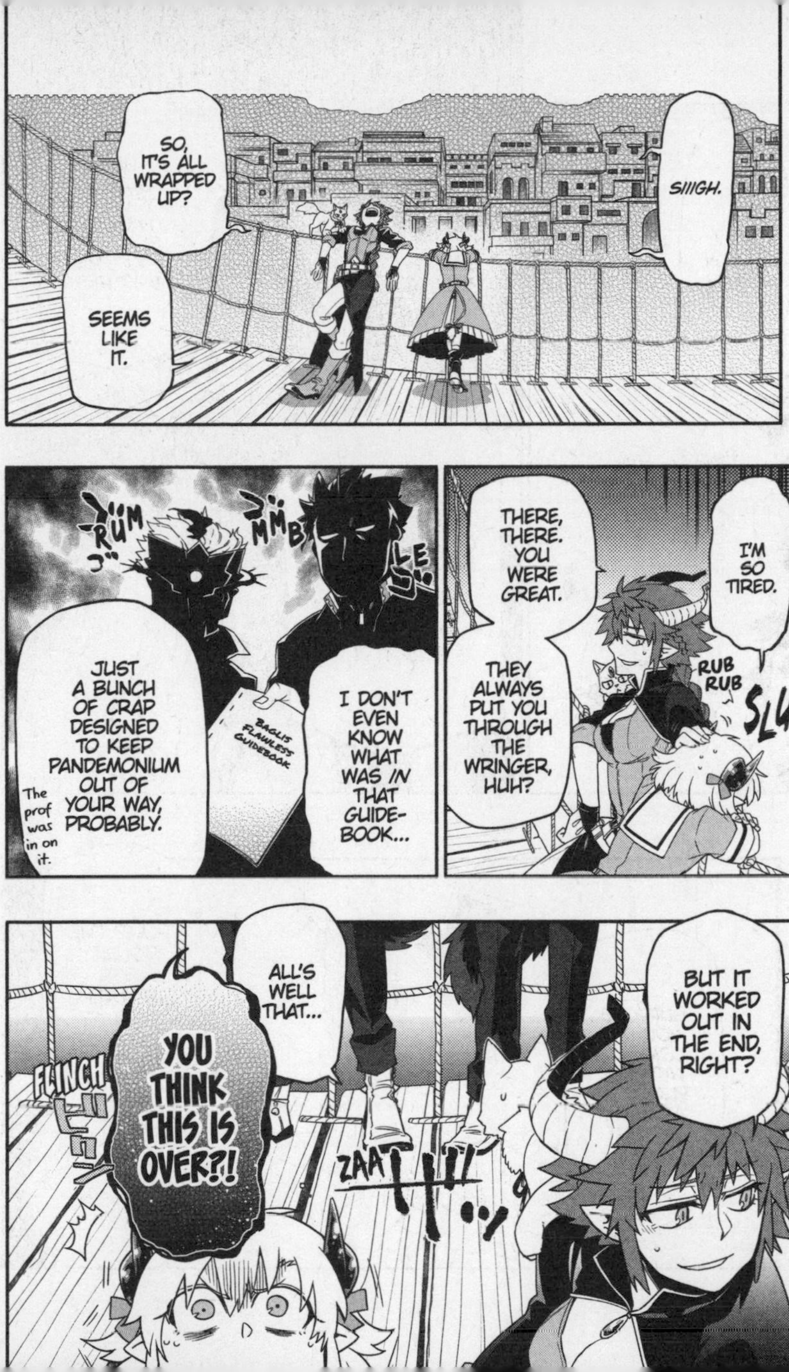
SIIIGH.
SO, IT'S ALL WRAPPED UP?
SEEMS LIKE IT.
I'M SO TIRED.
THERE, THERE. YOU WERE GREAT.
THEY ALWAYS PUT YOU THROUGH THE WRINGER, HUH?
RUB RUB
SLUMP
RUMBLE
I DON'T EVEN KNOW WHAT WAS IN THAT GUIDE-BOOK...
BAGLIS FLAWLESS GUIDEBOOK
JUST A BUNCH OF CRAP DESIGNED TO KEEP PANDEMONIUM OUT OF YOUR WAY, PROBABLY.
The prof was in on it.
BUT IT WORKED OUT IN THE END, RIGHT?
ALL'S WELL THAT...
YOU THINK THIS IS OVER?!
FLINCH
ZAAT

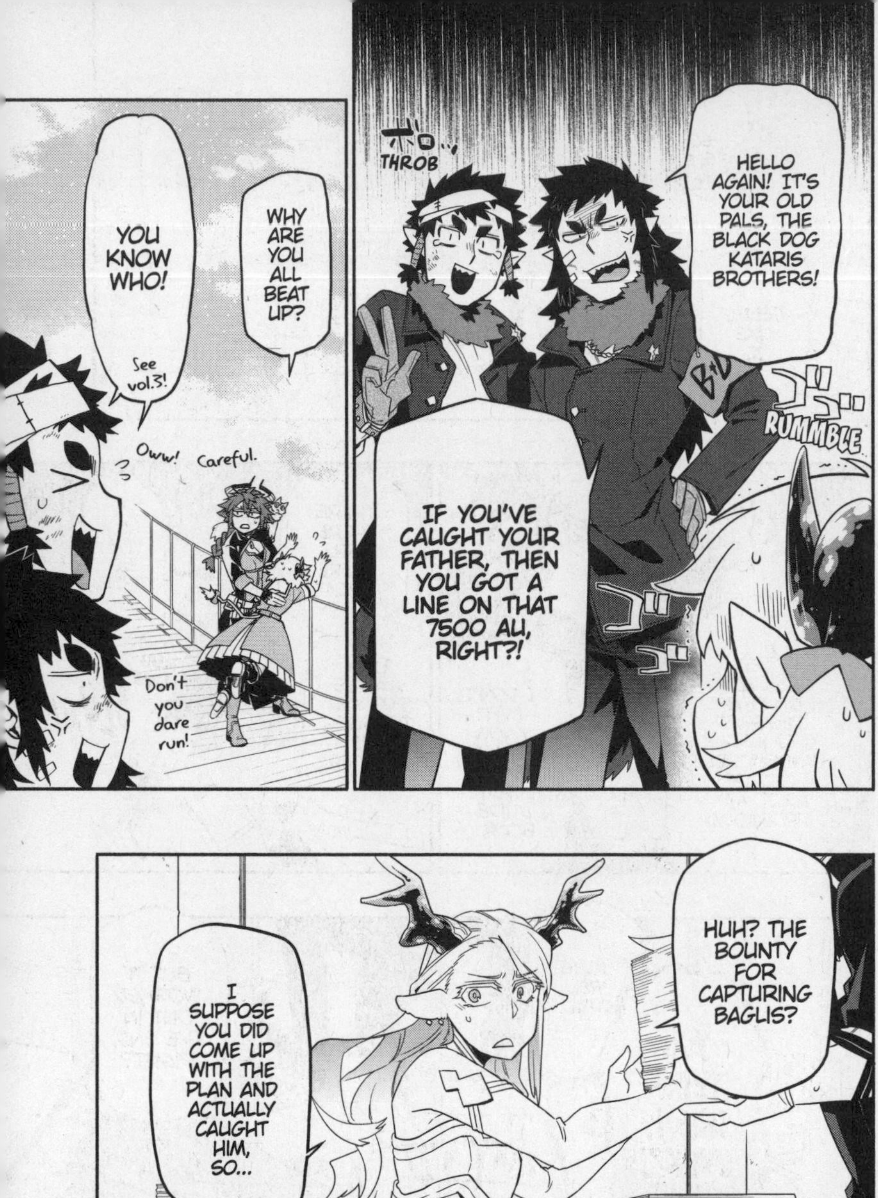
HELLO AGAIN! IT'S YOUR OLD PALS, THE BLACK DOG KATARIS BROTHERS!
ボロ… THROB
ゴゴゴ RUMMBLE
IF YOU'VE CAUGHT YOUR FATHER, THEN YOU GOT A LINE ON THAT 7500 AU, RIGHT?!
WHY ARE YOU ALL BEAT UP?
YOU KNOW WHO!
See vol.3!
Oww!
Careful.
Don't you dare run!
HUH? THE BOUNTY FOR CAPTURING BAGLIS?
I SUPPOSE YOU DID COME UP WITH THE PLAN AND ACTUALLY CAUGHT HIM, SO...

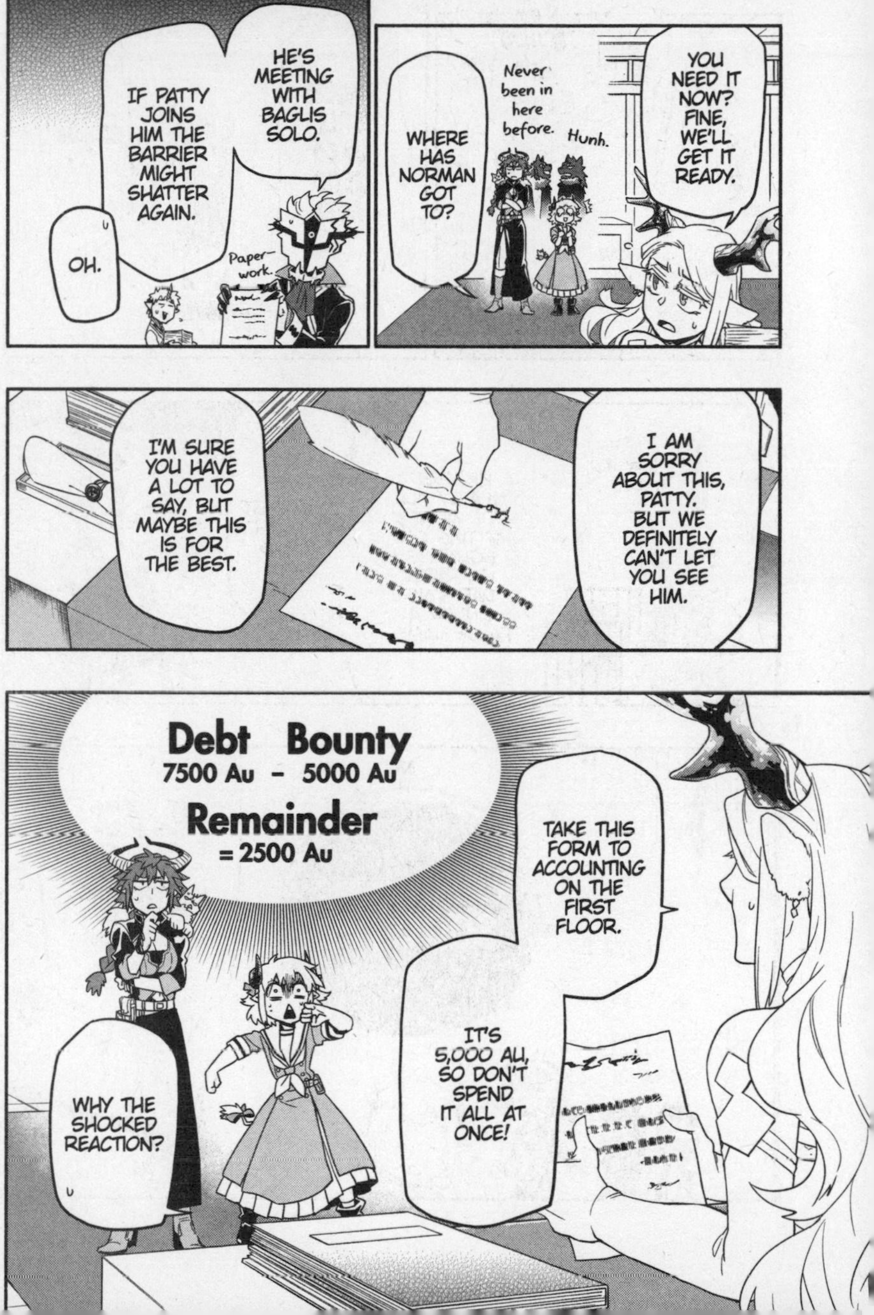
YOU NEED IT NOW? FINE, WE'LL GET IT READY.
Hunh.
Never been in here before.
WHERE HAS NORMAN GOT TO?
HE'S MEETING WITH BAGLIS SOLO.
Paper-work.
IF PATTY JOINS HIM THE BARRIER MIGHT SHATTER AGAIN.
OH.
I AM SORRY ABOUT THIS, PATTY. BUT WE DEFINITELY CAN'T LET YOU SEE HIM.
I'M SURE YOU HAVE A LOT TO SAY, BUT MAYBE THIS IS FOR THE BEST.
TAKE THIS FORM TO ACCOUNTING ON THE FIRST FLOOR.
IT'S 5,000 AU, SO DON'T SPEND IT ALL AT ONCE!
Debt Bounty
7500 Au - 5000 Au
Remainder
= 2500 Au
WHY THE SHOCKED REACTION?

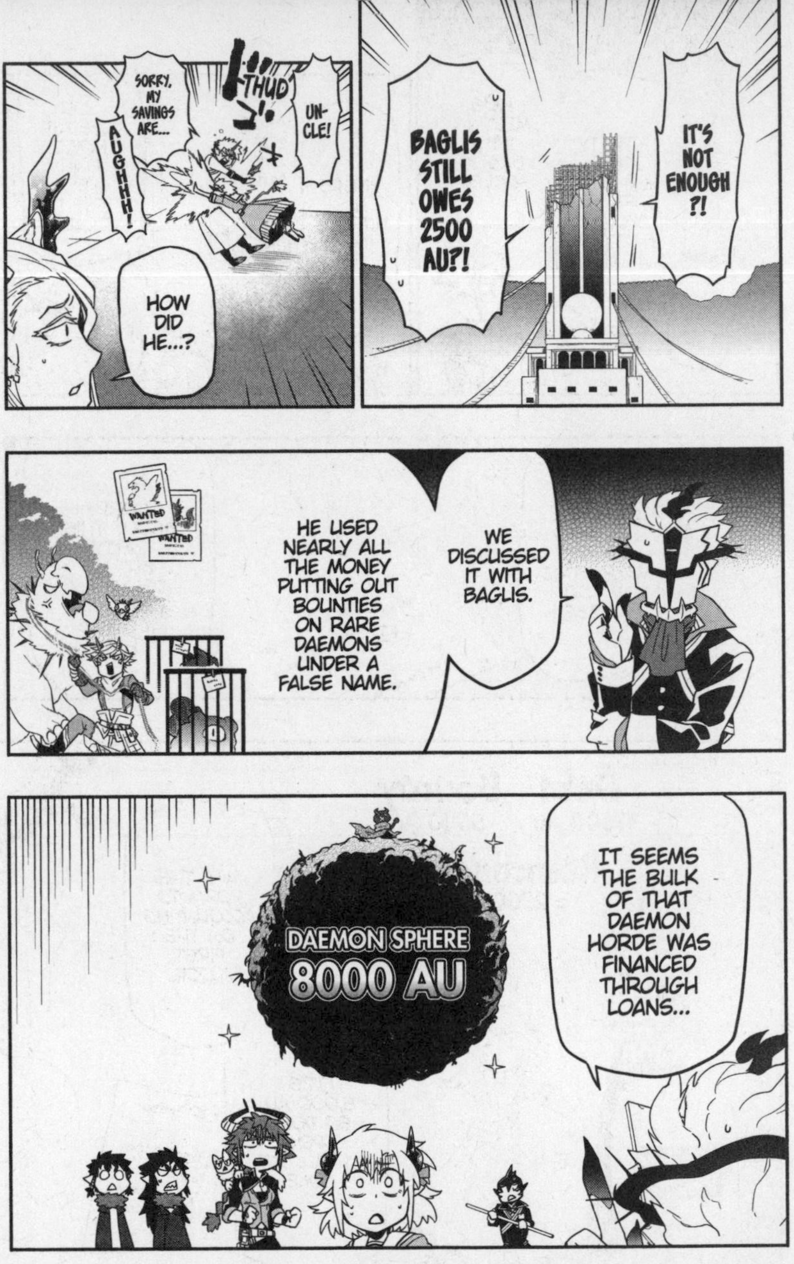
IT'S NOT ENOUGH ?!
BAGLIS STILL OWES 2500 AU?!
UN-CLE!
THUD
SORRY, MY SAVINGS ARE...
AUGHHH!
HOW DID HE...?
WE DISCUSSED IT WITH BAGLIS.
HE USED NEARLY ALL THE MONEY PUTTING OUT BOUNTIES ON RARE DAEMONS UNDER A FALSE NAME.
WANTED
WANTED
IT SEEMS THE BULK OF THAT DAEMON HORDE WAS FINANCED THROUGH LOANS...
DAEMON SPHERE
8000 AU

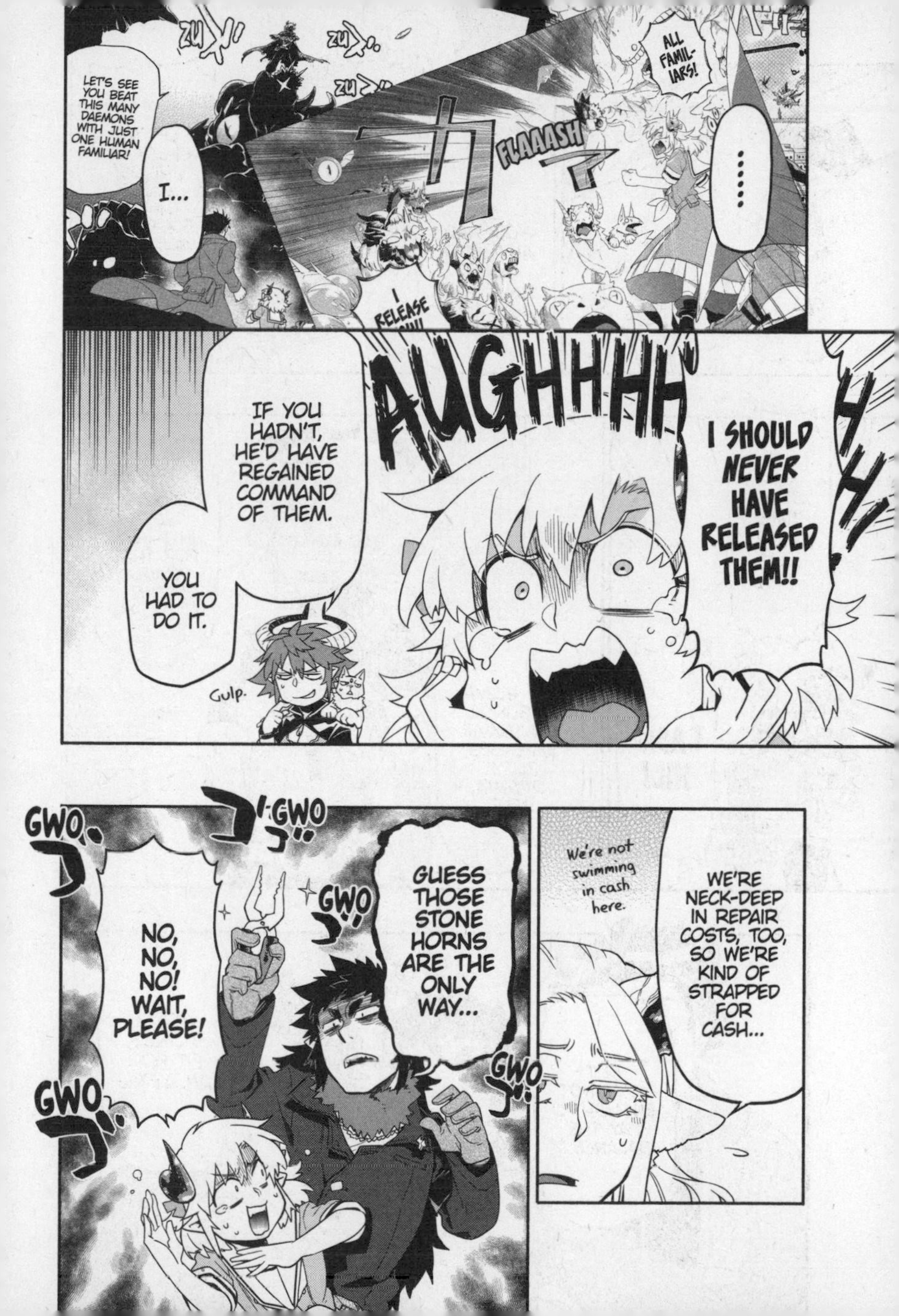
ALL FAMILIARS!
......
I RELEASE
FLAAASH
ZU
ZU
ZU
LET'S SEE YOU BEAT THIS MANY DAEMONS WITH JUST ONE HUMAN FAMILIAR!
I...
I SHOULD NEVER HAVE RELEASED THEM!!
AUGHHHHH
IF YOU HADN'T, HE'D HAVE REGAINED COMMAND OF THEM.
YOU HAD TO DO IT.
Gulp.
WE'RE NECK-DEEP IN REPAIR COSTS, TOO, SO WE'RE KIND OF STRAPPED FOR CASH...
We're not swimming in cash here.
GWO
GUESS THOSE STONE HORNS ARE THE ONLY WAY...
GWO
GWO
NO, NO, NO! WAIT, PLEASE!
GWO
GWO

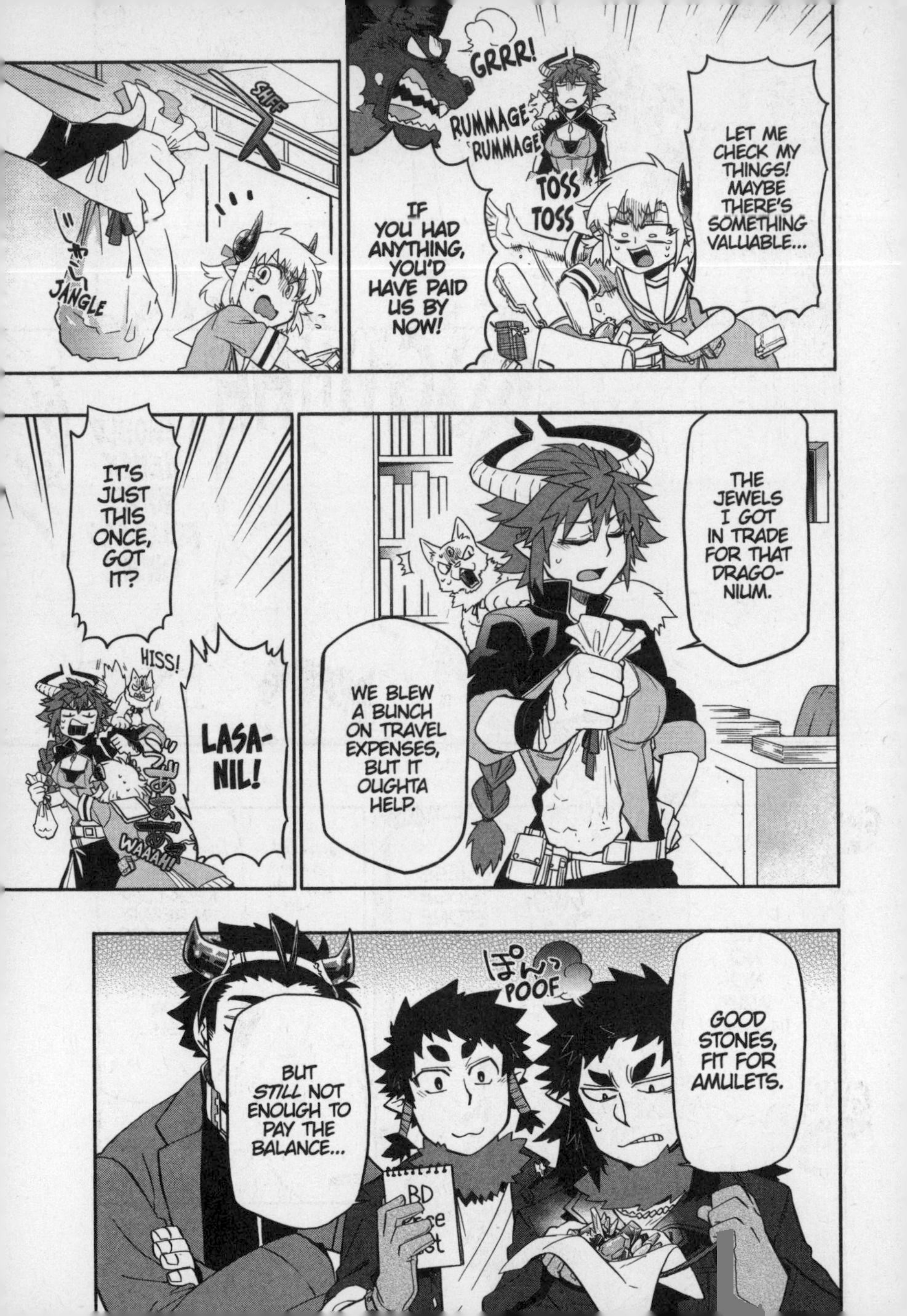
GRRR!
RUMMAGE RUMMAGE
TOSS TOSS
LET ME CHECK MY THINGS! MAYBE THERE'S SOMETHING VALUABLE...
IF YOU HAD ANYTHING, YOU'D HAVE PAID US BY NOW!
SHFF
...
JANGLE
THE JEWELS I GOT IN TRADE FOR THAT DRAGO-NIUM.
WE BLEW A BUNCH ON TRAVEL EXPENSES, BUT IT OUGHTA HELP.
IT'S JUST THIS ONCE, GOT IT?
HISS!
LASA-NIL!
WAAAH!
POOF
GOOD STONES, FIT FOR AMULETS.
BUT STILL NOT ENOUGH TO PAY THE BALANCE...

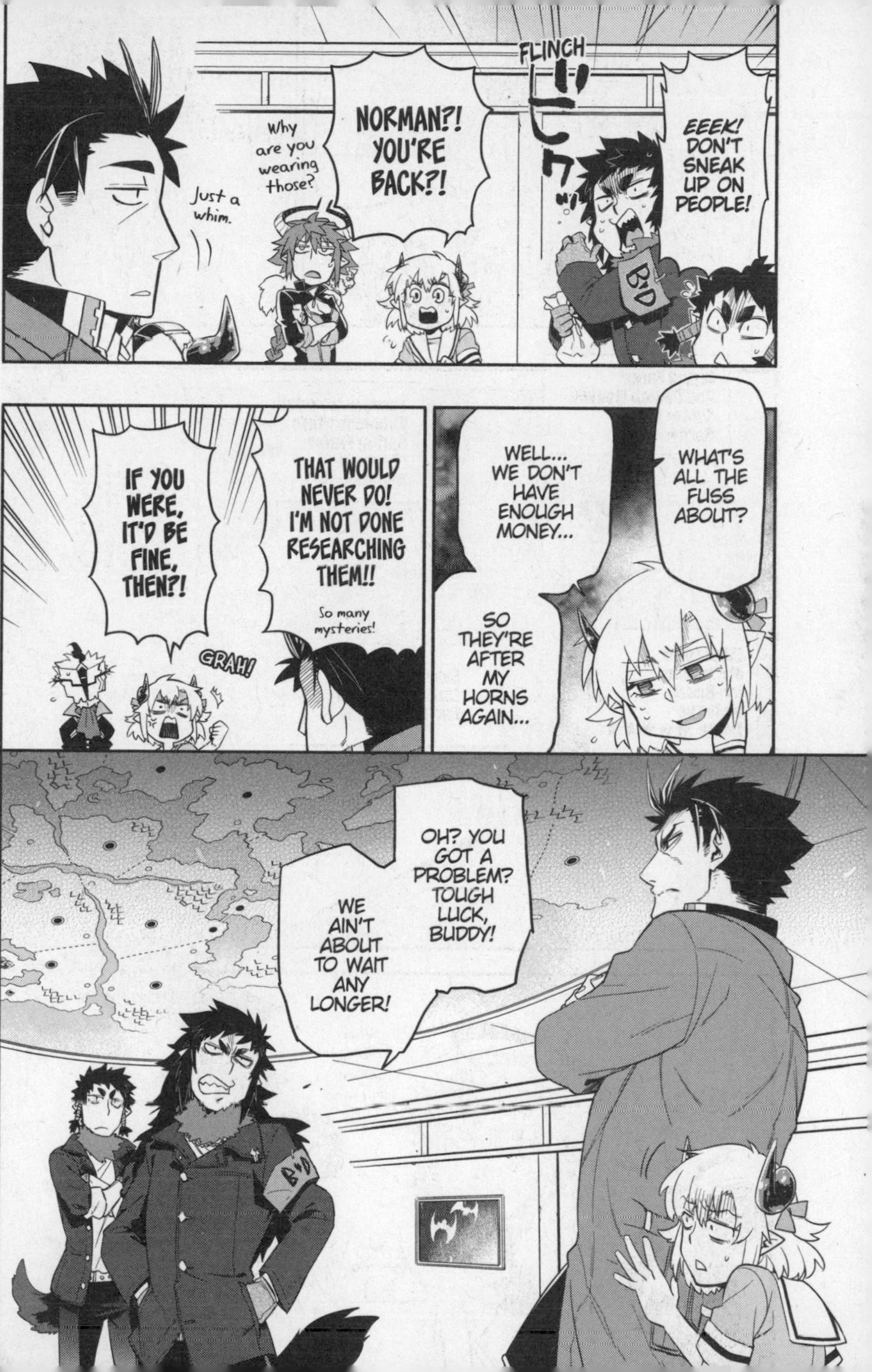
FLINCH
EEEK! DON'T SNEAK UP ON PEOPLE!
NORMAN?! YOU'RE BACK?!
Why are you wearing those?
Just a whim.
WHAT'S ALL THE FUSS ABOUT?
WELL... WE DON'T HAVE ENOUGH MONEY...
SO THEY'RE AFTER MY HORNS AGAIN...
THAT WOULD NEVER DO! I'M NOT DONE RESEARCHING THEM!!
So many mysteries!
IF YOU WERE, IT'D BE FINE, THEN?!
GRAH!
OH? YOU GOT A PROBLEM? TOUGH LUCK, BUDDY!
WE AIN'T ABOUT TO WAIT ANY LONGER!

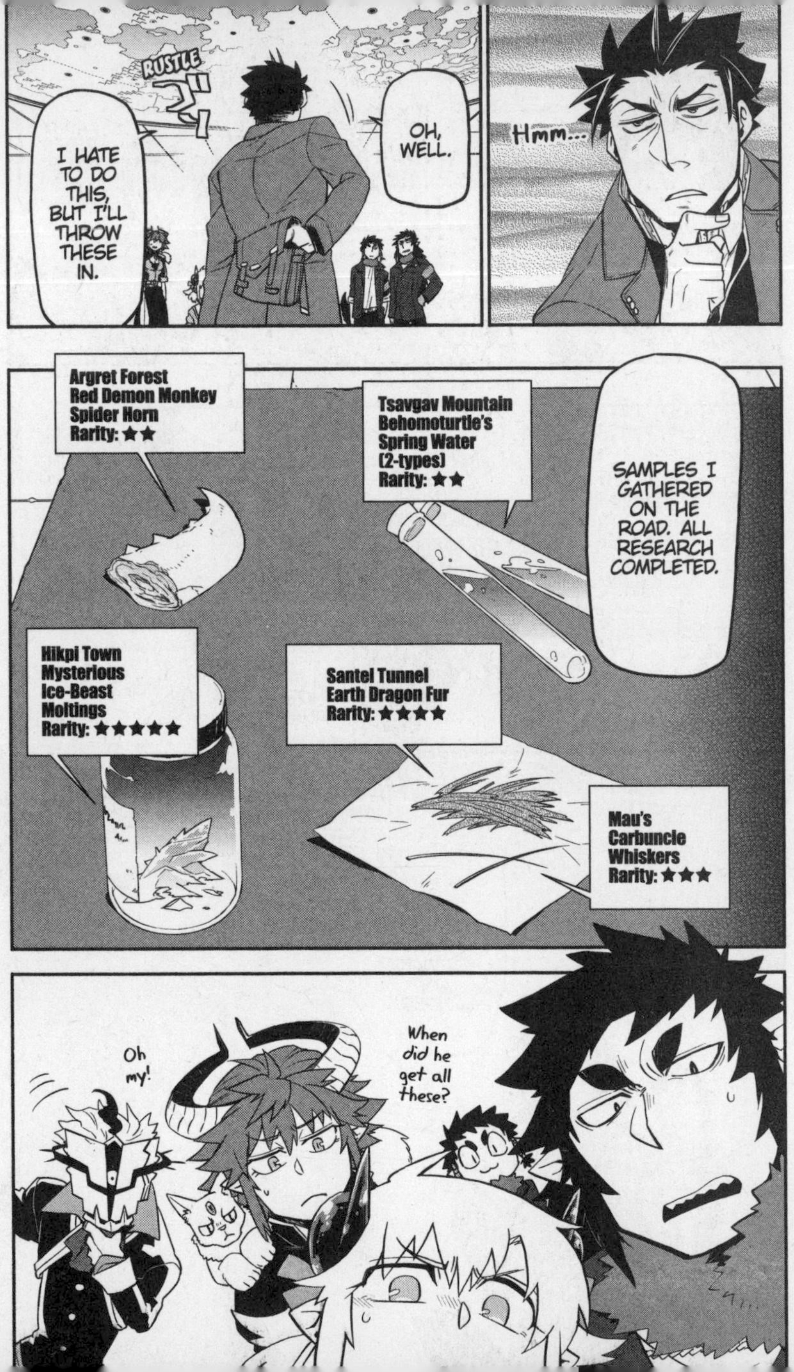
Hmm...
OH, WELL.
RUSTLE
I HATE TO DO THIS, BUT I'LL THROW THESE IN.
SAMPLES I GATHERED ON THE ROAD. ALL RESEARCH COMPLETED.
Tsavgav Mountain Behomoturtle's Spring Water (2-types) Rarity: ★★
Argret Forest Red Demon Monkey Spider Horn Rarity: ★★
Santel Tunnel Earth Dragon Fur Rarity: ★★★★
Hikpi Town Mysterious Ice-Beast Moltings Rarity: ★★★★★
Mau's Carbuncle Whiskers Rarity: ★★★
When did he get all these?
Oh my!

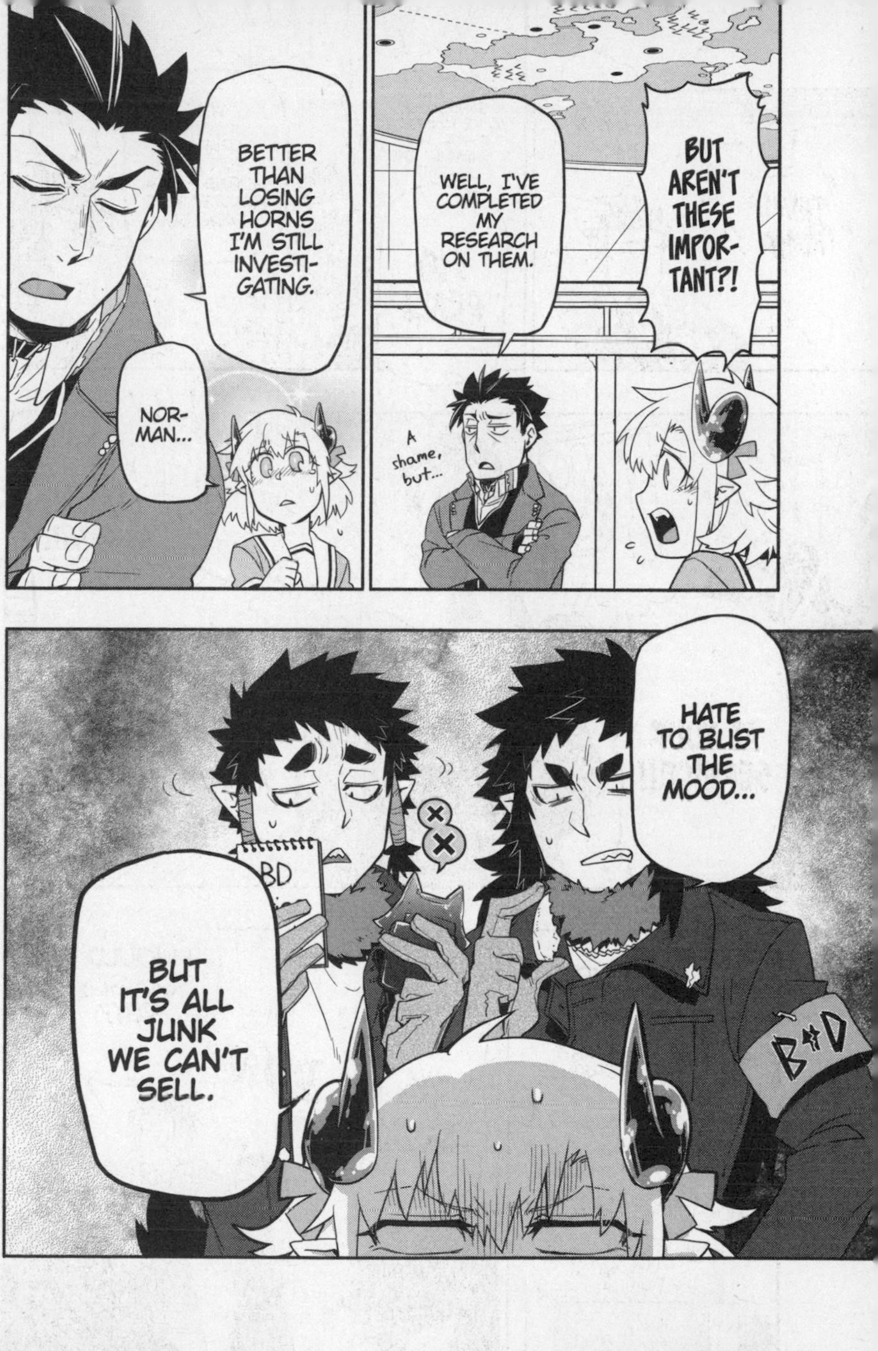
BUT AREN'T THESE IMPORTANT?!
WELL, I'VE COMPLETED MY RESEARCH ON THEM.
A shame, but...
BETTER THAN LOSING HORNS I'M STILL INVESTIGATING.
NORMAN...
HATE TO BUST THE MOOD...
BUT IT'S ALL JUNK WE CAN'T SELL.
B*D

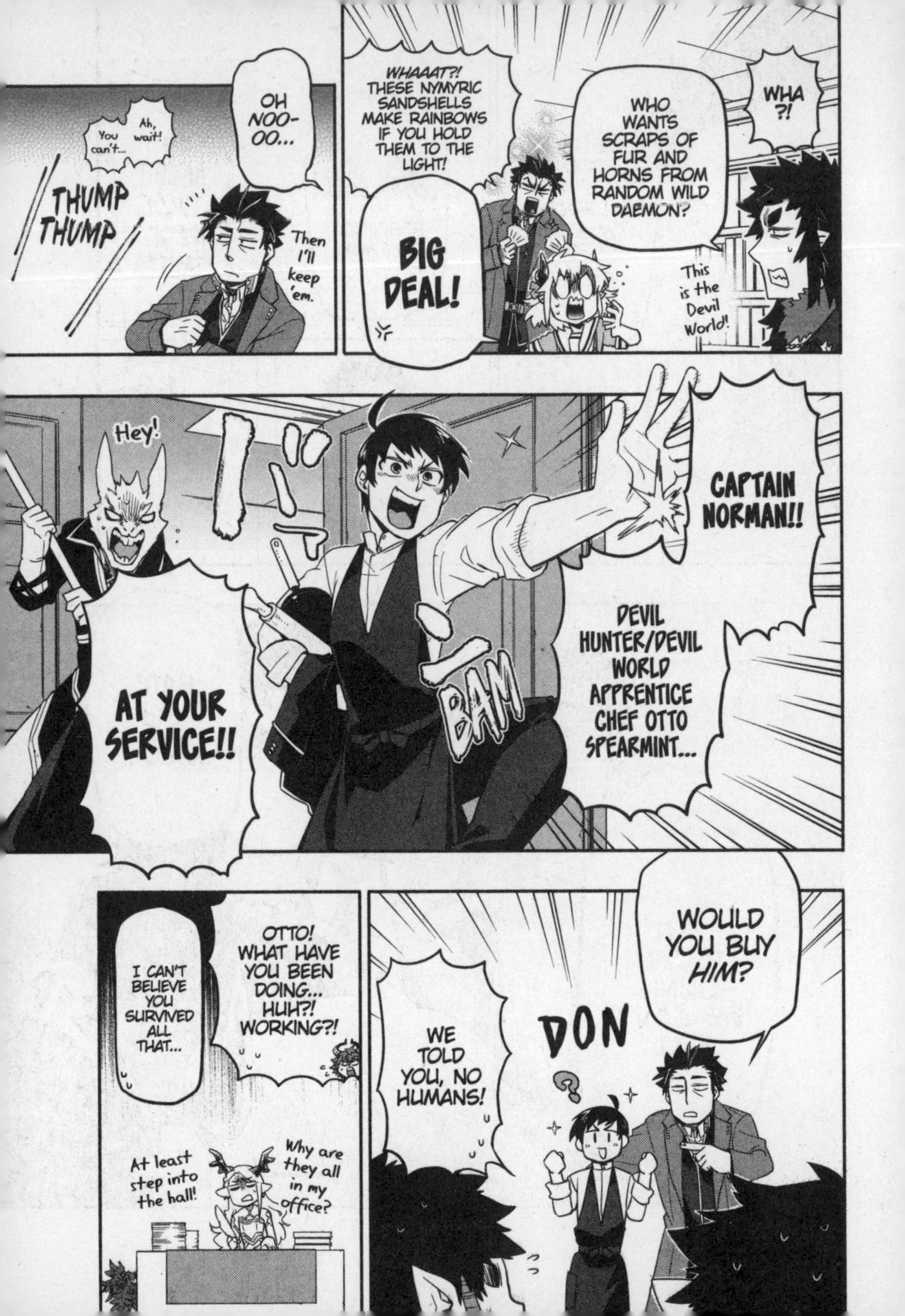
WHA ?!
WHO WANTS SCRAPS OF FUR AND HORNS FROM RANDOM WILD DAEMON?
WHAAAT?! THESE NYMYRIC SANDSHELLS MAKE RAINBOWS IF YOU HOLD THEM TO THE LIGHT!
This is the Devil World!
BIG DEAL!
OH NOO-OO...
Ah, wait!
You can't...
THUMP THUMP
Then I'll keep 'em.
CAPTAIN NORMAN!!
DEVIL HUNTER/DEVIL WORLD APPRENTICE CHEF OTTO SPEARMINT...
Hey!
BAM
AT YOUR SERVICE!!
WOULD YOU BUY HIM?
DON
WE TOLD YOU, NO HUMANS!
OTTO! WHAT HAVE YOU BEEN DOING... HUH?! WORKING?!
I CAN'T BELIEVE YOU SURVIVED ALL THAT...
Why are they all in my office?
At least step into the hall!

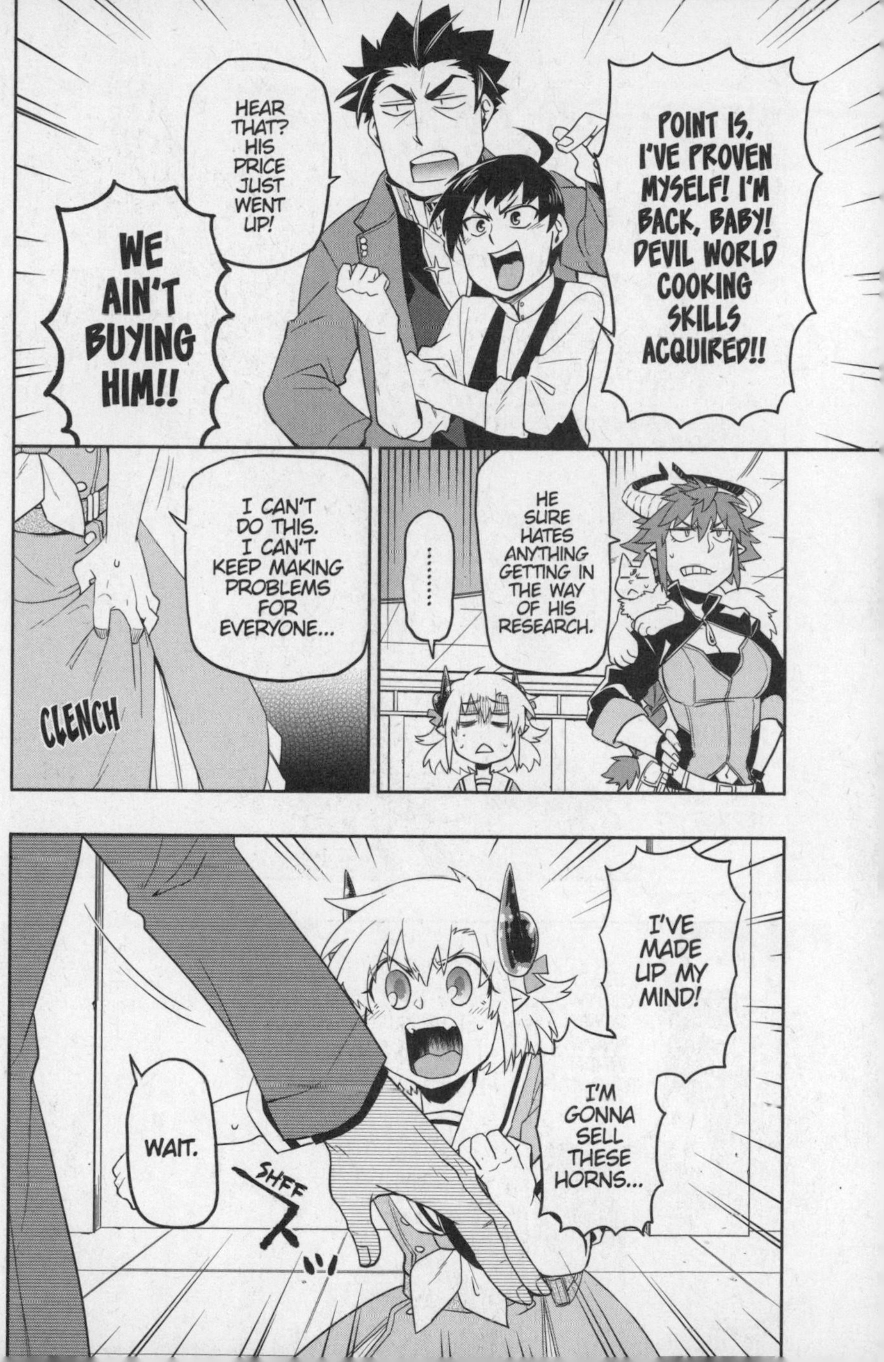
POINT IS, I'VE PROVEN MYSELF! I'M BACK, BABY! DEVIL WORLD COOKING SKILLS ACQUIRED!!
HEAR THAT? HIS PRICE JUST WENT UP!
WE AIN'T BUYING HIM!!
HE SURE HATES ANYTHING GETTING IN THE WAY OF HIS RESEARCH.
....
I CAN'T DO THIS. I CAN'T KEEP MAKING PROBLEMS FOR EVERYONE...
CLENCH
I'VE MADE UP MY MIND!
I'M GONNA SELL THESE HORNS...
WAIT.
SHFF

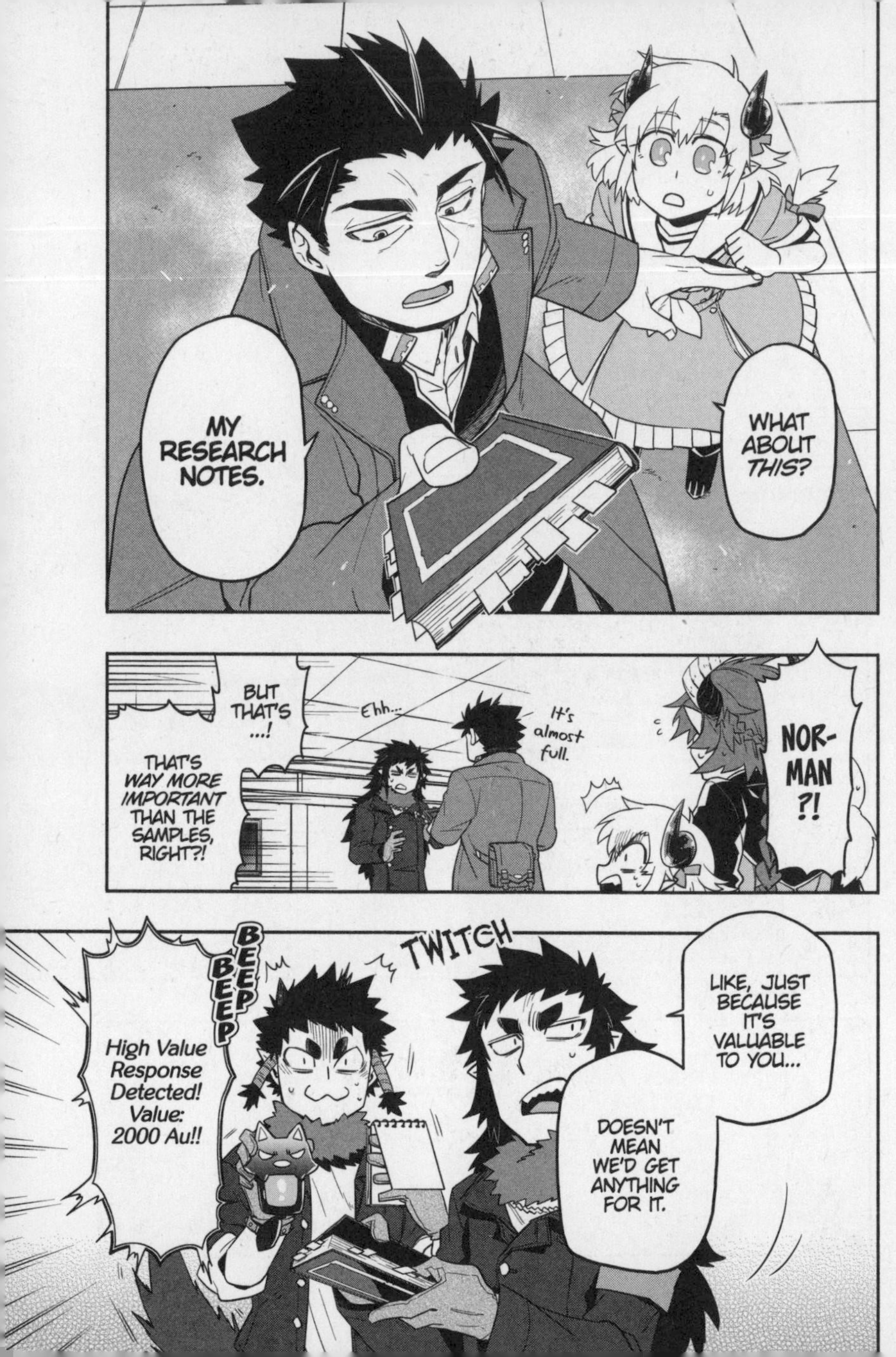
WHAT ABOUT THIS?
MY RESEARCH NOTES.
NOR-MAN?!
It's almost full.
Ehh...
BUT THAT'S ...!
THAT'S WAY MORE IMPORTANT THAN THE SAMPLES, RIGHT?!
LIKE, JUST BECAUSE IT'S VALUABLE TO YOU...
DOESN'T MEAN WE'D GET ANYTHING FOR IT.
TWITCH
BEEP BEEP
High Value Response Detected! Value: 2000 Au!!

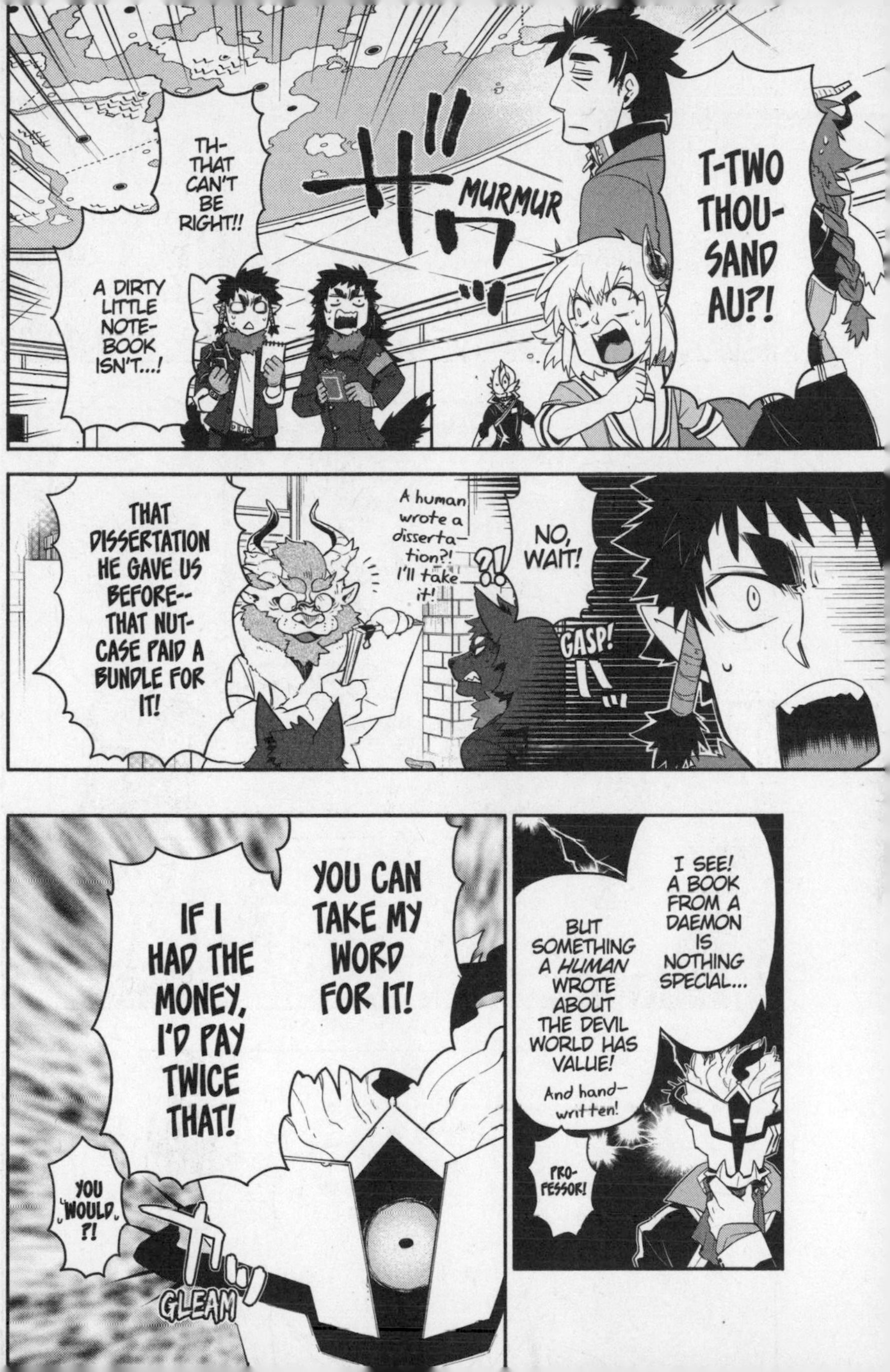
T-TWO THOUSAND AU?!
MURMUR
TH-THAT CAN'T BE RIGHT!!
A DIRTY LITTLE NOTEBOOK ISN'T...!
GASP!
NO, WAIT!
A human wrote a dissertation?! I'll take it!
THAT DISSERTATION HE GAVE US BEFORE-- THAT NUTCASE PAID A BUNDLE FOR IT!
I SEE! A BOOK FROM A DAEMON IS NOTHING SPECIAL...
BUT SOMETHING A *HUMAN* WROTE ABOUT THE DEVIL WORLD HAS VALUE!
And handwritten!
PROFESSOR!
YOU CAN TAKE MY WORD FOR IT!
IF I HAD THE MONEY, I'D PAY TWICE THAT!
YOU WOULD?!
GLEAM

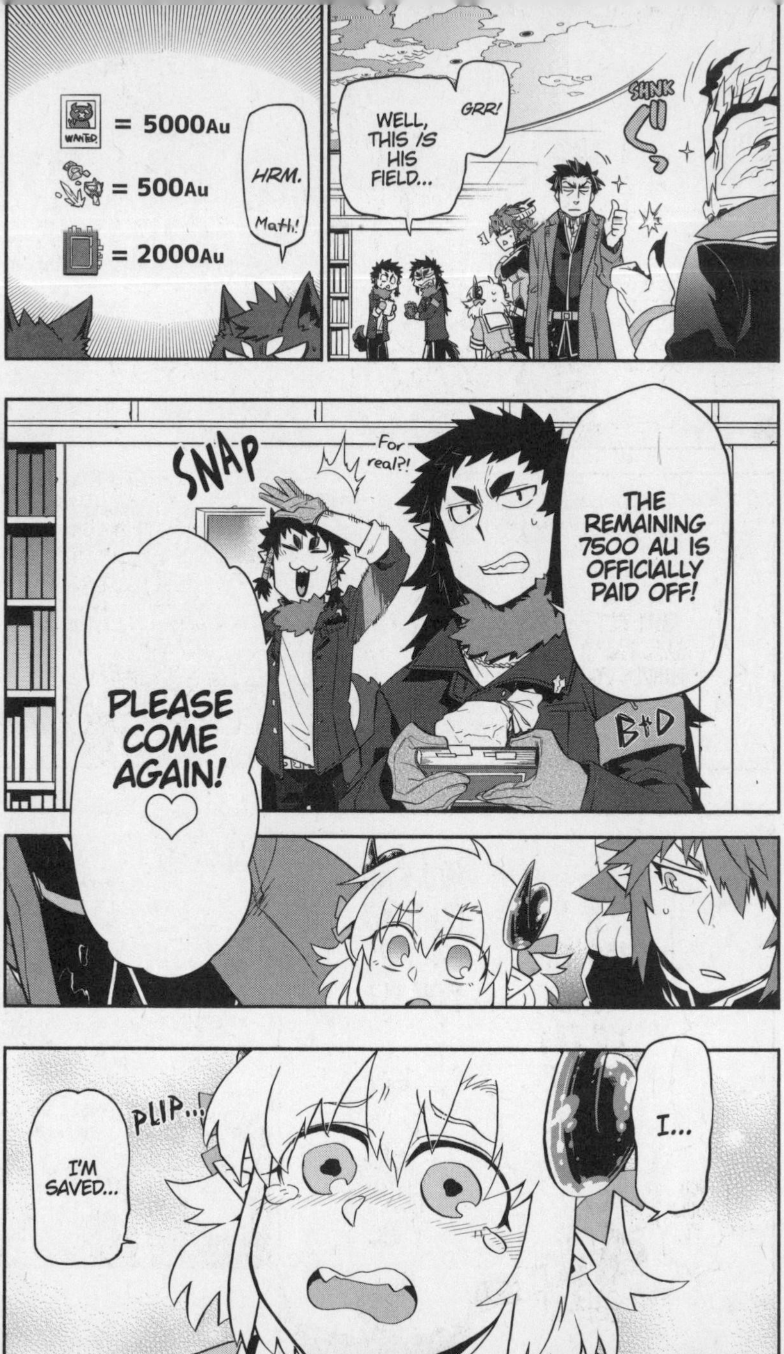
SHNK
GRR!
WELL, THIS IS HIS FIELD...
HRM.
Math!
WANTED
= 5000Au
= 500Au
= 2000Au
THE REMAINING 7500 AU IS OFFICIALLY PAID OFF!
For real?!
SNAP
PLEASE COME AGAIN!
I...
PLIP...
I'M SAVED...

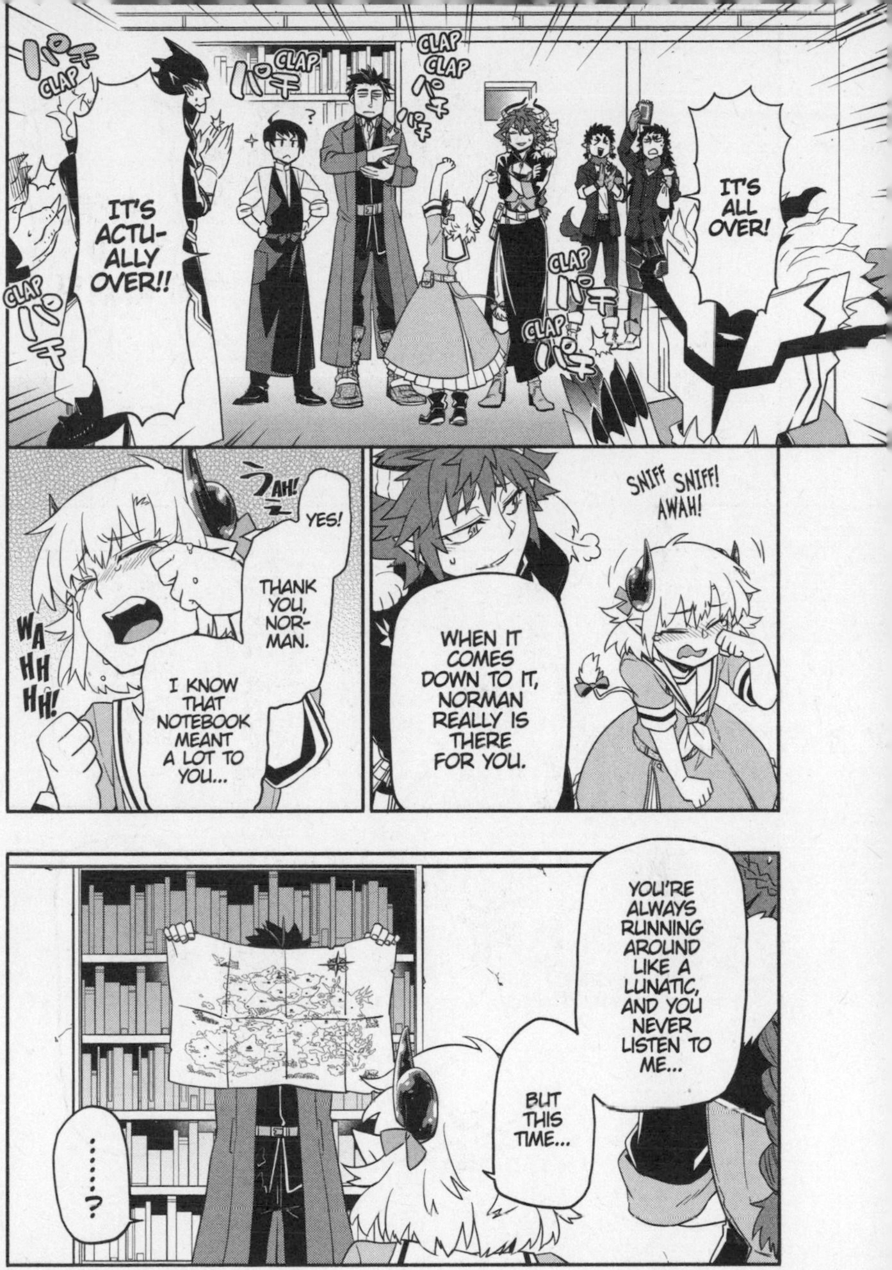
IT'S ALL OVER!
CLAP CLAP
CLAP
CLAP
CLAP
IT'S ACTUALLY OVER!!
CLAP
SNIFF SNIFF! AWAH!
WHEN IT COMES DOWN TO IT, NORMAN REALLY IS THERE FOR YOU.
AH!
YES!
THANK YOU, NORMAN.
I KNOW THAT NOTEBOOK MEANT A LOT TO YOU...
WAHHHH!
YOU'RE ALWAYS RUNNING AROUND LIKE A LUNATIC, AND YOU NEVER LISTEN TO ME...
BUT THIS TIME...
......?

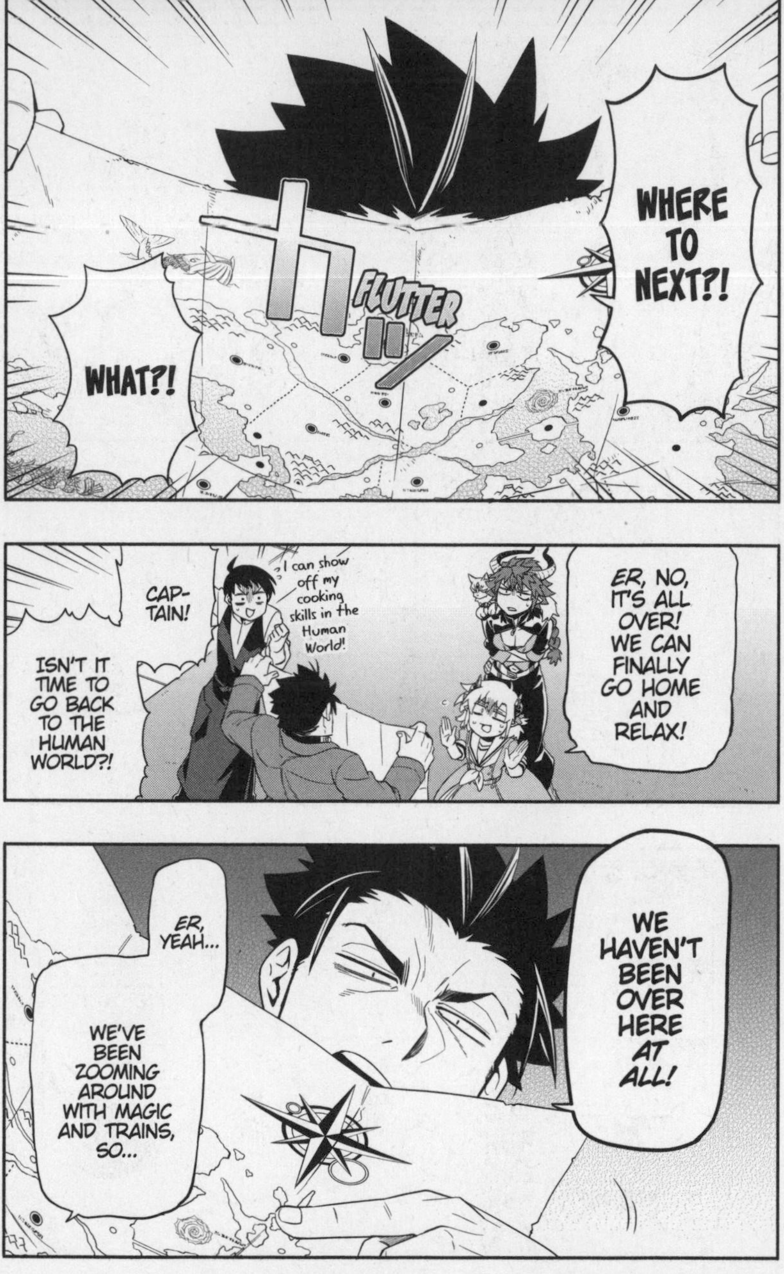
WHERE TO NEXT?!
カ
FLUTTER
WHAT?!
ER, NO, IT'S ALL OVER! WE CAN FINALLY GO HOME AND RELAX!
I can show off my cooking skills in the Human World!
CAP-TAIN!
ISN'T IT TIME TO GO BACK TO THE HUMAN WORLD?!
WE HAVEN'T BEEN OVER HERE AT ALL!
ER, YEAH...
WE'VE BEEN ZOOMING AROUND WITH MAGIC AND TRAINS, SO...

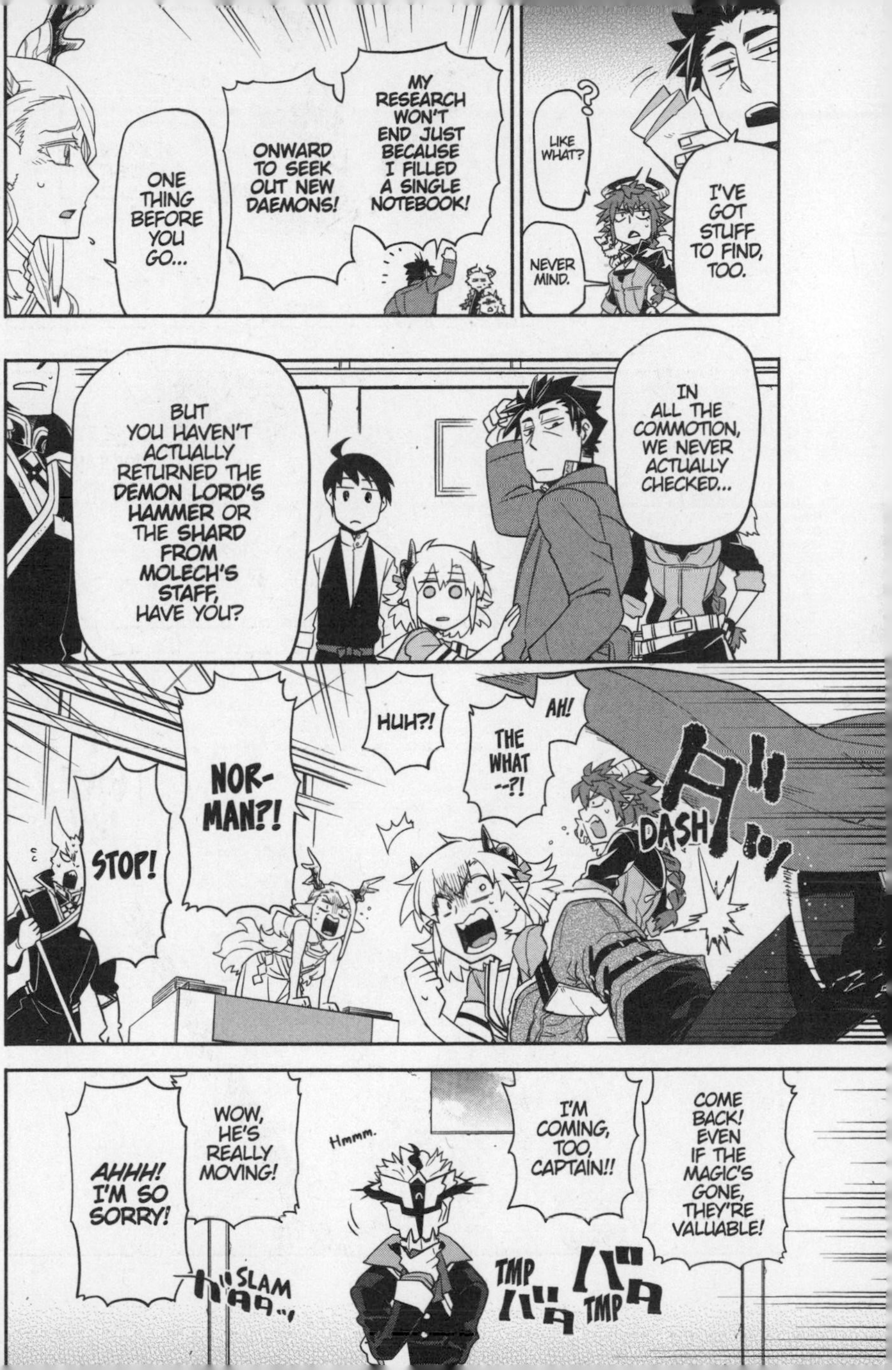
I'VE GOT STUFF TO FIND, TOO.
LIKE WHAT?
NEVER MIND.
MY RESEARCH WON'T END JUST BECAUSE I FILLED A SINGLE NOTEBOOK!
ONWARD TO SEEK OUT NEW DAEMONS!
ONE THING BEFORE YOU GO...
IN ALL THE COMMOTION, WE NEVER ACTUALLY CHECKED...
BUT YOU HAVEN'T ACTUALLY RETURNED THE DEMON LORD'S HAMMER OR THE SHARD FROM MOLECH'S STAFF, HAVE YOU?
DASH
AH!
THE WHAT--?!
HUH?!
NOR-MAN?!
STOP!
COME BACK! EVEN IF THE MAGIC'S GONE, THEY'RE VALUABLE!
I'M COMING, TOO, CAPTAIN!!
TMP
TMP
Hmmm.
WOW, HE'S REALLY MOVING!
AHHH! I'M SO SORRY!
SLAM

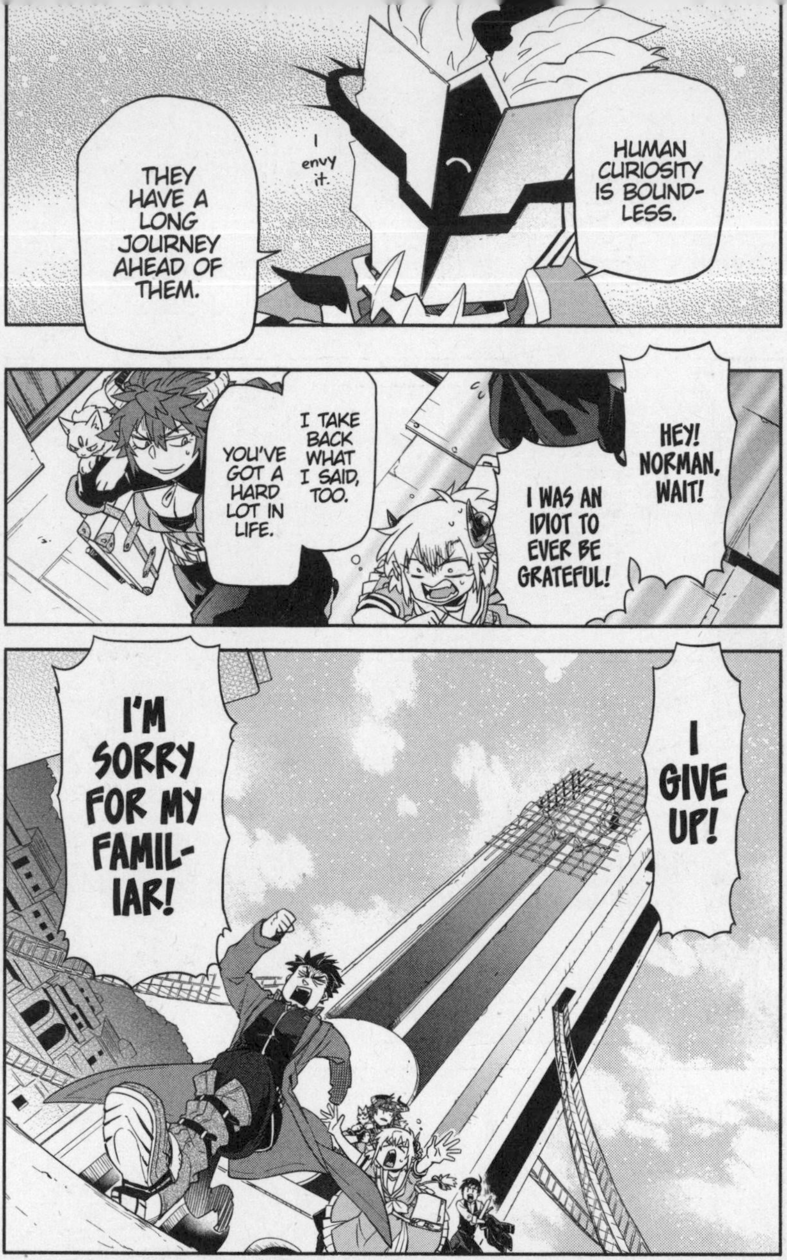
HUMAN CURIOSITY IS BOUNDLESS.
I envy it.
THEY HAVE A LONG JOURNEY AHEAD OF THEM.
HEY! NORMAN, WAIT!
I WAS AN IDIOT TO EVER BE GRATEFUL!
I TAKE BACK WHAT I SAID, TOO.
YOU'VE GOT A HARD LOT IN LIFE.
I GIVE UP!
I'M SORRY FOR MY FAMILIAR!

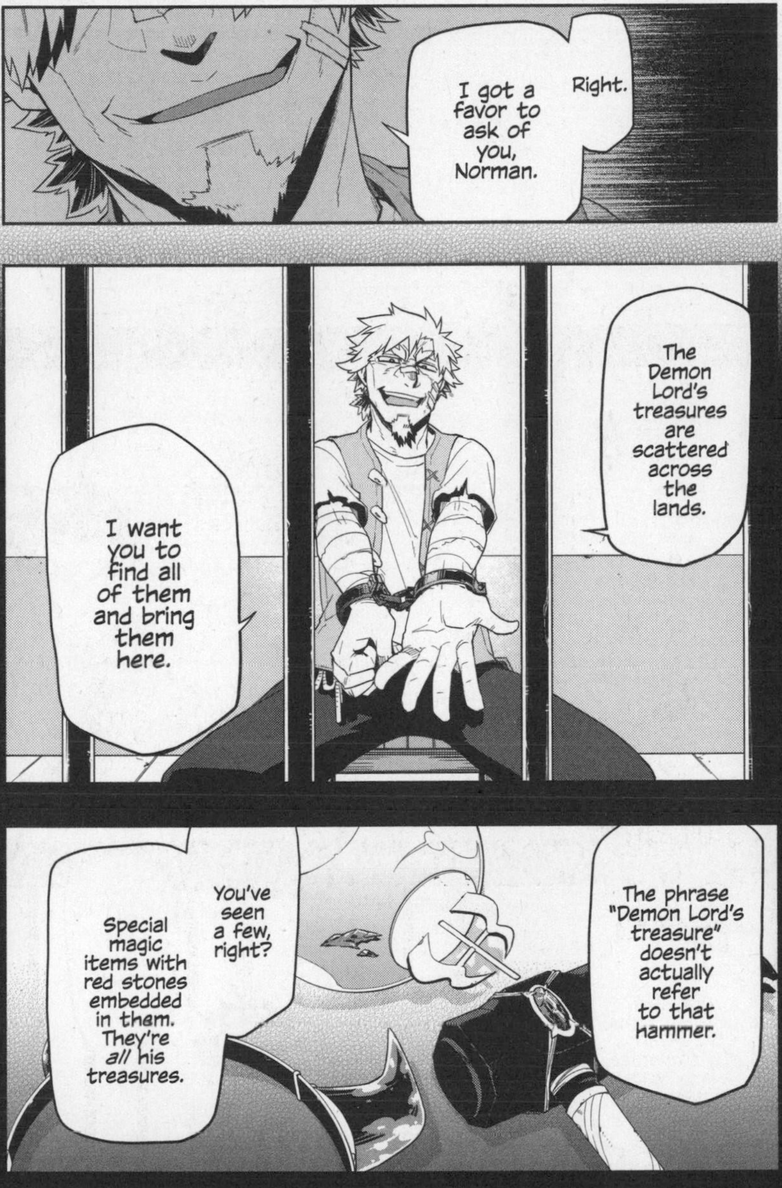
Right.
I got a favor to ask of you, Norman.
The Demon Lord's treasures are scattered across the lands.
I want you to find all of them and bring them here.
The phrase "Demon Lord's treasure" doesn't actually refer to that hammer.
You've seen a few, right?
Special magic items with red stones embedded in them. They're *all* his treasures.

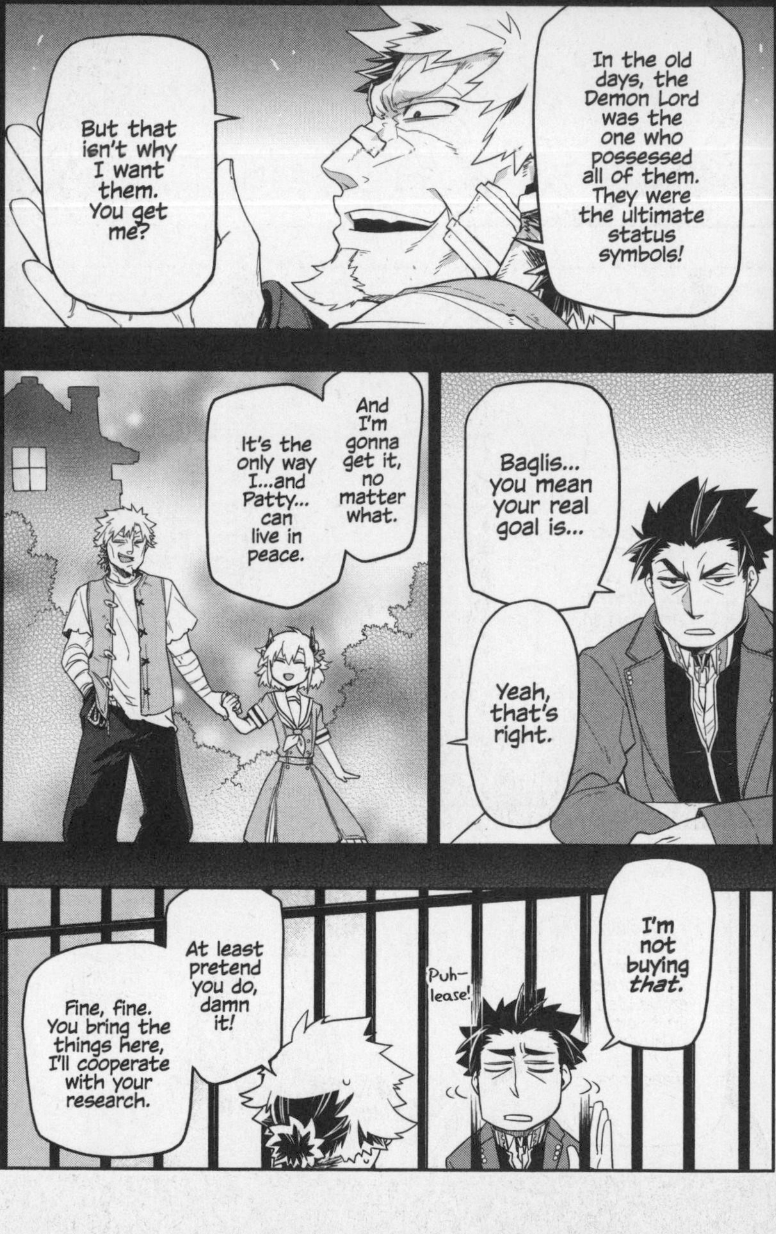
In the old days, the Demon Lord was the one who possessed all of them. They were the ultimate status symbols!
But that isn't why I want them. You get me?
Baglis... you mean your real goal is...
Yeah, that's right.
And I'm gonna get it, no matter what.
It's the only way I...and Patty... can live in peace.
I'm not buying *that*.
Puh-lease!
At least pretend you do, damn it!
Fine, fine. You bring the things here, I'll cooperate with your research.

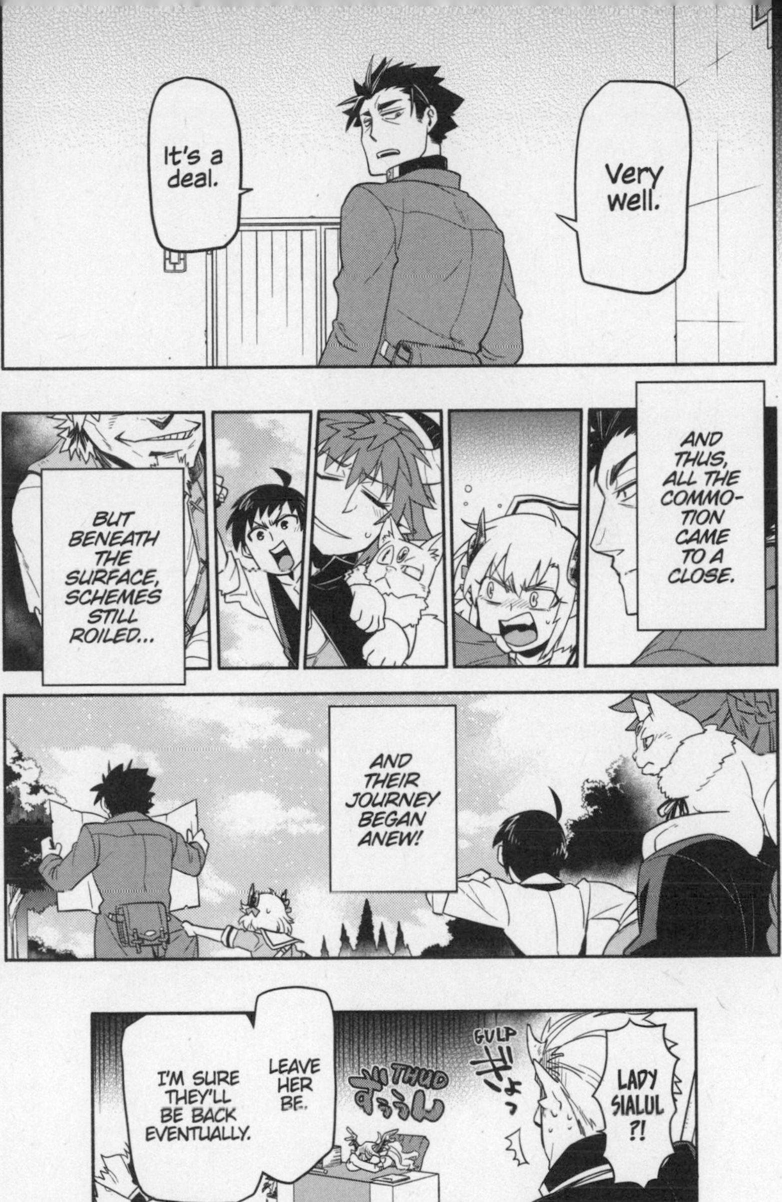
Very well.
It's a deal.
AND THUS, ALL THE COMMOTION CAME TO A CLOSE.
BUT BENEATH THE SURFACE, SCHEMES STILL ROILED...
AND THEIR JOURNEY BEGAN ANEW!
LADY SIALUL?!
GULP
THUD
LEAVE HER BE.
I'M SURE THEY'LL BE BACK EVENTUALLY.

Sorry For My Familiar

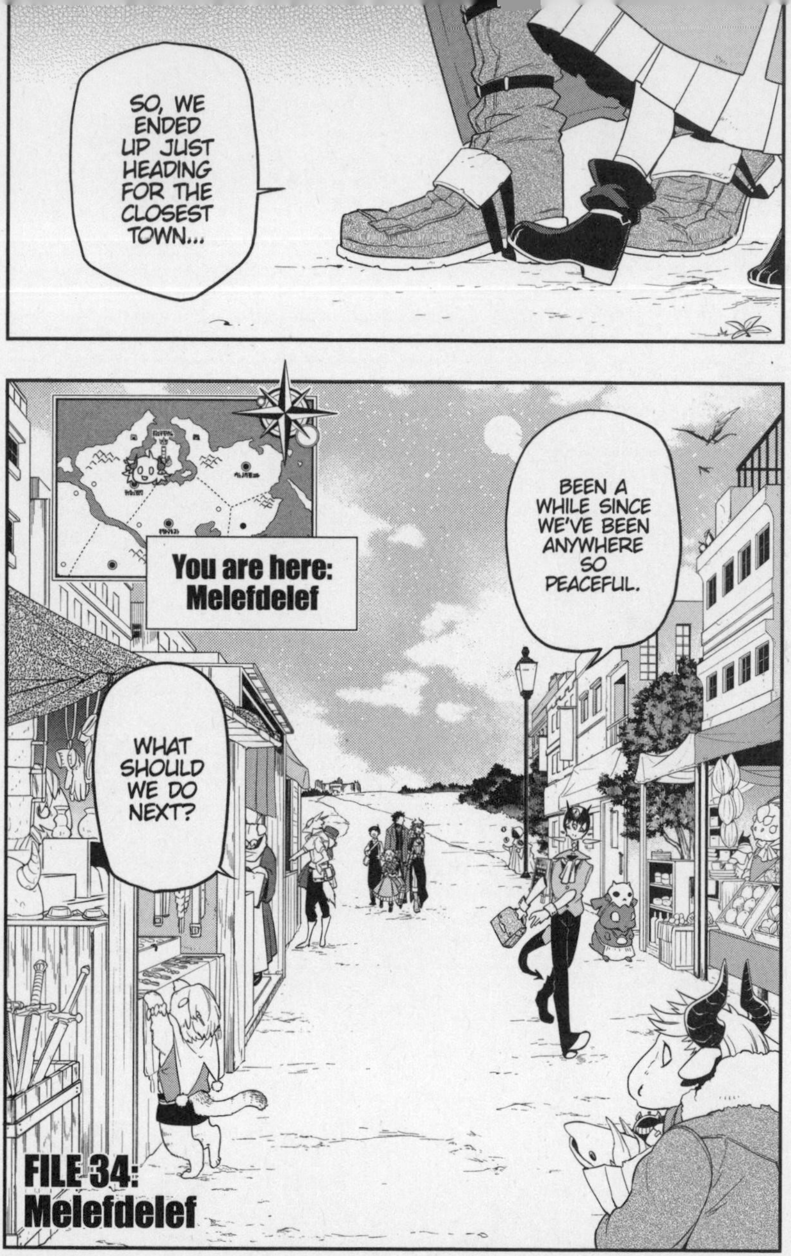
SO, WE ENDED UP JUST HEADING FOR THE CLOSEST TOWN...
BEEN A WHILE SINCE WE'VE BEEN ANYWHERE SO PEACEFUL.
You are here: Melefdelef
WHAT SHOULD WE DO NEXT?
FILE 34: Melefdelef

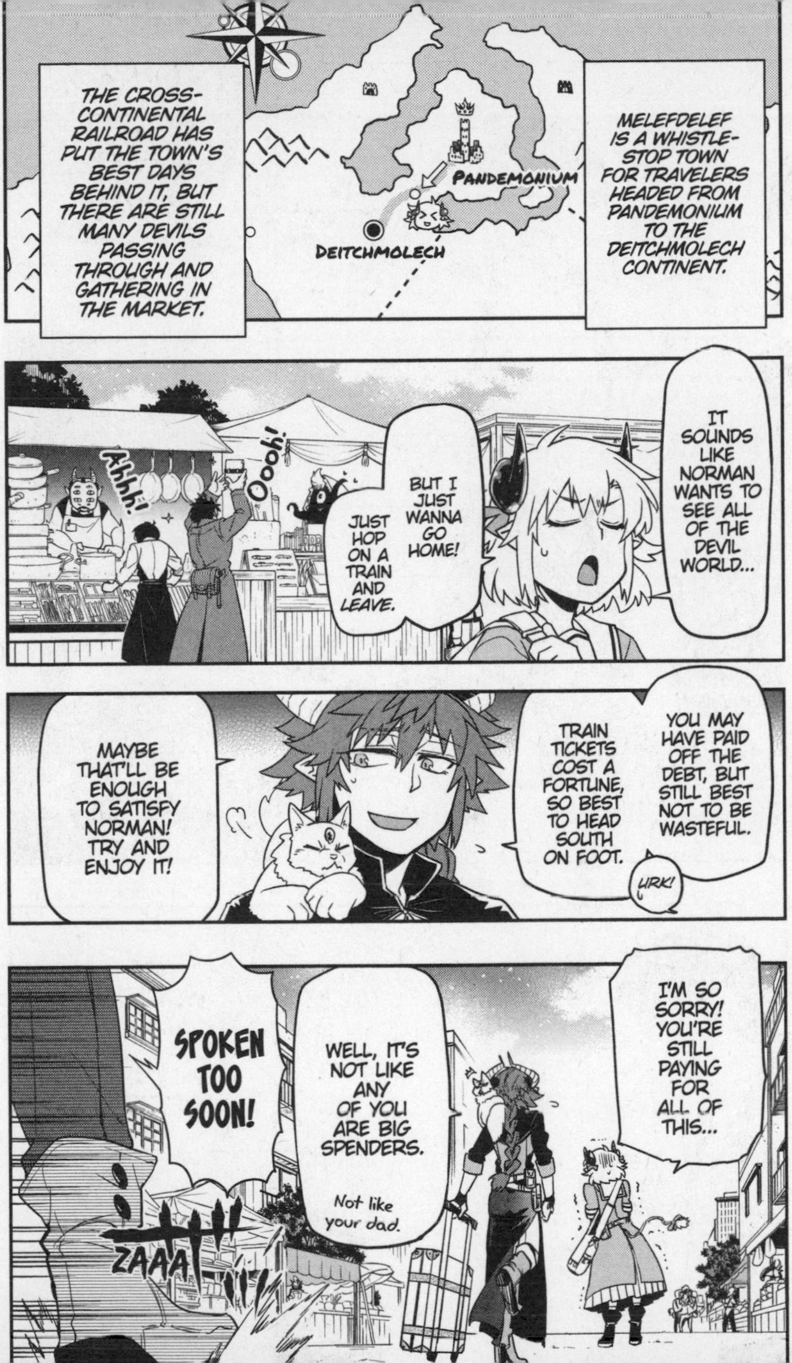
MELEFDELEF IS A WHISTLE-STOP TOWN FOR TRAVELERS HEADED FROM PANDEMONIUM TO THE DEITCHMOLECH CONTINENT.
PANDEMONIUM
DEITCHMOLECH
THE CROSS-CONTINENTAL RAILROAD HAS PUT THE TOWN'S BEST DAYS BEHIND IT, BUT THERE ARE STILL MANY DEVILS PASSING THROUGH AND GATHERING IN THE MARKET.
IT SOUNDS LIKE NORMAN WANTS TO SEE ALL OF THE DEVIL WORLD...
BUT I JUST WANNA GO HOME!
JUST HOP ON A TRAIN AND LEAVE.
Ooooh!
Ahhh!
YOU MAY HAVE PAID OFF THE DEBT, BUT STILL BEST NOT TO BE WASTEFUL.
TRAIN TICKETS COST A FORTUNE, SO BEST TO HEAD SOUTH ON FOOT.
URK!
MAYBE THAT'LL BE ENOUGH TO SATISFY NORMAN! TRY AND ENJOY IT!
I'M SO SORRY! YOU'RE STILL PAYING FOR ALL OF THIS...
WELL, IT'S NOT LIKE ANY OF YOU ARE BIG SPENDERS.
Not like your dad.
SPOKEN TOO SOON!
ZAAA

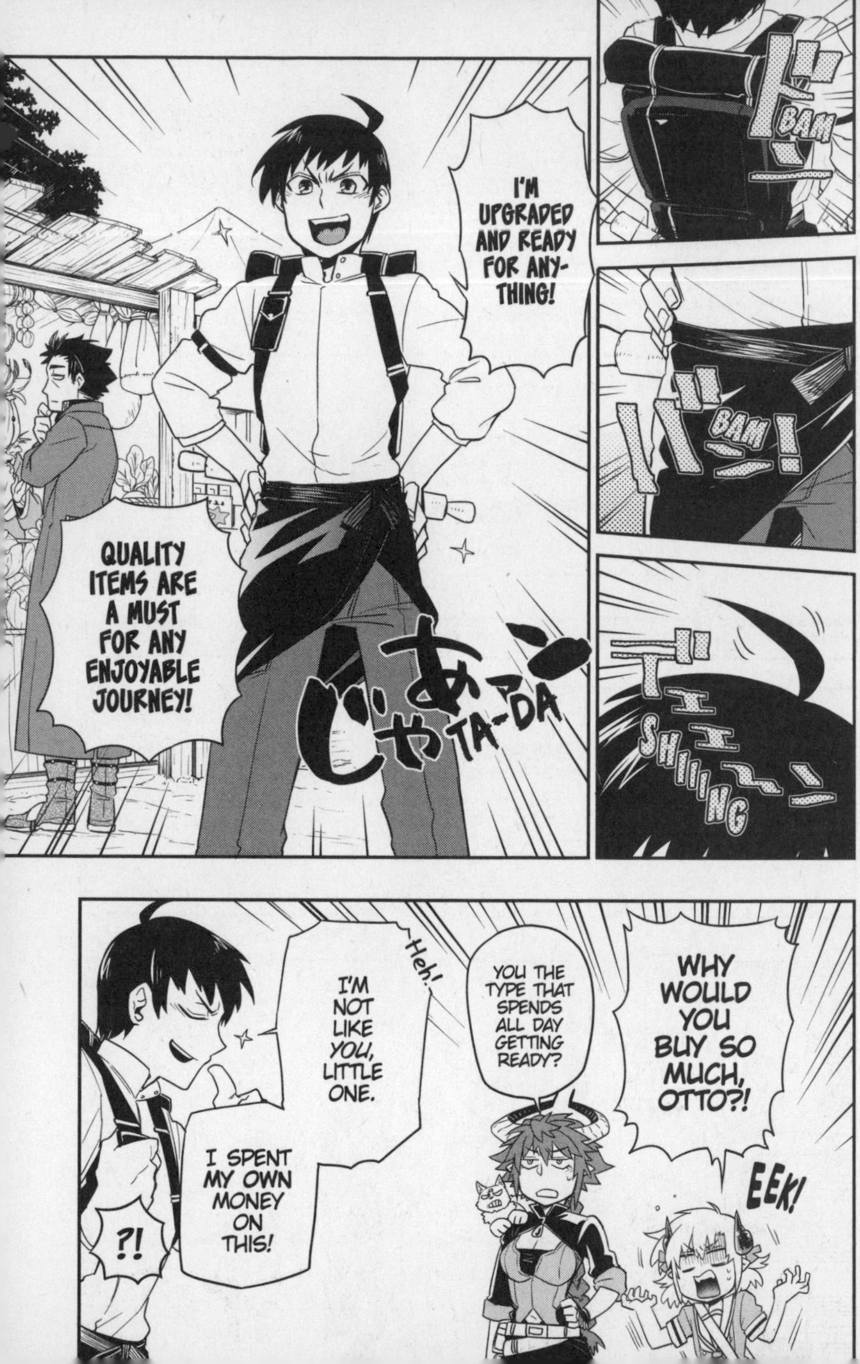
BAM
BAM!
SHIIIING
I'M UPGRADED AND READY FOR ANY-THING!
QUALITY ITEMS ARE A MUST FOR ANY ENJOYABLE JOURNEY!
TA-DA
WHY WOULD YOU BUY SO MUCH, OTTO?!
EEK!
YOU THE TYPE THAT SPENDS ALL DAY GETTING READY?
Heh!
I'M NOT LIKE YOU, LITTLE ONE.
I SPENT MY OWN MONEY ON THIS!
?!

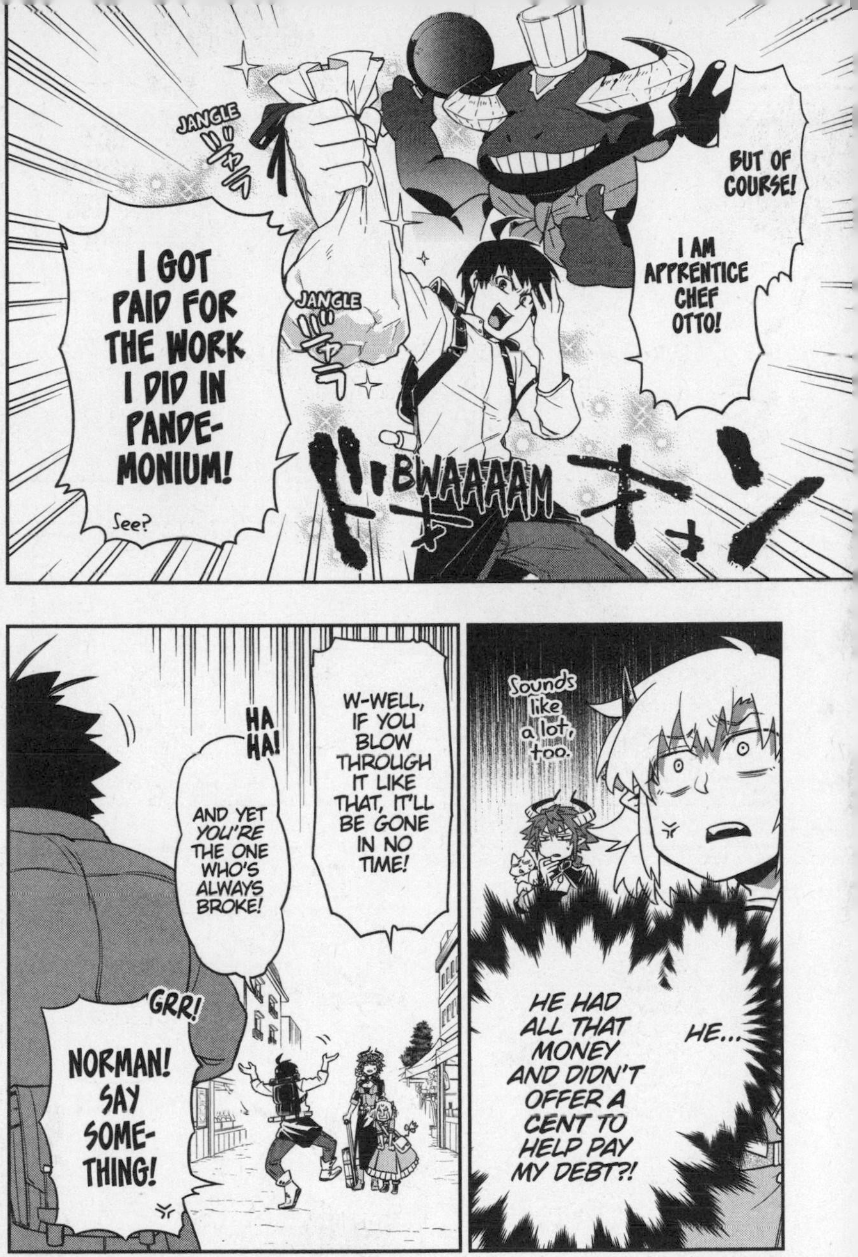
BUT OF COURSE!
I AM APPRENTICE CHEF OTTO!
JANGLE
JANGLE
I GOT PAID FOR THE WORK I DID IN PANDE-MONIUM!
See?
BWAAAAM
Sounds like a lot, too.
HE...
HE HAD ALL THAT MONEY AND DIDN'T OFFER A CENT TO HELP PAY MY DEBT?!
W-WELL, IF YOU BLOW THROUGH IT LIKE THAT, IT'LL BE GONE IN NO TIME!
HA HA!
AND YET YOU'RE THE ONE WHO'S ALWAYS BROKE!
GRR!
NORMAN! SAY SOME-THING!

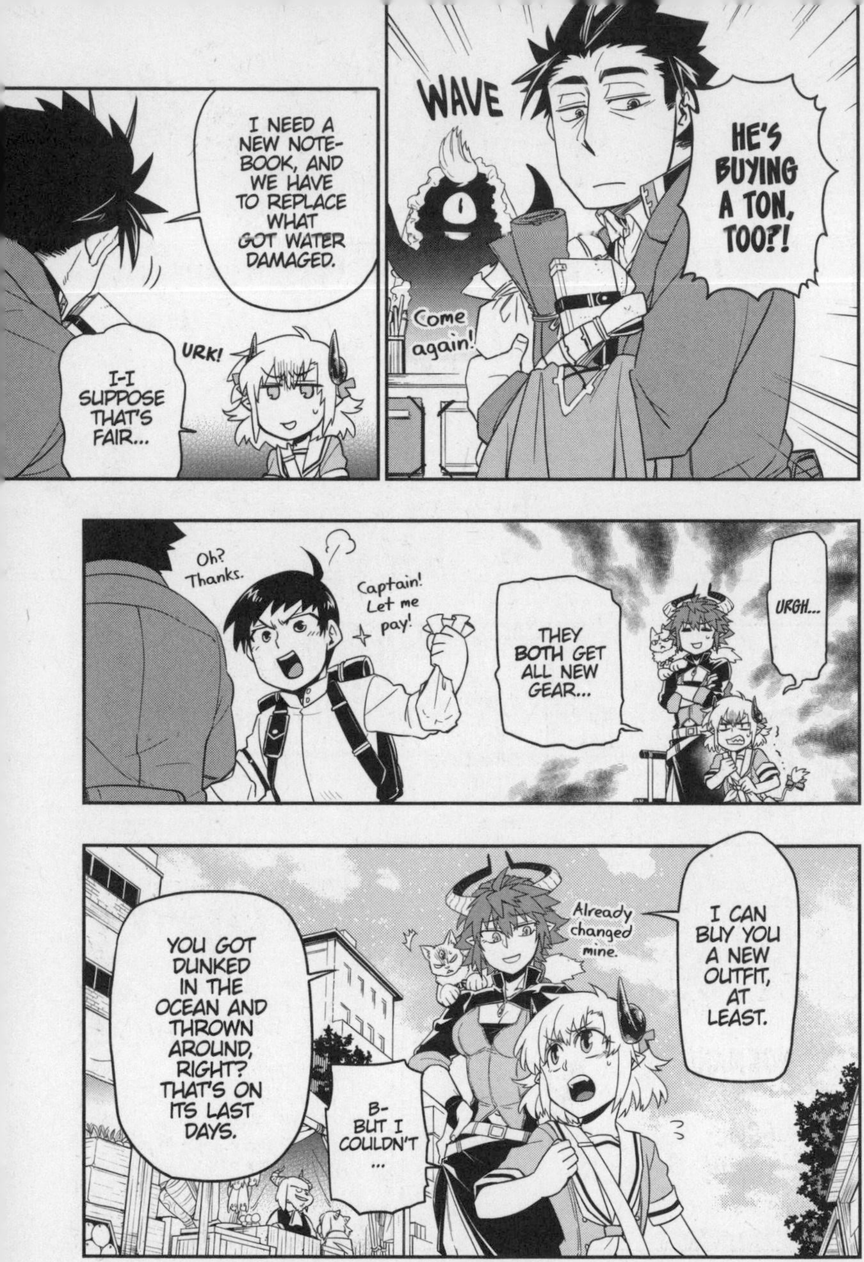
WAVE
HE'S BUYING A TON, TOO?!
Come again!
I NEED A NEW NOTE-BOOK, AND WE HAVE TO REPLACE WHAT GOT WATER DAMAGED.
URK!
I-I SUPPOSE THAT'S FAIR...
URGH...
THEY BOTH GET ALL NEW GEAR...
Captain! Let me pay!
Oh? Thanks.
I CAN BUY YOU A NEW OUTFIT, AT LEAST.
Already changed mine.
YOU GOT DUNKED IN THE OCEAN AND THROWN AROUND, RIGHT? THAT'S ON ITS LAST DAYS.
B-BUT I COULDN'T ...

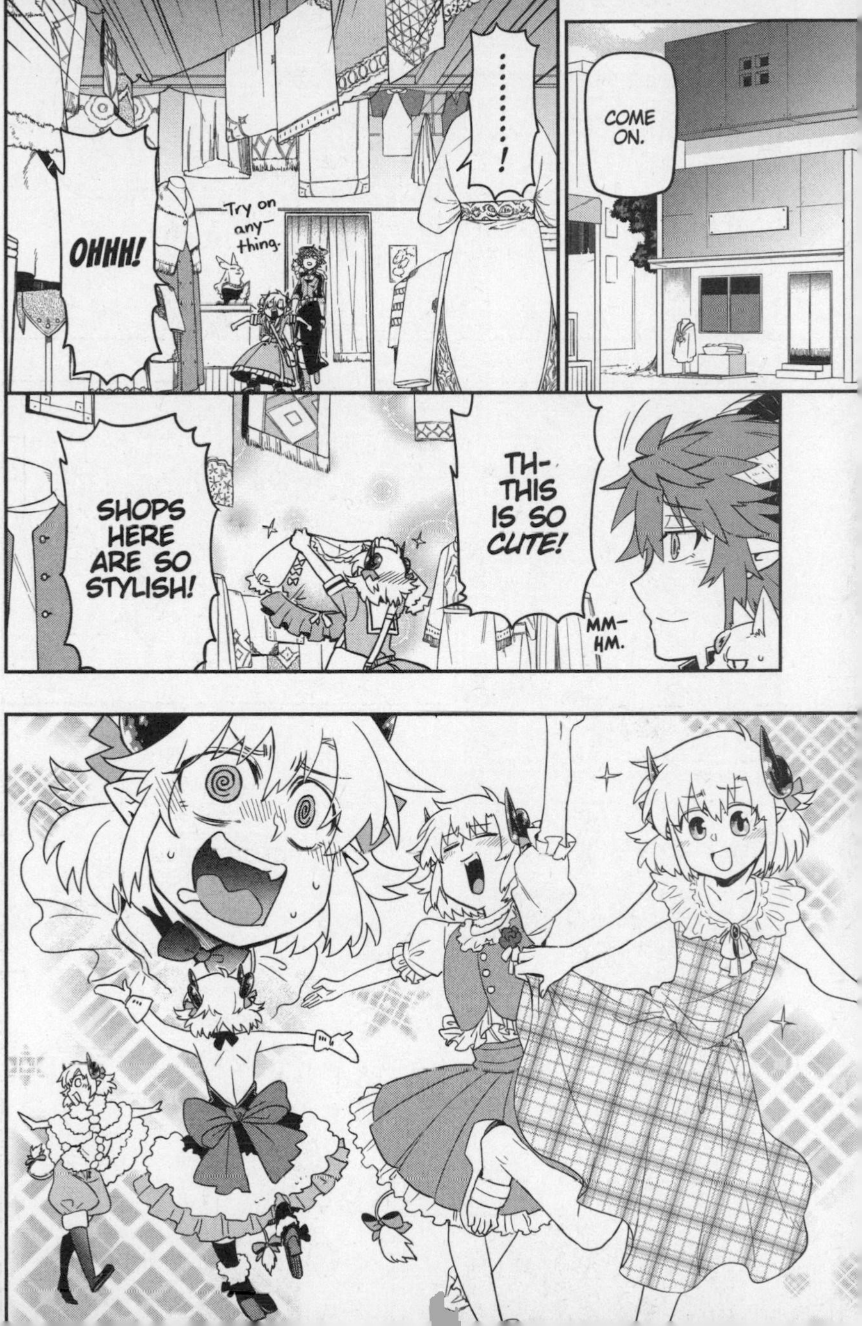
COME ON.
......!
Try on any-thing.
OHHH!
TH-THIS IS SO CUTE!
MM-HM.
SHOPS HERE ARE SO STYLISH!

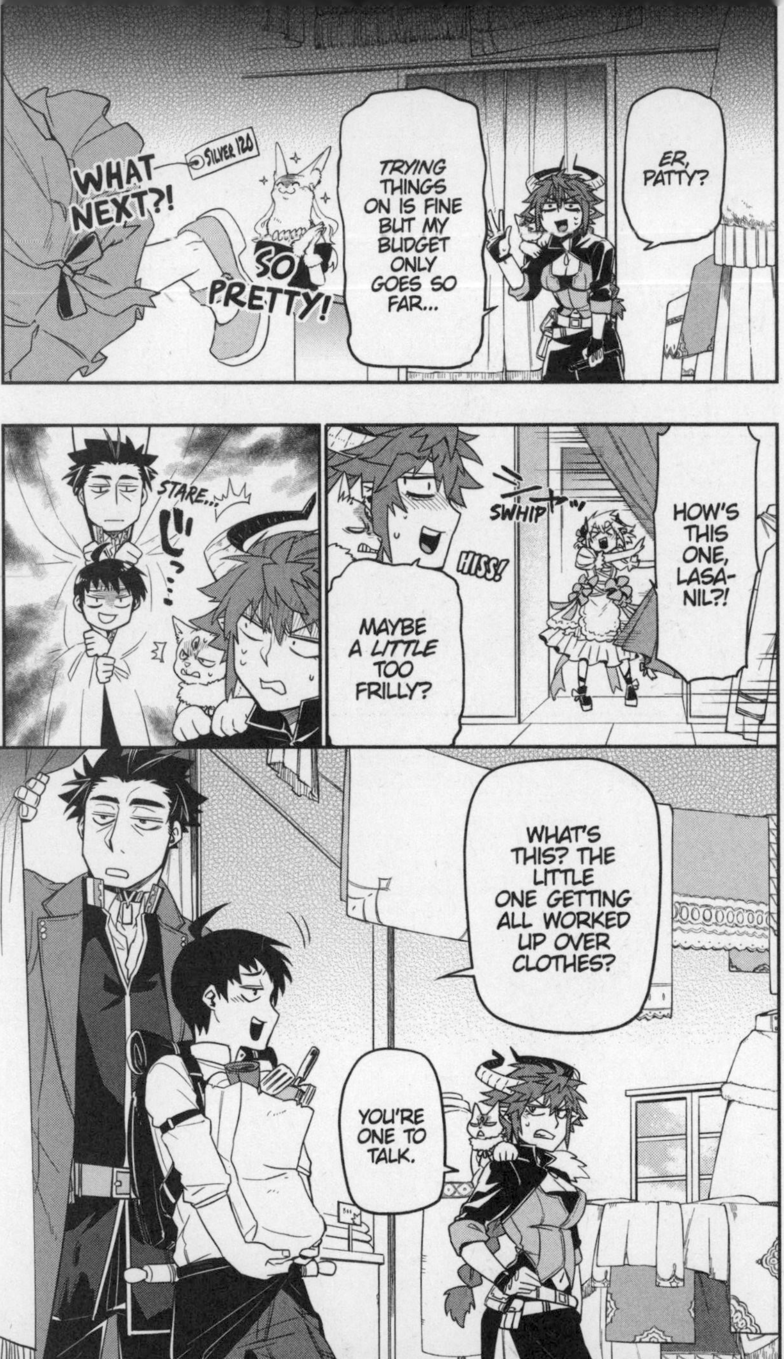
ER, PATTY?
TRYING THINGS ON IS FINE BUT MY BUDGET ONLY GOES SO FAR...
SILVER 120
WHAT NEXT?!
SO PRETTY!
HOW'S THIS ONE, LASA-NIL?!
SWHIP
HISS!
MAYBE A *LITTLE* TOO FRILLY?
STARE...
WHAT'S THIS? THE LITTLE ONE GETTING ALL WORKED UP OVER CLOTHES?
YOU'RE ONE TO TALK.

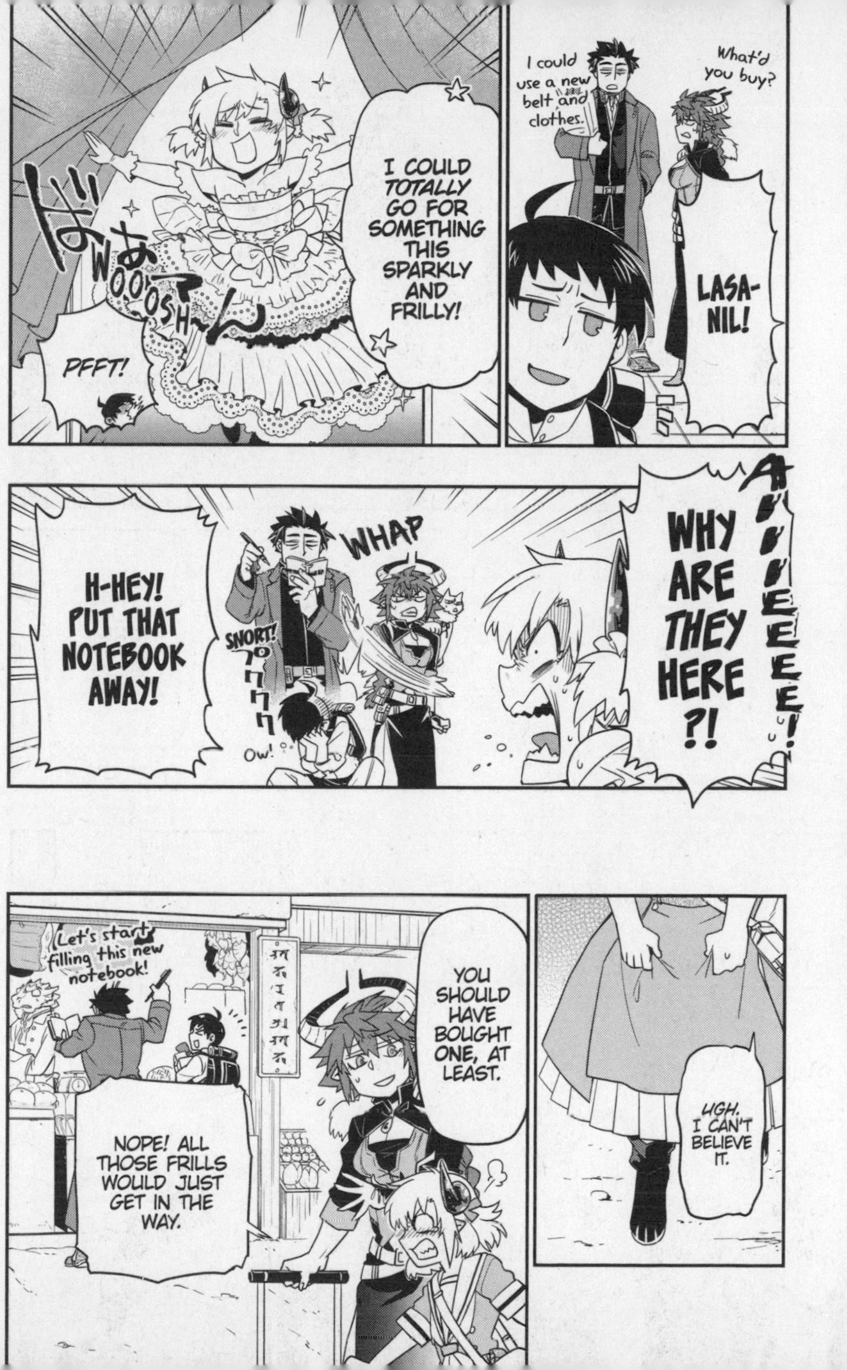
What'd you buy?
I could use a new belt and clothes.
LASA-NIL!
I COULD TOTALLY GO FOR SOMETHING THIS SPARKLY AND FRILLY!
WOOOOSH
PFFT!
AIIIEEEEE!
WHY ARE THEY HERE?!
WHAP
H-HEY! PUT THAT NOTEBOOK AWAY!
SNORT!
Ow!
UGH. I CAN'T BELIEVE IT.
YOU SHOULD HAVE BOUGHT ONE, AT LEAST.
NOPE! ALL THOSE FRILLS WOULD JUST GET IN THE WAY.
Let's start filling this new notebook!

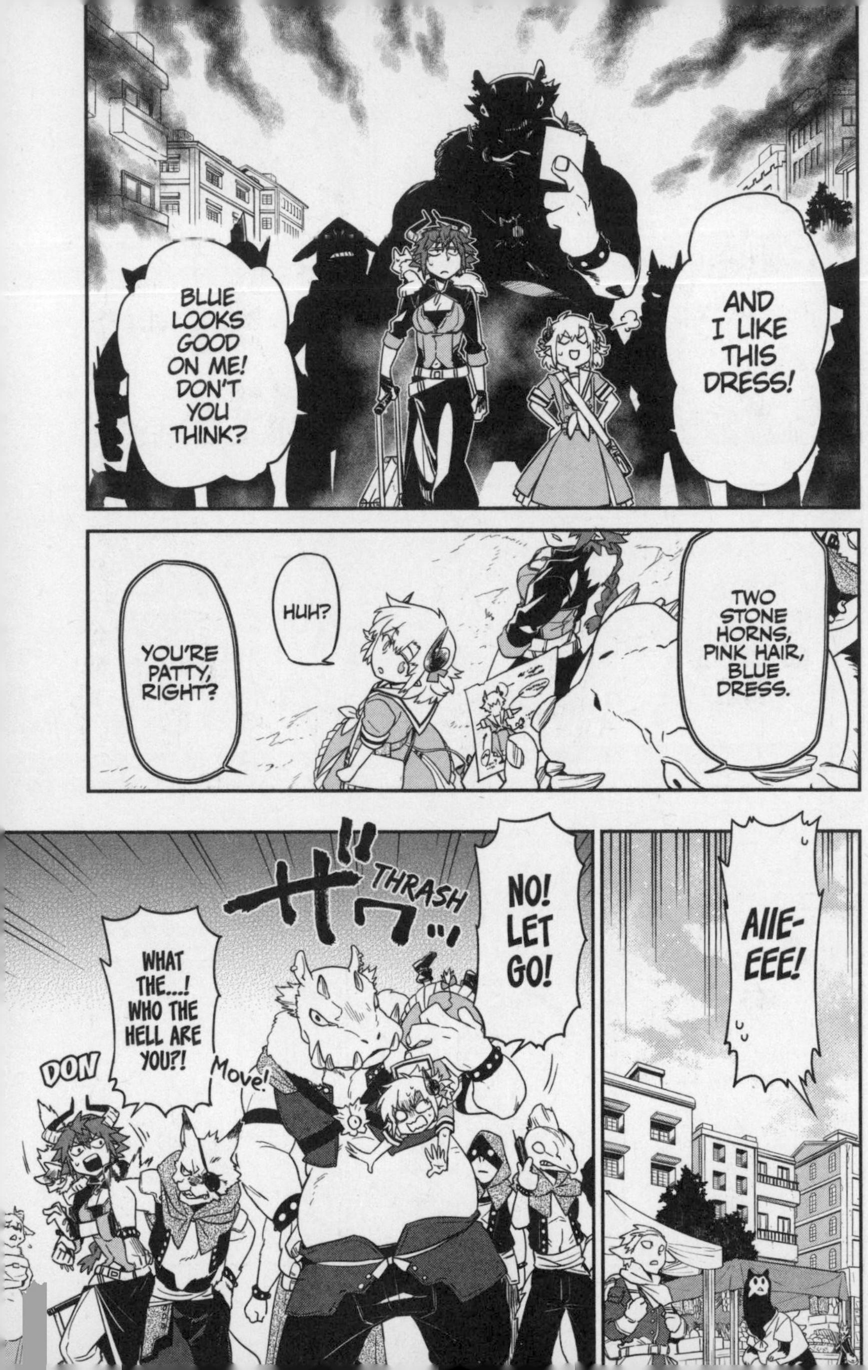
BLUE LOOKS GOOD ON ME! DON'T YOU THINK?
AND I LIKE THIS DRESS!
TWO STONE HORNS, PINK HAIR, BLUE DRESS.
HUH?
YOU'RE PATTY, RIGHT?
AIIE-EEE!
NO! LET GO!
ザワッ
THRASH
WHAT THE...! WHO THE HELL ARE YOU?!
Move!
DON

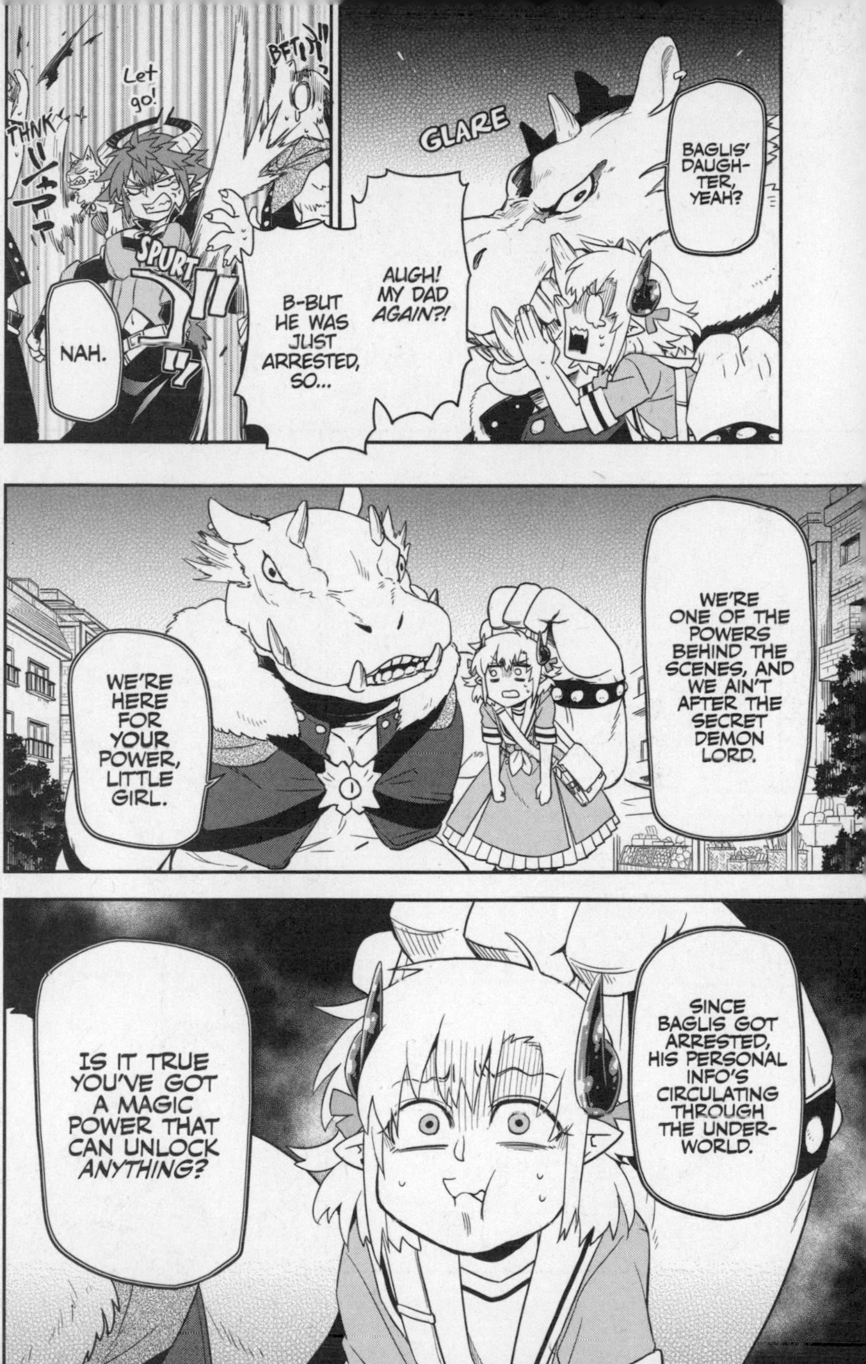
BAGLIS' DAUGHTER, YEAH?
GLARE
AUGH! MY DAD AGAIN?!
B-BUT HE WAS JUST ARRESTED, SO...
BFT!
Let go!
THNK
SPURT
NAH.
WE'RE ONE OF THE POWERS BEHIND THE SCENES, AND WE AIN'T AFTER THE SECRET DEMON LORD.
WE'RE HERE FOR YOUR POWER, LITTLE GIRL.
SINCE BAGLIS GOT ARRESTED, HIS PERSONAL INFO'S CIRCULATING THROUGH THE UNDERWORLD.
IS IT TRUE YOU'VE GOT A MAGIC POWER THAT CAN UNLOCK *ANYTHING*?

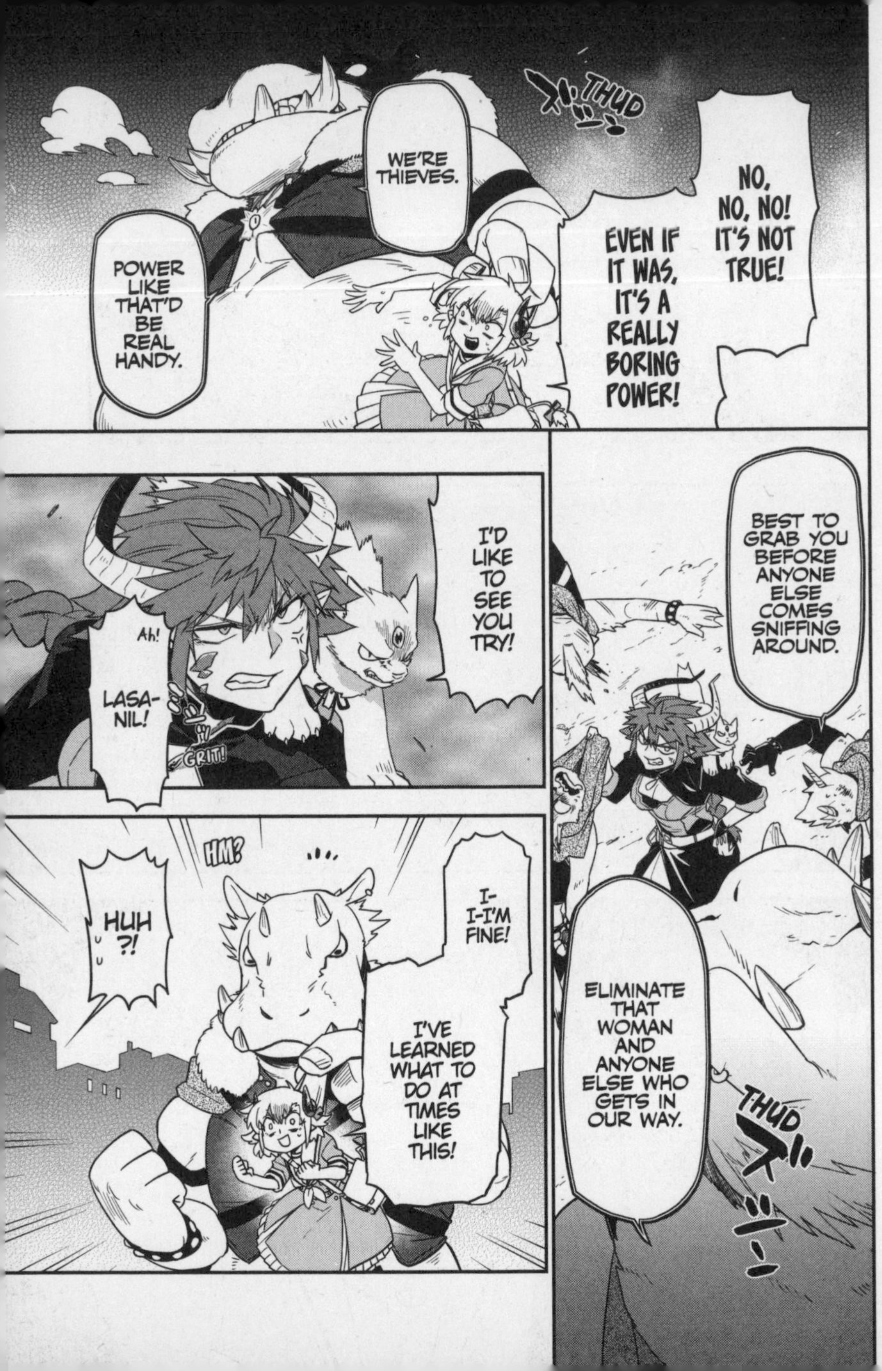
THUD
NO, NO, NO! IT'S NOT TRUE!
EVEN IF IT WAS, IT'S A REALLY BORING POWER!
WE'RE THIEVES.
POWER LIKE THAT'D BE REAL HANDY.
BEST TO GRAB YOU BEFORE ANYONE ELSE COMES SNIFFING AROUND.
ELIMINATE THAT WOMAN AND ANYONE ELSE WHO GETS IN OUR WAY.
THUD
I'D LIKE TO SEE YOU TRY!
Ah!
LASA-NIL!
GRIT!
I- I-I'M FINE!
I'VE LEARNED WHAT TO DO AT TIMES LIKE THIS!
HM?
HUH ?!

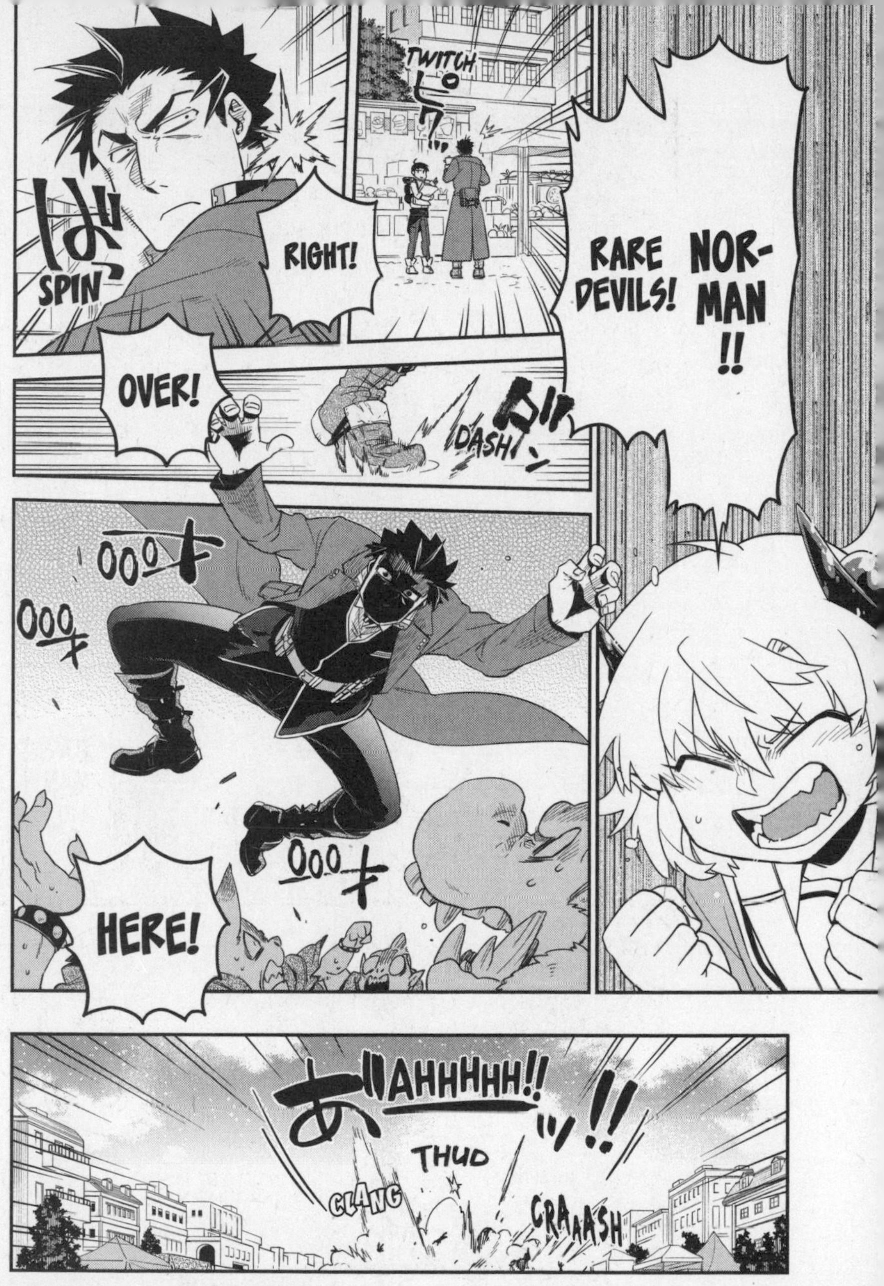
NOR-MAN!!
RARE DEVILS!
TWITCH
RIGHT!
SPIN
OVER!
DASH
OOO
OOO
OOO
HERE!
AHHHHH!!
THUD
CLANG
CRAAASH

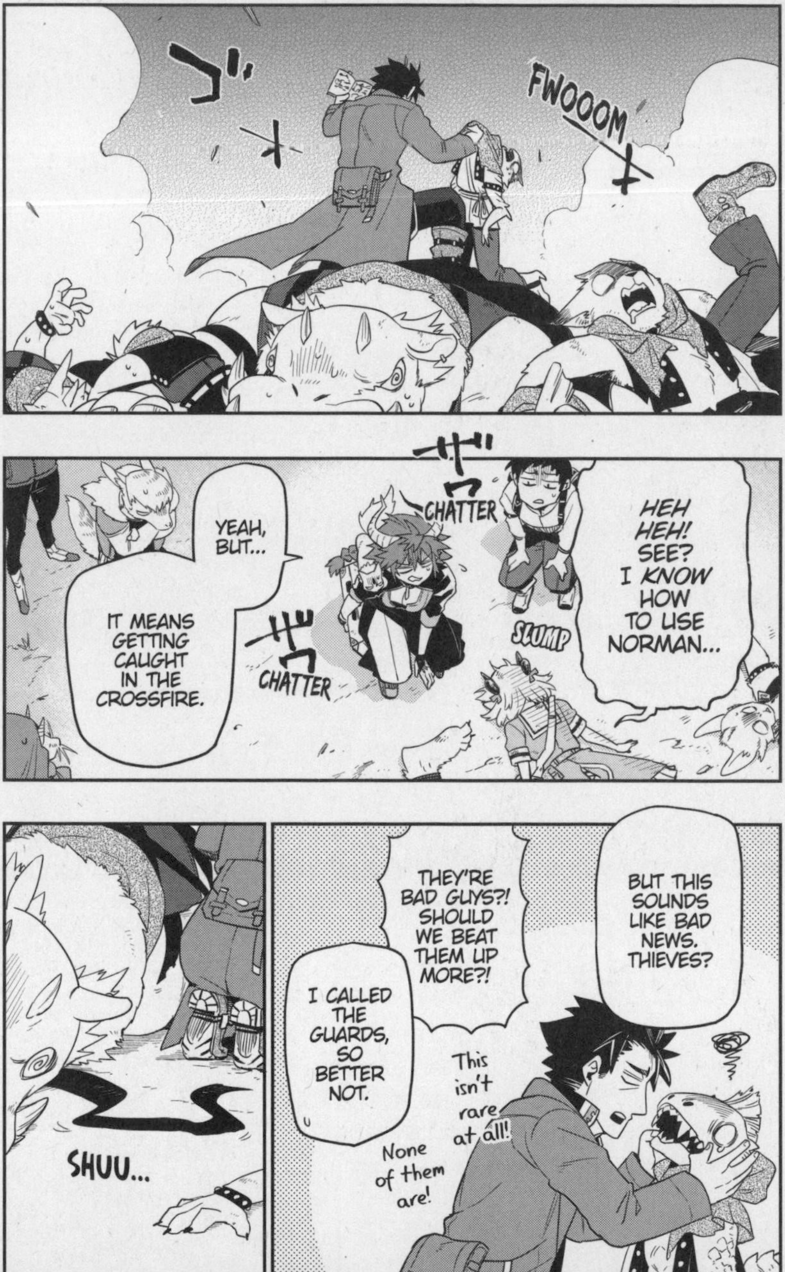
FWOOOM
HEH HEH! SEE? I KNOW HOW TO USE NORMAN...
SLUMP
CHATTER
YEAH, BUT...
IT MEANS GETTING CAUGHT IN THE CROSSFIRE.
CHATTER
BUT THIS SOUNDS LIKE BAD NEWS. THIEVES?
THEY'RE BAD GUYS?! SHOULD WE BEAT THEM UP MORE?!
I CALLED THE GUARDS, SO BETTER NOT.
This isn't rare at all!
None of them are!
SHUU...

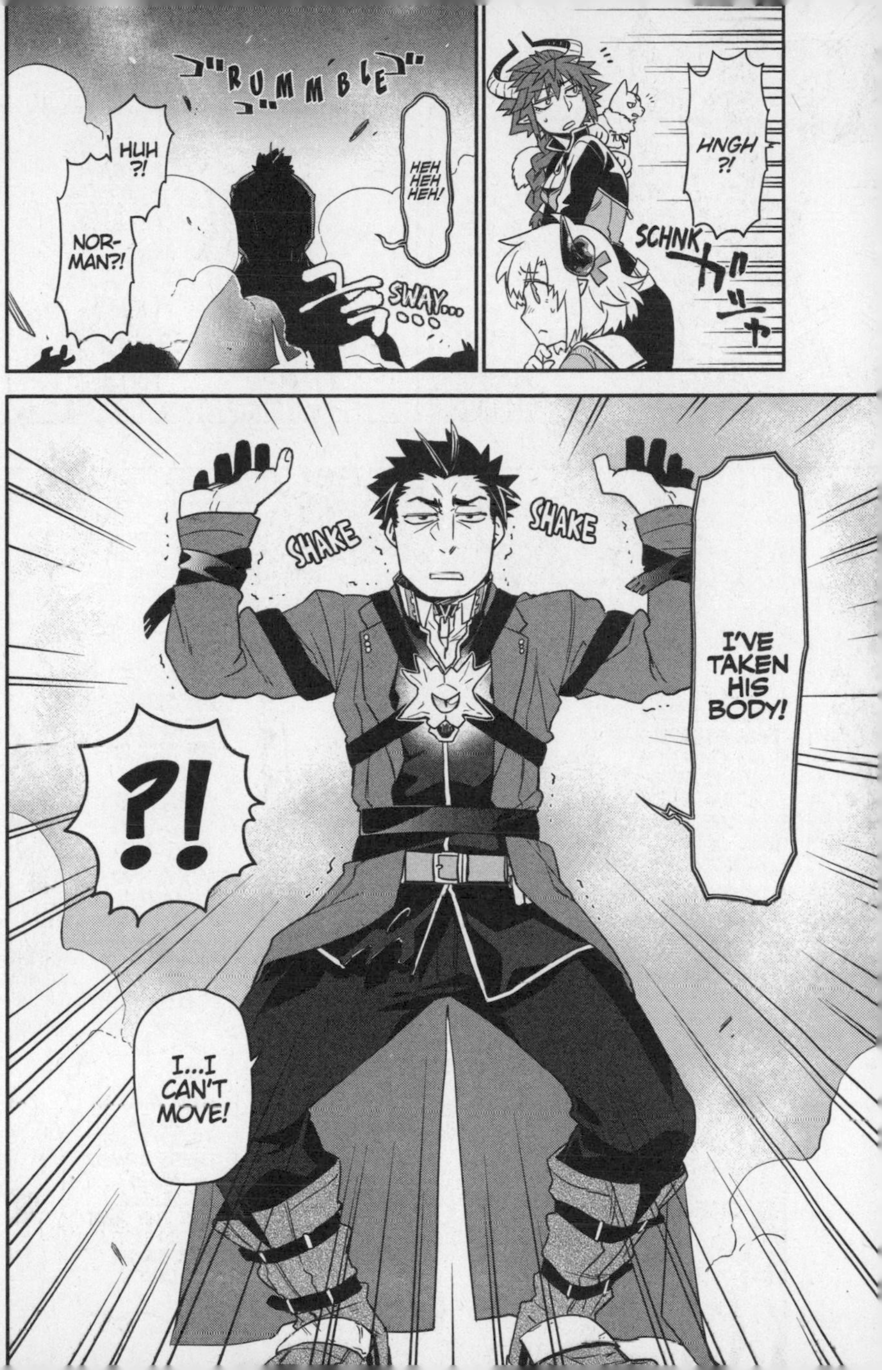
HNGH?!
SCHNK
RUMMBLE
HEH HEH HEH!
HUH?!
NOR-MAN?!
SWAY...
I'VE TAKEN HIS BODY!
SHAKE
SHAKE
?!
I...I CAN'T MOVE!

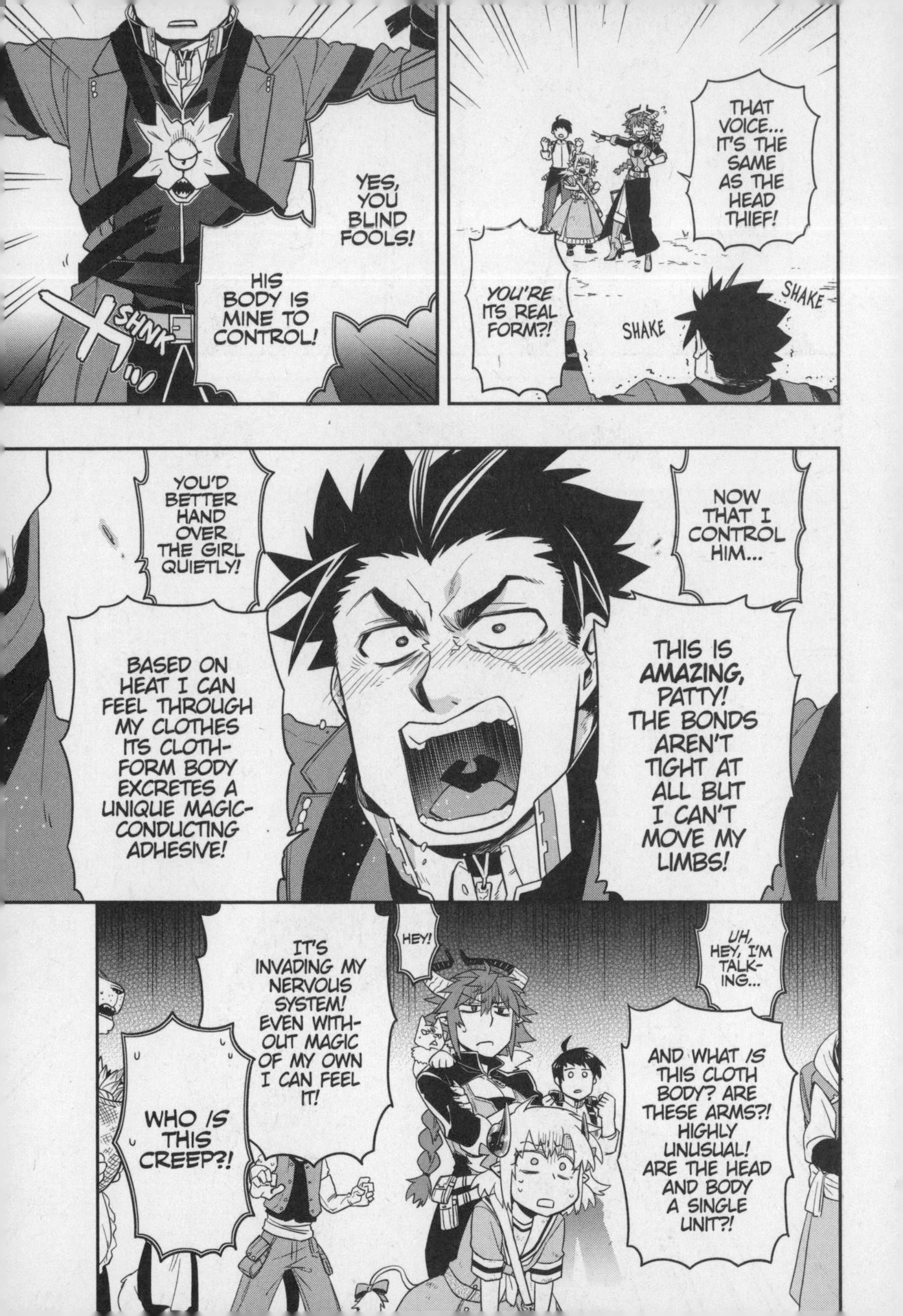
THAT VOICE... IT'S THE SAME AS THE HEAD THIEF!
YOU'RE ITS REAL FORM?!
SHAKE
SHAKE
YES, YOU BLIND FOOLS!
HIS BODY IS MINE TO CONTROL!
SHNK
NOW THAT I CONTROL HIM...
YOU'D BETTER HAND OVER THE GIRL QUIETLY!
THIS IS AMAZING, PATTY! THE BONDS AREN'T TIGHT AT ALL BUT I CAN'T MOVE MY LIMBS!
BASED ON HEAT I CAN FEEL THROUGH MY CLOTHES ITS CLOTH-FORM BODY EXCRETES A UNIQUE MAGIC-CONDUCTING ADHESIVE!
UH, HEY, I'M TALKING...
HEY!
IT'S INVADING MY NERVOUS SYSTEM! EVEN WITHOUT MAGIC OF MY OWN I CAN FEEL IT!
AND WHAT IS THIS CLOTH BODY? ARE THESE ARMS?! HIGHLY UNUSUAL! ARE THE HEAD AND BODY A SINGLE UNIT?!
WHO IS THIS CREEP?!

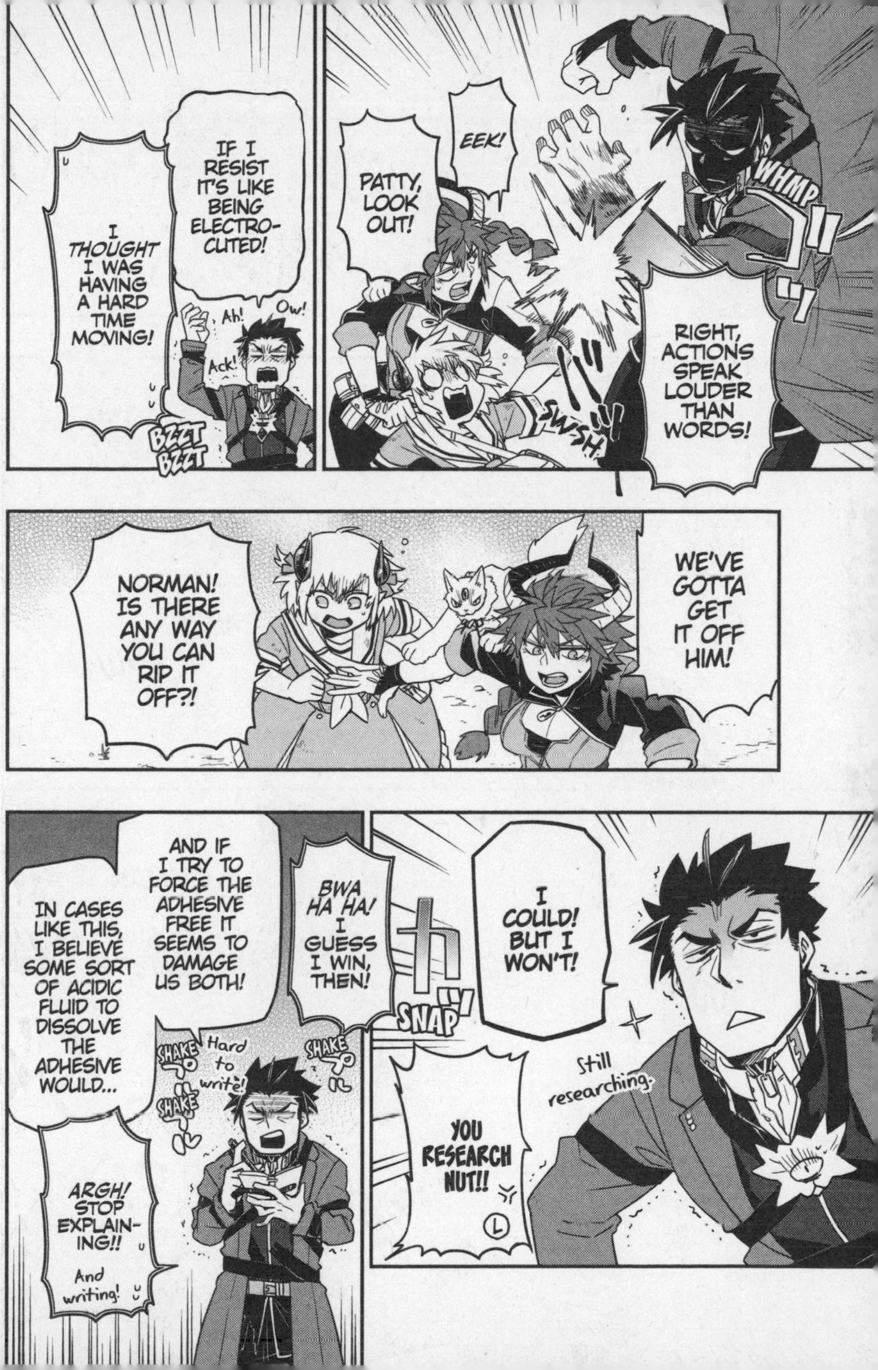
WHMP
RIGHT, ACTIONS SPEAK LOUDER THAN WORDS!
SWISH
EEK!
PATTY, LOOK OUT!
IF I RESIST IT'S LIKE BEING ELECTROCUTED!
Ow!
Ah!
Ack!
I THOUGHT I WAS HAVING A HARD TIME MOVING!
BZZT BZZT
WE'VE GOTTA GET IT OFF HIM!
NORMAN! IS THERE ANY WAY YOU CAN RIP IT OFF?!
I COULD! BUT I WON'T!
SNAP
Still researching.
YOU RESEARCH NUT!!
BWA HA HA! I GUESS I WIN, THEN!
AND IF I TRY TO FORCE THE ADHESIVE FREE IT SEEMS TO DAMAGE US BOTH!
IN CASES LIKE THIS, I BELIEVE SOME SORT OF ACIDIC FLUID TO DISSOLVE THE ADHESIVE WOULD...
SHAKE
Hard to write!
SHAKE
SHAKE
ARGH! STOP EXPLAINING!!
And writing!

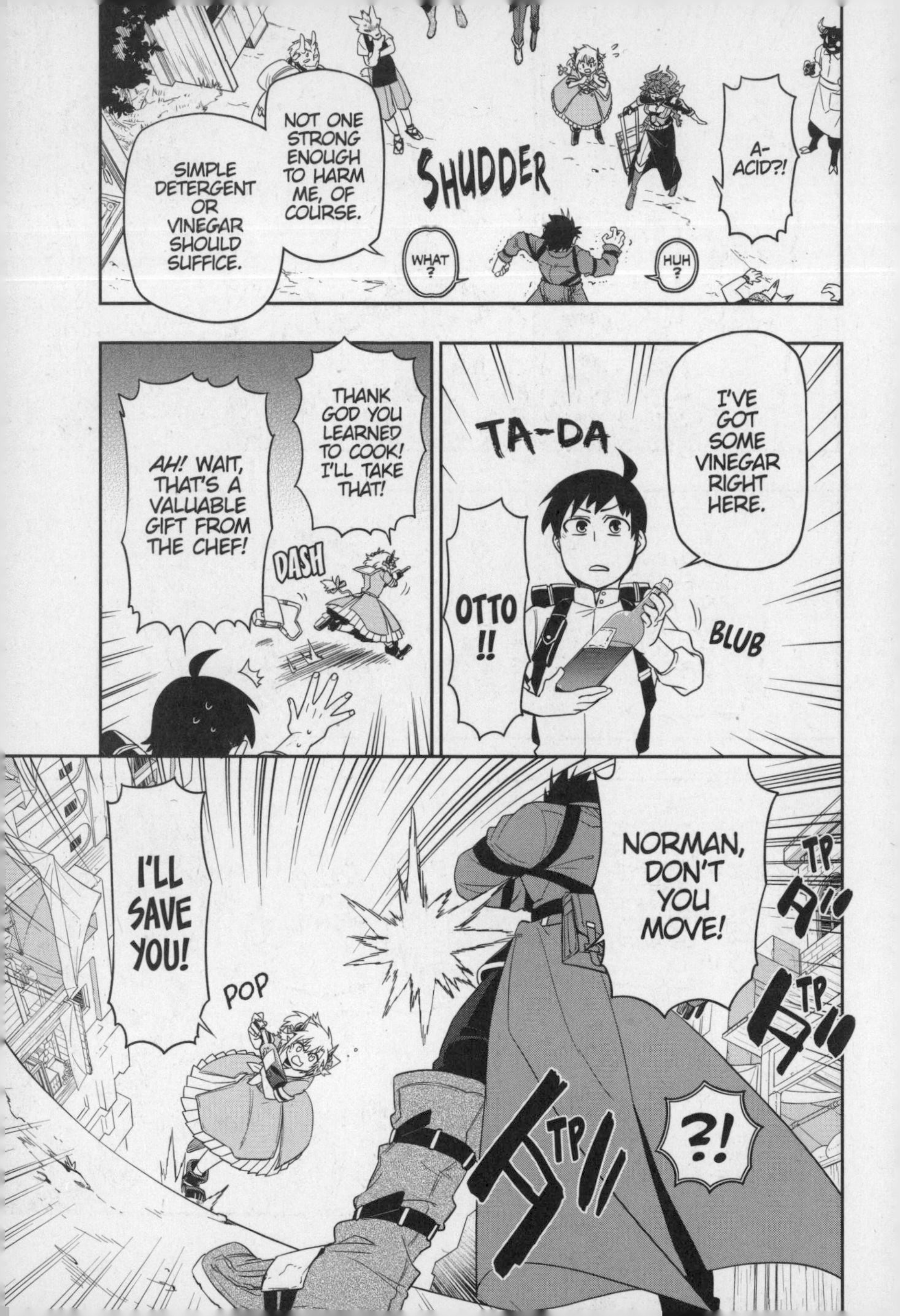
A- ACID?!
NOT ONE STRONG ENOUGH TO HARM ME, OF COURSE.
SIMPLE DETERGENT OR VINEGAR SHOULD SUFFICE.
SHUDDER
HUH?
WHAT?
I'VE GOT SOME VINEGAR RIGHT HERE.
TA-DA
OTTO!!
BLUB
THANK GOD YOU LEARNED TO COOK! I'LL TAKE THAT!
AH! WAIT, THAT'S A VALUABLE GIFT FROM THE CHEF!
DASH
NORMAN, DON'T YOU MOVE!
TP
TP
?!
TP
I'LL SAVE YOU!
POP

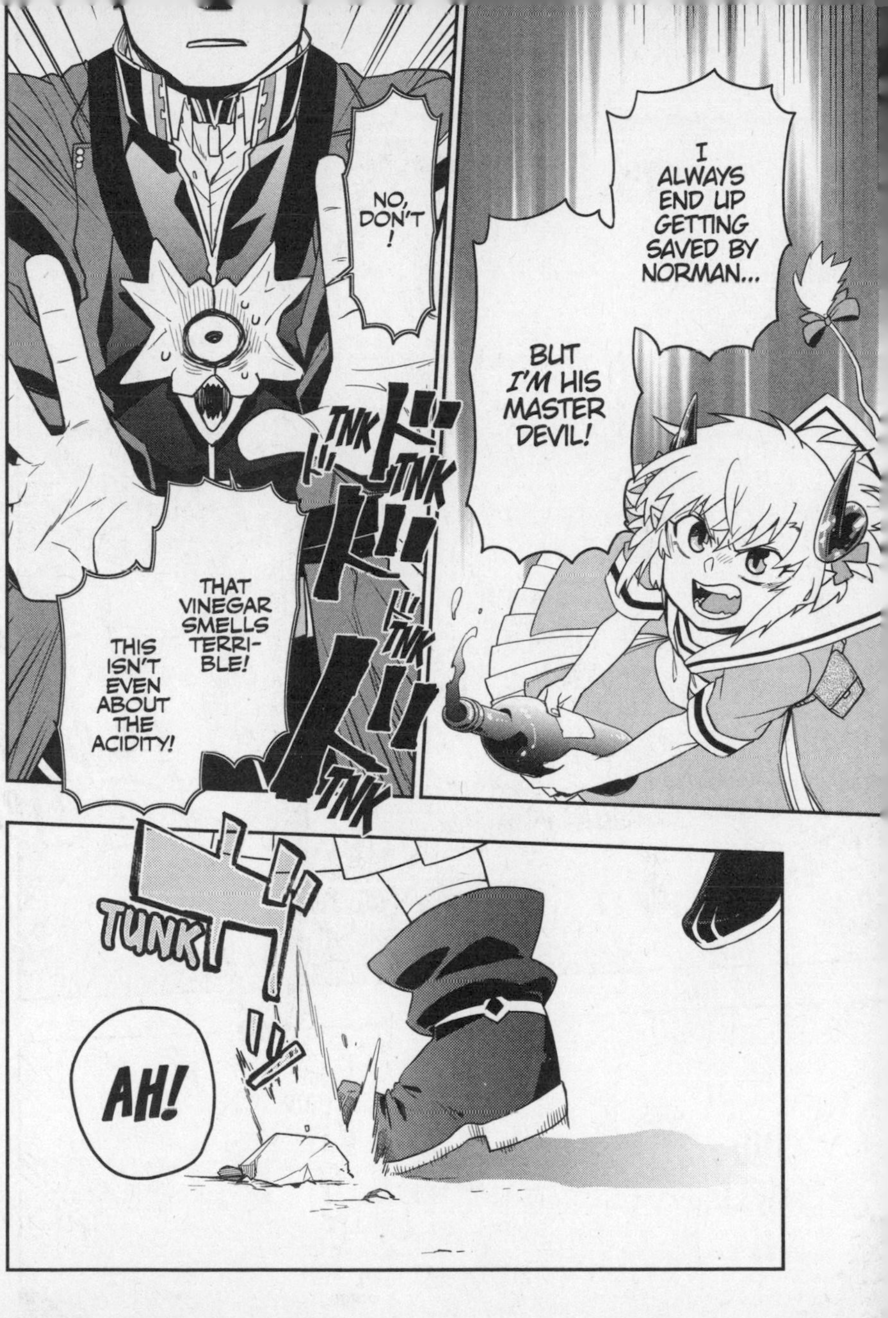
I ALWAYS END UP GETTING SAVED BY NORMAN...
BUT I'M HIS MASTER DEVIL!
TNK
TNK
TNK
TNK
NO, DON'T!
THAT VINEGAR SMELLS TERRIBLE!
THIS ISN'T EVEN ABOUT THE ACIDITY!
TUNK
AH!

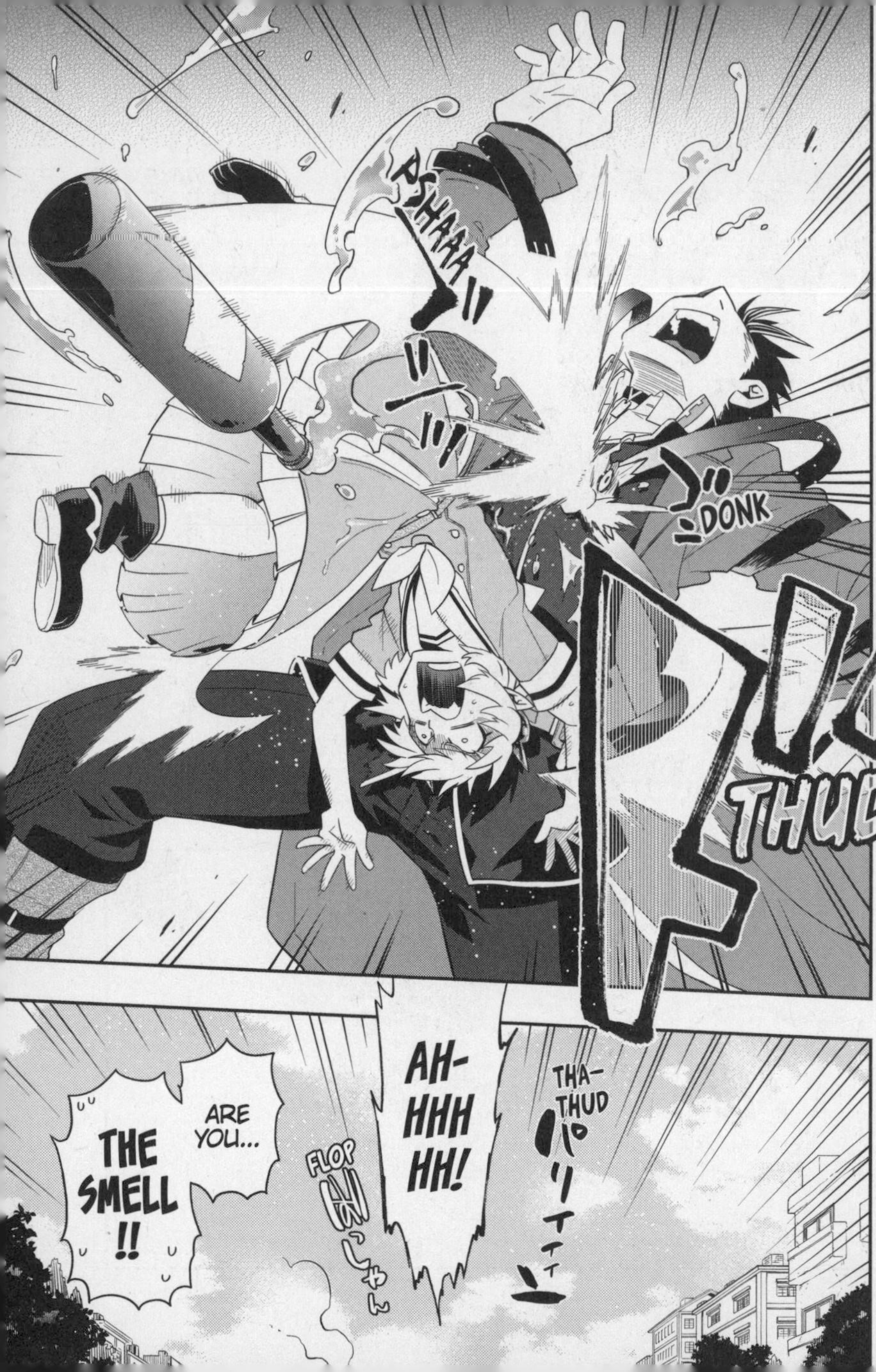
PSHAAA
DONK
THUD
THA-THUD
AH-HHHHH!
FLOP
ARE YOU...
THE SMELL!!

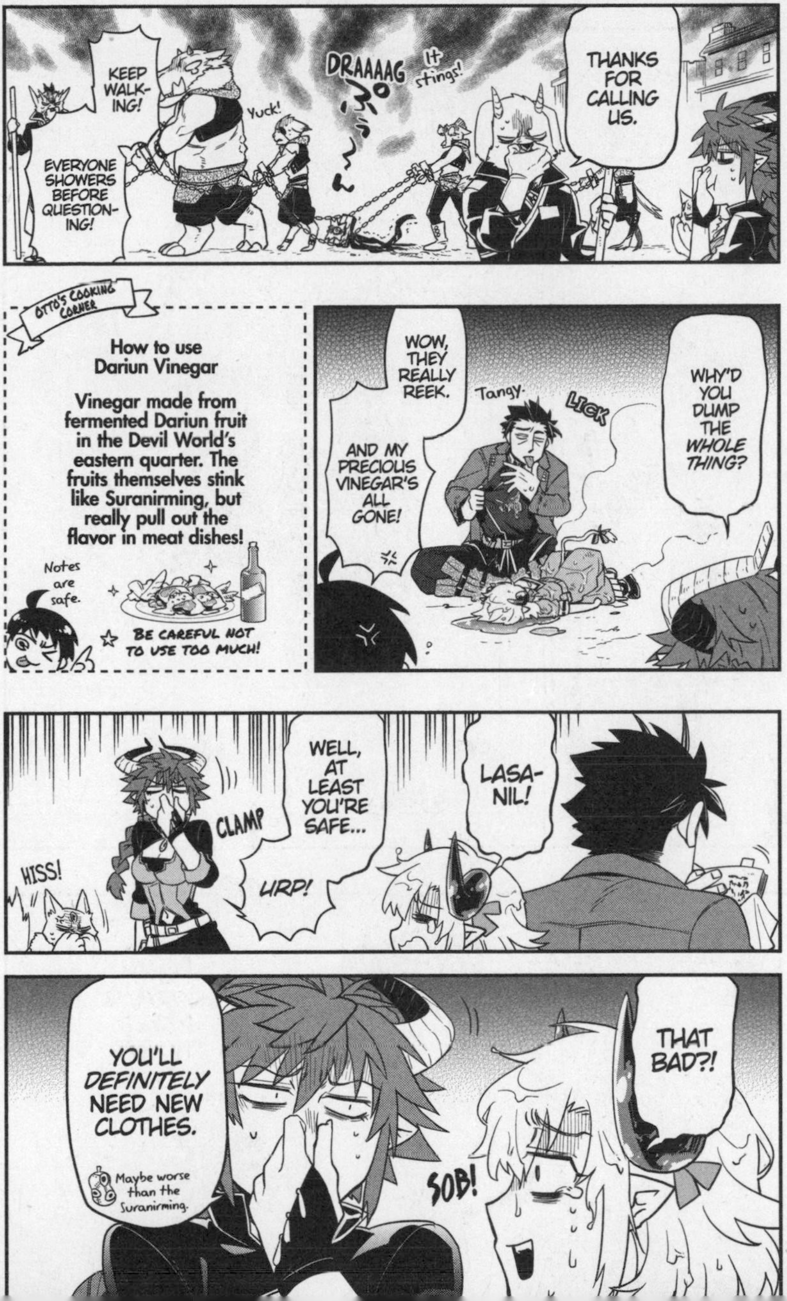
THANKS FOR CALLING US.
It stings!
DRAAAAG
ぷ〜ん
Yuck!
KEEP WALKING!
EVERYONE SHOWERS BEFORE QUESTIONING!
WHY'D YOU DUMP THE WHOLE THING?
LICK
Tangy.
WOW, THEY REALLY REEK.
AND MY PRECIOUS VINEGAR'S ALL GONE!
OTTO'S COOKING CORNER
How to use Dariun Vinegar
Vinegar made from fermented Dariun fruit in the Devil World's eastern quarter. The fruits themselves stink like Suranirming, but really pull out the flavor in meat dishes!
Notes are safe.
BE CAREFUL NOT TO USE TOO MUCH!
LASA-NIL!
WELL, AT LEAST YOU'RE SAFE...
URP!
CLAMP
HISS!
THAT BAD?!
SOB!
YOU'LL DEFINITELY NEED NEW CLOTHES.
Maybe worse than the Suranirming.

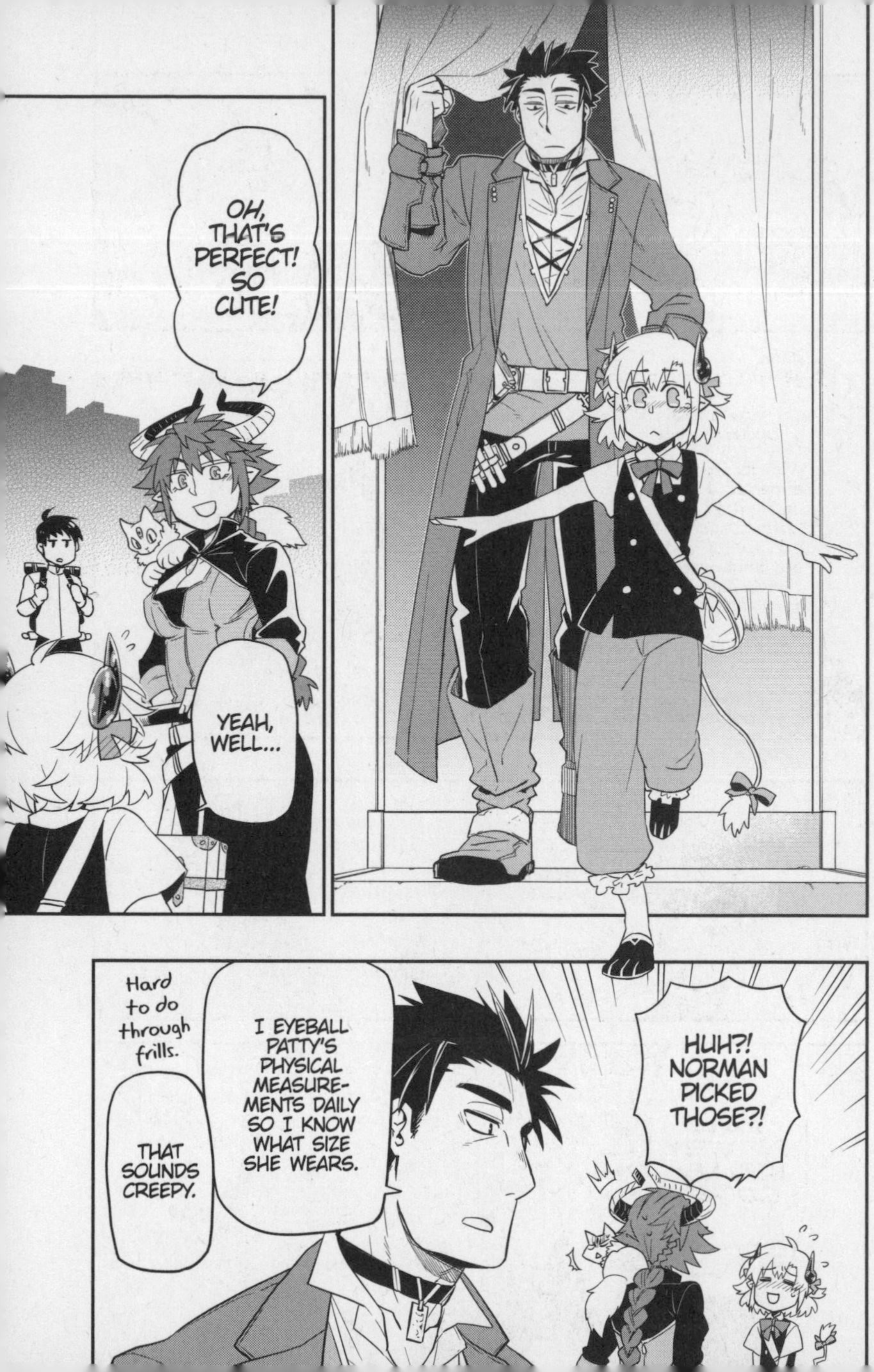
OH, THAT'S PERFECT! SO CUTE!
YEAH, WELL...
HUH?! NORMAN PICKED THOSE?!
I EYEBALL PATTY'S PHYSICAL MEASUREMENTS DAILY SO I KNOW WHAT SIZE SHE WEARS.
Hard to do through frills.
THAT SOUNDS CREEPY.

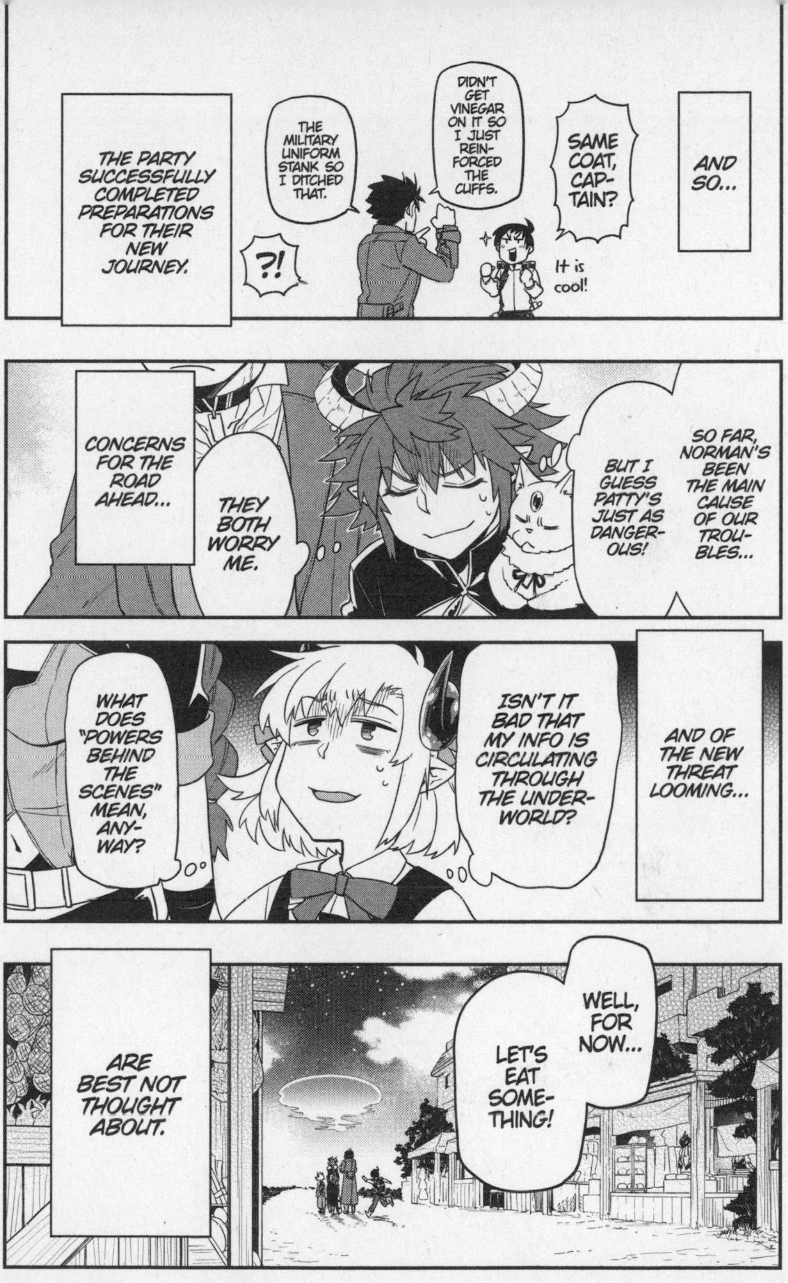
AND SO...
SAME COAT, CAPTAIN?
It is cool!
DIDN'T GET VINEGAR ON IT SO I JUST REINFORCED THE CUFFS.
THE MILITARY UNIFORM STANK SO I DITCHED THAT.
?!
THE PARTY SUCCESSFULLY COMPLETED PREPARATIONS FOR THEIR NEW JOURNEY.
SO FAR, NORMAN'S BEEN THE MAIN CAUSE OF OUR TROUBLES...
BUT I GUESS PATTY'S JUST AS DANGEROUS!
THEY BOTH WORRY ME.
CONCERNS FOR THE ROAD AHEAD...
AND OF THE NEW THREAT LOOMING...
ISN'T IT BAD THAT MY INFO IS CIRCULATING THROUGH THE UNDERWORLD?
WHAT DOES "POWERS BEHIND THE SCENES" MEAN, ANYWAY?
WELL, FOR NOW...
LET'S EAT SOMETHING!
ARE BEST NOT THOUGHT ABOUT.

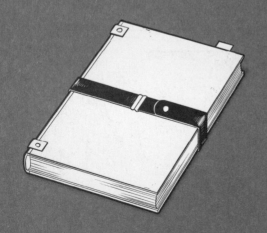

Sorry For My Familiar

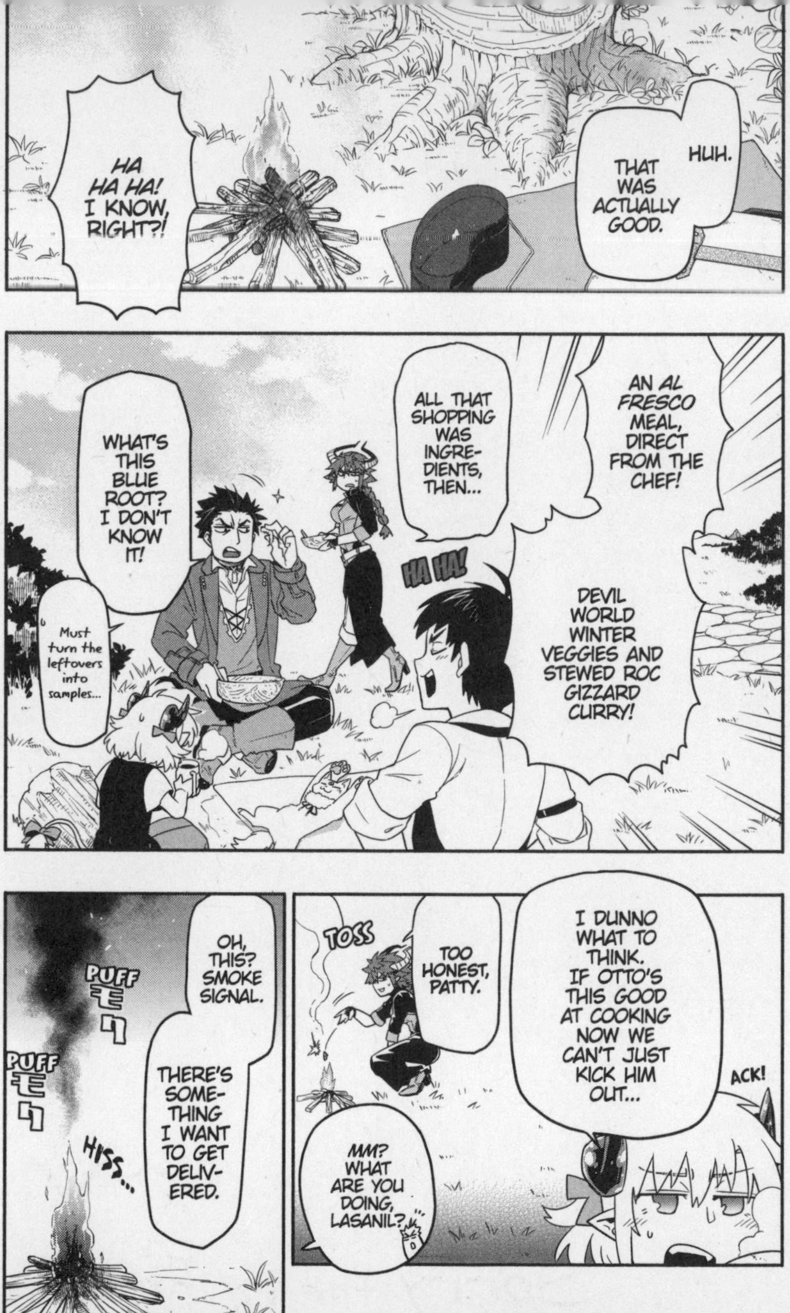
HUH.
THAT WAS ACTUALLY GOOD.
HA HA HA! I KNOW, RIGHT?!
AN AL FRESCO MEAL, DIRECT FROM THE CHEF!
DEVIL WORLD WINTER VEGGIES AND STEWED ROC GIZZARD CURRY!
HA HA!
ALL THAT SHOPPING WAS INGRE-DIENTS, THEN...
WHAT'S THIS BLUE ROOT? I DON'T KNOW IT!
Must turn the leftovers into samples...
I DUNNO WHAT TO THINK. IF OTTO'S THIS GOOD AT COOKING NOW WE CAN'T JUST KICK HIM OUT...
ACK!
TOO HONEST, PATTY.
TOSS
MM? WHAT ARE YOU DOING, LASANIL?
OH, THIS? SMOKE SIGNAL.
THERE'S SOME-THING I WANT TO GET DELIV-ERED.
PUFF モク
PUFF モク
HISS...

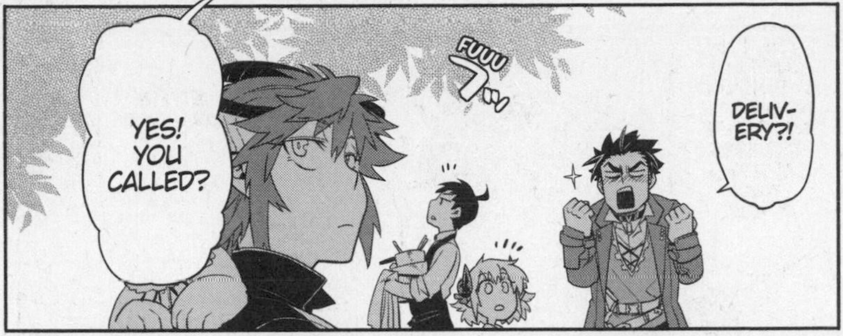
DELIV-ERY?!
FUUU
YES! YOU CALLED?

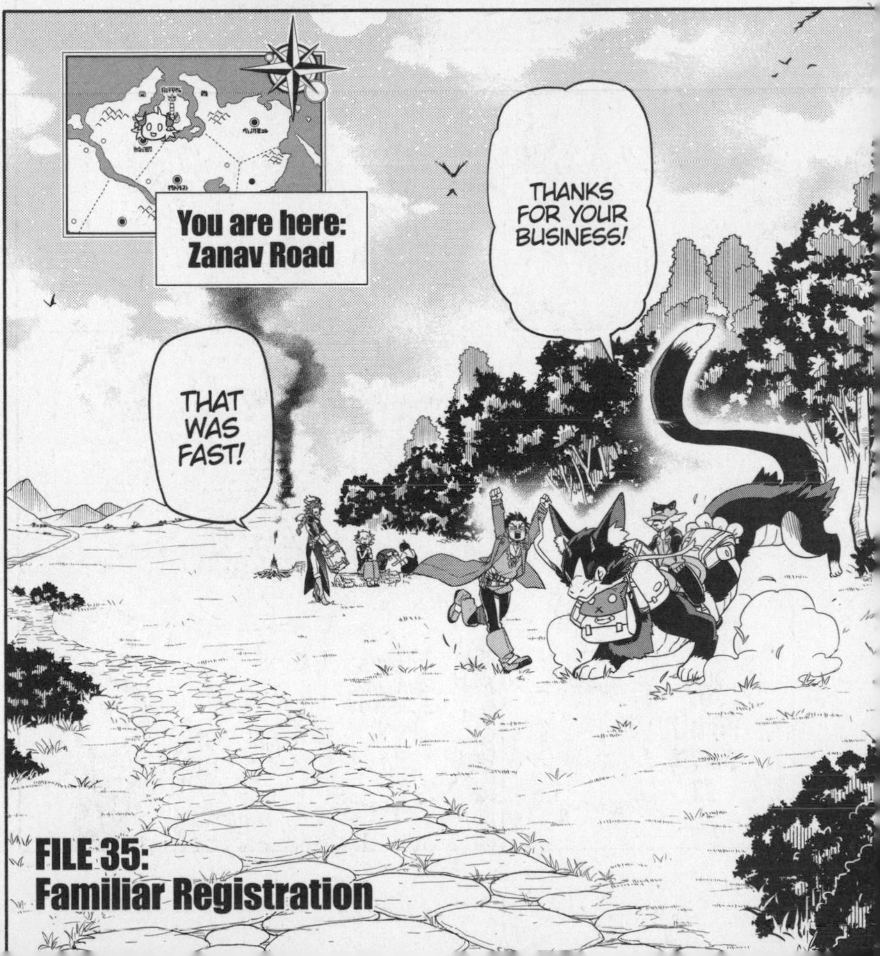
THANKS FOR YOUR BUSINESS!
You are here: Zanav Road
THAT WAS FAST!

FILE 35: Familiar Registration

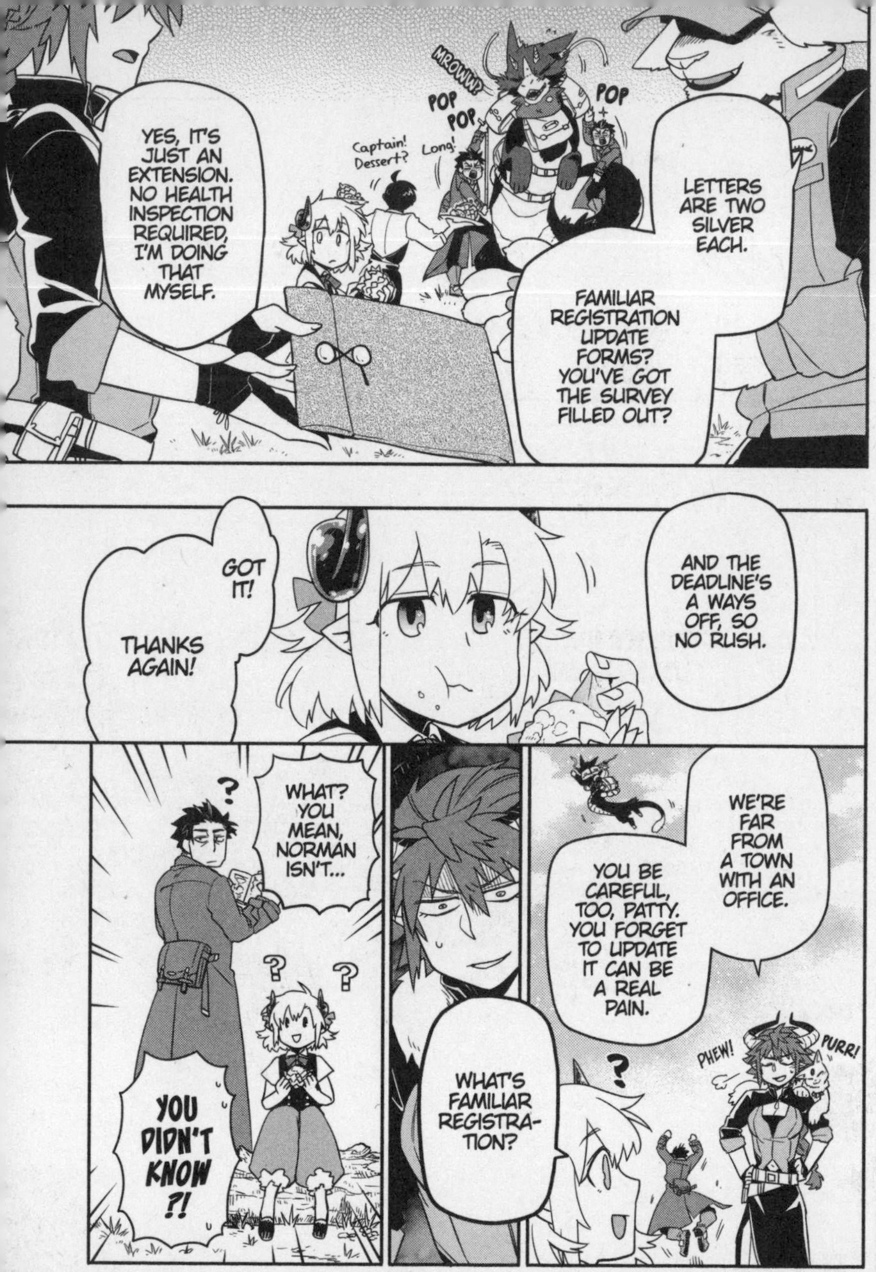
LETTERS ARE TWO SILVER EACH.
FAMILIAR REGISTRATION UPDATE FORMS? YOU'VE GOT THE SURVEY FILLED OUT?
MROWW!
POP
POP POP
Long!
Captain! Dessert?
YES, IT'S JUST AN EXTENSION. NO HEALTH INSPECTION REQUIRED, I'M DOING THAT MYSELF.
AND THE DEADLINE'S A WAYS OFF, SO NO RUSH.
GOT IT!
THANKS AGAIN!
WE'RE FAR FROM A TOWN WITH AN OFFICE.
YOU BE CAREFUL, TOO, PATTY. YOU FORGET TO UPDATE IT CAN BE A REAL PAIN.
PURR!
PHEW!
WHAT'S FAMILIAR REGISTRA-TION?
WHAT? YOU MEAN, NORMAN ISN'T...
YOU DIDN'T KNOW?!

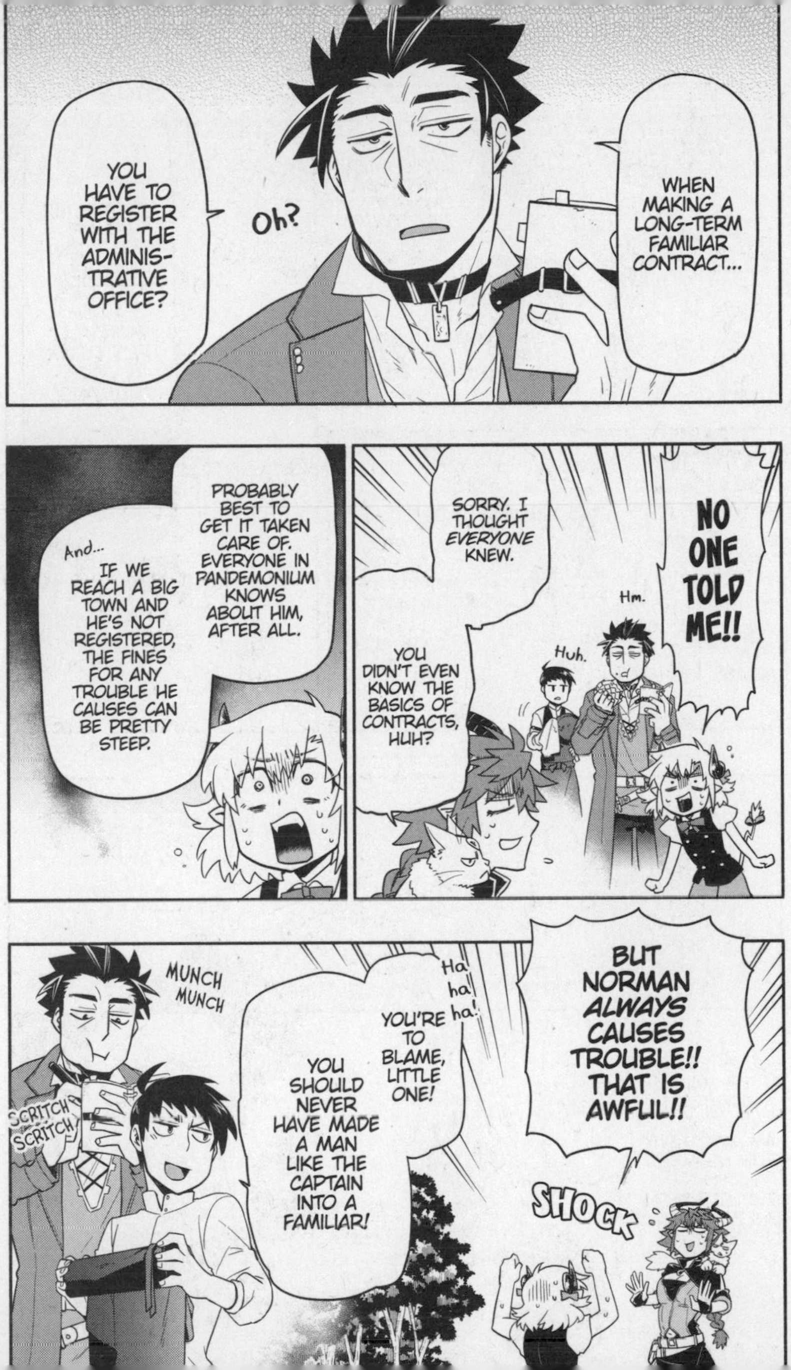
WHEN MAKING A LONG-TERM FAMILIAR CONTRACT...
Oh?
YOU HAVE TO REGISTER WITH THE ADMINIS-TRATIVE OFFICE?
NO ONE TOLD ME!!
SORRY. I THOUGHT *EVERYONE* KNEW.
Hm.
Huh.
YOU DIDN'T EVEN KNOW THE BASICS OF CONTRACTS, HUH?
PROBABLY BEST TO GET IT TAKEN CARE OF. EVERYONE IN PANDEMONIUM KNOWS ABOUT HIM, AFTER ALL.
And... IF WE REACH A BIG TOWN AND HE'S NOT REGISTERED, THE FINES FOR ANY TROUBLE HE CAUSES CAN BE PRETTY STEEP.
BUT NORMAN *ALWAYS* CAUSES TROUBLE!! THAT IS AWFUL!!
SHOCK
Ha ha ha!
YOU'RE TO BLAME, LITTLE ONE!
YOU SHOULD NEVER HAVE MADE A MAN LIKE THE CAPTAIN INTO A FAMILIAR!
MUNCH MUNCH
SCRITCH SCRITCH

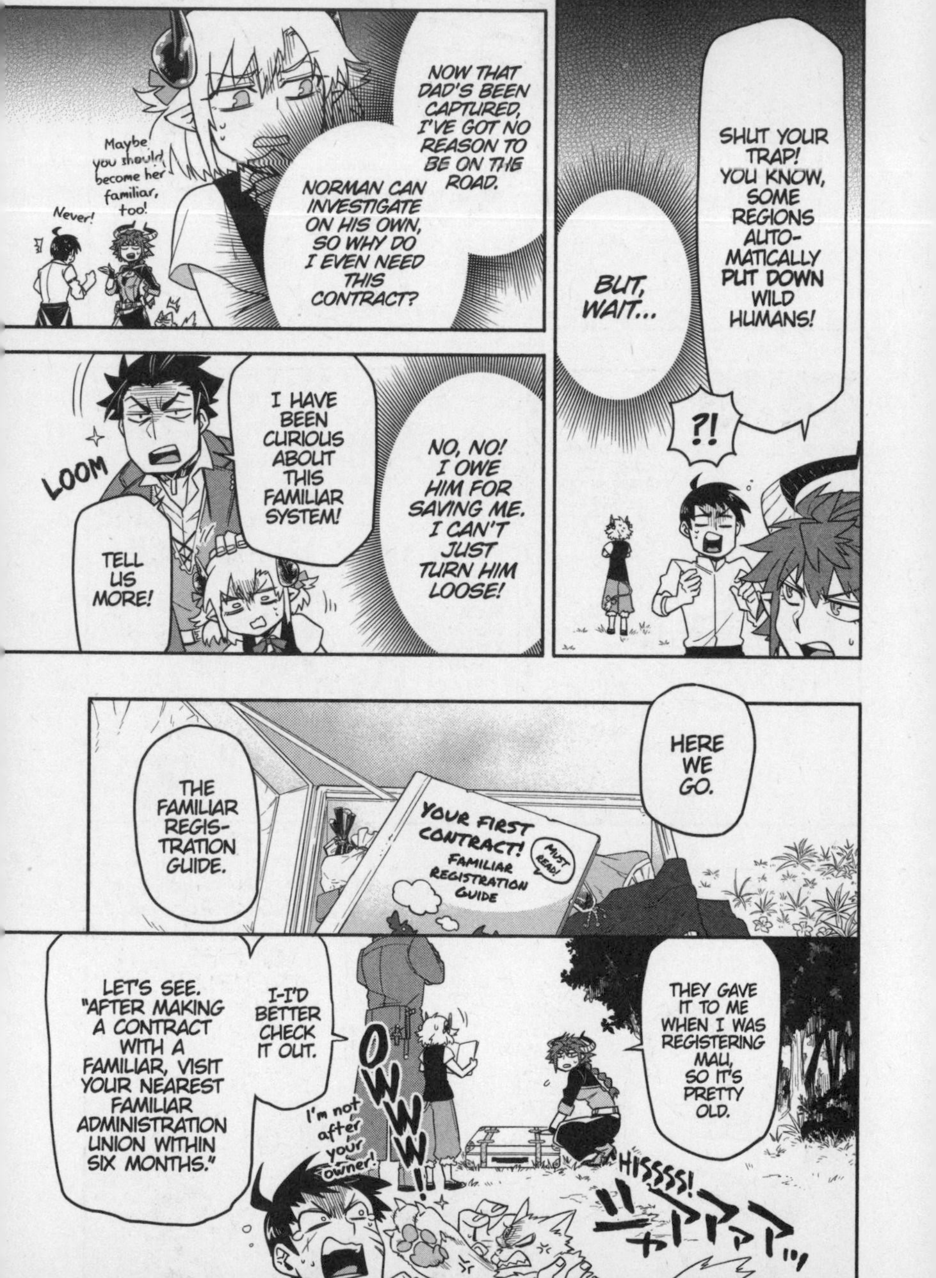
SHUT YOUR TRAP! YOU KNOW, SOME REGIONS AUTO-MATICALLY PUT DOWN WILD HUMANS!
BUT, WAIT...
?!
NOW THAT DAD'S BEEN CAPTURED, I'VE GOT NO REASON TO BE ON THE ROAD.
NORMAN CAN INVESTIGATE ON HIS OWN, SO WHY DO I EVEN NEED THIS CONTRACT?
Maybe you should become her familiar, too!
Never!
NO, NO! I OWE HIM FOR SAVING ME. I CAN'T JUST TURN HIM LOOSE!
I HAVE BEEN CURIOUS ABOUT THIS FAMILIAR SYSTEM!
LOOM
TELL US MORE!
HERE WE GO.
THE FAMILIAR REGIS-TRATION GUIDE.
YOUR FIRST CONTRACT! FAMILIAR REGISTRATION GUIDE
MUST READ!
THEY GAVE IT TO ME WHEN I WAS REGISTERING MAU, SO IT'S PRETTY OLD.
HISSSS!
I-I'D BETTER CHECK IT OUT.
OWWW!!
I'm not after your owner!
LET'S SEE. "AFTER MAKING A CONTRACT WITH A FAMILIAR, VISIT YOUR NEAREST FAMILIAR ADMINISTRATION UNION WITHIN SIX MONTHS."

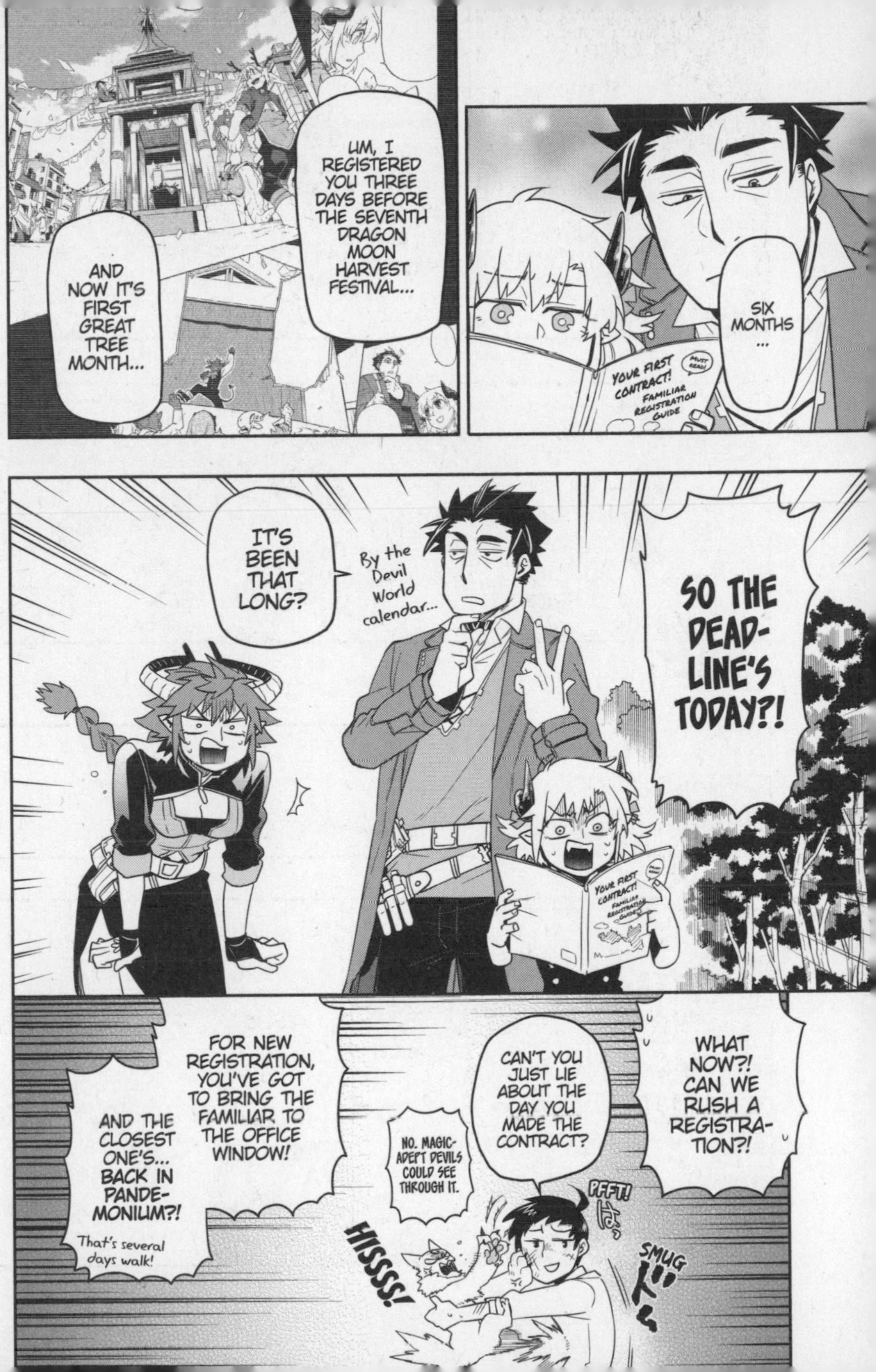
YOUR FIRST CONTRACT!
MUST READ!
FAMILIAR REGISTRATION GUIDE
SIX MONTHS ...
UM, I REGISTERED YOU THREE DAYS BEFORE THE SEVENTH DRAGON MOON HARVEST FESTIVAL...
AND NOW IT'S FIRST GREAT TREE MONTH...
SO THE DEAD-LINE'S TODAY?!
IT'S BEEN THAT LONG?
By the Devil World calendar...
WHAT NOW?! CAN WE RUSH A REGISTRA-TION?!
CAN'T YOU JUST LIE ABOUT THE DAY YOU MADE THE CONTRACT?
NO. MAGIC-ADEPT DEVILS COULD SEE THROUGH IT.
FOR NEW REGISTRATION, YOU'VE GOT TO BRING THE FAMILIAR TO THE OFFICE WINDOW!
AND THE CLOSEST ONE'S... BACK IN PANDE-MONIUM?!
That's several days walk!
PFFT!
SMUG
HISSSS!

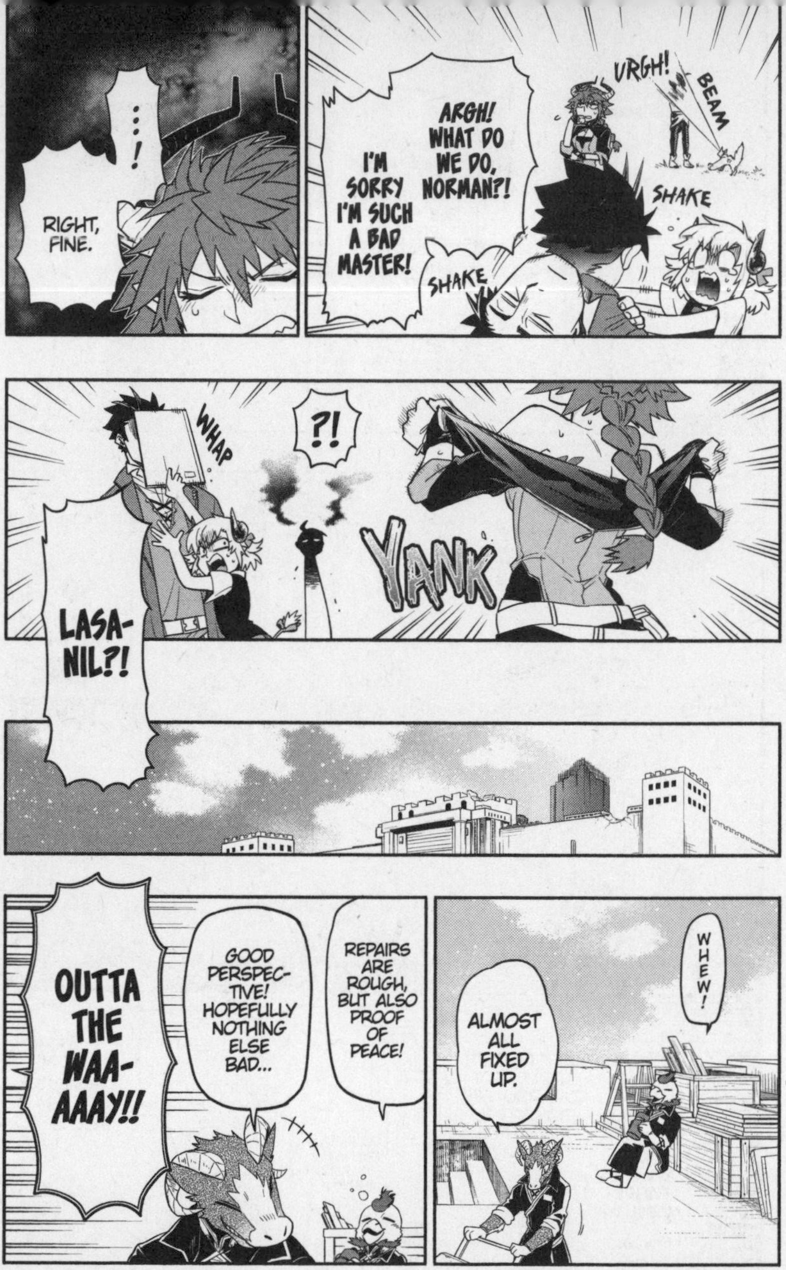
URGH!
BEAM
SHAKE
ARGH! WHAT DO WE DO, NORMAN?!
I'M SORRY I'M SUCH A BAD MASTER!
SHAKE
...!
RIGHT, FINE.
YANK
?!
WHAP
LASA-NIL?!
WHEW!
ALMOST ALL FIXED UP.
REPAIRS ARE ROUGH, BUT ALSO PROOF OF PEACE!
GOOD PERSPEC-TIVE! HOPEFULLY NOTHING ELSE BAD...
OUTTA THE WAA-AAAY!!

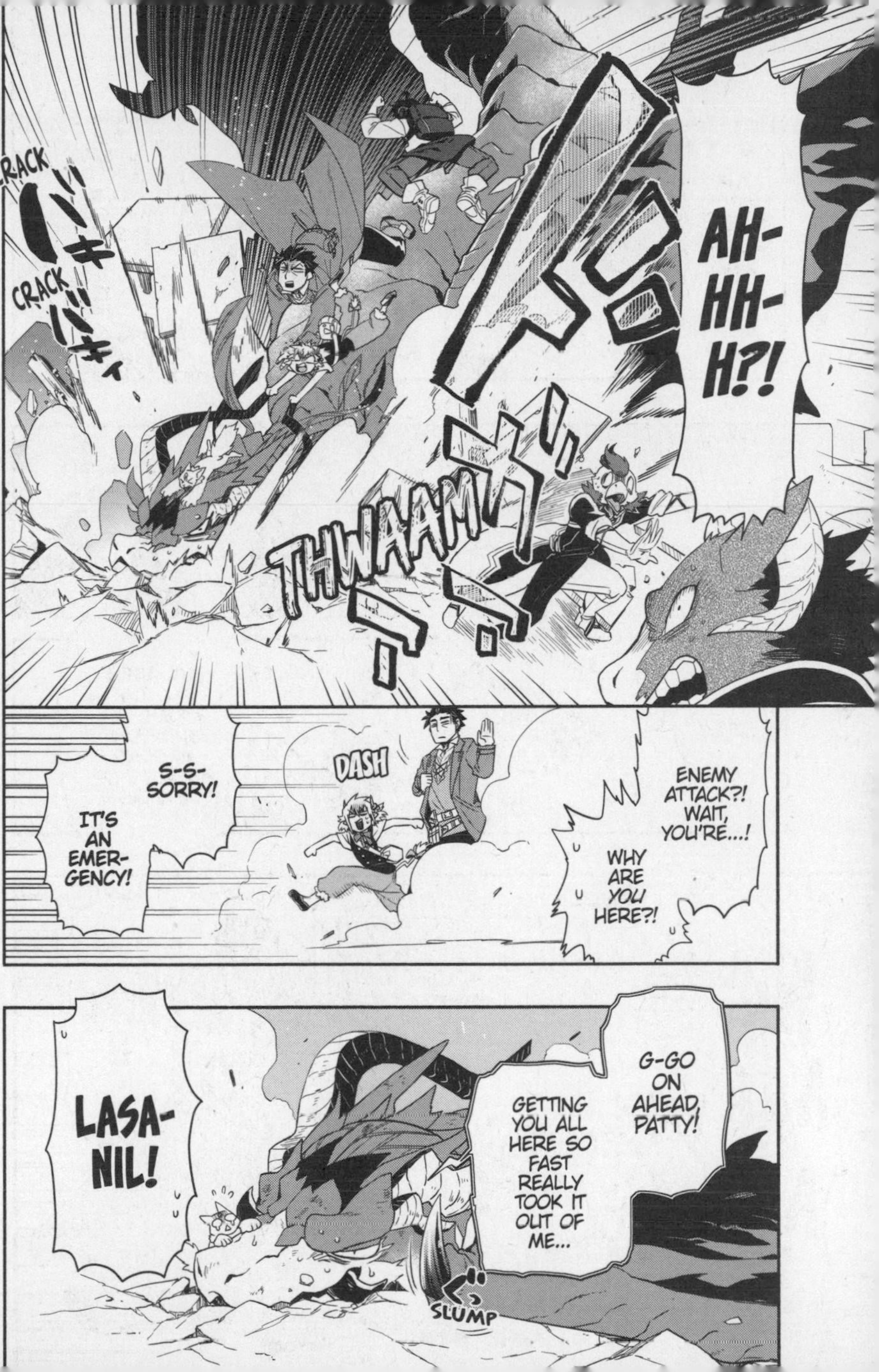
AH-HHH-H?!
THWAAM
CRACK
バキ
CRACK
バキィ
ENEMY ATTACK?! WAIT, YOU'RE...!
WHY ARE YOU HERE?!
DASH
S-S-SORRY!
IT'S AN EMERGENCY!
G-GO ON AHEAD, PATTY!
GETTING YOU ALL HERE SO FAST REALLY TOOK IT OUT OF ME...
SLUMP
LASA-NIL!

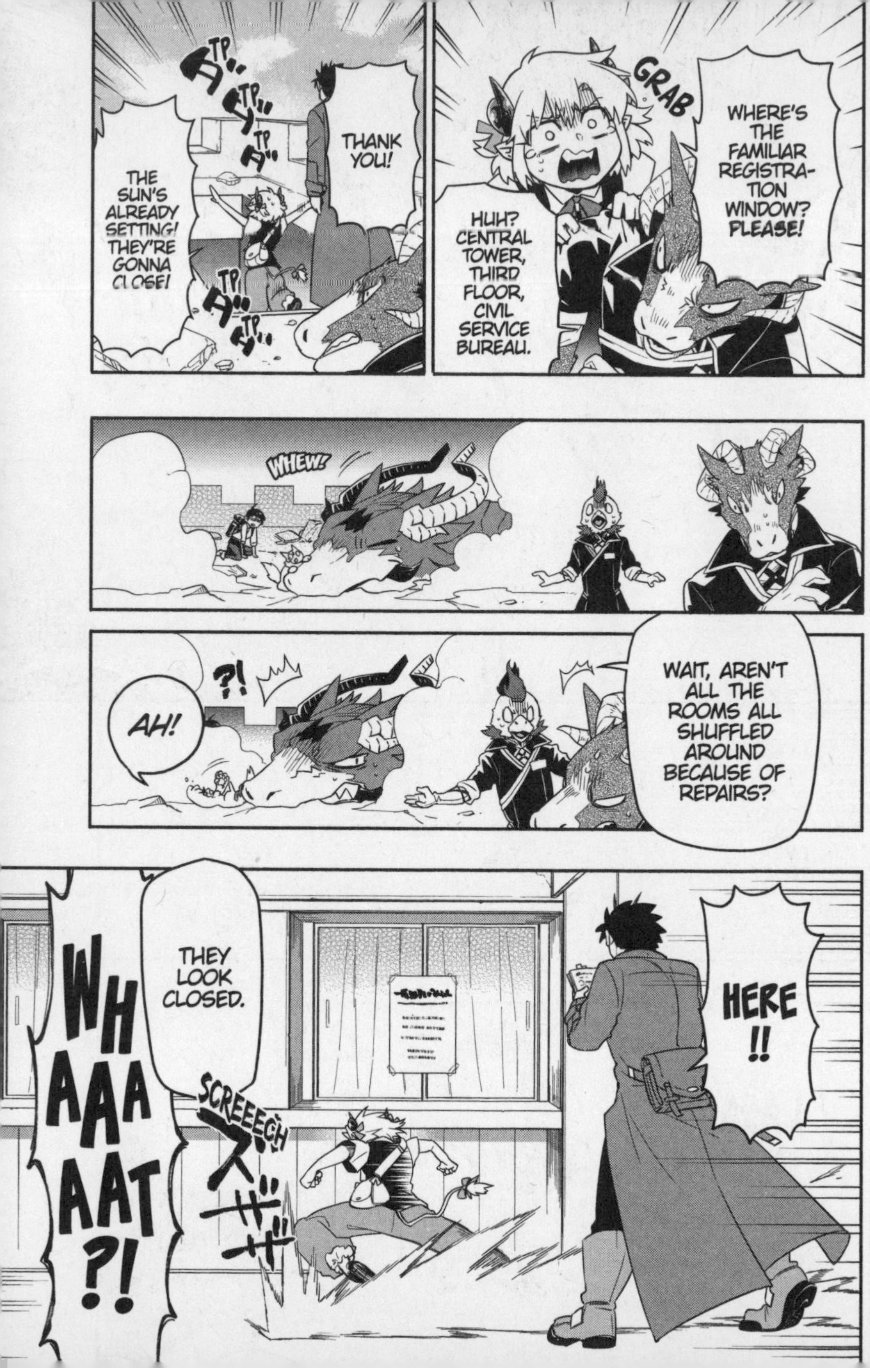
GRAB
WHERE'S THE FAMILIAR REGISTRATION WINDOW? PLEASE!
HUH? CENTRAL TOWER, THIRD FLOOR, CIVIL SERVICE BUREAU.
THANK YOU!
TP TP TP
THE SUN'S ALREADY SETTING! THEY'RE GONNA CLOSE!
TP TP
WHEW!
WAIT, AREN'T ALL THE ROOMS ALL SHUFFLED AROUND BECAUSE OF REPAIRS?
?!
AH!
HERE!!
THEY LOOK CLOSED.
SCREEECH
WHAAAAAT?!

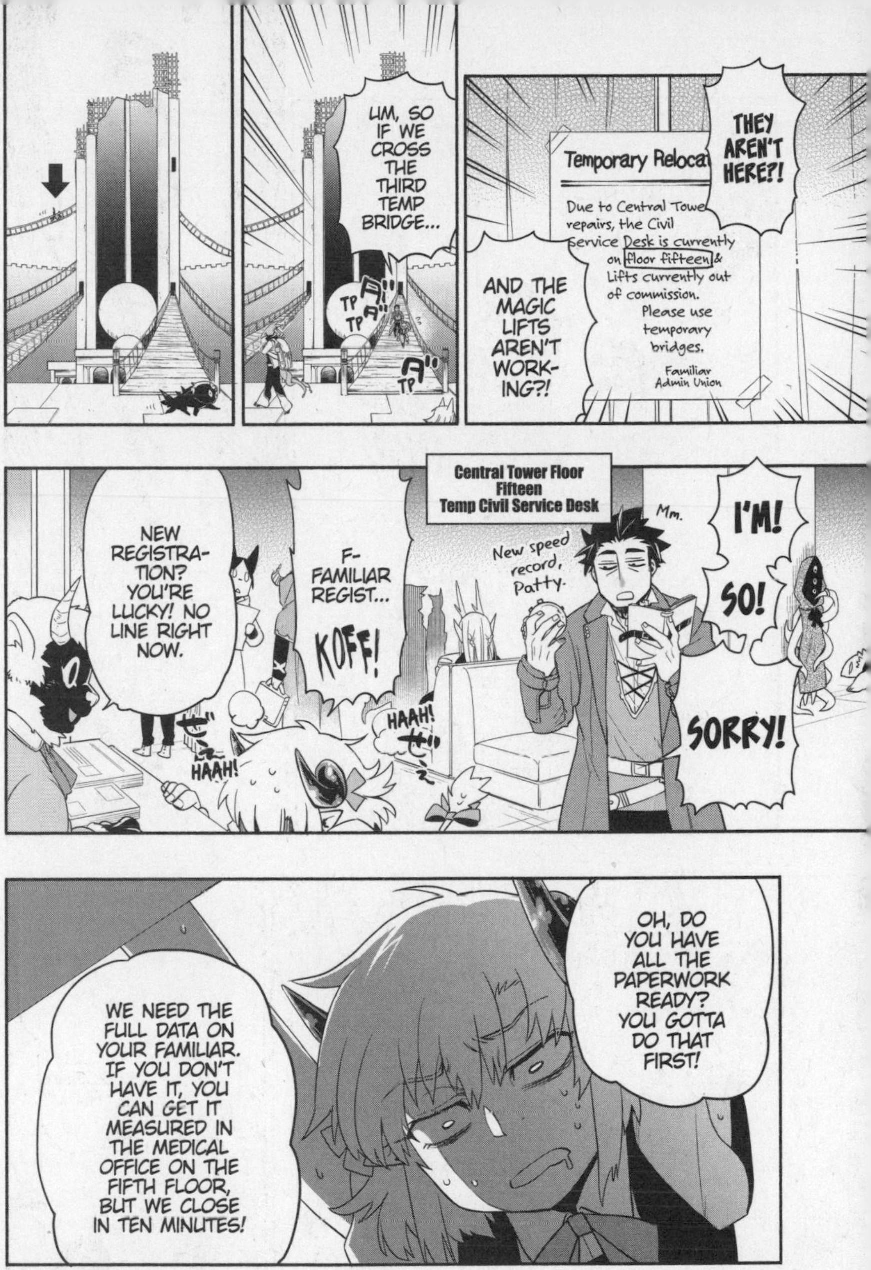
THEY AREN'T HERE?!
Temporary Relocat
Due to Central Towe repairs, the Civil Service Desk is currently on floor fifteen & Lifts currently out of commission. Please use temporary bridges.
Familiar Admin Union
AND THE MAGIC LIFTS AREN'T WORK-ING?!
UM, SO IF WE CROSS THE THIRD TEMP BRIDGE...
TP TP
TP
Central Tower Floor Fifteen Temp Civil Service Desk
I'M!
SO!
SORRY!
Mm.
New speed record, Patty.
F- FAMILIAR REGIST...
KOFF!
HAAH!
HAAH!
NEW REGISTRA-TION? YOU'RE LUCKY! NO LINE RIGHT NOW.
OH, DO YOU HAVE ALL THE PAPERWORK READY? YOU GOTTA DO THAT FIRST!
WE NEED THE FULL DATA ON YOUR FAMILIAR. IF YOU DON'T HAVE IT, YOU CAN GET IT MEASURED IN THE MEDICAL OFFICE ON THE FIFTH FLOOR, BUT WE CLOSE IN TEN MINUTES!

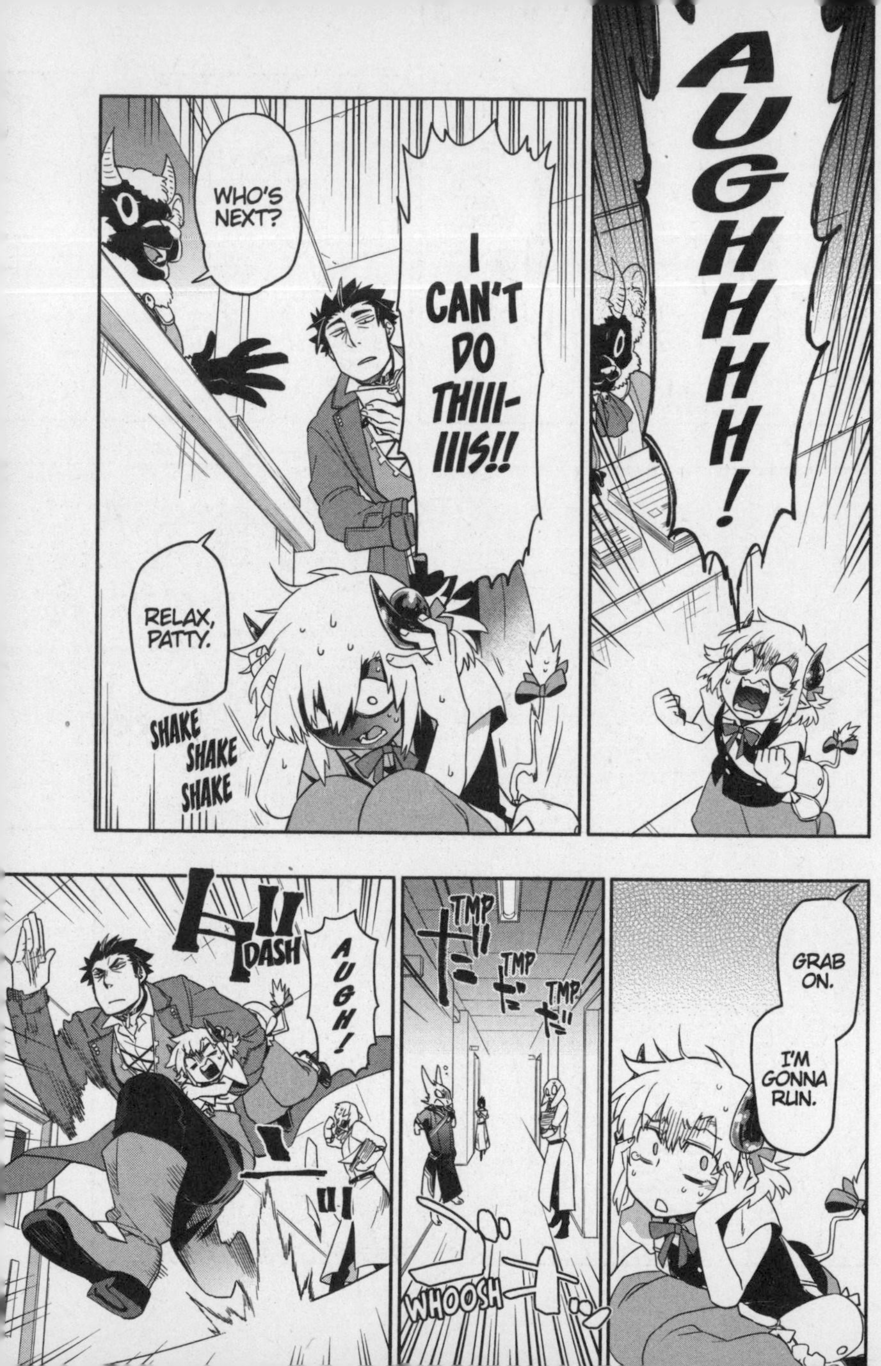
AUGHHHH!
WHO'S NEXT?
I CAN'T DO THIIII-IIIS!!
RELAX, PATTY.
SHAKE SHAKE SHAKE
GRAB ON.
I'M GONNA RUN.
TMP
TMP
TMP
WHOOSH
DASH
AUGH!

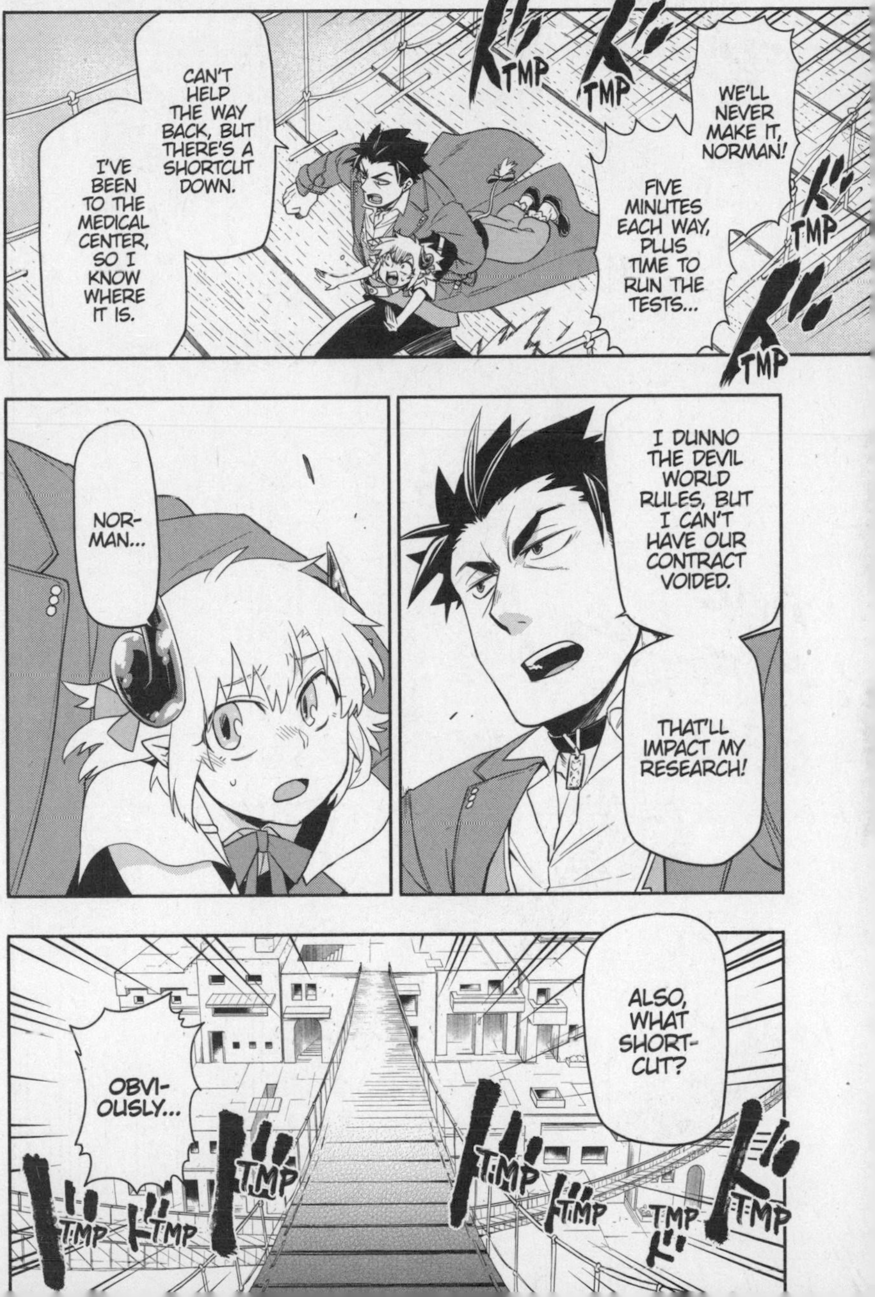
TMP TMP
WE'LL NEVER MAKE IT, NORMAN!
FIVE MINUTES EACH WAY, PLUS TIME TO RUN THE TESTS...
TMP TMP
CAN'T HELP THE WAY BACK, BUT THERE'S A SHORTCUT DOWN.
I'VE BEEN TO THE MEDICAL CENTER, SO I KNOW WHERE IT IS.
I DUNNO THE DEVIL WORLD RULES, BUT I CAN'T HAVE OUR CONTRACT VOIDED.
THAT'LL IMPACT MY RESEARCH!
NOR-MAN...
ALSO, WHAT SHORT-CUT?
OBVI-OUSLY...
TMP TMP TMP TMP
TMP TMP TMP TMP

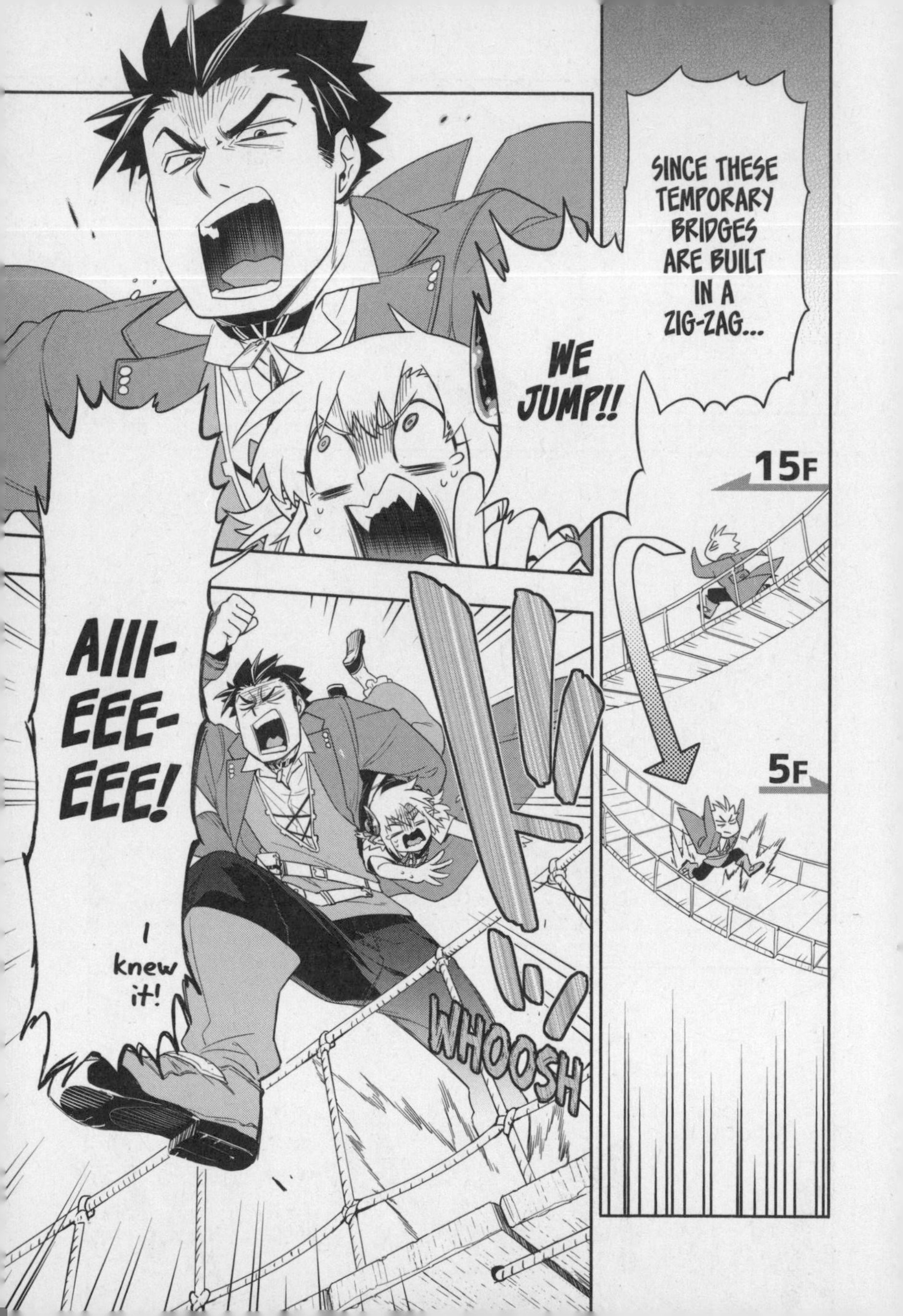
SINCE THESE TEMPORARY BRIDGES ARE BUILT IN A ZIG-ZAG...
15F
5F
WE JUMP!!
AIII-EEE-EEE!
I knew it!
WHOOSH

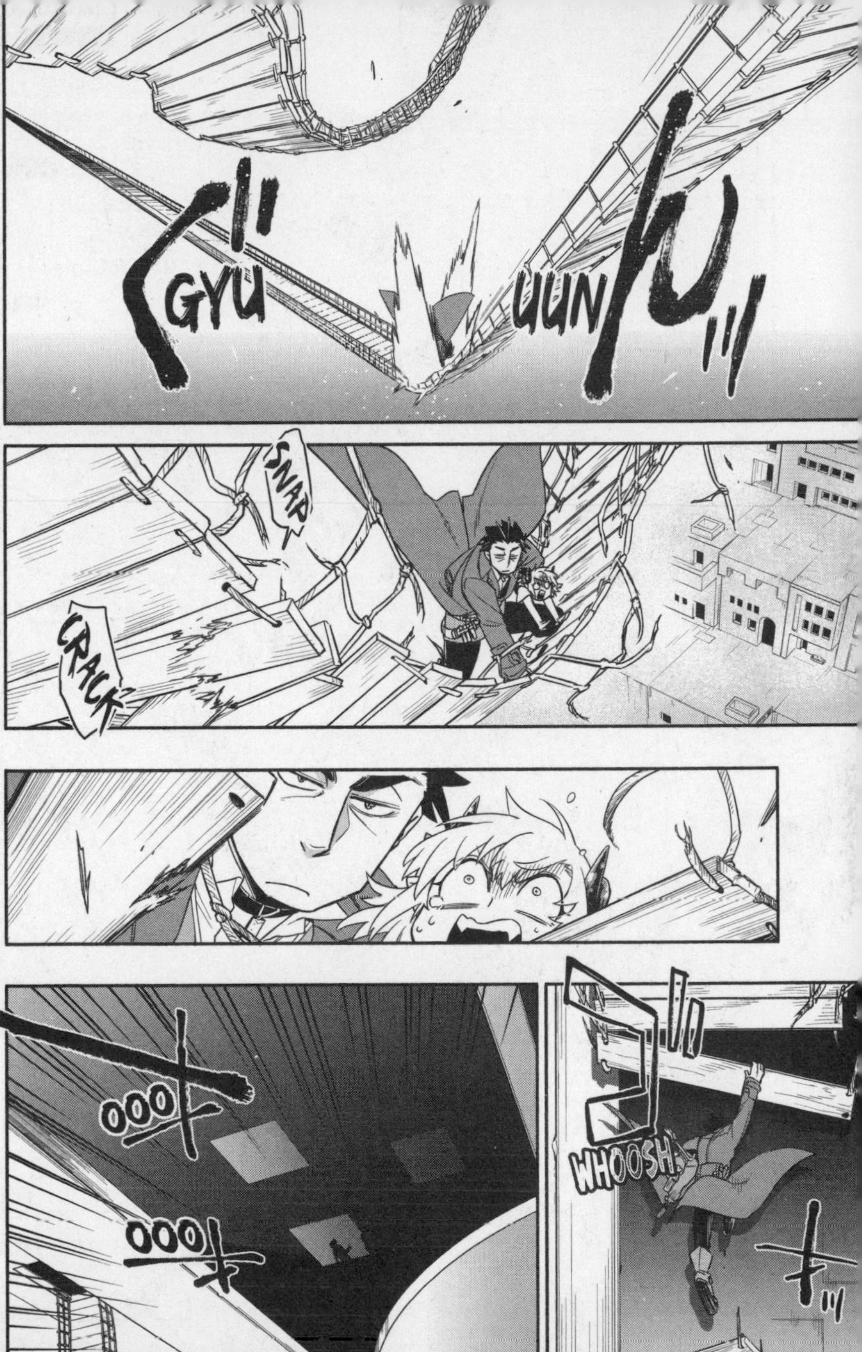
GYU
UUN
SNAP
CRACK
WHOOSH
OOO
OOO

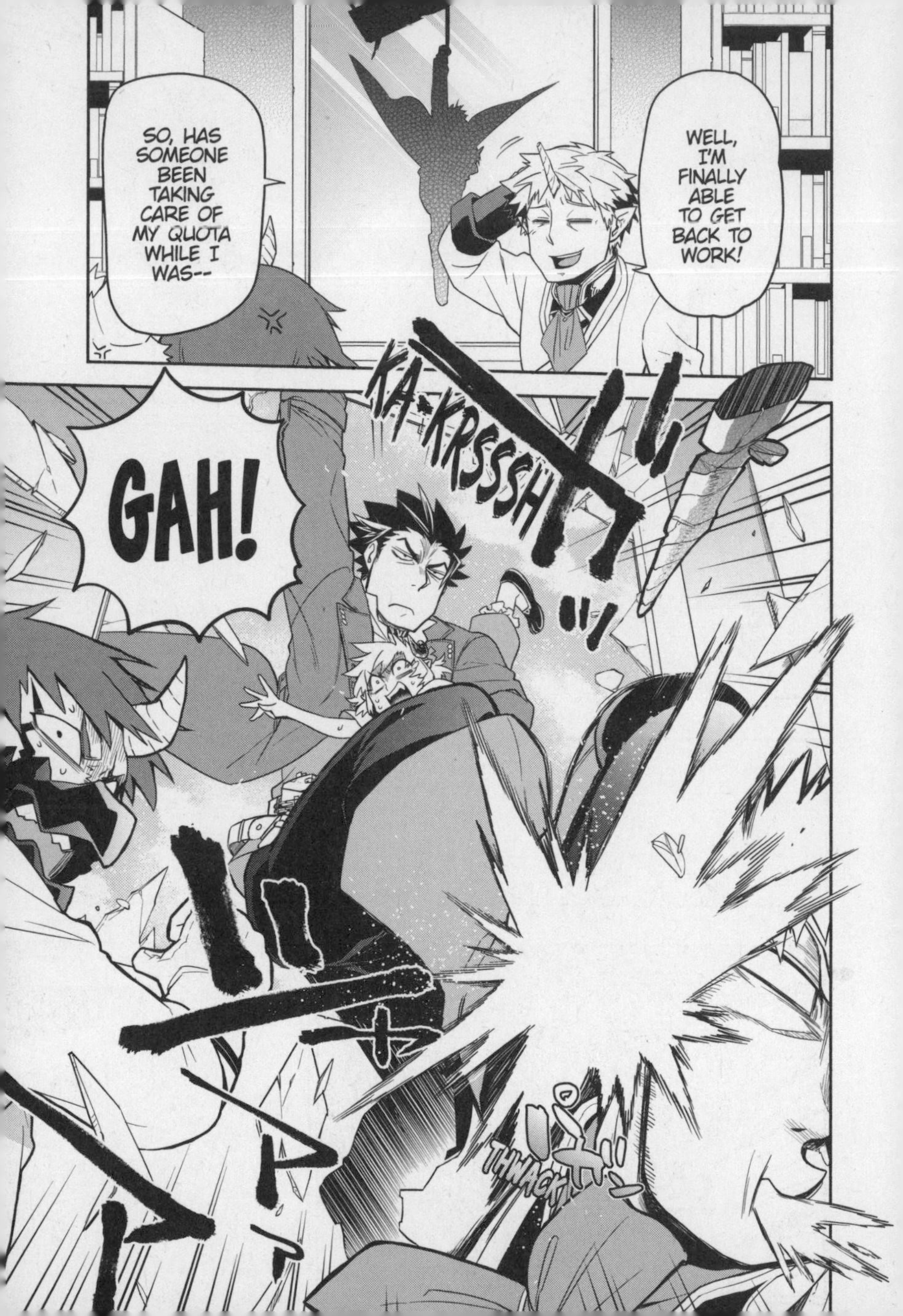
WELL, I'M FINALLY ABLE TO GET BACK TO WORK!
SO, HAS SOMEONE BEEN TAKING CARE OF MY QUOTA WHILE I WAS--
KA-KRSSSH
GAH!
THWACK!

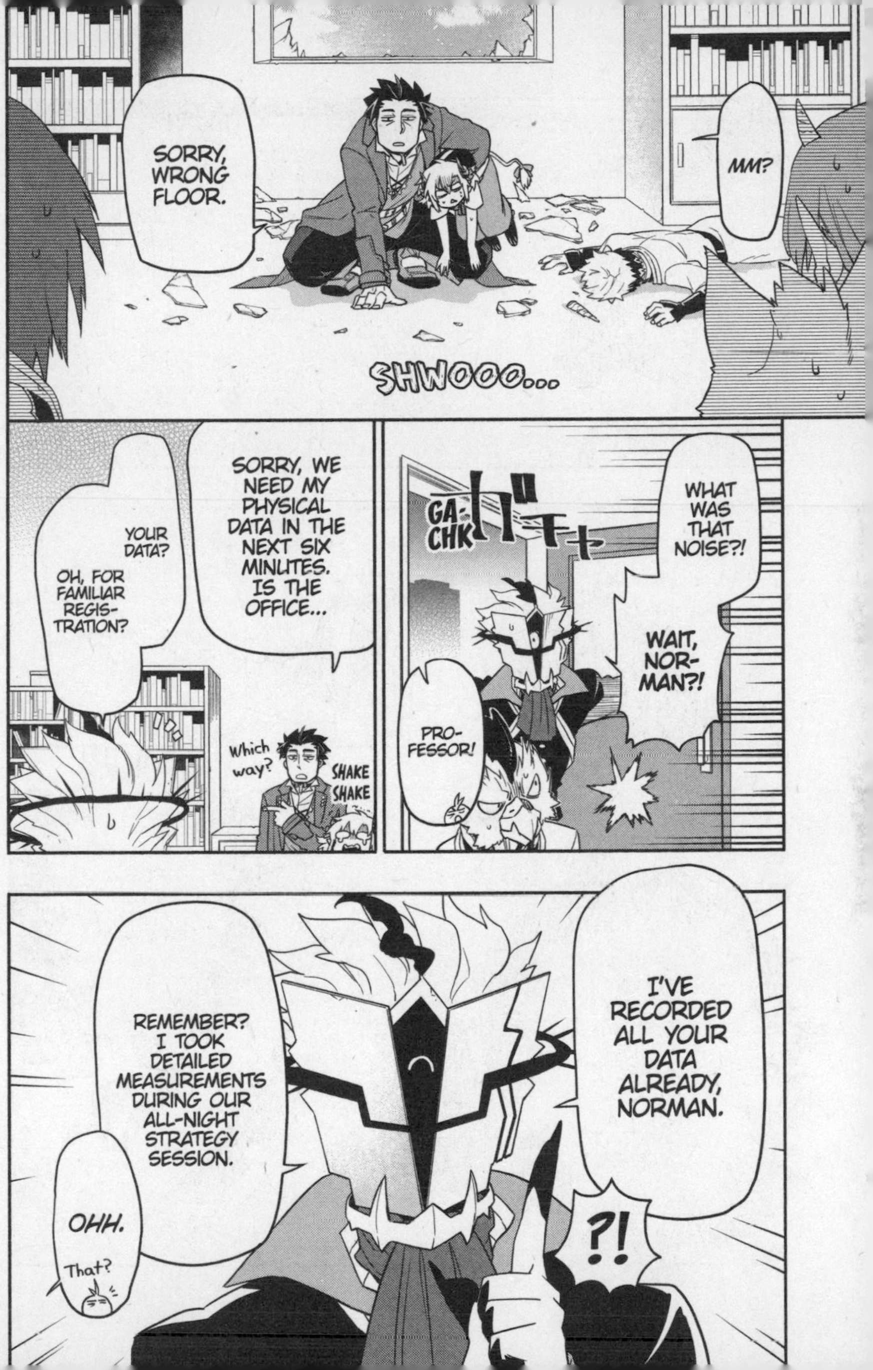
MM?
SORRY, WRONG FLOOR.
SHWOOO...
WHAT WAS THAT NOISE?!
GA-CHK
WAIT, NOR-MAN?!
PRO-FESSOR!
SORRY, WE NEED MY PHYSICAL DATA IN THE NEXT SIX MINUTES. IS THE OFFICE...
YOUR DATA?
OH, FOR FAMILIAR REGIS-TRATION?
Which way?
SHAKE SHAKE
I'VE RECORDED ALL YOUR DATA ALREADY, NORMAN.
?!
REMEMBER? I TOOK DETAILED MEASUREMENTS DURING OUR ALL-NIGHT STRATEGY SESSION.
OHH.
That?

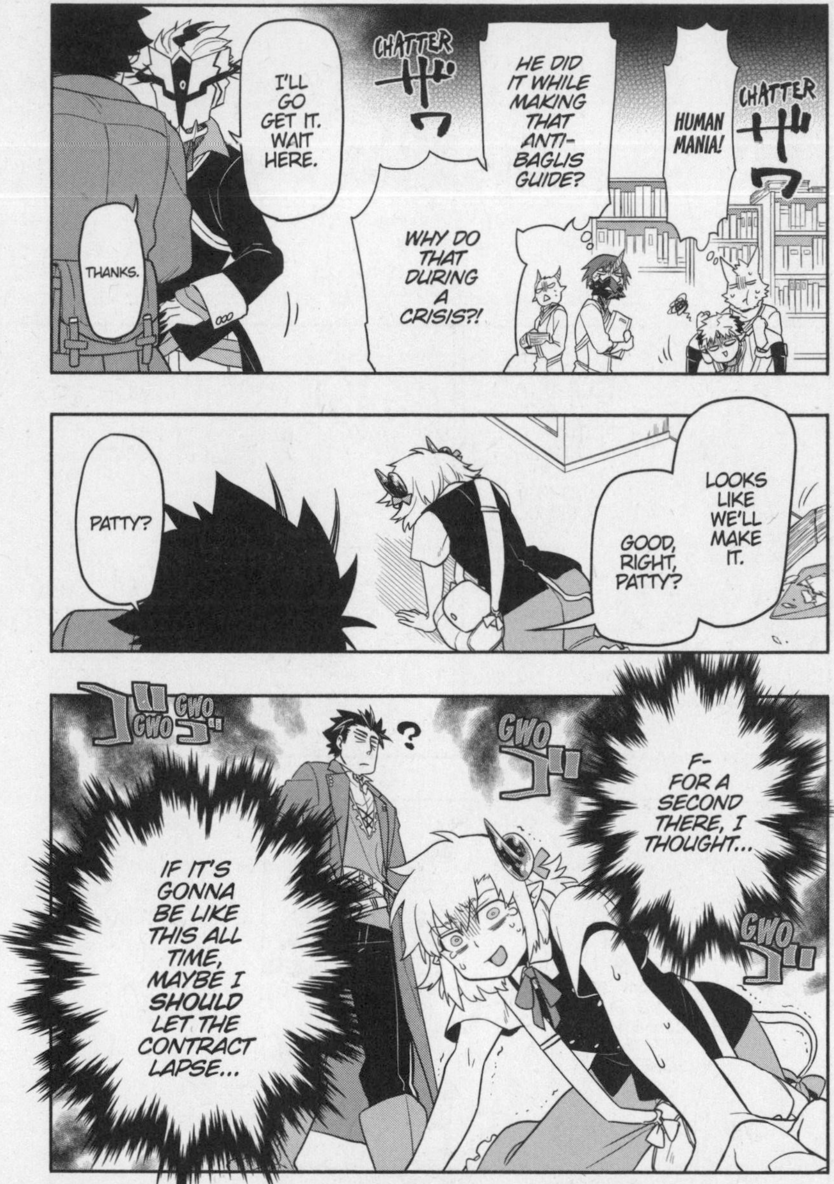
CHATTER
HUMAN MANIA!
HE DID IT WHILE MAKING THAT ANTI-BAGLIS GUIDE?
WHY DO THAT DURING A CRISIS?!
CHATTER
I'LL GO GET IT. WAIT HERE.
THANKS.
LOOKS LIKE WE'LL MAKE IT.
GOOD, RIGHT, PATTY?
PATTY?
F- FOR A SECOND THERE, I THOUGHT...
GWO
GWO
GWO GWO
?
IF IT'S GONNA BE LIKE THIS ALL TIME, MAYBE I SHOULD LET THE CONTRACT LAPSE...

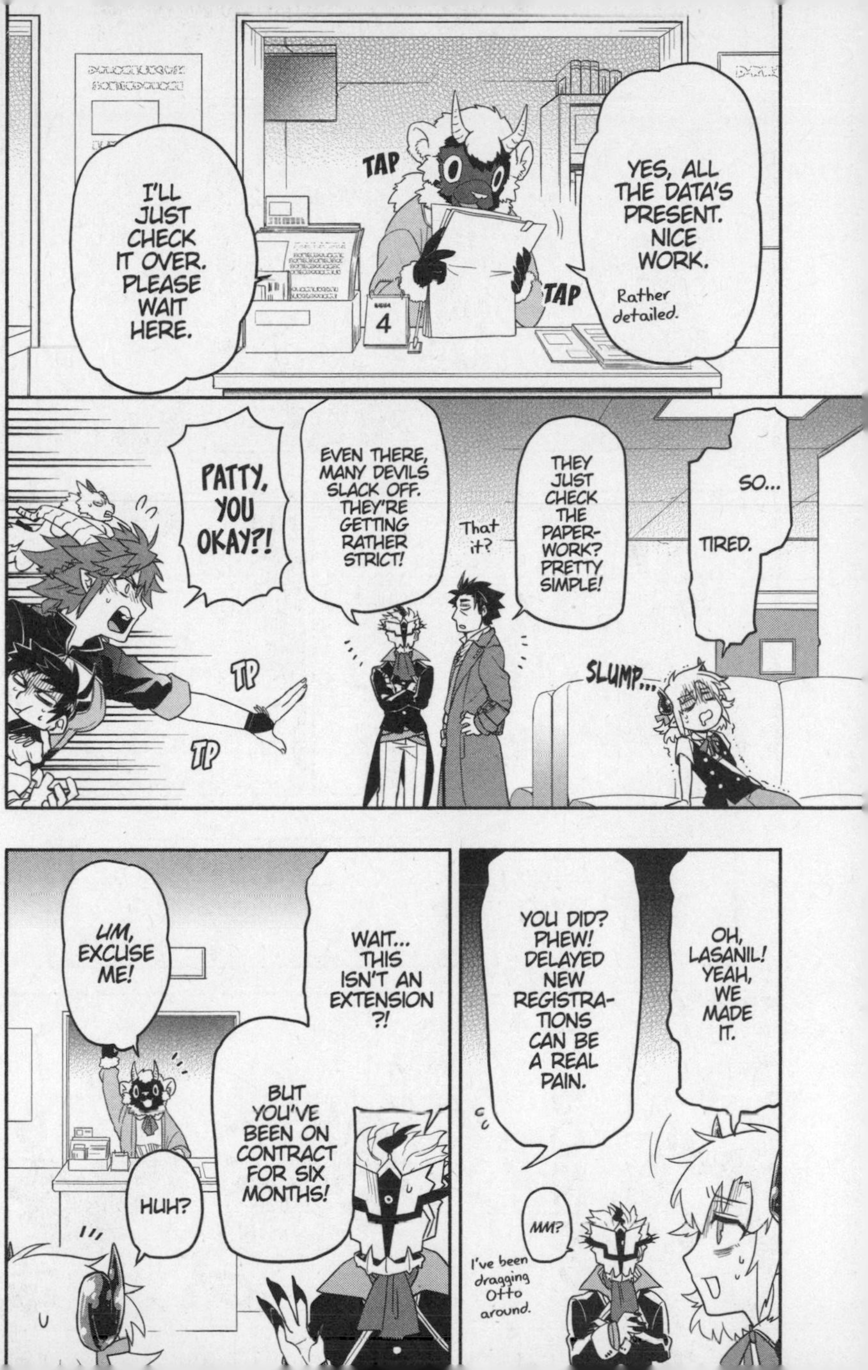
YES, ALL THE DATA'S PRESENT. NICE WORK.
Rather detailed.
TAP
TAP
I'LL JUST CHECK IT OVER. PLEASE WAIT HERE.
4
SO... TIRED.
SLUMP...
THEY JUST CHECK THE PAPER-WORK? PRETTY SIMPLE!
That it?
EVEN THERE, MANY DEVILS SLACK OFF. THEY'RE GETTING RATHER STRICT!
PATTY, YOU OKAY?!
TP
TP
OH, LASANIL! YEAH, WE MADE IT.
YOU DID? PHEW! DELAYED NEW REGISTRA-TIONS CAN BE A REAL PAIN.
MM?
I've been dragging Otto around.
WAIT... THIS ISN'T AN EXTENSION?!
UM, EXCUSE ME!
BUT YOU'VE BEEN ON CONTRACT FOR SIX MONTHS!
HUH?

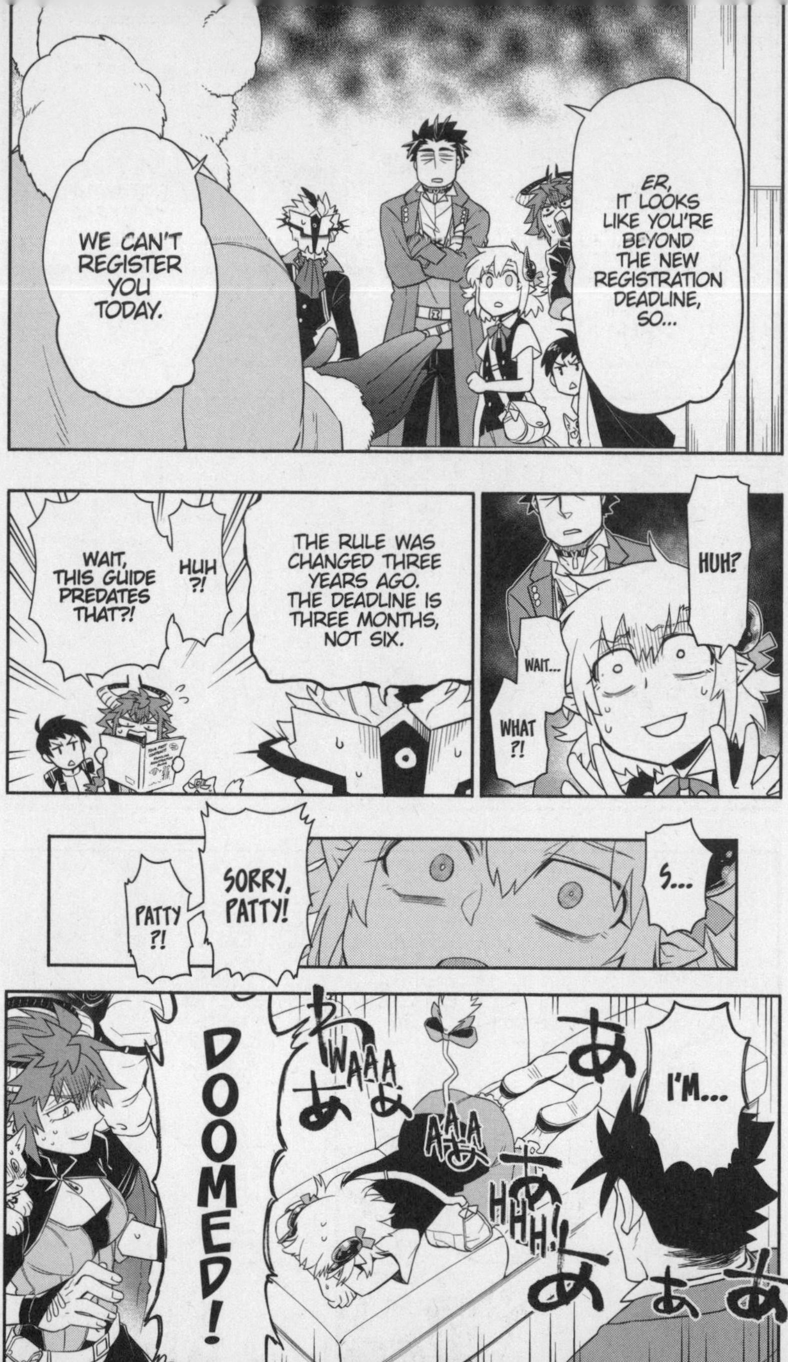
ER, IT LOOKS LIKE YOU'RE BEYOND THE NEW REGISTRATION DEADLINE, SO...
WE CAN'T REGISTER YOU TODAY.
HUH?
WAIT... WHAT?!
THE RULE WAS CHANGED THREE YEARS AGO. THE DEADLINE IS THREE MONTHS, NOT SIX.
HUH?!
WAIT, THIS GUIDE PREDATES THAT?!
S...
SORRY, PATTY!
PATTY?!
I'M...
WAAA AAA HHH!
DOOMED!

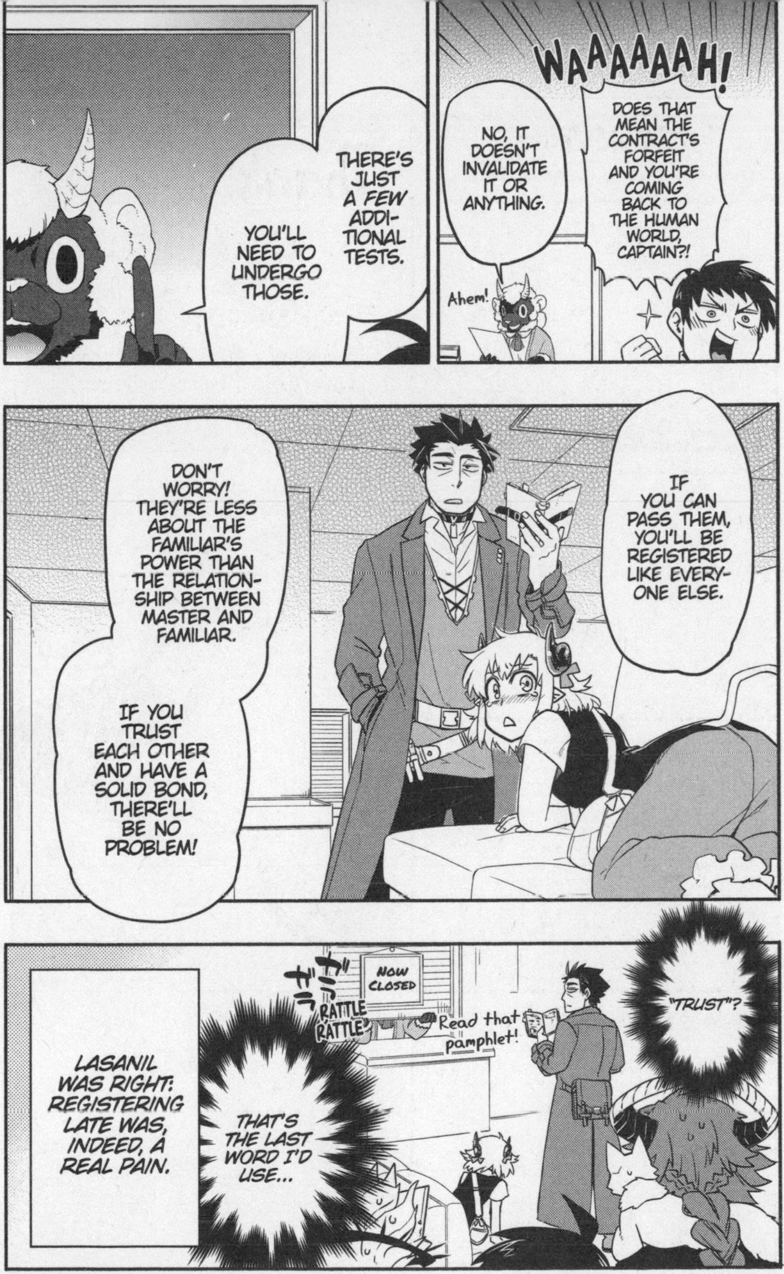
WAAAAAAH!
DOES THAT MEAN THE CONTRACT'S FORFEIT AND YOU'RE COMING BACK TO THE HUMAN WORLD, CAPTAIN?!
NO, IT DOESN'T INVALIDATE IT OR ANYTHING.
Ahem!
THERE'S JUST A *FEW* ADDITIONAL TESTS.
YOU'LL NEED TO UNDERGO THOSE.
IF YOU CAN PASS THEM, YOU'LL BE REGISTERED LIKE EVERYONE ELSE.
DON'T WORRY! THEY'RE LESS ABOUT THE FAMILIAR'S POWER THAN THE RELATIONSHIP BETWEEN MASTER AND FAMILIAR.
IF YOU TRUST EACH OTHER AND HAVE A SOLID BOND, THERE'LL BE NO PROBLEM!
"TRUST"?
Read that pamphlet!
NOW CLOSED
ガラ ガラ
RATTLE RATTLE
THAT'S THE LAST WORD I'D USE...
LASANIL WAS RIGHT: REGISTERING LATE WAS, INDEED, A REAL PAIN.

To be continued!

Thank you for reading!

Yagura

-Special Thanks-

Assistants: Nanami-san, Kuroichi-san
Cover/Logo Design: Sugita-san
Editors: T-san, F-san, I-san

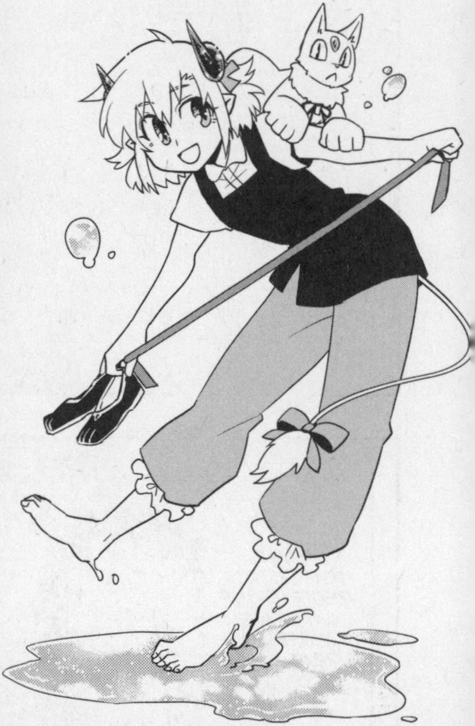

NEW COSTUMES

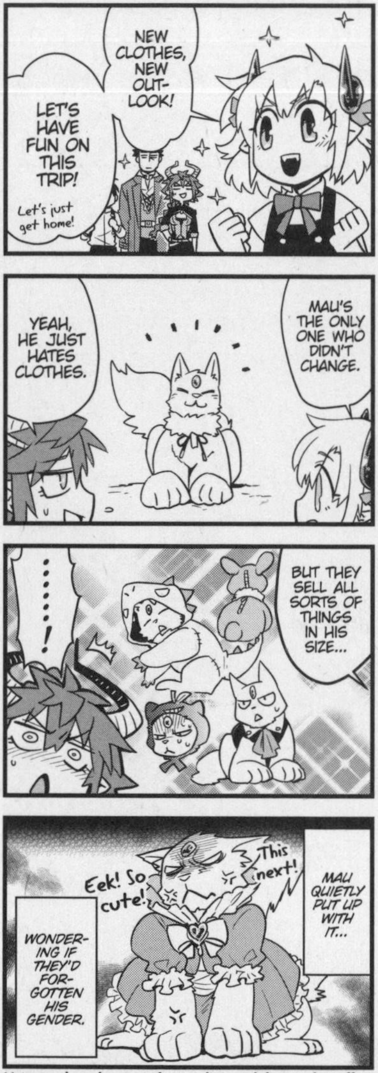
NEW CLOTHES, NEW OUT-LOOK!
LET'S HAVE FUN ON THIS TRIP!
Let's just get home!
MAU'S THE ONLY ONE WHO DIDN'T CHANGE.
YEAH, HE JUST HATES CLOTHES.
BUT THEY SELL ALL SORTS OF THINGS IN HIS SIZE...
......!
MAU QUIETLY PUT UP WITH IT...
This next!
Eek! So cute!
WONDERING IF THEY'D FORGOTTEN HIS GENDER.

Moments later he started struggling and they took it off.

Character Design Intro

This time I pulled out design documents for our supporting cast! Lasanil was originally supposed to be frostier but since she ended up reacting a lot I went with the current design. (I reused the single horn for Suphlatus.)

The other characters have other tiny differences, so have fun comparing!

Tekka Yaguraba

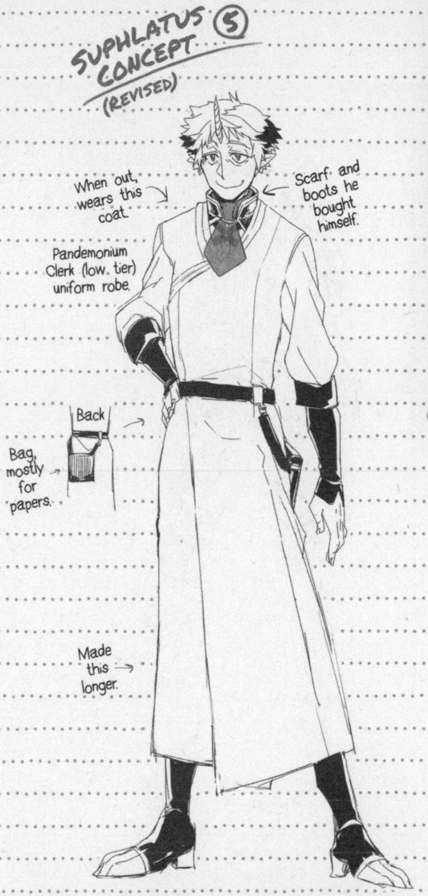

SUPHLATUS CONCEPT 5
(REVISED)
When out, wears this coat.
Scarf and boots he bought himself.
Pandemonium Clerk (low tier) uniform robe.
Back
Bag, mostly for papers.
Made this longer.

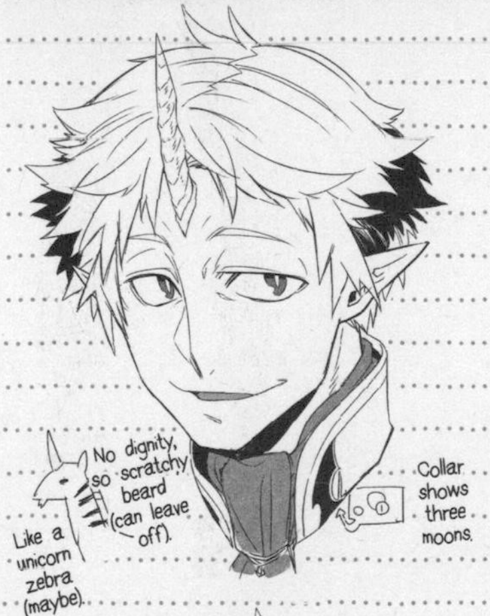

No dignity, so scratchy beard (can leave off).
Like a unicorn zebra (maybe).
Collar shows three moons.

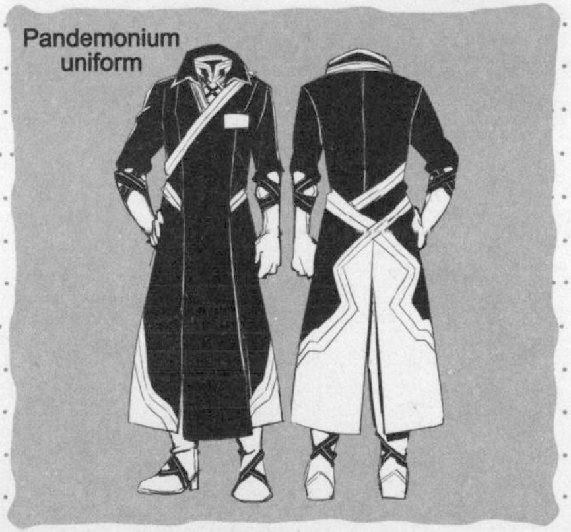

Pandemonium uniform

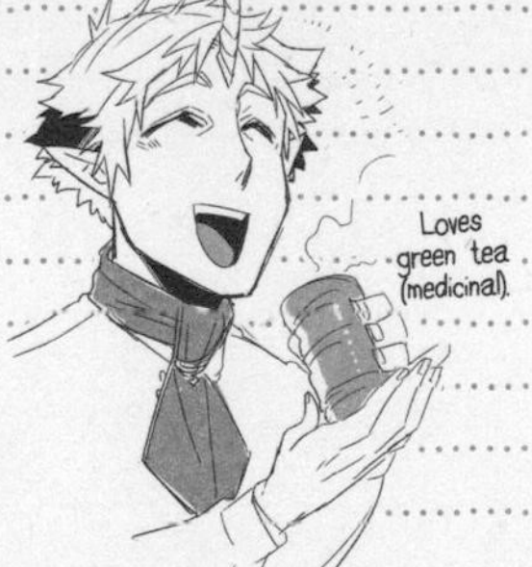

Loves green tea (medicinal).

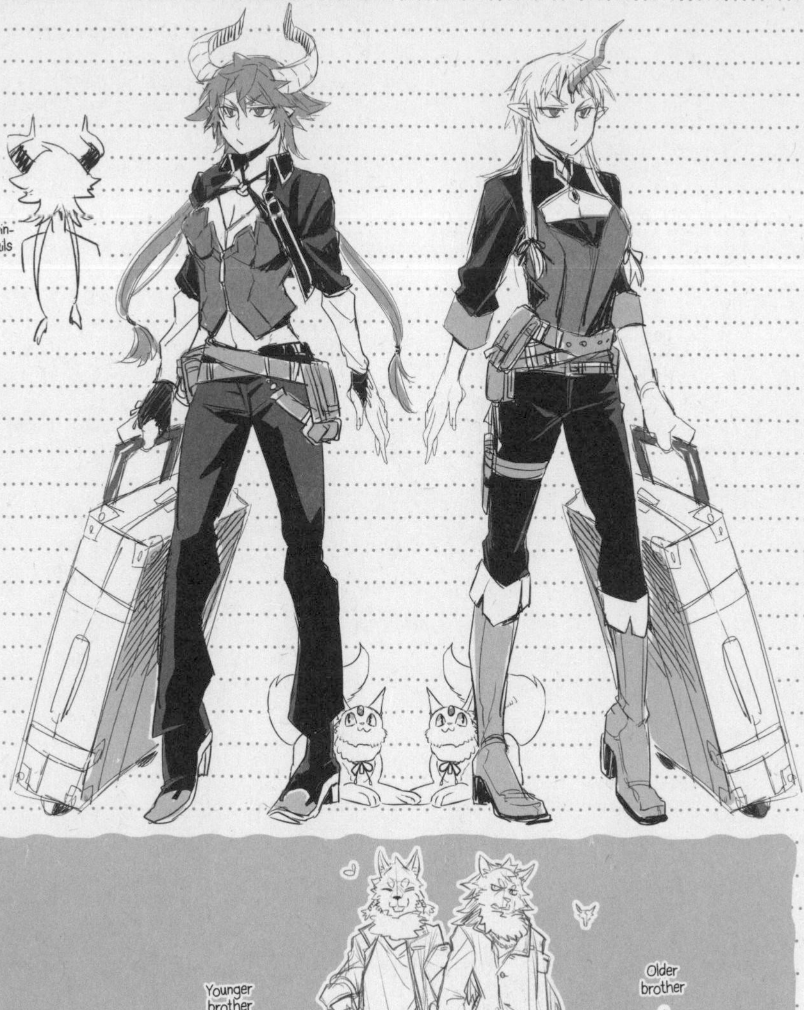
Twin-
tails

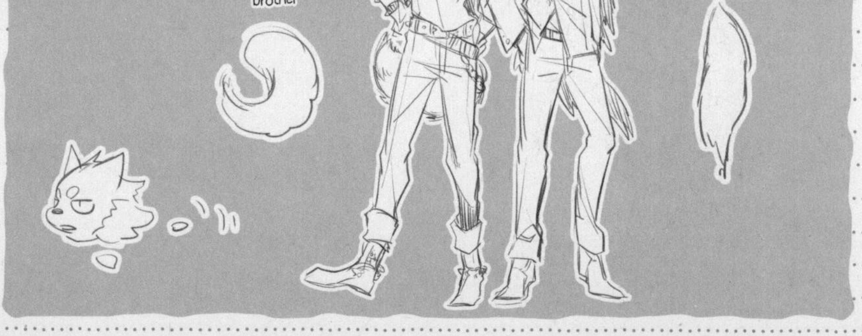
Younger
brother
Older
brother

NORMAN'S PROTÉGÉ DESIGN DRAFT

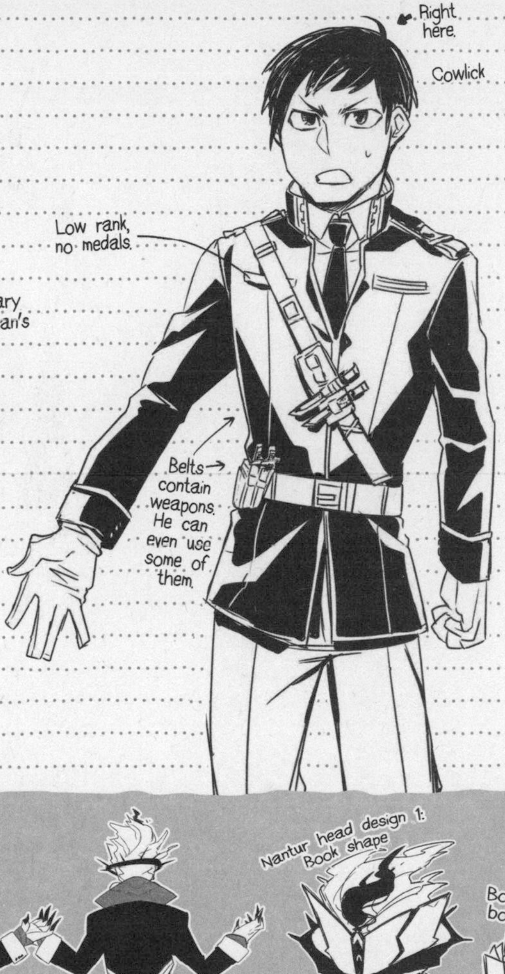
Right here.
Cowlick
☆ Basis is the military uniform from Norman's youth
Low rank, no medals.
Belts contain weapons. He can even use some of them.

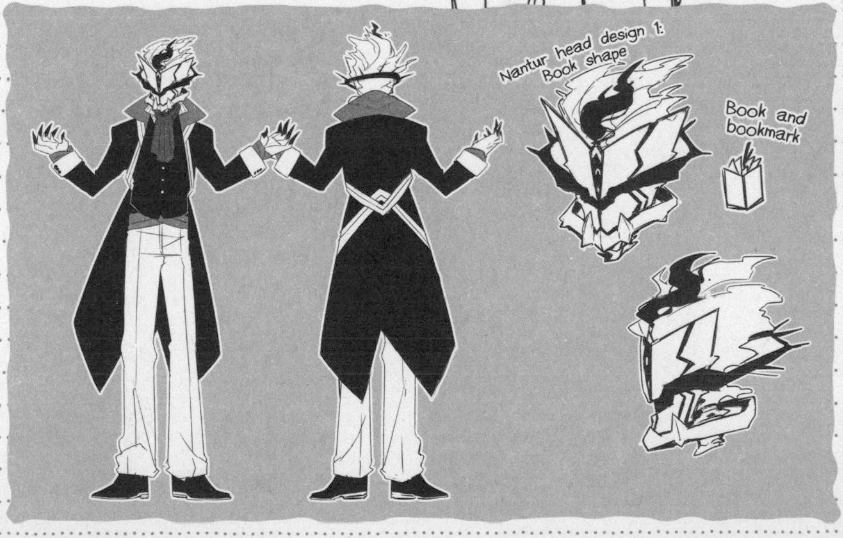
Nantur head design 1: Book shape
Book and bookmark

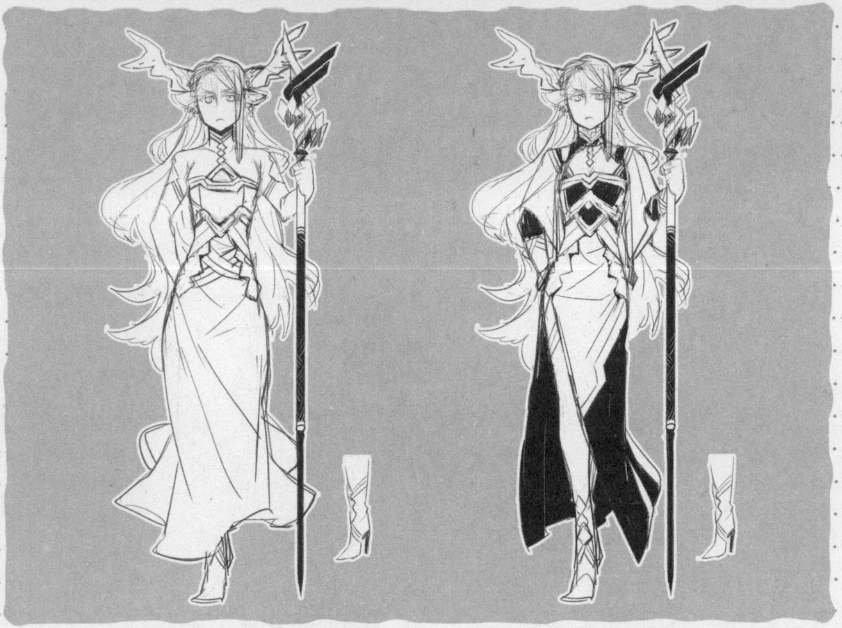

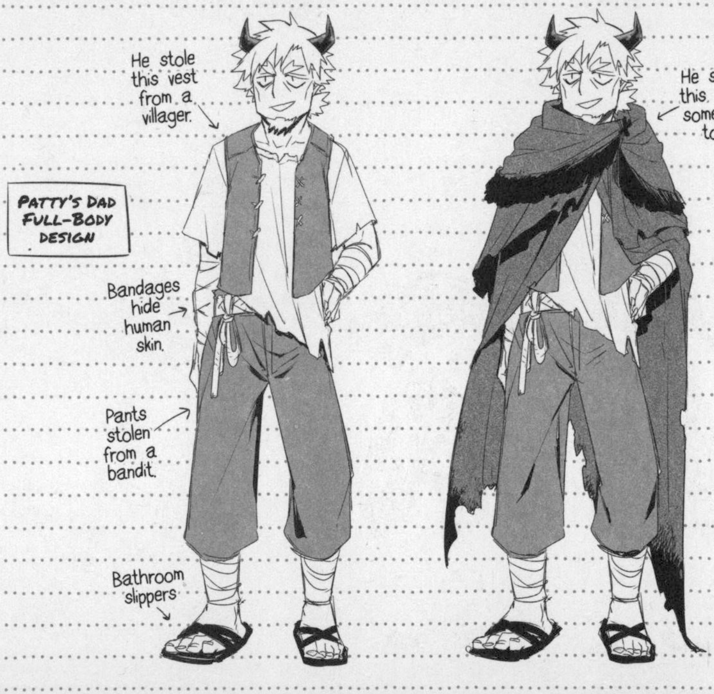

PATTY'S DAD FULL-BODY DESIGN
He stole this from someone, too.
He stole this vest from a villager.
Bandages hide human skin.
Pants stolen from a bandit.
Bathroom slippers

Next Time

What Lasanil called a "pain"...

The Familiar Registration Test!

Get Ready!!

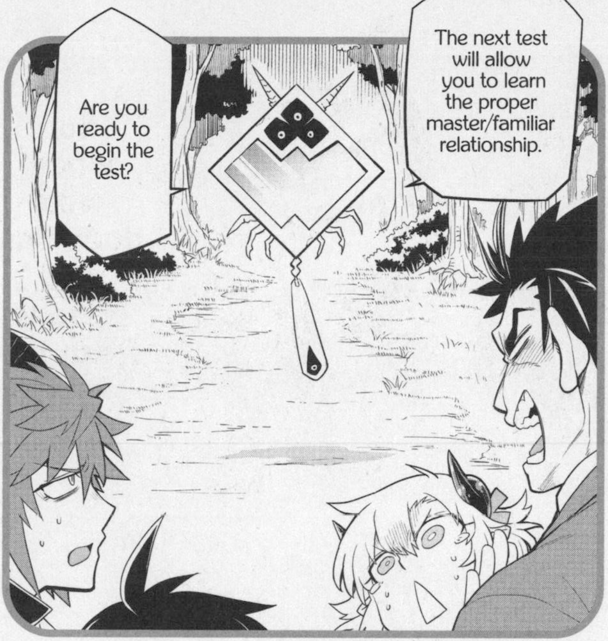
The next test will allow you to learn the proper master/familiar relationship.
Are you ready to begin the test?

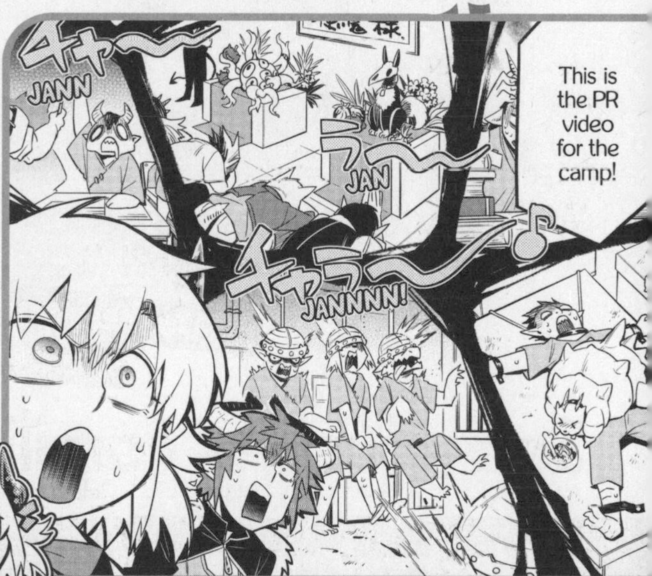
This is the PR video for the camp!
キャ〜
JANN
ら〜〜
JAN
キャら〜〜♪
JANNNN!

If they fail... a sinister camp awaits!

Do or die time!!!

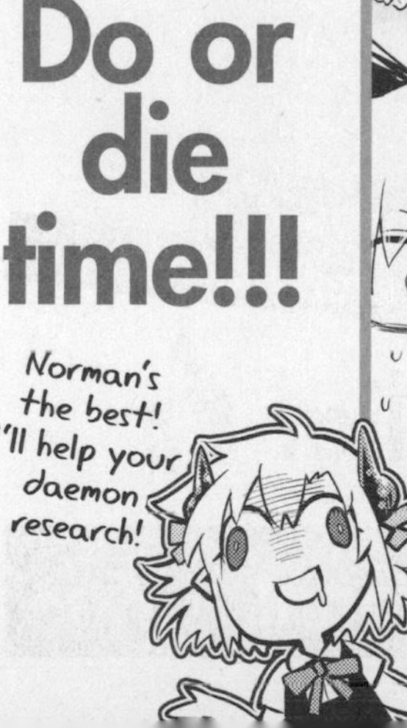
Norman's the best! I'll help your daemon research!

RUSTLE

DON—

But when wild daemons and bandits crash the party...

WHY IS THERE A HUGE DAEMON?!

NORMAN!!

AHHHH!

Will Patty and Norman's bonds pull them through?!

Do these bonds... even exist?!

Sorry for My Familiar 6
Tekka Yaguraba

Next volume coming soon!

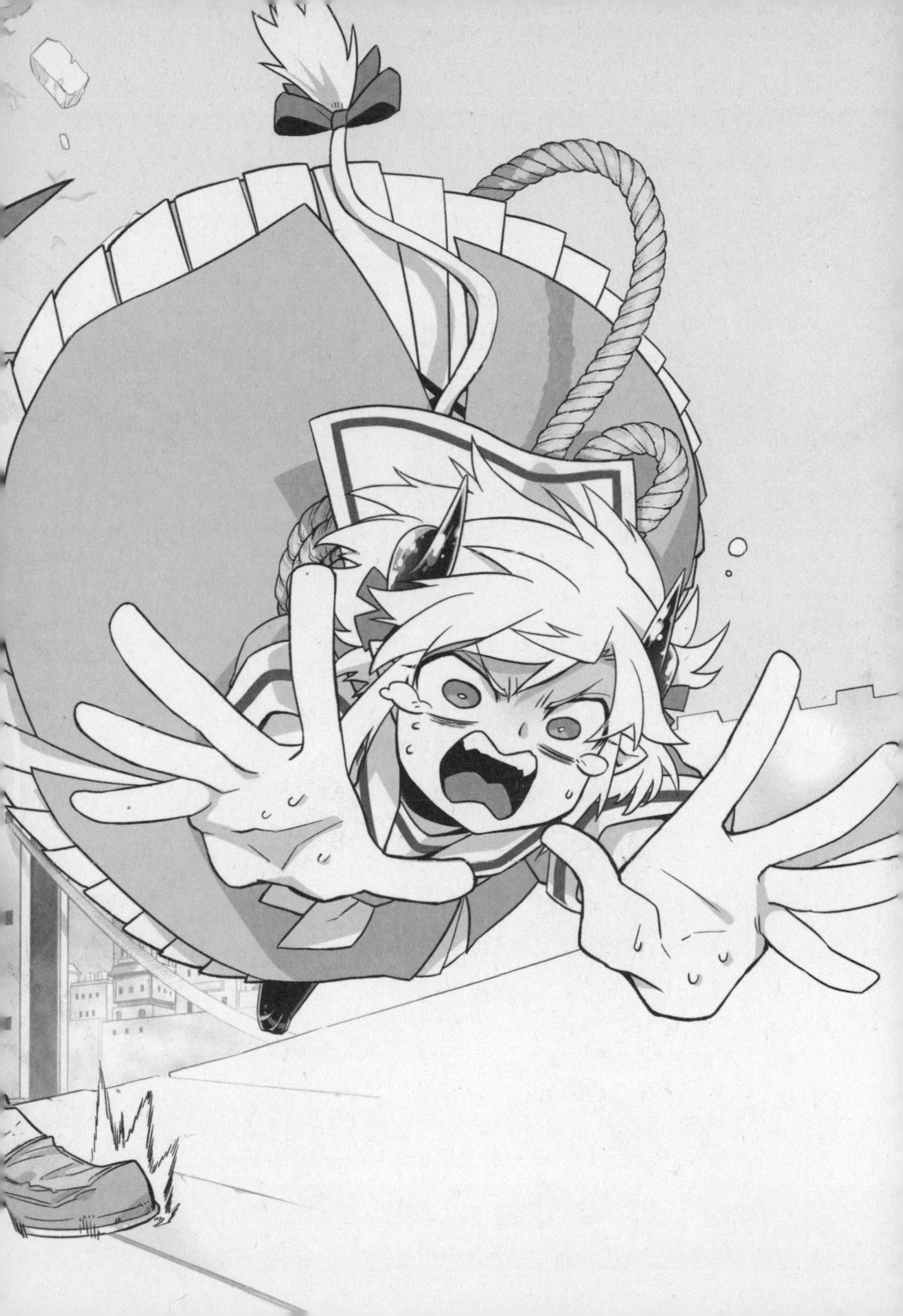

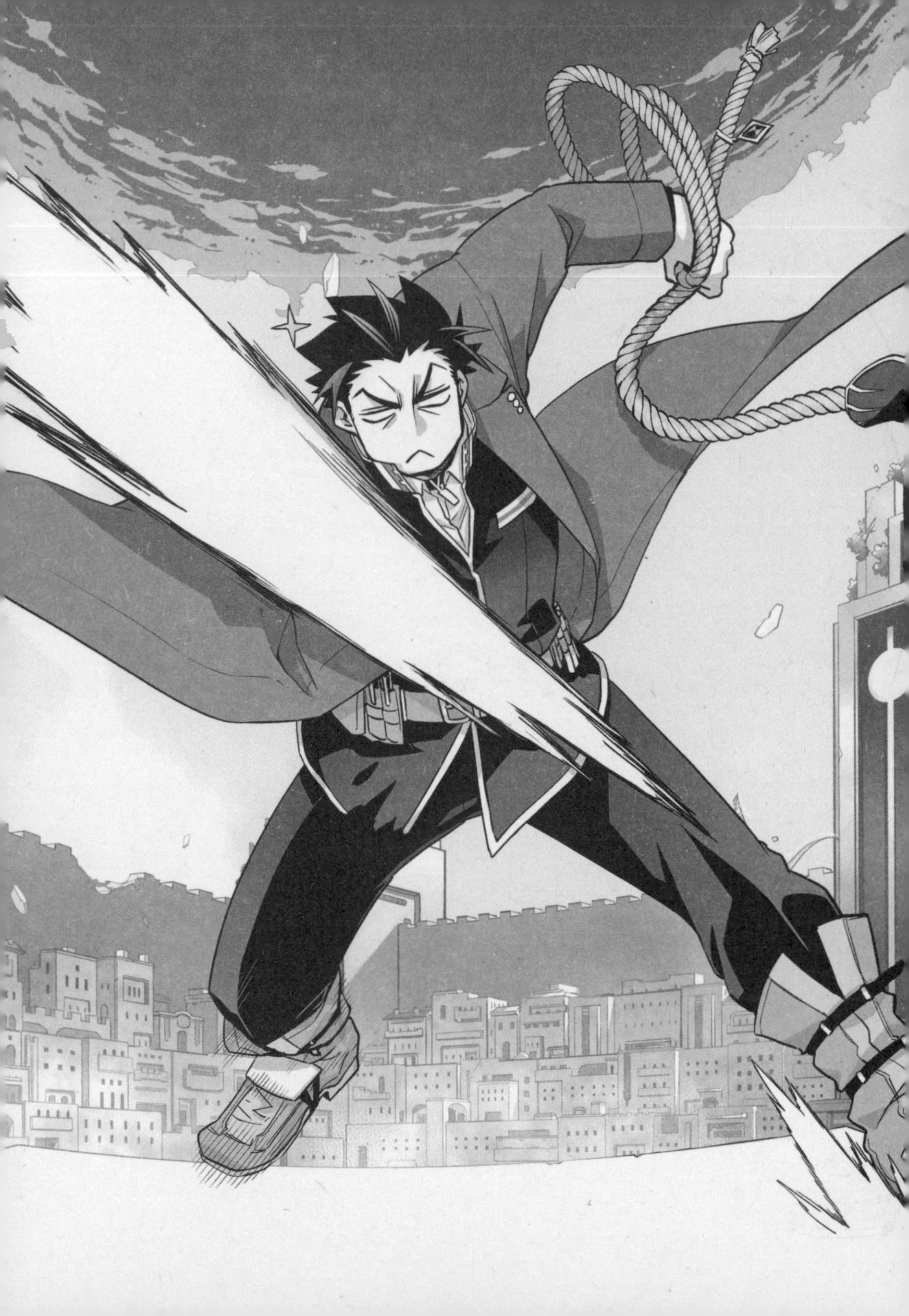

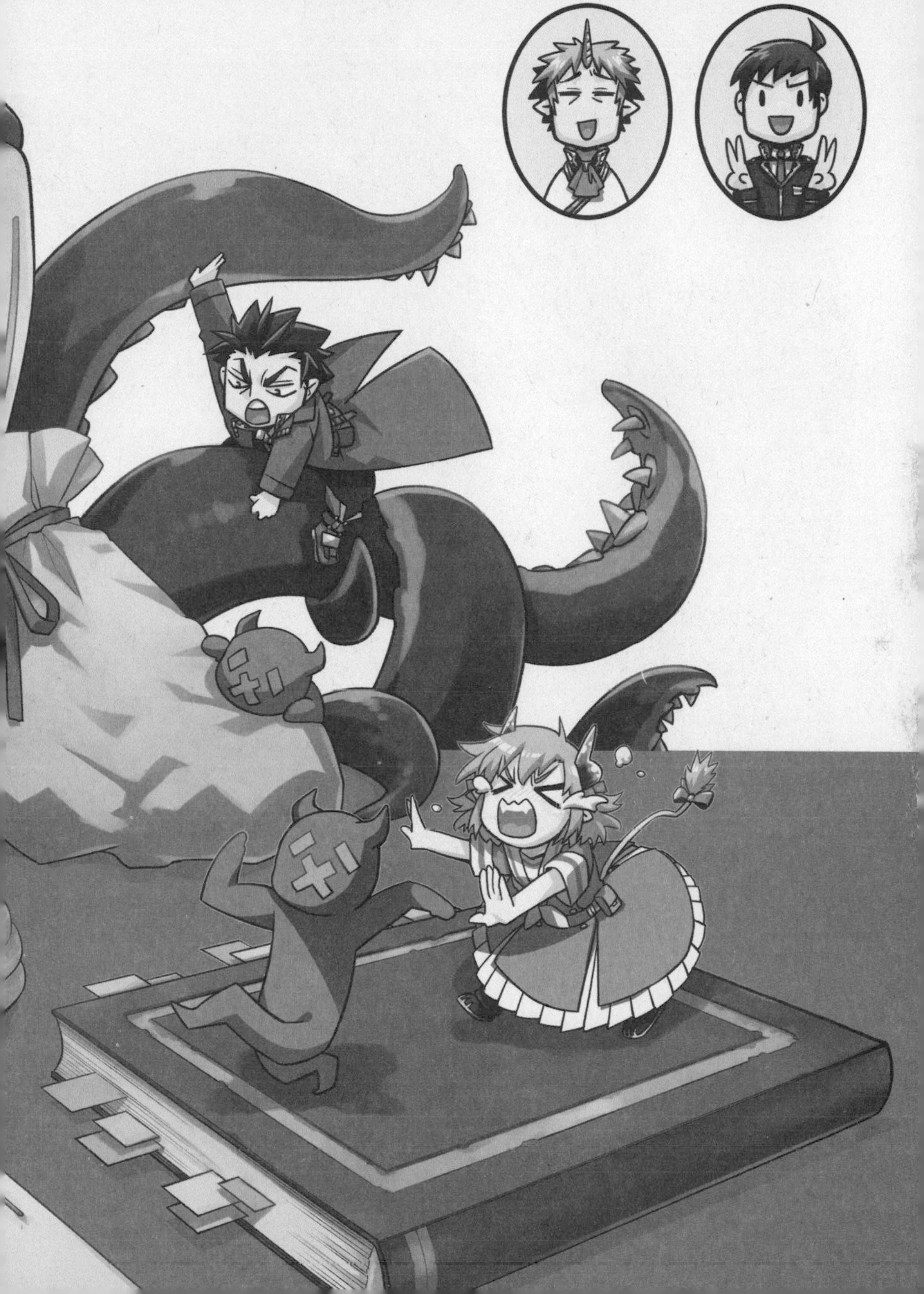

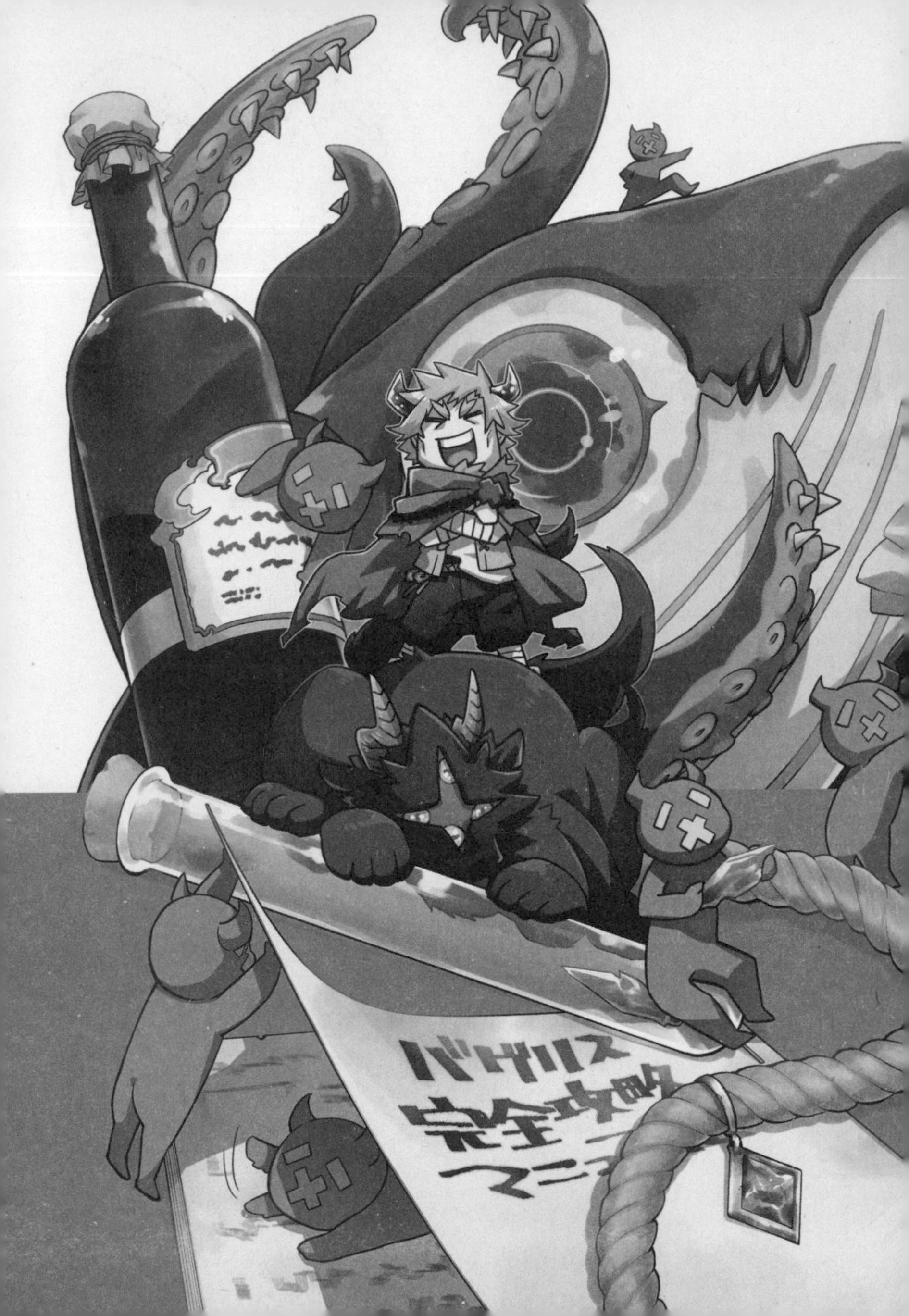

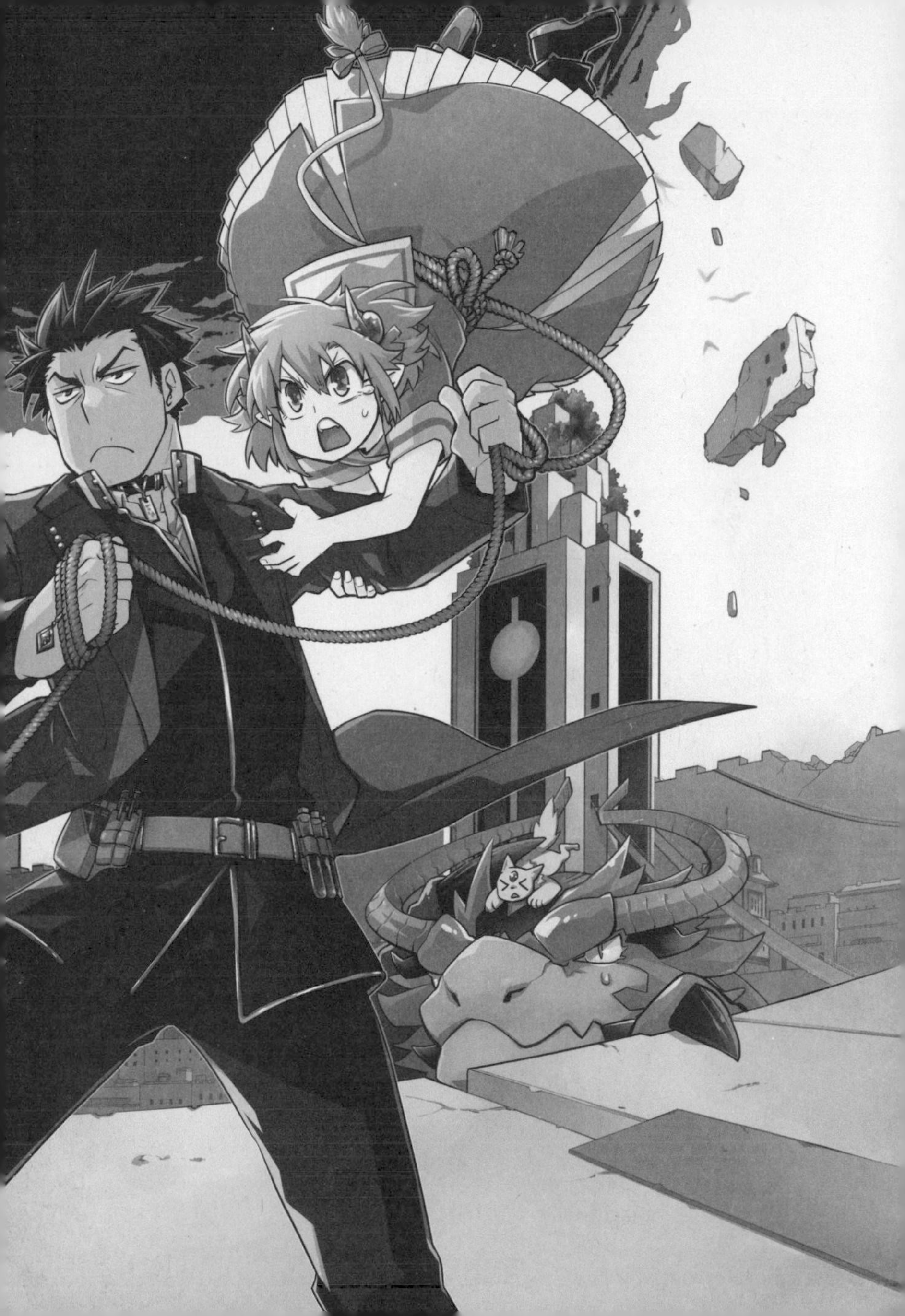

SEVEN SEAS ENTERTAINMENT PRESENTS

Sorry For My Familiar

story and art by **TEKKA YAGURABA**   **VOLUME 5**

TRANSLATION
Andrew Cunningham

ADAPTATION
Betsy Aoki

LETTERING AND RETOUCH
Kaitlyn Wiley

COVER DESIGN
KC Fabellon

PROOFREADER
Stephanie Cohen
Marykate Jasper

EDITOR
Shannon Fay

PRODUCTION MANAGER
Lissa Pattillo

MANAGING EDITOR
Julie Davis

EDITOR-IN-CHIEF
Adam Arnold

PUBLISHER
Jason DeAngelis

SORRY FOR MY FAMILIAR VOLUME 5
© Tekka Yaguraba 2018
All rights reserved.
First published in Japan in 2018 by Kodansha Ltd., Tokyo.
Publication rights for this English edition arranged through Kodansha Ltd.,
Tokyo.

No portion of this book may be reproduced or transmitted in any form without
written permission from the copyright holders. This is a work of fiction. Names,
characters, places, and incidents are the products of the author's imagination
or are used fictitiously. Any resemblance to actual events, locales, or persons,
living or dead, is entirely coincidental.

Seven Seas press and purchase enquiries can be sent to Marketing Manager
Lianne Sentar at press@gomanga.com. Information regarding the distribution
and purchase of digital editions is available from Digital Manager CK Russell
at digital@gomanga.com.

Seven Seas and the Seven Seas logo are trademarks of
Seven Seas Entertainment. All rights reserved.

ISBN: 978-1-64275-126-0

Printed in Canada

First Printing: August 2019

10 9 8 7 6 5 4 3 2 1

FOLLOW US ONLINE: *www.sevenseasentertainment.com*

READING DIRECTIONS

This book reads from ***right to left***, Japanese style.
If this is your first time reading manga, you start
reading from the top right panel on each page and
take it from there. If you get lost, just follow the
numbered diagram here. It may seem backwards at
first, but you'll get the hang of it! Have fun!!

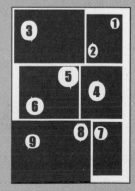

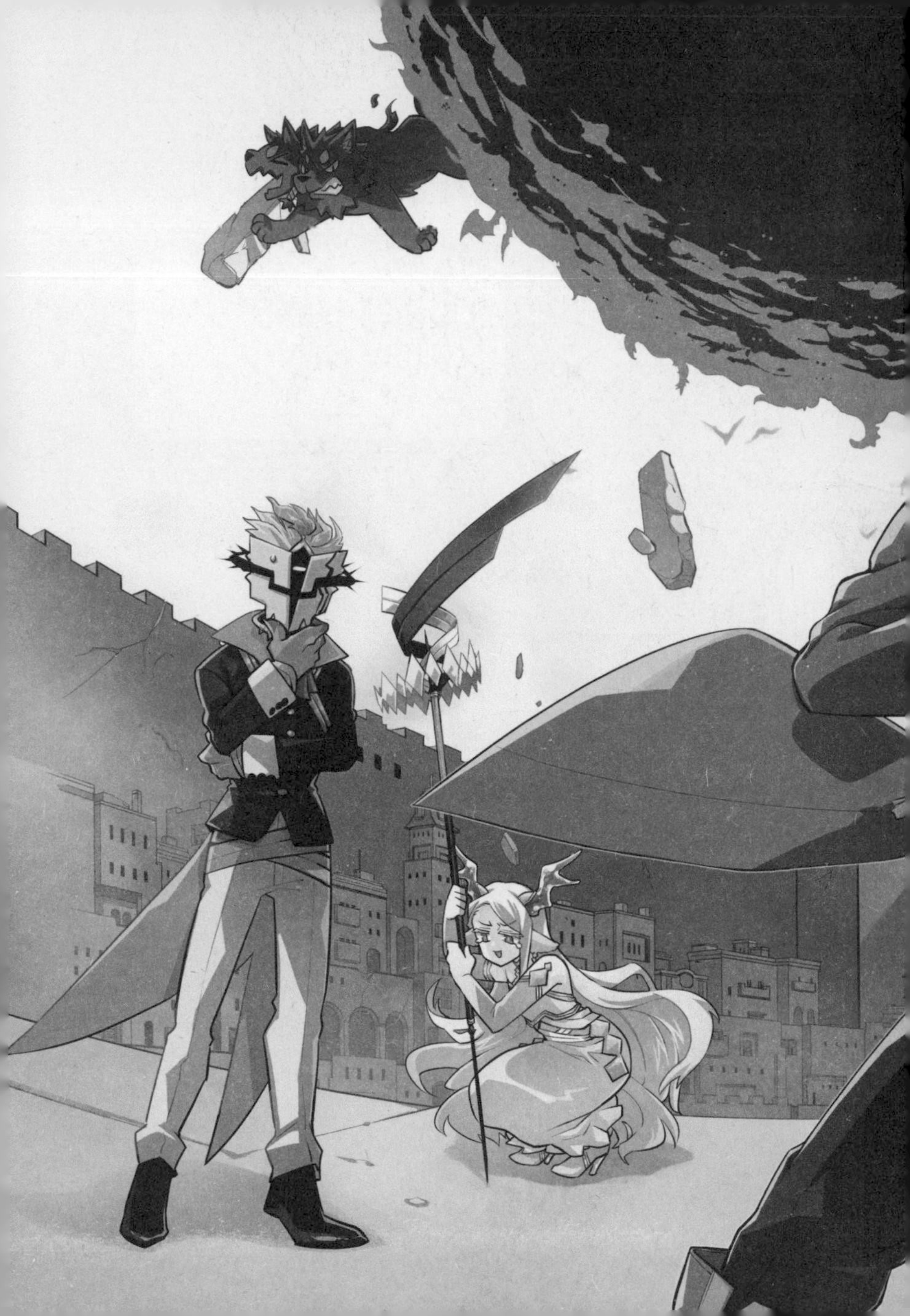

Sorry For My Familiar